Femicide
The Politics of Woman Killing

Femicide
The Politics of Woman Killing

edited by
JILL RADFORD AND DIANA E. H. RUSSELL

Twayne Publishers ❖ New York

Maxwell Macmillan Canada ❖ Toronto

Maxwell Macmillan International ❖ New York Oxford Singapore Sydney

"Female Genocide" on page 67 originally appeared in Marielouise Janssen-Jurreit, *Sexismus: Uber die Abtreibung der Frauenfrage* (Munich: Carl Hanser Verlag, 1976). Reprinted by permission of the publisher.

Twayne Publishers
Macmillan Publishing Company
866 Third Avenue
New York, New York 10022

Maxwell Macmillan Canada, Inc.
1200 Eglinton Avenue East
Suite 200
Don Mills, Ontario M3C 3N1

Macmillan Publishing Company is a part of the Maxwell Communication Group of Companies.

Library of Congress Cataloging-in-Publication Data

Femicide: the politics of woman killing / edited by Jill Radford and Diana E. H. Russell
    p. cm.
  Includes bibliographical references (p.   ) and index.
  ISBN 0-8057-9026-8 (cloth). — ISBN 0-8057-9028-4 (paper)
  1. Murder—History. 2. Women—Crimes against—History.
3. Uxoricide—History. I. Radford, Jill, 1947– . II. Russell, Diana E. H.
HV6511.F46 1992
364.1'523'082—dc20

            92-7036
            CIP

The paper used in this publication meets the minimum requirements of American National Standard for Information Sciences—Permanence of Paper for Printed Library Materials. ANSI Z3948–1984. ⊖™

10 9 8 7 6 5 4 3 2 1 (alk. paper)

10 9 8 7 6 5 4 3 2 1 (pbk: alk. paper)

PRINTED IN THE UNITED STATES OF AMERICA

My dedication is to the memory of my friend Mary and to other women who have died as a result of the violence of men; to survivors struggling to regain control in their lives; to women and children who are coping with violence in their lives; to women engaged in the global struggles to challenge, resist, and fight back against male sexual violence; and to women whose visions include a world free of all forms of violence, oppression, and femicide. It is out of hopes and visions that new realities become possible.

—J. R.

I dedicate this book to Nikki Craft for her ground-breaking actions against femicide long before there was a word for it; to Chris Domingo for her dedication to raising awareness about femicide and for her establishment of the Clearinghouse on Femicide, the first organization of its kind in the United States; to all the other women, known and unknown, who have denounced and organized against the slaughter of women throughout centuries of patriarchal rule; and finally, to all those women who will open their hearts and minds to the reality of the femicidal age in which we live and will take the bold steps necessary to end it.

—D. E. H. R.

Contents

PART 2 ❖ THE PATRIARCHAL HOME: THE MOST LETHAL PLACE FOR WOMEN

PART 3 ❖ FEMICIDE AND RACISM

SUMMARY AND CONCLUSION

Preface

The killing of individual women has sometimes generated feminist anger and inspired acts of protest. But femicide itself—the misogynist killing of women by men—has rarely been the subject of feminist analysis. This anthology represents an attempt to fill this void by bringing together and making more accessible existing writings on femicide and by presenting new material on this subject. Together the contributors address the problem of femicide in the United States, the United Kingdom, and India. We hope that their collective influence will persuade readers to recognize femicide as an urgent problem, advance feminist thinking about this issue, increase the general understanding of it, and, perhaps most important, generate resistance to it.

The book is divided into six parts. Like many organizational schemes, this one has an element of arbitrariness. Many of the readings could be accommodated in more than one section. Part 1 explores the history of femicide, demonstrating that femicide is as old as patriarchy itself. Part 2 explodes one of the most pervasive myths of patriarchal culture—that the home provides a safe haven for women. The readings here show that the home is the place where women are at greatest risk when that home is shared by a man, be he husband, male lover, father, or brother. In Part 3 the complex interactions of racism and femicide are explored. The contributions in this section demonstrate that femicide is no respecter of race, class, or culture and acknowledge the compound effects of racism and misogyny on women of color. In the interest of respecting the preferred terminology regarding race and ethnicity of women in England and the United States, contributions from each country use their own terms. Hence, original contributions from England often use the term *black and minority ethnic women*, while those from the United States use African-American, Asian-

American, American Indian, and so forth. Reprinted articles preserve the style in which the writings were first published.

Part 4 examines media representations of femicide, showing that the media generally fail to identify the sexual politics of femicide and often sympathize with the male murderer at the expense of the female victim. The important subject of sexual violence in pornography is also addressed. Parts 5 and 6 illustrate the arbitrary nature of our classification scheme: most of the readings in this anthology recount "Travesties of Justice" (part 5), and most include descriptions of "Women Fighting Back against Femicide" (part 6). But part 5 focuses specifically on the response of criminal justice systems to femicide, while part 6 concentrates exclusively on the ways in which women have begun to fight back and calls for feminist activism. Recognizing that the struggle against femicide is already under way may be an important source of strength and empowerment, countering the feelings of despair generated by a singular focus on the problem itself.

Because the subject of femicide is so disturbing, work on this volume has not been easy. One strengthening aspect of the work, however, was meeting either in person or through their writing other women who not only know the pain and anger caused by femicide but are also committed to confronting this extreme form of sexual violence.

This anthology is the product of a collaborative effort on Jill Radford's part in the United Kingdom and Diana Russell's in the United States. In compiling it we were overwhelmed by the wealth of material on woman killing available to us, both in the form of previously published and newly written works. We finally had to acknowledge that our oversized manuscript had become two books. This led to our decision to separate the analytical articles about misogynist murder from the straightforward narratives about woman killing, titling the former, a more scholarly and theoretical collection, *Femicide: The Politics of Woman Killing*, and the latter, *Fatal Attractions*.

Since the difficulties of transatlantic communication had led us each to write an introduction and conclusion for the original manuscript, and since we felt unable to merge them, we decided to use Jill's more academic contributions for *Femicide* and Diana's for *Fatal Attractions*. Many of Diana's ideas and arguments have, however, been incorporated into the introduction and conclusion to this volume. Following are individual statements from Jill and then Diana that express our particular concerns about femicide.

For more than 15 years I have been active in the feminist struggle against male violence. My concern about femicide has a personal origin. On the night of 29 October 1981 a close friend, Mary Bristow, was killed in her Winchester home by a former boyfriend, Peter Wood. Wood had harassed and threatened Mary before finally killing her. His stated reason for killing her was Mary's refusal to reenter a relationship with him.

It is a cruel irony that in the previous year the Winchester Women's Liberation Group, including myself and Mary, who was a founding member, began to work against male violence. Soon after beginning this work we saw press reports of the killing of a local woman, Jane Asher, and of the trial and ultimate release by the courts of her husband and killer. We began a campaign focusing on how both the courts and the press had blamed Jane Asher for her murder. None of us had known her, but we realized the death of any woman could be represented in this way. We began to recognize the power of a patriarchal ideology that seeks to control women, to punish those who resist violence, and to then blame women for provoking that violence. This ideology was shared by Jane Asher's killer and his judge, and its power was such that it allowed a man to walk free after killing his wife.

Almost a year to the day later the Winchester Group again responded to a misogynist killing. We felt the same anger, but this time we also experienced the shock and pain of personal loss. It was one of us, Mary Bristow, who had died at the hands of a man. Later it was Mary's life that was put on trial and distorted by a male judicial system and a male-dominated press.

Like many in our group, I left Winchester after the trial. I moved to London and became active in Central London WAVAW (Women against Violence against Women), one of the many WAVAW groups active in the United Kingdom in the early 1980s. We took to the streets to protest the hatred of women expressed in pornography; we marched to "reclaim the night" for women; we picketed courtrooms that had handed down rulings holding women responsible for violence against them and sentencing decisions trivializing male violence. I also began some research.

With a grant from the Greater London Council and support from a community police monitoring group, I undertook a research project on the problem of male violence in the London borough of Wandsworth. This project demonstrated the extent to which the threat and reality of male sexual violence routinely constrained, albeit in a range of ways, the lives of the 300 women interviewed. It was during the concluding stage of this project that I met Diana Russell and the idea of producing an anthology on the politics of woman killing was born.

A feminist approach to femicide makes it possible for this extreme form of male sexual violence to be linked with the more routine forms of harassment, abuse, and violence around which many women's lives are structured. In taking femicide as its subject, this anthology aims to contribute to feminist understandings of and resistance to male violence.

—J. R.

I first encountered the term *femicide* when an acquaintance told me in 1974 that American writer Carol Orlock was preparing an anthology on femicide. Although her book was never published and I had no idea how she had defined this new word, it resonated powerfully with me as one that might refer to the killing of women by men *because* they are women. We have long needed such a term as an alternative to the gender-neutral *homicide*. Establishing a word that signifies the killing of females is an important step toward making known this ultimate form of violence against women. Naming an injustice, and thereby providing a means of thinking about it, usually precedes the creation of a movement against it.

I first used the term *femicide* when testifying about misogynist murder before the 1976 International Tribunal on Crimes against Women. After the tribunal I started using it in my teaching and public lectures. Unfortunately, few are familiar with the word even now; more troubling, misogyny is rarely recognized as a factor in many cases of woman killing. The reality of femicide is implicitly denied by the common view of feminists and nonfeminists that rape and battery are the most extreme forms of violence against women.

During the process of researching my 1982 book, *Rape in Marriage*, I discovered that the threat of femicide by American husbands is disturbingly pervasive. Of the total 930 San Francisco women aged 18 and older interviewed by my research team, 644 had been married. Of these 644, 87 had been raped by a husband or exhusband at least once. Twenty-two percent (19) of these wife rape victims volunteered that their husbands had threatened to kill them. Although these threats had obviously not been carried out at the time of the interview, there is no way of knowing what percentage of such threats will be carried out.

Not surprisingly, organizing against femicide has not been easy. On 6 December 1981, I addressed a small crowd of mostly women who had gathered to protest the killing of several women in Marin County, an upper-class, low-crime area just north of San Francisco. David Carpenter, the serial killer later convicted of these and other femicides, had murdered these women when they were hiking in the Marin countryside. Women who continued to hike in or nearby the area felt even more than their usual fear of attack—confronted by the familiar female choice between freedom of movement and safety.

In my speech on femicide that day, I pointed out that women in the United States live at risk of being killed for no reason other than being female. I urged those present to start organizing to raise awareness about femicide. A handful of feminists responded by forming a group whose goal was to organize a national conference on femicide. Sadly, after a lot of hard work, the group disintegrated without having achieved its goal. It was not until eight years later that Chris Pocock founded the Clearinghouse on Femicide and made use of the information that she and the other members of the fledgling group had begun to amass so long ago.

Coincidentally, my address to that small gathering in Marin County took place eight years to the day before 14 female engineering students were shot and killed in a massacre at the University of Montreal in 1989. The explicitness of Marc Lépine's misogyny, both in targeting solely women and calling them "fucking feminists," made the existence of the phenomenon of femicide, at least for some, impossible to ignore. Since then, use of the term *femicide* has been growing. I hope that this anthology will institutionalize its use in the English language and that the naming of this extreme form of sexual violence will predicate widespread resistance to it.

—D. E. H. R.

Acknowledgments

I would like to thank the women who contributed to this book, my colleague Diana E. H. Russell, and all the women who through the years have helped me develop my thinking and provided emotional support at times of crisis. The ideas I express here are the product of 15 years of work with other women on the problem of men's sexual violence. I particularly want to acknowledge the support of the Winchester Women's Liberation Group, Women against Violence against Women, the Lesbian Policing Project, Rights of Women (ROW), the Sexual Violence Group and the Law Group at ROW, the British Sociological Association, the Women's Caucus, the Violence against Women Study Group, the workers at the North London Polytechnic Child Sexual Abuse Research Unit, and my other friends.

—J. R.

I was impressed on reading some of Jill Radford's articles on the murder of women in England, so I asked my friend Sheila Jeffries to introduce us when I visited London in 1986. It was at our first meeting that Jill and I decided to collaborate on the preparation of this book. Most feminists—even those dedicated to working on violence against women—have been silent about its ultimate form: femicide. It was to break this silence that Jill and I felt it necessary to work on this anthology.

I am grateful to Chris Domingo, the organizer of the Clearinghouse on Femicide in Berkeley, California, for the many ways in which she supported this project. She brought numerous articles to my attention, loaned me her Clearinghouse files, generously donated her time to library research, helped obtain permissions to publish reprinted contributions, put in hours around the clock to help prepare the final manuscript, and searched for answers to numerous niggling factual questions that I needed answered. Chris is one of the few women I know who shares my profound concern with femicide.

In October 1989 I had the good fortune to meet Jane Caputi, the first person in the United States to write a feminist analysis of serial killing: *The Age of Sex Crime* (1987). Since she spent her sabbatical in Berkeley, where I live, we had the opportunity to become friends and collaborators on various action and writing projects on femicide. It is often lonely working on the frontier of feminist awareness, on a problem that few feminists are willing to face or to take with the seriousness it deserves. It was a joy to meet a kindred spirit and wonderfully affirming to share with her the numerous experiences both of us have had of people thinking there must be something wrong with us for spending so much of our time and energy on the still-taboo subject of woman killing. Jane also helped me greatly by bringing many useful newspaper stories and references to my attention and by providing a stimulating discussion partner on theories of femicide and many related topics.

I am also grateful to Catharine MacKinnon, who reviewed the entire manuscript and offered many invaluable suggestions. Several others helped in different ways during the many months of writing and manuscript preparation: Marny Hall, Priscilla Camp, and Joan Balter read drafts of one or more chapters; Marny, Joan, Sandy Butler, and Maryel Norris leant a sympathetic ear whenever I needed it; Sydelle Kramer located an interested publisher at a time when there was little interest in woman killing; Jan Dennie, Dennis Bell, Veronica Jordan, Catha Worthman, Steve McCoy, and Felicity Wood helped with word processing or clerical work; and Candida Ellis plied her editorial skills to my contributions. To all of them, my heartfelt thanks. And to Roberta Harmes I would like to reserve a special thanks for the many ways she assisted me with this work, completing references and finding articles, books, and photographs, often at the last minute. She saved me many frustrating hours of work and did so with an enviable patience and calm. Thanks also to Ann Forfreedom for telling me where to find an illustration of the persecution of women as witches.

I also appreciate the efforts of Twayne editors Carol Chin and India Koopman for the careful and thoughtful work they put into transforming our manuscript into a book. I hope that all of us will feel our efforts have been worthwhile when this work is finally available to concerned readers.

—D. E. H. R.

Femicide
The Politics of Woman Killing

Take Back the Night march in Cambridge, Massachusetts, 1980. Photo Ellen Shub.

Introduction

JILL RADFORD

Femicide, the misogynous killing of women by men, is a form of sexual violence. Liz Kelly has defined sexual violence as "any physical, visual, verbal or sexual act" experienced by a woman or girl, "at the time or later, as a threat, invasion, or assault, that has the effect of hurting or degrading her and/or takes away her ability to control intimate contact" (1988, 41). Underlying this definition is a recognition of the dissonance between women's and men's perceptions and experiences of the social world and of sexual violence. It gives women's experiences and understandings priority over men's intentions and as such is consistent with one of the basic tenets of feminism—women's right to name our experience.

The concept of sexual violence is valuable because it moves beyond earlier feminist debates over whether rape, for example, should be seen as an act of violence or of sexual assault. The limitations of this debate center on a narrow definition of the term *sexual,* one that rests on whether the man is seeking sexual pleasure. In contrast, the term *sexual violence* focuses on the man's desire for power, dominance, and control. This definition enables sexual aggression by men to be seen in the context of the overall oppression of women in a patriarchal society. It also allows feminist analysis to distance itself from legal discourse that is based on discrete and narrow definitions of the sexual and the violent, definitions that can distort and deny women's experience. Such distancing is especially important given the moralistic, racist, heterosexist conservatism that dominated law and order debates in the 1980s.

The concept of sexual violence also makes it possible to make connections between its various forms, establishing what Kelly has called "a continuum of sexual violence" (1988, 97). Rape, sexual harassment, pornography, and physical abuse of women and children are all different expressions of male sexual violence rather than discrete, disconnected issues. This reconceptualization is theoretically significant: it provides a broader perspective that more sensitively

3

reflects the experiences of male violence as named and defined by women and children. Rather than forcing experience of sexual abuse into discrete legal categories, the concept of a continuum allows us to identify and address a range of forced or coercive heterosexual experiences. The notion of a continuum further facilitates the analysis of male sexual violence as a form of control central to the maintenance of patriarchy.

Furthermore, locating femicide within this continuum enables us to draw on radical feminist analyses of sexual violence and to compare the treatment of femicide in law, social policy, and the media with the treatment of other expressions of sexual violence. This is important, because feminist discussions of femicide have been limited in comparison with discussions of other forms of sexual violence. This neglect is particularly disturbing given the extensive media coverage of murders of women by men, including the increasing number of serial killings. The misogynist motivations of these killings are often ignored by the media, which may blame the women or deny the humanity, and therefore the masculinity, of the killer, who is frequently portrayed as a beast or an animal. Such press coverage masks the sexual politics of femicide. Relocating femicide within the continuum of sexual violence establishes its significance in terms of sexual politics.

But this is no easy task. Many feminists still consider rape to be the most extreme form of sexual violence. There are more books on women who kill (for example, Browne 1987; Jones 1980; Walker 1989) than there are on men who kill women. The ground-breaking work in 1987 of Deborah Cameron and Elizabeth Frazer in *The Lust to Kill: A Feminist Investigation of Sexual Murder* and of Jane Caputi in *The Age of Sex Crime* has not been sufficient to break through the general resistance to acknowledging the existence of femicide. Neither Women's Aid in the United Kingdom nor the National Coalition against Domestic Violence (NCADV) and the National Coalition against Sexual Assault, both in the United States, have done much work on the murder of wives by their husbands, on the murder of rape victims, or on misogynist murder in general.

The limited discussion of woman killing in feminist literature does not mean, however, that feminists are unaware of this issue. Many groups have organized around particular instances of femicide in their communities. Examples are the Combahee River Collective in Boston and the Repeat Attacks and Murders of Women groups in Britain. Still, these responses have been largely ad hoc; as an issue femicide is not yet firmly placed on feminist agendas. Most feminist writing has focused on the survivors of male violence rather than on its perpetrators.

One reason for the reluctance to acknowledge femicide is its finality. This finality puts it outside traditional feminist modes of working. When a woman is killed, there may be no survivor to tell her story. There is no way of sharing the experience of violent death; all that can be shared are the pain and anger of those who have known such a loss. And this pain, far from being a basis for unity and strength—as it is in support groups for women who have survived sexual violence—can be undermining and silencing. In many cultures coming to terms with death is considered a private matter. Women who do speak out have had to be mindful of the impact their words may have on those close to the dead woman. There is also the danger of being faced with the accusation of making "political capital" out of grief. For these reasons femicide is perhaps one of the most harrowing and sensitive dimensions of male violence for feminists to address.

Unfortunately, feminist silence on this important subject, however understandable, leaves it open to justification or denial by the larger culture. In the sixteenth and seventeenth centuries the dominant thinking justified the killing of women believed to be witches on the grounds that they were inherently evil. In more recent times prevailing thought has led to a legal system that takes the killing of certain women—lesbians, wives suspected of adultery, prostitutes—less seriously than it does other murders. Denial of femicide is especially evident in its representation on film—both in television thrillers and in pornography—where the torture and killing of women is portrayed for male sexual gratification. In so-called snuff movies, the production of pornography results in the actual killing of women, usually black or Third World women deceived or coerced into participation. What each of the above examples has in common is its objectification of women. When viewed solely as a witch, a lesbian, a body employed for male sexual gratification, a woman becomes less than a woman—less than human. She becomes an object that can be disposed of or easily replaced. The treatment of women as objects and the denial of their subjective experience—an issue that lies at the heart of much feminist discourse—is a theme running repeatedly through the readings in this volume.

The writings collected here also challenge laws, legal practices, and ideologies that allow men who have killed their wives to walk away free or to serve only token sentences. The trivializing of femicide is often justified by the claim that the women concerned are in some way to blame for their deaths. This form of "victimology" is currently quite prevalent.

Victimology is a way of explaining crime that is popular within criminology. It holds that those victimized by crime are often responsible for it. It has been used in a range of criminological contexts but has been most powerful in explaining interpersonal violence, particularly violence against women. In the early 1970s feminists gave considerable attention to identifying and challenging victimology's myths of rape by strangers—that women "ask for it," enjoy it, or provoke it in how we dress, what we say, how we behave. Despite feminist exposure of these myths about rape, they have resurfaced in relation to sexual violence against women and girls in the home. Here, too, the actions of women and girls are scrutinized and often pathologized, and they are ultimately held responsible for the violence and abuse.

In the case of the 14 female college engineering students killed in Montreal in December 1989 by Mark Lépine, it was not only the victims—whom Lépine referred to as "fucking feminists"—who were blamed but also another woman, Lépine's mother. A psychologist quoted in *Today* (London) suggested a motive for the killings: perhaps "the boy's mother was unavailable to lavish attention on him for a short while through depression or illness. That could have started the emotional sickness. Or maybe the mother unconsciously seduced her child leading to him feeling rage at being spurned in favour of the father" (1989, 9). The article then cites the director of the Centre for Crisis Psychology, in the United Kingdom, who

> agrees that mass murderers like Marc frequently harbour a hatred of women.
> But why this man should have it in for feminists I have really no idea. I would imagine he has something in common with many sexual offenders in that he probably felt an intense sense of humiliation by women.
> In sexual offenders this often comes from a powerful dominant mother.

In countering woman blaming, most feminist analyses of male sexual violence have drawn on radical feminist theory. These analyses are political, interpreting male sexual violence in relation to the gendered power relations of patriarchal society. In the radical feminist formulations of the 1970s, societies characterized by male dominance and female subordination were identified as *patriarchal.* Gender relations were identified as *power relations,* which were defined structurally through the social or political construction of masculinity as active and aggressive and the social construction of femininity as receptive and passive. Male sexual violence has been identified as a defining characteristic of patriarchal societies (Kelly and Radford 1987), a central means by which men maintain power over women and children. Patriarchal oppression, like other forms of oppression, may manifest itself in legal and economic discrimination, but like all oppressive structures, it is rooted in violence.

In the context of radical feminist analysis, femicide has great political significance. As a form of capital punishment, it affects the women who are its victims and their families and friends. More generally, it serves as a means of controlling women as a sex class, and as such it is central to the maintenance of the patriarchal status quo. Femicide, as reenacted in courtroom trials and as represented in the media, is surrounded by the mythology of woman blaming. It is women's behavior that is scrutinized and found wanting when measured against men's idealized constructions of femininity and standards of female behavior. The message of the myth is clear. For women, it reads, "Step out of line and it may cost you your life"; for men, "You can kill her and get away with it."

These messages can be read in the advice police and others often offer to protect women from violent crime. Women are routinely advised not to live alone; not to go out at night unaccompanied (meaning without a man); not to go to certain areas of a city. In the United Kingdom, for a six-year period, night and day, the whole of West Yorkshire was defined as unsafe for women because of the Yorkshire Ripper. Such advice seeks to control women by placing limits on where they may go and how they may behave in public, a reminder that public space is men's space and women's presence in it is conditional on male approval. Woman's place, according to patriarchal ideologies, is in the home. But even there women are not safe—a fact that is rarely mentioned. The home is the most lethal place for women living in nuclear families.

The task of identifying femicide as a subject of feminist concern, analysis, and action has certain parallels with the task undertaken by feminists working around violence against women in the 1970s. Before that time, feminists, like nonfeminists, failed to perceive the ubiquity of rape and domestic violence and the threat they represent to women. Feminists led the way in calling public attention to this threat and demanding that it be addressed. By publishing evidence of femicide in a gender-sensitive way, Diana Russell and I hope that once more feminists will find the courage to challenge yet another form of sexual violence. By going beyond an academic discussion of the evidence, by making the fight against femicide a major theme of this anthology, we hope it will play a strategic role in consolidating feminist resistance to femicide.

Femicide has many different forms: for example, racist femicide (when black women are killed by white men); homophobic femicide, or lesbicide, (when lesbians are killed by heterosexual men); marital femicide (when women are killed by their husbands); femicide committed outside the home by a stranger; serial femicide; and mass femicide. In this era of AIDS, femicide includes the deliberate transmission of the HIV virus by rapists. The concept of femicide also extends itself beyond legal definitions of murder to include situations in which women are permitted to die as a result of misogynous attitudes or social practices.

Where the right of women to control their own fertility is not recognized, for example, women die from botched abortions. In 1970, when the U.S. Supreme Court declared the death penalty unconstitutional, Kate Millett pointed out that, "indirectly, one form of 'death penalty' still obtains even in America today. Patriarchal legal systems in depriving women of control over their own bodies drive them to illegal abortions; it is estimated that between two and five thousand women die each year from this cause" (1970, 43–44). Although abortions were legalized in the United States in 1973, the right to choose has subsequently been curtailed in individual states and may be further restricted. Many countries deny or restrict women's access to abortion; consequently, thousands of women die each year. Other examples of femicide include deaths from unnecessary surgeries, including hysterectomies and clitorectomies; from infanticide, in which more female babies are killed than males; and even from the deliberate preference given to boys over girls in many cultures, resulting in deaths from neglect and starvation. This listing is illustrative, not definitive, as the forms taken by femicide are shaped by changing cultures and contexts.

Among the forms that are addressed here are racist femicide and homophobic femicide. As feminism developed through the 1980s, it was forced to consider the impact of competing patriarchal power structures on the lives—and in this context, deaths—of women different in race, culture, and class. Black women have had to insist that attention be paid to the complex interactions between racism and sexism. White feminists have had to be told how racism compounds and shapes black women's experiences of sexual violence—how, for example, racism and misogyny are often inseparable dimensions of the violence. White feminists have had to acknowledge that black women's experiences are rooted in histories different from white women's. White colonial and imperial rule considered the rape of black women to be the slave owner's privilege. The influence of this history persists today: it is expressed in the stereotypes of black women portrayed in the media and in pornographic celebrations of violence against black women, and it is expressed in the response of the police and other professionals in the legal system to black women experiencing male violence—a response often dictated by racism. Analyses that fail to acknowledge differences in women's experiences, cultures, and histories replicate the white- and male-dominated society's failure to acknowledge broader categories of difference—what it means, for instance, to be black, lesbian, or poor. Any strategy for change that does not recognize these power relations is likely to benefit only certain women at the expense of others.

An awareness of the complexities of racism, of the historical legacies of colonialism and imperialism, and of the sensitivity of the topic of sexual violence has led us to think carefully about how to address the femicide of black women in the United States and the United Kingdom. As white women, we are aware of the trap of appropriating black women's experiences to advance the political agendas of white feminism. Yet we do want to identify the complex ways in which racism interacts with misogyny in shaping both black women's experiences of sexual violence and white society's response to it. This is an essential starting point for understanding racist femicide. We want to address the racist femicide of black women by white men and the existence of sexual violence and femicide within black communities. Racism has made the latter issue a sensitive one for many women. Sexual violence in black communities has often been addressed in ways that either exaggerate the problem—perpetuating the stereotype that black men are more prone to violence than white men—or minimize its importance—suggesting that sexual violence is more acceptable in these communities, which are then viewed as pathological.

Recognition of heterosexuality as an oppressive social institution, rather than a private sexual preference, informs our understanding of femicide, and of homophobic femicide specifically. Awareness of heterosexism as a powerful oppressive force is integral to radical feminist analysis.

> Heteroreality is used to describe the world view that woman exists in relation to man (Raymond 1986). In Britain "heteropatriarchy" is beginning to be used to signify a system of social relations based on male dominance or supremacy, in which men's structured relationships to women underpin all other systems of exploitation.

> Male supremacy is not the only power structure in capitalist, neocolonial societies that adversely affects women. While all women are affected by an inferior social status in relation to men, an adequate theoretical analysis must recognise other power structures based on systemic inequality, in particular those of class, race and sexuality. These power structures are not mutually exclusive but interactive. (Hanmer, Radford, and Stanko 1989, 6)

Recognizing heterosexuality as a power structure is theoretically important, but following this up with explicitly lesbian writings about femicide is not as easy. We were able to find few accounts in which the victim was openly defined as a lesbian. In a heterosexist culture, such an admission by the family and friends of the victim would only compound the stigma associated with murder. In the United Kingdom, heterosexism has been encoded in recently enacted laws.[1] In this political climate, which has seen a rise in violent attacks on lesbians, it is important to recognize the issue of antilesbian femicide, but it is not hard to explain the limited number of lesbian contributions on the topic.

Cultural differences among various patriarchal societies can give rise to different forms of femicide. While recognizing femicide as a global issue, in this volume we explore its different forms in two Western, industrialized, patriarchal countries, the United Kingdom and the United States, and in one developing country, India. A comprehensive review of femicide would cross all cultures, but such coverage is beyond the scope of this anthology, which is limited by our current knowledge and by constraints of time and space. Facing the questions of inclusion and exclusion, our decisions were shaped by a desire to avoid producing a volume global in scope but superficial and voyeuristic in analysis. By limiting the scope of discussions in the way we have, we aimed to do justice to the historical and contemporary complexities of femicide and women's resistance to it in the United Kingdom, the United States, and India. At the same time, we are aware of the impact of femicide on the lives and deaths of women in other parts of the world—Africa, Central and South America, the Arab world, Southeast Asia, and Eastern Europe. Each of these regions, and many of the communities within them, has its own history of femicide and of resistance that must be acknowledged to generate a fully antiracist and international struggle by women against femicide.

In addressing femicide in India in an anthology produced primarily by and for women living in the Western world, we have tried to avoid voyeurism and cultural stereotyping. In anthropology the term *ethnocentrism* is used to describe the presentation of Third World experiences through First World eyes to a First World readership. With a view to minimizing this problem, yet establishing that femicide is a global issue, we have included writings from Indian women belonging to the cultures they represent.

Having addressed the definition of femicide and some of its forms and contexts, some discussion of its prevalence is needed. We should establish that, while our concern is with femicide, we do not claim that women are murdered

TABLE 1 Chances of Being Murdered in the United States

Total		1 in 133
Men		1 in 84
White	1 in 131	
Black	1 in 21	
Women		1 in 282
White	1 in 369	
Black	1 in 104	

Source: *San Francisco Chronicle*, 6 May 1985.

more frequently than men. In the United States, for example, homicide statistics compiled by the National Center for Health Statistics of the U.S. Public Health Service indicate that the estimated chance of being murdered is 1 in 282 for all females and 1 in 84 for all males (*San Francisco Chronicle* 1985). As table 1 illustrates, a person's chance of being murdered in the United States differs in accordance with gender and race. These statistics are not a measure of femicide, as they do not indicate the gender of the murderer.

Our argument is that while men are murdered more frequently than women, men are rarely murdered simply because they are men. Even in the rare cases of women killing men, it is unlikely that they kill because the victim is male. Most murders by women are in self-defense or represent a desperate attempt at self-preservation.[2] In both the United Kingdom and the United States the right to self-defense was constructed to reflect situations of violence between men in public places. The law protecting this right excludes the situation of a woman who, after years of violence, kills a partner at a point of desperation, feeling this is the only way she can survive. It is rarely possible for a woman to act in a way that the law recognizes as self-defense—an immediate response to a life-threatening situation without using a weapon, as the legal definition requires a proportionality of force. Feminists in the United Kingdom are campaigning for a new formal defense of self-preservation.

Statistics from both the United States and the United Kingdom show that women most at risk of femicide are women living with their husbands and children. The high risk of femicide facing women living in a heterosexual family may be explained in part by the difficulties facing women wanting to leave violent partners. Law enforcement agencies, like the nonfeminist public, are more prepared to assist women attacked by strangers than to women attacked by husbands or male partners. The widespread assumptions that domestic violence is a private matter that women provoke and that women are the property of their husbands contribute to the prevalence of this form of femicide.

It is hard to tell whether or not this form of femicide is increasing. For example, in the early 1980s in the United States, FBI figures suggested some decrease in the murder of wives (Russell 1982, 294). Diana Russell has argued that the increase in the divorce rate may have accounted for some of this decline. On the other hand, considerable anecdotal evidence suggests that wives are at an increased risk of femicide when they indicate they want to leave or initiate divorce proceedings.

There is clearer evidence from the United States to suggest that serial killings of women and girls have become more frequent. Although precise figures are unavailable, law enforcement experts estimate that "as many as two thirds [or 3,500] of the estimated 5,000 unsolved homicides in the nation each year may be committed by serial murderers" (Starr 1984, 100). Jane Caputi reports that by the mid-1980s police officials' estimate of the total number of serial killings had risen to 4,000 per year (1987, 117). While some serial murderers kill males, most experts agree that the vast majority of the victims are female (Caputi 1987, 203). Assuming that approximately four fifths of the victims of male serial killers are female,[3] and assuming that the law enforcement experts of the mid-1980s are correct in estimating that 4,000 serial murders take place each year, about 3,200 femicides occur annually, 32,000 per decade.

Mass murder, a single crime that involves the killing of a number of people, is less often directed exclusively at women and so is not usually interpreted as femicide. There are some notable cases of femicidal mass murder, however, such as Marc Lépine's massacre of 14 women at the University of Montreal in 1989.

While official statistics have been of only limited assistance in assessing the extent of femicide, its existence—in the form of outright murder, denial of abortion rights, or misogynous social practices—is undeniable. It is our intention in this volume not to induce despair over this urgent and extensive problem but to elicit resistance to it.

Notes

1. In 1988 the Local Government Act outlawed the "promotion of homosexuality" in state education. In 1990 the Human Embryology and Fertilization Act excluded lesbians from access to donor insemination and treatments for infertility. A consultative document, "Guidelines to the Children's Act 1989," attempts to prevent lesbians from taking children into foster care by stating that "equal rights and gay rights" have no place in fostering services. For further information see Rights of Women (1991).

2. In 1991 some feminists in the United Kingdom began to discuss the possibility of a new defense for women who kill—that of self-preservation—recognizing that the existing defenses, "not guilty by reason of self-defense" and "manslaughter defenses of provocation," rarely cover the situation in which women have been repeatedly subject to violent abuse and consequently kill their abuser. We are reluctant to support those advocating recognition of a "battered woman syndrome" in the defense of diminished responsibility. The problem with this label is that it reproduces the language and images of victimology, which represents women as not being responsible for their actions and pathologizes women's anger and resistance.

3. An assumption supported by serial murder expert Jane Caputi, personal communication, 19 December 1989.

References

Browne, Angela. 1987. When Battered Women Kill. New York: Free Press.

Cameron, Deborah, and Elizabeth Frazer. 1987. *The Lust to Kill: A Feminist Investigation of Sexual Murder*. New York: New York University Press; London: Polity Press.

Caputi, Jane. *The Age of Sex Crime*. 1987. Bowling Green, Ohio: Bowling Green State University Popular Press; London: Women's Press.

Hanmer, Jalna, Jill Radford, and Elizabeth A. Stanko. 1989. *Women, Policing, and Male Violence*. London: Routledge.

Jeffreys, Sheila. 1990. *Anticlimax: A Feminist Perspective on the Sexual Revolution*. London: Women's Press.

_____, and Jill Radford. 1984. "Contributory Negligence: Being a Woman." In *Causes for Concern*, ed. P. Scraton and P. Gordon. New York: Penguin.

Jones, Ann. 1980. *Women Who Kill*. New York: Holt, Rinehart & Winston.

Kelly, Liz. 1988. *Surviving Sexual Violence*. London: Polity Press.

_____. 1990. " 'Nothing Really Happened': The Invalidation of Women's Experience of Sexual Violence." *Critical Social Policy* 30 (Winter 1990–91).

_____, and Jill Radford. 1987. "The Problem of Men." In *Law, Order, and the Authoritarian State*, ed. P. Scraton. Milton Keynes, England: Open University Press.

MacKinnon, Catherine A. 1987. *Feminism Unmodified: Discourses on Life and Law*. Cambridge, Mass.: Harvard University Press.

Mama, Amina. 1989. *The Hidden Struggle: Statutory and Voluntary Sector Responses to Violence against Black Women in the Home*. London: London Race and Housing Unit, c/o Runnymede Trust.

Millett, Kate. 1970. *Sexual Politics*. New York: Doubleday.

Radford, Jill. 1987. "Policing Male Violence: Policing Women." In *Violence and Social Control*, ed. J. Hanmer and M. Maynard. New York: Macmillan.

Raymond, Janice. 1986. *A Passion for Friends*. London: Women's Press.

Rights of Women. 1991. "Backlash against Lesbian Parenting," briefing paper. London (January).

Russell, Diana E. H. 1982. *Rape in Marriage*. New York: Macmillan; 2d ed., Bloomington: Indiana University Press, 1990.

_____. 1984. *Sexual Exploitation: Rape, Child Sexual Abuse, and Workplace Harassment*. Beverly Hills, Calif.: Sage Publications.

_____. 1988. "Pornography and Rape: A Causal Model." *Political Psychology* 9, no. 1: 41–73.

_____, and Nicole Van de Ven. 1976. *Crimes against Women: The Proceedings of the International Tribunal*. Millbrae, Calif.: Les Femmes; repr. ed., Palo Alto, Calif.: Frog in the Well, 1984.

San Francisco Chronicle, 6 May 1985.

Starr, Mark. 1984. "The Random Killers: An Epidemic of Serial Murder Sparks Growing Concern." *Newsweek*, 26 November.

Today (London), 9 December 1989.

Walker, Lenore. 1989. *Terrifying Love: Why Battered Women Kill and How Society Responds*. New York: Harper & Row.

Femicide: Sexist Terrorism against Women

JANE CAPUTI AND DIANA E. H. RUSSELL

Kill Feminist Bitches

> —Graffito, University of Western Ontario, after Marc Lépine's
> murder of 14 women in Montreal, 1989

Canadian novelist Margaret Atwood once asked a male friend why men feel threatened by women. He replied: "They are afraid women will laugh at them." She then asked a group of women why they felt threatened by men. They answered: "We're afraid of being killed."

However wildly disproportionate, these fears are profoundly linked, as was demonstrated on 6 December 1989 at the University of Montreal. On that day, 25-year-old combat magazine aficionado Marc Lépine suited up for war and rushed the school of engineering. In one classroom, he separated the women from the men, ordered the men out, and, shouting "You're all fucking feminists," opened fire on the women. During a half-hour rampage, Lépine killed 14 young women, wounded 9 other women and 4 men, then turned his gun on himself. A three-page suicide note blamed all of his failures on women, whom he felt had rejected and scorned him. Also found on his body was a hit-list of 15 prominent Canadian women.

Unable to complete an application to the school of engineering, Lépine felt humiliated ("laughed at") by women he defined as "feminists" because they had entered traditional male territory. His response to the erosion of white male exclusivity and privilege was lethal. It was also eminently political.

Another version of this article appeared as "Femicide: Speaking the Unspeakable," in *Ms.* magazine, (September/October 1990). Although references are not included here, *Ms.* required documentation of all sources. We would like to thank Joan Balter, Sandy Butler, Phyllis Chesler, Candida Ellis, Marny Hall, Robin Morgan, and Helen Vann for their comments and/or editorial suggestions.

In the aftermath of the massacre, media reports regularly denied the political nature of Lépine's crimes, citing comments such as that of Canadian novelist Mordecai Richler, "It was the act of an absolutely demented man [that does not] lend itself to any explanation." Richler ignored Lépine's explanation of his actions. He hated women, particularly feminists. Whether such a killer is "demented" is beside the point. Fixation on the pathology of perpetrators of violence against women only obscures the social control function of these acts. In a racist and sexist society, psychotic as well as supposedly normal men frequently act out the ubiquitous racist, misogynist, and homophobic attitudes with which they are raised and which they repeatedly see legitimized.

Lépine's murders were hate crimes targeting victims by gender, not race, religion, ethnicity, or sexual orientation. In the cases of lynchings and pogroms, no one wastes time wondering about the mental health of the perpetrators or about their previous personal experiences with African-Americans or Jews. Most people today understand that lynchings and pogroms are forms of politically motivated violence, the objectives of which are to preserve white and gentile supremacy. Similarly, the goal of violence against women—whether conscious or not—is to preserve male supremacy.

Early feminist analysts of another form of sexist violence—rape—asserted that it is not, as common mythology insists, a crime of frustrated attraction, victim provocation, or uncontrollable biological urges. Nor is rape perpetrated only by an aberrant fringe. Rather, rape is a direct expression of sexual politics, an

Take Back the Night march in San Francisco, 1990, commemorating the mass femicide of 14 engineering students in Montreal in 1989. Photo Jane Philomen Cleland.

act of conformity to masculinist sexual norms (as "humorist" Ogden Nash put it, "Seduction is for sissies. A he-man wants his rape"), and a form of terrorism that serves to preserve the gender status quo.

Like rape, most murders of women by husbands, lovers, fathers, acquaintances, and strangers are not the products of some inexplicable deviance. They are femicides, the most extreme form of sexist terrorism, motivated by hatred, contempt, pleasure, or a sense of ownership of women. Femicide includes mutilation murder, rape murder, battery that escalates into murder, the immolation of witches in Western Europe and of brides and widows in India, and "crimes of honor" in some Latin and Middle Eastern countries, where women believed to have lost their virginity are killed by their male relatives. Calling misogynist killings femicide removes the obscuring veil of nongendered terms such as homicide and murder.

Widespread male identification with killers demonstrates how rooted femicide is in sexist culture. For example, engineering student Celeste Brousseau, who had complained about sexism in the engineering faculty at the University of Alberta, was subjected to chants of "Shoot the bitch!" from hundreds of her "fellow" students when she participated in an engineering society skit-night shortly after the Lépine killings.

Misogyny not only motivates violence against women but distorts the press coverage of such crimes as well. Femicide, rape, and battery are variously ignored or sensationalized in the media, depending on the victim's race, class, and attractiveness (by male standards). The police, media, and public response to crimes against women of color, poor women, lesbians, women prostitutes, and women drug users is particularly abysmal—generally apathy laced with pejorative stereotyping and victim blaming (for example, "All women of color are drug addicts and/or prostitutes who put themselves in danger"). Moreover, public interest is disproportionately focused on cases involving nonwhite assailants and white middle-class victims, such as the uproar in Boston over the 1989 murder of Carol Stuart, a pregnant white woman who, her husband falsely claimed, was shot by an African-American robber. Carol Stuart was not murdered by a Willie-Horton-like phantasm of her husband's concoction, but by her affluent, white husband.

Femicide is on the extreme end of a continuum of antifemale terror that includes a wide variety of verbal and physical abuse, such as rape, torture, sexual slavery (particularly in prostitution), incestuous and extrafamilial child sexual abuse, physical and emotional battery, sexual harassment (on the phone, in the streets, at the office, and in the classroom), genital mutilation (clitoridectomies, excision, infibulations), unnecessary gynecological operations (gratuitous hysterectomies), forced heterosexuality, forced sterilization, forced motherhood (by criminalizing contraception and abortion), psychosurgery, denial of food to women in some cultures, cosmetic surgery, and other mutilations in the name of beautification. Whenever these forms of terrorism result in death, they become femicides.

THE MAGNITUDE OF SEXIST TERRORISM IN THE UNITED STATES

Federal statistics do not reveal the scope of violence against women. One feminist researcher, Mary Koss, has described the federal government's efforts to gather national statistics on rape as "a cruel hoax that covers up rather than reveals women's risk of victimization." Surveys by independent researchers indicate shattering rates of female victimization. In Diana Russell's probability sample survey of 930 San Francisco women, for example, 44 percent reported being victimized by rape or attempted rape, 38 percent by incestuous and extrafamilial child sexual abuse and 16 percent by incestuous abuse, and 14 percent by wife rape.

As with rape and child sexual abuse, femicide is most likely to be perpetrated by a male family member, friend, or acquaintance. Ironically, the patriarchy's ideal domestic arrangement (heterosexual coupling) holds the greatest potential for femicide. Although it is not legitimate to assume that a misogynist element is present in all murders of women by men, it is probable that this is the case for most murders of women by their legal or common-law husbands. Table 1 shows that women murdered by their husbands outnumber all other categories of victims where information about the relationship is available. Specifically, in those cases where it is possible to determine the relationship between the murdered women and their murderers, husbands constituted a third of the murderers during the 12-year period analyzed.

Violent crimes against women have escalated in recent decades. Some believe this increase is due to increased reporting. But Russell's research on (largely unreported) rape, for example, establishes a dramatic escalation during

---

TABLE 1 Statistics on the Murder of Women Fifteen Years and Older by Relationship: 1976–1987

Relationship	No. of Women Murdered	Percentage	Percentage in Known Relationships[a]
Husband/common law	11,236	22.81	33.10
Other family	2,937	5.96	8.65
Other intimates[b]	5,318	10.80	15.67
Acquaintances	9,930	20.16	29.26
Strangers	4,521	9.18	13.32
Undetermined	15,320	31.10	
TOTAL	49,262	100.01	100.00

Source: James A. Mercy, "Men, Women, and Murder: Gender-Specific Differences in Rates of Fatal Violence and Victimization," *Journal of Trauma*. Forthcoming.
a. (N=33,942)
b. Friend, date, cohabiting relationship

the last 50 years. Although it is not yet possible to assess the number of sex murders in any given year, virtually all experts agree that there has been a substantial rise in such killings since the early 1960s. A surge in serial murder (when one perpetrator kills a number of victims in separate incidents) is recognized by criminologists to have begun in the 1950s and has become a characteristic phenomenon of the late twentieth century in the United States.

We see this escalation of violence against females as part of male backlash against feminism. This doesn't mean it's the *fault* of feminism: patriarchal culture terrorizes women whether we fight back or not. Still, when male supremacy is challenged, that terror is intensified. While many women who stepped out of line in early modern Europe were grotesquely tortured and killed as witches (with estimates ranging from 200,000 to 9 million killed), today such women are regarded as cunts or bitches, deserving whatever happens to them. "Why is it wrong to get rid of some fuckin' cunts?" Kenneth Bianchi, convicted "Hillside Strangler," demanded.

Many law enforcement officials have commented on the growing viciousness in slayings. As Justice Department official Robert Heck said, "We've got people out there now killing 20 and 30 people and more, and some of them don't just kill. They torture their victims in terrible ways and mutilate them before they kill them." For example:

- Teenager Shirley Ledford screamed for mercy while Roy Norris and Lawrence Bittaker of Los Angeles raped and mutilated her with a pair of locking pliers, hit her with a sledgehammer, and jabbed her ear with an ice pick. The men audiotaped the torture-femicide from beginning to end.

- Sixty-five-year-old Jack King virtually destroyed the face of 16-year-old Cheryl Bess by pouring acid on her head after he tried to rape her. Bess survived the attack, permanently blinded, her hearing severely damaged, and her face totally disfigured.

- One victim of a sexual femicide was found "with stab wounds in her vagina and groin and with her throat slashed. Her nipples had been removed and her face severely beaten; her cut-off hair was found hanging from a nearby branch.

- In 1987, police found three half-naked, malnourished African-American women "shackled to a sewer pipe in a basement that doubled as a secret torture chamber" in the home of Gary Heidnik, a white Philadelphian; "24 pounds of human limbs were discovered stock-piled in a freezer and other body parts were found in an oven and a stew pot." (See part 3 of this volume, "Slavery and Femicide.")

Such atrocities also are enacted upon women by their male intimates. Joel Steinberg—who murdered his adopted daughter, Lisa, and tortured his companion, Hedda Nussbaum, for years—and Curtis Adams are extreme, but not unique, examples:

- "Steinberg had kicked her [Nussbaum] in the eye, strangled her, beaten her sexual organs, urinated on her, hung her in handcuffs from a chinning bar, lacerated a tear duct by poking his finger in the corner of her eye, broken her nose several times and pulled out clumps of hair while throwing her about their apartment. 'Sometimes he'd take the blowtorch we used for freebasing and move it around me, making me jump [said Nussbaum] . . . I have burn marks all over my body from that. Joel told me he did this to improve my coordination.' "

- In 1989, Curtis Adams was sentenced to 32 years in prison for torturing his wife in a 10-hour attack. After she refused anal sex, Adams handcuffed his wife, repeatedly forced a bottle and then a broomstick into her anus, and hung her naked out the window—taking breaks to make her read Bible passages adjuring women to obey their husbands.

The sex-and-violence culture of the late twentieth century is a breeding ground for such amateur torturers and executioners, who have emerged as the shock troops of male dominance.

A sense of entitlement is another cause of sexual terrorism. Many males believe they have a right to get what they want from females. If girls or women thwart them, some become violent, sometimes to the extent of committing femicide. Consider the extraordinary hatred exhibited in response to a complaint by female students at the University of Iowa about the loud stereos of male students who lived on the floor above them. A list in graffito, titled "The Top Ten Things to Do to the Bitches Below," was found in the men's bathroom and subsequently published in the university newspaper. The list included exhortations to beat women "into a bloody pulp with a sledgehammer and laugh" and instructions on "how to mutilate female genitalia with an electric trimmer, pliers, and a 'red-hot soldering iron.' " In a similar display of contempt for women, a suggestion was made in the University of Toronto engineering students' newspaper that women "cut off their breasts if they were sick of sexual harassment."

To see where these students get such gruesome ideas, we need only look to pornography and mass media "gorenography" (movies and magazines featuring scenes of sensationalized and eroticized violence). Like many feminists, we believe pornography is a form of antifemale propaganda, peddling a view of women as objects, commodities, "things" to be owned, used, and consumed while also promoting the logical correlates: all women are whores and therefore fair game; sexual violence is normal and acceptable; women deserve and want to be hurt, raped, or even killed. Research indicates that objectifying, degrading, and violent images of women in pornography and gorenography predispose certain males to be turned on by rape and other violence against women and and/or undermine their inhibitions against acting out sexualized violence.

An FBI study of 36 sex killers found that pornography was ranked highest in a list of many sexual interests by an astonishing 81 percent. Such notorious killers as Edmund Kemper (the "Coed Killer"), Ted Bundy, David Berkowitz (the "Son of Sam"), and Kenneth Bianchi and Angelo Buono (the "Hillside Stranglers") were all heavy pornography consumers. Bundy maintains that pornography "had an impact on me that was just so central to the development of the violent behavior that I engaged in." His assessment is consistent with testimony from many other sex offenders, as well as research on the effects of pornography.

Femicidal mayhem is the essential subject matter of slasher films, "splatterpunk" horror novels, or the endless outpouring of sex killer paperback thrillers—all genres that count the vast majority of their fans among men, particularly young men. In contemporary superhero comic books, graphic femicidal visuals abound. For example, a recent issue of "Green Arrow" depicts a near-naked prostitute, tortured and crucified. As a comic book distributor/apologist explained: "The readers are teen-aged boys, so what you have is a lot of repressed anger. . . . They do like to see the characters sliced and diced."

We do not mean to imply that one must go into the side-pockets of culture to encounter femicidal themes. Mainstream filmmaker Brian DePalma once whined, "I'm always attacked for having an erotic, sexist approach—chopping up women, putting women in peril. I'm making suspense movies! What else is going to happen to them?" In *Harlem Nights*, a "comedy," Eddie Murphy first beds, then blows away, Jasmine Guy, the film's object of desire. Misogynist and femicidal themes abound as well in rock and roll. Twenty years ago, Mick Jagger threatened, "Rape, murder, it's just a kiss away." Currently, Guns 'N' Roses croon, "Well I used to love her / but I had to kill her / she bitched so much / she drove me nuts."

Femicidal atrocity is everywhere normalized, explained away as a joke, and rendered into standard fantasy fare. Although the annihilation of women has not been formally institutionalized, our annihilation in media portrayals has been—from comic books through Nobel-prize-winning literature, from box-office smashes through snuff films. "C'mon girls," the refrain goes, "it's just entertainment." Meanwhile the FBI terms sex killings "recreational murder."

Most Americans refuse to recognize the gynocidal period in which we are living—and dying—today. To traverse the streets is often to walk a gauntlet. The nuclear family is a prison for millions of girls and women. Some husbands and fathers act as full-time guards who threaten to kill if defied, a threat all too often carried out. "Dedicated Bible reader" John List was convicted for mass murder in New Jersey in 1990 after escaping detection for 18 years. In a letter to his pastor, List complained that his wife refused to attend church, an action he "knew would harm the children." Moreover, his daughter wanted to pursue an acting career, making him "fearful as to what that might do to her continuing to be a Christian." In a rage over his loss of control of his family, this godly man slaughtered his wife, daughter, mother, and two sons.

If all femicides were recognized as such and accurately counted, if the massive incidence of nonlethal sexual assaults against women and girls were taken into account, if incestuous abuse and battery were recognized as torture (frequently prolonged over years), if the patriarchal home were seen as the inescapable prison it so frequently becomes, if pornography and gorenography were recognized as hate literature, then we in the United States might have to acknowledge that we live in the midst of a reign of sexist terror comparable in magnitude, intensity, and intent to the persecution, torture, and annihilation of European women as witches from the fourteenth to the seventeenth centuries.

REMEMORY AND RESISTANCE

Basically, I worshipped him. He was the most wonderful man I had ever met. I believed he had supernatural, godlike powers.

—Hedda Nussbaum on Joel Steinberg

We do not worship them.
We do not worship what they have made.
We do not trust them.
We do not believe what they say . . .
We do not worship them.

—Alice Walker, "Each One, Pull One"

It is unspeakably painful for most women to think about men's violence against us, whether individually or collectively. And when we do attempt to think about the unthinkable, speak about the unspeakable, as we must, the violence, disbelief, and contempt we encounter is often so overwhelming that we retreat, denying or repressing our experiences.

In November 1989, 28-year-old Eileen Franklin-Lipsker of Foster City, California, suddenly remembered having witnessed her father sexually abuse her 8-year-old friend, Susan Nason, then bludgeon her to death. Twenty years later, she turned her father in to the police. Such remembrance and denunciation is the work of the entire feminist movement against violence against women: to disobey the fathers' commandments to forget, deny, and maintain silence, and instead to turn in abusive fathers, husbands, brothers, lovers, sons, and friends. The recollection and acknowledgment of the history and experience that has been so profoundly repressed is what Toni Morrison, in her masterpiece *Beloved*, calls *rememory*. *Beloved* concerns the unthinkably painful subject of slavery. In an interview about the book, Morrison noted that there is virtually no remembrance—no lore, songs, or dances—of the African people who died en route to the Americas. "I suspect the reason is that it was not possible to survive on certain levels and dwell on it," Morrison suggested. "People who did dwell on it, it probably killed them, and the people who did not dwell on it probably went forward. . . . There is a necessity for remembering the horror, but . . . in a manner in which the memory is not destructive." Morrison's concept of rememory, though developed to describe the psychic torment inflicted on African-Americans, is crucial for women grappling with a femicidal world. We too must be able to face horror in ways that do not destroy, but save us.

Following the mass femicide carried out by Marc Lépine in Montreal, Quebec prime minister M. Bourassa rejected petitions to close the legislature and universities on the day of the funerals. A day of official mourning was only appropriate, he insisted, "when someone important to the State had died." Some Canadian feminists are working to establish 6 December as a national day of remembrance for the slaughtered women. We encourage women worldwide to join our Canadian sisters in declaring 6 December an international day of mourning and rage, a "Rememory Day" for all women who have been victims of sexual violence. As Ntozake Shange writes, "We shall have streets and monuments named after / these women & children they died for their country."

Still, such commemorations remain palliatives, modes of healing, but not cures. Feminists, collectively and internationally, must take on the urgent task of formulating strategies of resistance to femicide. Progressive people rightly favor an international boycott of South Africa so long as apartheid reigns; why then does no one consider the potential efficacy of boycotting violent and abusive men and their culture? The women in Aristophanes' *Lysistrata* engage in a sexual boycott of men to compel an end to war. In 1590, Iroquois women gathered in Seneca to demand the cessation of war among the nations. We must now demand an end to the global patriarchal war on women.

A femicidal culture is one in which the male is worshipped. This worship is obtained through tyranny, subtle and overt, over our bruised minds, our battered and dead bodies, and our co-optation into supporting even batterers, rapists, and killers. "Basically, I worshipped him," said Hedda Nussbaum. "We do not worship them . . . we do not trust them," writes Alice Walker. In myriad ways, let us refuse nurture, solace, support, and approval. Let us withdraw our worship.

Part 1

❖ ❖ ❖

FEMICIDE IS AS OLD AS PATRIARCHY

Women being hanged as witches during witch-craze that plagued Europe in the sixteenth and seventeenth centuries. On horseback is the bellman, on the ladder the hangman, below him two sargeants, and at right the witch finder taking money for his work. Print first published 1655. Reprinted by permission of the British Library.

Introduction

It is often claimed that the problem of violence against women is new or has recently become worse. It is said that women can no longer safely go out at night, implying that once, in some golden age, the streets were safe for women. It has even been suggested that violence against women in a domestic context was not a problem before feminists uncovered it in the 1970s. Historical comparisons are difficult since so much of women's experience is hidden from history. Similarly, such general statements are impossible to validate, because they lack reference to specific historical and cultural contexts.

If it is difficult to document the very existence of violence against women historically, documenting the extent of the violence is even more problematic. Femicide is not a recognized legal category, so no official statistics are available from the past or the present. Our aim in part 1 of this anthology is to demonstrate that while the concept of femicide is new, the phenomenon it describes is as old as patriarchy itself. Here we have brought together a series of articles that demonstrate that femicide, like other forms of sexual violence, has historically been used by men to secure the social relations of patriarchy, that is, male dominance and female subordination. Further, we aim to show that femicide reflects other hierarchies within specific patriarchal societies and affects women differently according to their positions in these other power structures, be they defined in terms of religion, race, relationship to heterosexuality, or class.

A historical discussion of femicide in different cultures illustrates both continuities and changes in the forms taken by femicide at different points in the histories of patriarchal societies. Some forms, such as the persecution of women suspected of using witchcraft, discussed by Marianne Hester, are quite specific to their particular cultural, political, and economic contexts. Similarly, as Diana

Russell shows, the lynching of African-American women in the southern United States was clearly shaped by the specific nature of racism in that culture. Marielouise Janssen-Jurreit explores yet another form of femicide, female infanticide, which she identifies as a gendered phenomenon practiced widely in patriarchal societies. Other forms of femicide, such as the torture and killing of women by their husbands, identified in 1878 by Frances Power Cobbe, have clear parallels in contemporary experience. In drawing together historical discussions of femicide from Europe in the Middle Ages, the American South, and eighteenth- and nineteenth-century India, part 1 of this volume shows that while all of these patriarchal societies were characterized by femicide, its forms were shaped by the social, political, and economic arrangements of the different cultures in different periods.

This evidence lends support to the argument that all patriarchal societies have used—and continue to use—femicide as a form of punishment or social control of women by men. For example, men have employed femicide as a means of punishing women who choose not to live their lives according to men's definitions of what constitutes a woman's proper role. For instance, Ruthan Robson documented little-known cases of legal lesbicide—the legal murder of women because of their lesbianism—that have occurred in Anglo-European patriarchy. This form of capital punishment of women who challenge or appear to challenge male notions of womanhood also serves as a form of threat or social control for a wider group of women by showing what can happen to women who step out of line—a line drawn by men.

Examining these accounts also enables us to study the legal responses to femicide. Some forms of femicide have been endorsed by law, as shown by Marianne Hester's reading on what is commonly termed the "witch-craze." (This term is an unfortunate euphemism for the persecution and massacre of women as witches.) In other situations femicide may be a subject of conflict or controversy in law and the legal process. This is shown in different ways in Dorothy Stein's discussion of suttee, or bride burning, and Diana Russell's discussion of lynching.

Perhaps most important, the writings in part 1 suggest that historically femicide has been challenged by women. The form of resistance has been limited by the possibilities open to women within the different cultures. In short, the history of femicide is paralleled by a history of women's resistance.

The Witch-craze in Sixteenth- and Seventeenth-Century England as Social Control of Women

MARIANNE HESTER

During the sixteenth and seventeenth centuries, primarily in continental Europe and Scotland, but also in England, thousands of people were condemned to imprisonment and death, accused of the crime of "witchcraft." This period of rampant "witch"-hunting has aptly been called the "witch-craze" (Trevor-Roper 1969). What is so striking about the witch-craze period, and the reason it is such an important area for feminists to examine and understand, is that the vast majority of those deemed guilty of witchcraft were women. More than 90 percent of the accused in England were women, and the few men who were also accused tended to be married to an accused witch or to appear jointly with a woman (MacFarlane 1970, 160).

There are many different explanations for the witch-craze, but apart from a few, mainly feminist, contributions (Daly 1979; Ehrenreich and English 1976; Dworkin 1974; Karlsen 1987; Larner 1983), the fact that it was almost exclusively *women* who were accused is either not questioned at all or tends to be dealt with very inadequately.[1] It is my contention that the witch-craze cannot be adequately explained without focusing specifically on the problem of why primarily women were affected, because I believe the craze was—however unconsciously—an attempt at maintaining and restoring male supremacy. The form that this took, using the accusation of witchcraft, was a product of the socio-historical context. Only certain women—usually older, lower-class, poor, and often single or widowed—were directly affected, and this was also a product of the historically specific context. The witch-craze may be seen as an example of femicide where the use of violence against women by men was reliant on a particular construct of female sexuality. To understand why the social control of women took this particular form at this particular time we need to examine the events leading up to, and taking place during, the witch-craze period—which in England was largely from the middle of the sixteenth century to the middle of the seventeenth.

The time during and before the witch-craze was very complex, mainly because it was a period of great change and restructuring of society. Prior to the witch-craze, and laying the framework for the witch-hunts, was the (mainly European) Inquisition. This attempted to eradicate deviance from, and opposition to, the Catholic Church—what was termed "heresy." It is particularly interesting that the accusation of heresy often involved charges of what may be seen as "gender deviation" or "sexual deviation" from the Church's doctrine or ideology. Groups that elevated women's social status—such as the Albigensians, who were also accused of homosexuality (see Karlen 1971),[2] and the female religious order of Beguines (Gracia Clark 1981)[3]—were persecuted, as was Joan of Arc, who was accused of wearing supposedly "male" attire (Lea 1906).

The Catholic Church's view of women, which also formed the dominant ideology regarding gender before and during the witch-craze, was based on the creation story in Genesis. Eve was conceived from the rib of Adam and was therefore inferior to him. Eve, representive of womankind, had also sinned in the Garden of Eden, thus making all women by nature sinful. It was particularly female *sexuality* that made women sinful; women were considered sexually insatiable and led men into damnation through association with their bodies. This view was to remain dominant until the end of the witch-craze, and indeed the change in ruling-class gender ideology, which devalued women in a different but equally oppressive way, was very important in facilitating the decline of the craze. The "new ideology" changed the perception of women from that of "powerful and threatening witch" to that of "hysterical woman" and emphasized women's subordinate place in marriage (Karlsen 1987; Hester 1988, 1992).

The belief in witchcraft and magic existed prior to the witch-craze but was not a cause for concern in the earlier period as it was to become later. This was both because witchcraft was not considered sinister and because the legal apparatus for prosecuting it did not exist until the late Middle Ages (Cohn 1975, 163). What is also important is that within the traditional belief in witchcraft among the lower classes (the group against whom the witch-craze accusations were primarily directed), the witch was specifically seen as a woman. As Cohn explains, "For centuries before the great witch-hunt the popular imagination, in many parts of Europe, had been familiar with women who could bring down misfortune by a glance or a curse. It was popular imagination that saw the witch as an old woman who was the enemy of new life, who killed the young, caused impotence in men and sterility in women, blasted the crops" (153).

This was to be the stereotype of the witch outlined in the *Malleus Maleficarum* (1486), one of the most often printed and widely distributed manuals of witch spotting and woman hunting (see Kramer and Sprenger 1971); it was also echoed in the English witch accusations. It was a stereotype by which women were presented as a potential threat to the general well-being of the populace and in need of control.

So what was specific to sixteenth- and seventeenth-century England that allowed the change from informal accusations of witchcraft to a formal witch-hunt? The following features seem particularly important.

First, during the sixteenth and seventeenth centuries important changes were taking place in the religious, economic, and political dimensions of society. Very briefly, the Catholic, tenant-farming, and monarch-ruled social structure changed to Protestantism, greater reliance on wage labor, and greater influence by Parliament. The population was increasing at a rapid rate. The law was being transferred from ecclesiastical to secular administration, that is, from enforcement by the Church to enforcement by the State, although the Church (Protestant) continued to form the basis of the State. These changes led to tensions and conflicts and made society appear unstable (Pennington and Thomas 1978; Hill 1975). Sylvia Walby (1986) has found that when there are changes in the economic sphere, such as changes in production methods, conflict around male-female power relations also take place to ensure male dominance. It may be argued that other societal changes bring about a similar realignment regarding male power. If witch hunting is related to do woman hunting, as is being argued here, then we should expect that witch hunting intensifies at times of greatest change and instability. This is indeed the case, as Henry Kamen (1971) points out: "In every European country the most intensive outbreaks of witch persecution were in times of disaster" (276). Similarly, in England there was marked increase in witch accusations, for example, during the Civil War period.

An obvious area of male-female conflict at the time was around economic resources, particularly within the areas of the economy that were especially important to the development of capitalism. The textile industry was one such area. It grew considerably during the witch-craze period, and the textile areas were also centers of witchcraft prosecutions (although they were by no means the only such centers) (MacFarlane 1970, 149). The wool and textile industry was generally very important in sixteenth- and seventeenth-century England, and also crucial to the development of capitalism. It was women who did all the spinning of thread for the weaver; hence the term *spinster* for the women making their living by spinning. This work was badly paid, as Alice Clark (1982) observes: "Though these wages provided no margin for the support of children it was possible for a woman who could spin the better quality yarns to maintain herself in independence" (115). In other words, it was possible for the single woman without children to support herself in this way.

Although women spun the yarn, the weavers were increasingly men. "Women were excluded from cloth weaving on the grounds that their strength was insufficient to work the wide and heavy looms in use" (Clark 1982, 103). Only as the widow of a weaver could a woman carry out this trade, or even take on apprentices. However, such apprentices might not be accepted by the Company of Weavers (the trade organization) as apprentices trained by men, thus again placing women in a relatively inferior position (Lewenhak 1980, chap. 7).

Second, the demographic features of the population were changing. During the sixteenth and seventeenth centuries women outnumbered men, and for the lower classes specifically, marriage occurred very late. As Stone (1979) points out: "Among small property-owners and labourers the median age of first marriage was very high in the sixteenth century and went even higher in the 17th . . . rising from twenty-seven to twenty-eight for men and from twenty-five to twenty-seven for women" (44). The difficult economic circumstances meant that it was not financially possible to marry until late. The effect was the evolution of a population with large numbers of unmarried people, especially women, and women living outside the direct control of men (Wall 1981).[4] Within this context women were actively, if individually, competing with men for their livelihoods in spite of scarce resources and an increasing population. This was particularly the case for peasant women—the group most directly affected by the witch-craze (see Alice Clark 1982).

Third, by the mid-sixteenth century, when the witch-craze was emerging in England, women were visibly encroaching upon some formerly "male" domains. For example, it was an extraordinary period for the ascendancy of female monarchs: Mary Tudor, Elizabeth I, Mary Queen of Scots, Catherine de Medici, who ruled France on behalf of her sons, and also a number of female regents within the Hapsburg Empire. This rule by women was considered both unnatural and undesirable. It produced various condemnatory and misogynist reactions, such as the writings by John Knox (1558) against the "Monstrous Regiment of Women," directed specifically at Mary Queen of Scots but also published in England (Fraser 1969, 178).

Lastly, it should be noted that the threat posed by women to the male supremacist status quo, and men's reaction to it, was a specific concern of the literate upper strata of society throughout the period of the witch-craze. This is important—it was only by the upper classes sanctioning social control of women that the legal apparatus could be used against women as witches. The resultant debate about women's position vis-à-vis men is known as the "Popular Controversy."

The Popular Controversy debate was characterized by religious references to the "Original Sin" of Eve in the Garden of Eden and to Eve's construction by God from one of Adam's ribs, and generally by arguments meant to show women's inferiority to men and women's role as a "weaker vessel" fit only for the supposedly lesser task of carrying babies. The distinction between "good" and "bad" constituted an important aspect of this definition of women's nature and being. In the heavily religious context of the sixteenth and seventeenth centuries, the distinction was expressed in the following way: women were weak and more likely to sin (that is, be sexual) than men, and as a result women were also more likely to end up in league with the Devil, who would win them over by his sexual prowess and by promising them certain powers. Thus women, who were by nature *weak,* might actually become *stronger* than men through their allegience with the Devil. The dominant gender ideology thereby insisted that women could easily present a threat to society, and hence to men, unless female behavior was kept in check.

Within the Popular Controversy debate, this view of women is expressed, for example, by Joseph Swetnam, who, writing in 1615, exclaimed, "Then who can but say that women sprung from the devil, whose heads, hands and hearts, minds and souls are evil, for women are called the hook of all evil, because men are taken by them as fish is taken by the hook" (54). Swetnam also endorsed the idea that women were defective owing to their origin from the "crooked rib of Adam." It is interesting to see that, in a reply to Swetnam's misogynism, Ester Sowernam (1617) turned the idea around so that it is shown up to be both ludicrous and a condemnation of the men who produced such an idea in the first place. She suggested that, "if woman received her crookedness from the rib, and consequently from the man, how doth man excel in crookedness, who hath more of those crooked ribs?"(92). Despite reactions and resistance by literate women (and some men) at the time, the dominant gender ideology expressed through the Popular Controversy sanctioned what constituted a particularly brutal means of suppressing women. By inducing fear of violent interrogation, imprisoning in barbaric conditions, and sentencing to death, the ongoing witch-craze imposed social control of women in a way similar to the control arising out of both the threat of and actual sexual violence against women today. Moreover, as I mentioned previously, it was only through change in the dominant gender ideology that witchcraft prosecutions, and therefore the witch-craze, eventually declined.

THE ACCUSATIONS

The vast majority of witchcraft cases in England recorded as having come before the courts occurred during the reign of Elizabeth I (1563–1603). During James I's reign (1603–20), the recorded figures were much lower; and the underlying trend was a decrease in the number of formal accusations from then until the repeal of the witchcraft legislation in 1736. The number of executions throughout the witch-craze period in England was small compared with the European and Scottish experience; only a small proportion of English accusations ended in execution. The number of executions (as distinct from accusations) has been estimated by Ewen (1929) at "less than 1000" (122) between 1542 and 1736—that is, between the passing of the first witchcraft statute and the repeal of the last. It is generally difficult to provide figures for accusations, and for the outcomes of those accusations. Essex is one of the best documented areas in England: in the village of Hatfield Peveril—one of the densest areas of persecution—about 15 accusations of witchcraft reached the courts over a period of 30 years, in a population of approximately 600. Out of these 15 or so individuals, 6 were found not guilty, 2 were hanged for the crime of witchcraft, and the rest suffered either penury or prison (MacFarlane 1970, 95).

Informal accusations of witchcraft seem to have continued at a local level until the nineteenth century, and as mentioned earlier, they also occurred prior to the witch-craze period. We are familiar today with the word *witch* as a term of abuse. It might be argued that the term is still employed in a limited way as part of the mechanism of socially controlling women: women are sometimes accused of being "witches" when they step outside the "accepted" roles for women.

Unlike crimes such as theft or robbery, witchcraft was not merely a crime against an individual person—although that is often how it appeared in the English trials—it was a crime against *God,* and perhaps by inference, a crime against *man*kind. Furthermore, it was a crime almost impossible to deny once accused of it. Even if a woman accused of witchcraft was acquitted, the label of "witch" tended to linger; some such women were accused of another crime of witchcraft at a later date.[5]

The crimes, especially as outlined in the trial pamphlets,[6] do not appear to have been real crimes at all but seem to have been explanations for unpleasant events in the village. It was the general belief in supernatural powers that placed events in the lives of the villagers within the context of witchcraft, rather than the particular events themselves. In other words, witchcraft did not really exist, but was imagined to exist.

An examination of the trial material demonstrates the process by which women were accused of being "witches." For example, in the 1566 trial at the Chelmsford Assizes, Elizabeth Francis was one of three women accused of witchcraft. The others were Agnes Waterhouse, her sister, and Joan Waterhouse, Agnes's daughter.

The story of Elizabeth Francis, from the 1566 trial pamphlet, presents a very plausible scenario of one woman's life. Elizabeth was sexually abused by Andrew Byles, who she thought would marry her, but he refused. She then found herself pregnant, and facing the massive social and financial pressures of being a single parent with an illegitimate child, she set about procuring an abortion. Throughout the period described in the trial she was helped to get what she wanted (although this did not always turn out to her liking) by her "familiar," Sathan the cat. (A familiar was thought to have direct access to the Devil's power.) She was found guilty of causing injury to a fellow villager and sentenced to six months in prison.

Whether or not the trial of Elizabeth Francis, outlined in the contemporary pamphlet, represents her actual experience, the events mentioned and the way they are described can be seen as the product of a society in which men dominated women. In such a society we can expect that women tended to be financially dependent on men, that women were left with the responsibility for pregnancy, and that women were sexually abused by men rather than the other way around. Furthermore, it seems logical that women should have ended up trying to use, or being thought to use, supernatural power to "fight back" instead of using, for example, legal or financial retribution, which women tended not to have as much access to as men. Thus in some witch trials the accused appeared to admit that she *did* actually use witchcraft, presumably because this admission allowed her to feel she had some power over her life, but in other trials the accused *denied* using witchcraft—presumably to save her neck!

In another trial involving Elizabeth Francis, the 1579 trial at Chelmsford, the same interpretation can be applied, although the circumstances are somewhat different. As before, the story is one of unfulfilled wishes and retribution using witchcraft: Elizabeth Francis wanted yeast from one of her neighbors, "Poole's wife," who unfortunately would not give her any. As a result, Elizabeth Francis got an evil spirit in the form of a white dog to "pay her back" by giving her a seemingly endless pain in the head; the cost of the spirit's services was merely a crust of bread. Once again Elizabeth Francis was found guilty of causing injury by witchcraft; in addition to being imprisoned, she was placed in the pillory.

This scenario is, again, a common one in the trials: neighbors asking each other for help, not obtaining it, and using witchcraft to spite the ungiving individual. It was also common for women to accuse each other in this way, often incriminating other women in the process (which, indeed, Elizabeth Francis did, incriminating Widow Lorde and Mother Osborne as witches). It is not surprising that women should incriminate each other. Not only were they likely to believe, as members of a misogynist and superstitious society, that women were more prone than men to be in league with the Devil, but they would also want to accuse others of witchcraft to divert suspicion away from themselves.

From some of the trial material it appears that women would at times "confess" that they had used witchcraft as a result of pressure—promises of "deals" or harassment from the judge or members of the prosecution. Ursula Kempe's 1582 trial in Essex is one such instance. Ursula was pressured by the judge while she was being held in prison to confess to a number of crimes involving the use of witchcraft, including murder. The judge promised leniency if she confessed, a promise that he did not keep: Ursula Kempe was hanged after her eventual confession. Matthew Hopkins, also known as the "Witch-finder General," was particularly keen on the use of torture to obtain "evidence" against the accused and, partly as a result, managed to have a horrendous number of women killed for the crime of witchcraft—about 200 women during a period of only three years. Hopkins (who carried out his "witch-finding" during the 1640s) would subject the accused to enforced sleeplessness until she "saw" her familiars or imps, and this "evidence" was central to the subsequent trials.

THE WITCH-CRAZE AS SOCIAL CONTROL OF WOMEN

Throughout this reading I have been arguing that the witch-craze phenomenon involved the social control of women in the context of a society steeped in male supremacist religion and ideology and in which female sexuality was ideologically constructed as active and insatiable. I now want to show how the witch-craze as an instance of violence against women served to socially control women in the interests of men.

Within the analysis used here, the witch-craze is one form of violence against women as experienced by women during the sixteenth and seventeenth centuries (see also Bashar 1983). The witch-craze, of course, is not entirely similar to the violence experienced by women today. This is to be expected because the witch-craze occurred in a particular sociohistorical context different from today's society. What is important is that the general framework of analysis still applies. I will briefly outline this framework before using it to analyze the witch-craze phenomenon.

The analytical framework I use is concerned with the maintenance and perpetuation of power over women, and with understanding the longevity of male supremacy. By "male supremacy" I mean social systems where men are in a generally dominant position in relation to women, and where this dominance rests on a naturalized, albeit ideological, notion of male superiority, however defined. Drawing on contemporary women's experience of living in a male-supremacist society and using historical research, two areas of particular importance concerning the maintenance of male power over women have become apparent: sexuality, and male violence against women. Furthermore, these issues are intrinsically linked (see Jeffreys 1983, 1985; Jackson 1984, 1987; Hester 1988, 1992).

Hence, at the core of the feminist analysis used here is a focus on the "personal" as "political," particularly in the area of sexuality, which is seen as socially constructed rather than biologically given. Sexuality is seen as a fundamental aspect of the masculine and feminine constructs that define different behaviors for men and women; male and female sexual constructs may vary depending on the particular sociohistorical context. Thus within male-supremacist societies male and female sexualities tend to be constructed in such a way that male supremacy is maintained and continued.

The result is a system of male supremacy in which sexuality and "personal relations" are extremely crucial areas for acting out and maintaining male dominance, and in which these unequal power relations between men and women are institutionalized in many different ways as well as reflected in social relations generally. The institution of heterosexuality in particular is a linchpin of male dominance and control over women because it is in heterosexual relations that men are able to "do power over" women to the greatest effect (Jeffreys 1983, 1985; Jackson 1984, 1987; Hester 1992; Wise and Stanley 1987). In the formalized heterosexual relations of marriage and the family men may also benefit materially, as has been pointed out by various writers (Pahl 1980; Delphy 1984).

Violence against women by men (and the threat of such violence) relies on and reinforces the sexual constructs outlined above (Edwards 1987). In recent years feminists have argued that male violence against women in whatever form—harassment, rape, battering—is a crucial mechanism by which male dominance and control is maintained over women (Hanmer and Maynard 1987).

The construction of female sexuality discussed above entails its objectification. In the contemporary context this process reduces women to passive heterosexual objects compliant to male "needs," though at the same time objectification also presents women as sexually enticing and potentially threatening, necessitating the reassertion of male control. Women are thus implicated in the process of their own oppression. For example, the case of Peter Sutcliffe, the so-called Yorkshire Ripper, shows clearly how such a construct leads women to be seen as responsible for their own or other women's murders at the hands of men, while the male aggressor is placed in a less responsible role (Stanley 1985). Male dominance and control is asserted, then, by some men using violence against some women (Kelly 1987), while all women at the same time live with the threat of violence from potentially any man (LRCC 1984).

While the perspective outlined so far may give the impression that women tend to be passive victims in the male supremacist context, this is by no means the case. The social and ideological structures and institutions of male supremacy act to constrain women's behavior. But women are not passive. On the contrary, many women resist or fight back against their oppression and oppressors by using a number of strategies (Wise and Stanley 1987). Indeed, it may be argued that, without such activity by women, complex mechanisms of male control over women would be superfluous.

I will now show how this type of perspective provides a comprehensive, and also historically specific, analysis of the sixteenth- and seventeenth-century witch-craze in England.

The witch-craze constituted violence *against women* in the sense that the vast majority of the accused were women. Unlike rape, in which a man or group of men sexually violates a woman, the embodiment of male violence in the witch-craze is more complex: the legal apparatus, an essential ingredient of the craze, was entirely staffed by upper-class men. Individuals who made witch hunting their business, such as Matthew Hopkins, were also men. But more important was the general context of the witch-craze: it occurred during a period when the belief that women were inferior and sinful was widespread, and when the social structure reflected women's supposed inferiority and women were kept out of the important areas of societal power (for example, the Church and State hierarchies). Without this context it is highly unlikely that such an overwhelming proportion of women would have been blamed for village problems. At a general level, therefore, the witch-craze was violence against women within a context of male-dominant social relations, rather than violence by individual men against women.

As mentioned earlier, the definition of *witch* relied on a sexualized construct of female behavior, according to which female sexuality was defined as different and deviant from men's and as potentially threatening. This is reflected in many of the cases mentioned in the Essex trial pamphlets, for instance, where women were described in terms of sexual "deviance"—as "being lewd," having illegitimate children, and, in one instance, apparently being a lesbian (Hester

1988, 1992). As a result of the construction of women's behavior as deviant, accusing women of witchcraft seemed reasonable and necessary—as did imprisonment or death. Thus what we may call femicide was deemed a necessity to ensure social order—male social order. Furthermore, since it was part and parcel of female nature to be weak and sinful, women were themselves to blame for using witchcraft—just as today's myth is that women "ask" to be raped by supposedly presenting themselves as sexually enticing (LRCC 1984).

Women's lives were profoundly controlled through the threat of witchcraft accusation, as are women's lives today through the threat of violence (Hanmer and Saunders 1984). In sixteenth- and seventeenth-century society any conversation, request for help, or movement about the village could be construed as evidence of witch behavior. Doing good deeds as well as bad deeds opened a woman to the charge of witchcraft. A woman who knew a witch or was related to one was likely to be labeled a witch herself. In short, it was easy to be accused of witchcraft, and accusation could mean death. The fact that many women incriminated each other is indicative of the pressures they felt to avoid being accused of witchcraft, or of their attempts to reduce their own sentences.

In these ways, the framework for analyzing present-day violence against women outlined earlier can help us understand much of the witch-craze phenomenon. Within this framework it may be argued that *any* woman could be the target of male violence. Today some women may at times be more vulnerable, even if others are perceived as more directly threatening. As Susan Brownmiller (1976) writes about Albert De Salvo, the Boston Strangler, "he deliberately began his murdering career by 'dropping' older women, who would certainly present less physical resistance, and then, as he gained confidence, began testing his strength against younger women" (205). Similarly, at the time of the witch-craze it was perhaps easier to accuse those who were more vulnerable such as the old, widowed, and poor—although the craze itself was based on a religious and inherently male-supremacist ideology that saw all women generally as a threat and thus in need of control.

CONCLUSION

The witch-craze is not a unique event to be filed under "the historical and unrepeatable past." Rather, the witch-craze is part of the ongoing attempt by men—acting as a group and with the support of some women—to ensure the continuance of male supremacy. The witch-craze was particular to a specific historical period; very significantly, it was a product of a society with a prevalent superstitious belief in evil and magic. But it was also a response to an age-old problem, a part of the dynamic process whereby men as a group actively attempted to maintain dominance over women, who were rarely passively compliant. To understand the witch-craze it is necessary to look at its particular historical setting as well as to situate it within the wider, and ongoing, mechanisms of social control.

Notes

1. For English material see L'Estrange Ewen, *Witch Hunting and Witch Trials* (1929); Christina Hole, *Witchcraft in England* (1947); Wallace Notestein, *A History of Witchcraft in England from 1558 to 1718* (1968); and Keith Thomas, *Religion and the Decline of Magic* (1978). Alan MacFarlane's *Witchcraft in Tudor and Stuart England* (1970) is the most detailed work specifically on the Essex witch accusations; the court records, specifically the Assizes, have been compiled by James Cockburn, *Calender of Assize Records* (1978, 1982). See note 6.

2. The Albigensians were members of a medieval Christian religious group who considered themselves purer than the orthodox Church. They also allowed women to hold high-ranking positions within the group. They were outlawed as heretics (Karlen 1971).

3. The Beguines were a women-only Christian order established during the Middle Ages. They carried out religious activities deemed the province of men by the orthodox Church.

4. Single women were likely to be working as live-in servants in households that were headed by men. See Laslett (1977, 13–48).

5. Such, for example, was the case of Margaret Welles (or Gans), who was acquitted in 1579 after being accused of using witchcraft to cause murder. She appears in the records of the next Assizes accused of bewitching a pig, though she was again acquitted. See also the case of Elizabeth Francis, described below.

6. Material concerning the English witch-craze can be found in a variety of contemporary sources:

   1. Court records, mainly from the Assize courts, but also from the Quarter sessions, and to some extent from the Church Court and Borough Court records
   2. Pamphlets on some individual trials
   3. Literature discussing the nature and treatment of witchcraft, for example, *The Daemonology* by James I (see MacFarlane [1970])

There are five pamphlets for Essex of which I use two here; see "Essex Pamphlets" in the bibliography below.

References

Bashar, Nazite. 1983. "Rape in England between 1550 and 1700." In *The Sexual Dynamics of History: Men's Power, Women's Resistance,* ed. London Feminist History Group, 28–46. London: Photo Press.

Brownmiller, Susan. 1976. *Against Our Will.* Harmondsworth: Penguin.

Clark, Alice. [1919]. *The Working Life of Women in the Seventeenth Century.* London: Routledge & Kegan Paul, 1981.

Clark, Gracia. 1981. "The Beguines: A Medieval Women's Community." In *Building Feminist Theory,* ed. Quest, 236–42. London: Longman.

Cockburn, James. 1978. *Calendar of Assize Records: Essex Indictments: Elizabeth I.* London: Her Majesty's Stationery Office.

_____. 1982. *Calendar of Assize Records: Essex Indictments: James I.* London: Her Majesty's Stationery Office.

Cohn, Norman. 1975. *Europe's Inner Demons.* London: Chatto/Heinemann.

Crawford, Pat. 1983. *Exploring Women's Past.* London: Allen & Unwin.

Daly, Mary. 1979. *Gyn/Ecology: The Metaethics of Radical Feminism*. London: Women's Press.

Delphy, Christine. 1984. *Close to Home*. London: Hutchinson.

Dworkin, Andrea. 1974. *Woman-Hating*. New York: E. P. Dutton.

Edwards, Anne. 1987. "Male Violence in Feminist Theory: An Analysis of the Changing Conceptions of Sex/Gender Violence and Male Dominance." In Hanmer and Maynard 1987, 13–29.

Ehrenreich, Barbara, and Deirdre English. 1976. *Witches, Midwives, and Nurses*. London: Writers and Readers.

Essex Pamphlets:

    1. *A Detection of damnable driftes, practized by three Witches arraigned at Chelmisforde in Essex, at the late Assizes there holden, whiche were executed in Aprill 1579.* Copy in British Museum.

    2. *The examination and confession of certain Wytches at Chensforde in the Countie of Essex before the Quenes maiesties Judges, The xxvi daye of July Anno 1566.* Copy in British Museum; reprinted in *Miscellanies of the Philobiblon Society* 3 (1863–64).

Ewen, L'Estrange C. [1929]. *Witch Hunting and Witch Trials*. London: Frederick Miller, 1971.

Fraser, Antonia. 1972. *Mary Queen of Scots*. London: Book Club Associates.

Hanmer, Jalna, and Mary Maynard. 1987. *Women, Violence, and Social Control*. London: Macmillan.

_____, and Sheila Saunders. 1984. *Well Founded Fear*. London: Hutchinson.

Hester, Marianne. 1988. "The Dynamics of Male Domination." Ph.D. thesis (University of Leeds).

_____. 1992. *Lewd Women and Wicked Witches: The Dynamics of Male Domination*. London: Routledge.

Hill, Christopher. 1975. *The World Turned Upside Down*. Harmondsworth: Penguin.

Hole, Christina. 1947. *Witchcraft in England*. London: Batsford.

Jackson, Margaret. 1984. "Sexology and the Social Construction of Male Sexuality." In *The Sexuality Papers*, ed. Lal Coveney et al, 45–68. London: Hutchinson.

_____. 1987. " 'Facts of life' or the eroticization of women's oppression? Sexology and the social construction of heterosexuality." In *The Cultural Construction of Sexuality*, ed. Pat Caplan, 45–58. London: Tavistoc.

Jeffreys, Sheila. 1983. "Sex Reform and Anti-feminism in the 1920s." In *The Sexual Dynamics of History*, ed. London Feminist History Group, 98–112. London: Pluto Press.

_____. 1985. *The Spinster and Her Enemies*. London: Pandora.

Kamen, Henry. 1976. *The Iron Century: Social Change in Europe 1550–1660*. London: Sphere.

Karlen, Arno. 1971. *Sexuality and Homosexuality*. London: Norton.

Karlsen, Carol. 1987. *The Devil in the Shape of a Woman*. New York: Norton.

Kelly, Liz. 1987. "The Continuum of Sexual Violence." In Hanmer and Maynard 1987, 46–60.

Kramer, Heinrich, and James Sprenger. 1971. *Malleus Maleficarum* [1486]. New York: Dover.

Larner, Christina. (1983). *Enemies of God*. Oxford: Blackwell.

Laslett, Peter. 1977. *Family Life and Illicit Love in Earlier Generations*. Cambridge: Cambridge University Press.

_____, and Richard Wall. 1972. *Household and Family in Past Time*. Cambridge: Cambridge University Press.

Lea, Henry C. 1963. *The Inquisition of the Middle Ages*, vol 1. [1906]. London: Eyre & Spottiswode.

Lewenhak, Sheila. 1980. *Women and Work*. London: Fontana.

London Rape Crisis Centre (LRCC). 1984. *The Reality for Women*. London: The Women's Press.

MacFarlane, Alan. 1970. *Witchcraft in Tudor and Stuart England: A Regional and Comparative Study*. London: Routledge.

Notestein, Wallace. 1968. *A History of Witchcraft in England from 1558 to 1718*. New York: Thomas Y. Crowell.

Pahl, Jan. 1980. "Patterns of Money Management within Marriage." *Journal of Social Policy* 9, no. 3.

Pennington, Donald, and Keith Thomas. 1978. *Puritans and Revolutionaries*. Oxford: Oxford University Press.

Sowernam, Ester. 1617. *Ester hath hang'd Haman: or an Answere to a lewd Pamphlet, entituled, "The Arraignment of Women." With the arraignment of lewd, idle, froward and unconstant men, and husbands*. Copy in Fawcett Library, London.

Stanley, Liz (1985). "Accounting for the Fall of Peter Sutcliffe, and the Rise of the So-called Yorkshire Ripper." *Manchester University Occasional Papers* 15 (University of Manchester).

Stone, Lawrence. 1979. *The Family, Sex, and Marriage*. Harmondsworth: Penguin.

Swetnam, Joseph. 1615. *The Arraignment of Lewde, Idle, Froward and unconstant Women: or the vanitie of them, choose you whether. With a Commendacion of wise, vertuous, and honest Women. Pleasant for married Men, profitable for young Men, and hurtful for none*. Copy in Fawcett Library, London.

Thomas, Keith. 1978. *Religion and the Decline of Magic*. Harmondsworth: Penguin.

Trevor-Roper, Hugh. 1969. *The European Witch-craze of the Sixteenth and Seventeenth Centuries*. Harmondsworth: Penguin.

Walby, Sylvia. 1987. *Patriarchy at Work*. Cambridge: Polity.

Wall, Richard. 1981. "Women Alone in English Society." *Annales de Demographie Historique*, 25–40.

Wise, Sue, and Liz Stanley. 1987. *Georgie Porgie*. London: Pandora.

Legal Lesbicide

RUTHANN ROBSON

The legal murder of women because of their lesbianism has a long if unrenowned history within Anglo-European patriarchy.[1] Although it is popular to posit that lesbianism (especially as opposed to male homosexuality) has been traditionally legally irrelevant, or that lesbianism is not a historically intelligible concept prior to the nineteenth century "rise of the sexologists," my own work has led me to evidence of a tradition of legal lesbicide. Many legal systems have authorized death as an appropriate punishment for lesbian sexuality.

The historical indications of legal lesbicide are quixotic, abstract and accidental. In Roman civilization a married woman found engaged in any lesbian sexual activity (even mutual caressing) who had not produced the requisite number of children could be accused of adultery. If convicted, she could be killed by her husband as a "just penalty for her crime" (Ide 1985, 49). However, "lesbianism was excused by general Roman populace as being the result of drunkenness: women suspected of 'lesbian tendencies' were frequently forbidden access to the family wine cellar, and a married woman caught in the wine cellar could be forced to starve herself to death—even if she was not found in a compromising situation with another woman" (Ide 1985, 50). There is evidence of a "general blood bath" in which thousands of women were sentenced to death for participating in "Bacchic" rites and delivered to their male relatives to be put to death privately (Ide 1985, 50–52). Martial, an influential poet, argued that Roman lesbians should lose their property and possibly their lives.

Like ancient Rome, Christian Rome and medieval Europe continued to penalize lesbian sexuality, usually relying on Paul's epistle to the Romans concerning women changing the "natural into the unnatural"(1:26). In the Holy

---

This article is based upon a longer work, "Lesbianism in Anglo-European Legal History," 5 *Wisconsin, Women's Law Journal* (1990), and is also part of *Lesbian (Out)Law* (Ithica, N.Y.: Firebrand Books, 1992). The article has benefited immeasurably from the research of Sarah Valentine.

Roman Empire under Emperor Charles V (1519–56), the constitution explicitly stated that an impurity of "a woman with a woman" merited a sentence of death by burning (Faderman 1981, 49). Secular laws also mandated death for lesbianism. The famous 1260 Code of Orleans in France secularized the prohibition of lesbianism, mandating that for the first two offenses a woman would "lose her member"; for the third offense she would be burned (Bailey 1955, 142; Crompton 1981, 13). A small town near Venice, Italy, adopted a statute in 1574 that forbade sexual relations of "a woman with a woman if they are twelve or more," ordering as punishment that "she shall be fastened naked to a stake in the street of Locusts and shall remain there all day and night under a reliable guard and the following day shall be burned outside the city" (Crompton 1981, 16).

Burning alive was also the preferred punishment for lesbianism in Spain. A midsixteenth-century gloss on the country's basic law code of 1256 makes this explicit (Crompton 1981, 14). However, Spanish and Italian jurists devoted attention to tailoring the punishment to the nature of the lesbian activity (Faderman 1981, 36, 419n.14). For example, the Spanish jurist Antonio Gomez "felt that burning should be mandatory only in cases in which a woman has relations with another woman by means of any material instrument." (Faderman 1981, 36, 419n.14; Crompton, 17; Brown, 165–66 n.5) If a "woman has relations with another woman without an instrument" then her punishment was variable: she might, for example, be beaten as delinquent women were in Granada. (Crompton, 19). Similarly, in Italy, the jurist Farinaccius decreed that if a woman behaved "like a man with another woman she will be in danger of the penalties for sodomy and death" (Brown 1986, 14). However, if a woman only made overtures, she was to be publicly denounced; if she "behaves corruptly with another woman only by rubbing," she was to be "punished." If she "introduces some wooden or glass instrument into the belly of another," she was to be put to death (Brown 1986, 14).

In addition to legal texts mandating the punishment of lesbianism, there are references in European history to executions and other punishments of women for lesbian sexual acts and cross-dressing. In Spain, two nuns were burned for using "material instruments" (Crompton 1981, 17). In France, a woman was burned in 1536 for "counterfeit[ing] the office of husband" (Crompton 1981, 17; Faderman 1981, 51). A case of lesbian sexuality was brought before the parliament of Toulouse in 1553, and another in 1555 (Brown 1986, 6, 165n.5), and two other women were tried and tortured but eventually acquitted for insufficient evidence (Crompton 1981, 17). In Germany, a girl was drowned at Speier in 1477 for "lesbian love" (Crompton 1981, 17). In Italy, a woman was hanged in 1580 for "engaging in a lesbian love affair" (Brown 1986, 165n.5). All of these references are preserved through accident—for example, the last-mentioned hanging in Italy was recorded in Montaigne's diary (Crompton 1981, 18). Therefore the discoverable instances of lesbicide almost certainly do not accurately reflect the true numbers of legally sanctioned murders of women for lesbian acts.

The trial of Catharina Margaretha Linck and Catharina Margaretha Muhlhahn in 1721 is recorded in a rare transcript of criminal accusations of lesbianism (Ericksson 1981). The transcript gives an equally rare portrait of two working-class women attempting to live lesbian lives during an inhospitable time. The judicial proceedings interestingly obsess on the exact nature of the sexual acts between the two women, because "it is only fair to determine the penalty according to the seriousness of the crime" (Ericksson 1981, 39). That Catharina Linck would be killed was never in doubt: the issue the jurists deliberated was whether the punishment would be hanging with the body burned afterward, being put to death by the sword, or being burned alive.

Any discussion of lesbicide is incomplete without reference to the "witch-craze," which, despite the characterization of "craze," was most often systemized and legalized femicide. Authorities and popular opinion linked witchcraft, heresy, and homosexuality. An anonymous 1460 tract circulated during the trial of accused witches in France documents these connections: "Sometimes indeed indescribable outrages are perpetrated in exchanging women, by order of the presiding devil, by passing on a woman to other women and a man to other men, an abuse against the nature of women by both parties and similarly against the nature of men, or by a woman with a man outside the regular orifice and in another orifice" (Evans 1978, 76; Robbins 1959, 468). Earlier accounts of the orgies so plentiful in witchcraft accounts also include mentions of homosexuality and bisexuality, and the phrase *femina cum feminus* (woman with woman) was apparently often an accusation in witch trials (Russell 1972, 94–95, 239).

One of the most famous trials was that of Joan d'Arc, charged with heresy and witchcraft. At 16, Joan d'Arc refused to marry despite her father's wishes. Her betrothed sued her for breach of contract based upon her father's promise. She defended herself against this charge and won (Russell 1972, 86). During her successful career as a soldier, Joan d'Arc's wearing of male attire, including armor, served to protect her. After her capture, the Inquisition focused on her male attire as proof of criminality. The judges also inquired into her relationships with other women, including the woman whom with she lived after she left her parents and another woman with whom she admitted sleeping for two nights. (Evans 1978, 6). Whether or not Joan d'Arc engaged in lesbianism,[2] her refusal to succumb to heterosexualism resulted in her being burned at the stake.

Contemporaneously with the Inquisition's subjugation of witchcraft by legal means, the conquisitadors and other European colonists were quelling the lesbian sexuality they found among many native peoples of the New World. Of course, the indigenous peoples of the Americas were not monolithic in culture or custom. Contemporary Native American Paula Gunn Allen (1981) describes the tradition of the Lakota culture's *koskalaka:* women who do not want to marry and are said to be followers of *wiya numpa*, or Doublewoman, she who can link two women together (82).[3] However, there were laws among the Aztecs and "pre-Conquest Mexicans" that mandated the death penalty for lesbianism (Katz 1976, 283). Lesbian scholar Judy Grahn (1984) notes that "Gay people were often the first Indians killed and that even when tribes were tolerated by the white people, their Gay people were mocked and persecuted to the point of changing their behavior for the safety of their people" (56). Missionaries inquired about lesbian sexuality during confessions (Katz 1976, 283, 286–87). As the New World became colonized, European powers extended their laws prohibiting lesbianism. For example, the Portuguese extended their death penalty to Brazil in 1521 and broadened the list of crimes deserving of capital punishment to include lesbian acts in 1602 (Greenburg 1988, 304).

Like Catholic missionaries, the Protestants also sought to suppress lesbian sexual acts within their jurisdictions. In 1636, the Rev. John Cotton prepared, upon request from the General Court of Massachusetts, legislation for the Massachusetts Bay colony. Cotton included lesbianism—"woman with woman"—in his definition of the capital offense of sodomy, but this legislation was not adopted (Katz 1976, 20). Soon thereafter, the governor of Massachusetts Bay colony wrote to Plymouth theologians requesting an opinion concerning "what sodomitical acts" were to be punished by death. At least one theologian, the Rev. Charles Chauncy, who later became president of Harvard University, included "women with women" as a capital offense (Katz 1976, 20–21; Oaks 1981, 81). The recorded punishments for lesbian sexual acts in Massachusetts at that time, however, were apparently not capital.

Actual incidents of legal lesbicide may be camouflaged by the legal system's commitment to silence about lesbianism. Despite statutes and trials, there has long been an entrenched reluctance to acknowledge lesbianism. For example, fifteenth-century rector Jean Gerson relied upon St. Thomas Aquinas to conclude that lesbianism was a crime against nature but described it as a sin in which "women have each other by detestable and horrible means which should not be named or written" (Brown 1986, 7, 19). This silence was also practiced by secular authorities. Germain Colladon, a famous sixteenth-century jurist, advised Genevan authorities who had no prior experience with lesbian crimes, that the death sentence should be read publicly but that the customary description of the crime should be omitted: "A crime so horrible and against nature is so detestable and because of the horror of it, it cannot be named" (Monter 1981, 41). Thus, when a lesbian was drowned for her crime in 1568, Colladon stated: "it is not necessary to describe minutely the circumstances of such a case, but only to say that it's for the detestable crime of unnatural fornication" (Monter 1981, 48). Given such official silences, it is likely that more women were punished for lesbian sexual acts but their crimes were unnamed or misnamed in official records.

A modern statutory debate reproduces this commitment to silence. A 1921 amendment to a British bill sought to penalize any act "of gross indecency between female persons." As Sheila Jeffreys explains, the amendment failed to pass because of a deliberate choice to ignore lesbianism. Quoting from debates by the members of Parliament, Jeffreys posits that the choice to ignore lesbianism was a deliberate one selected as the best method for eradicating "perverts."

The members of Parliament argued that the death penalty would "stamp them out" and locking lesbians up as lunatics would "get rid of them," but that ignoring them was best because "these cases are self-exterminating." The Parliament members explicitly recognized the danger of lesbianism. They believed lesbianism caused the "destruction" of Greek civilization and the "downfall" of the Roman Empire; they feared lesbianism could cause the decline of "our race" and the sexual unavailability of women to men ("any woman who engages in this vice will have nothing whatsoever to do with the other sex") (Jeffreys 1985, 114). The decision of the lawmakers was that the danger of mentioning lesbian sexuality outweighed the danger of not criminalizing it.

Legal lesbicide has included the murder—by drowning, by burning, by starving, by hanging—of flesh-and-blood women. Such murders have been committed by both secular and religious powers. These institutions continue to endorse another type of legal lesbicide—the murder of the lesbian choice within women. Thus, while lesbianism is not a contemporary capital crime, lesbian sexuality is criminalized by many governments and condemned by most religions. Even without the backing of state or church power, lesbicide persists as a "private" act in much the same manner as the "private" starving of a woman to death was permitted to the husband by the laws of the Roman Empire. In researching modern legal instances of lesbian violence, I discovered an amazing number of cases in which men's violence toward women included verbal accusations of lesbianism. Since I was looking for the murder of "real" lesbians, at first I discounted these cases, in which the judicial opinions assumed the victim was heterosexual. But perhaps that is the essence of lesbicide: the murder of lesbian possibility, in flesh and in spirit.

Notes

1. This article is limited to European and Anglo-American legal history because of the limited nature of my historical research skills. I am trained as an attorney, not as a historian. Further, the purpose of the law review article upon which this article is based was to confront the often repeated statement in American legal literature that "lesbianism was never punished."

2. Rather than engaging in analysis of the "real" reason Joan d'Arc was executed, I think it is important to make connections between lesbian sexuality, cross-dressing and paganism, all of which are threats to male authority. Arthur Evans (1978) explicitly notes Joan d'Arc's relationship with women as constituting part of the charges against her (6) and also makes an important connection between cross-dressing and paganism: "For one thing, the emphasis on transvestism at Joan's trial is important because transvestism played a major role in the religion of Europe before Christianity. The historian Pennethorne Hughes [1965] put it this way: 'The wearing of clothes appropriate to the opposite sex was always one of the rites of witchcraft, as it has been of primitive [sic] peoples, during their fertility festivals throughout the history of the world' " (11).

3. See also Katz (1976), 293–98, 302–3, 304–11, 317–18, 320, 321–25, 327; Grahn (1984), 49–72.

References

Allen, P. G. 1981. "Lesbians in American Indian Culture." *Conditions* 7; reprinted in *Conditions: A Retrospective,* 1989.

Bailey, D. 1955. *Homosexuality and the Western Christian Tradition.* London: Longmans, Green.

Brown, J. 1986. *Immodest Acts.* Oxford: Oxford University Press.

Crompton, L. 1981. "The Myth of Lesbian Impunity." *Journal of Homosexuality* 6:11; reprinted in *The Gay Past: A Collection of Historical Essays,* ed. S. J. Licata and R. Petersen. New York: Haworth Press, 1985.

Ericksson, B., trans. 1981."A Lesbian Execution in Germany, 1721: The Trial Records." *Journal of Homosexuality* 6:27; reprinted in *The Gay Past: A Collection of Historical Essays,* ed. Licata and Petersen, 1985.

Evans, A. 1978. *Witchcraft and the Gay Counterculture.* Boston: Fag Rag Books.

Faderman, L. 1981. *Surpassing the Love of Men.* New York: William Morrow.

Grahn, J. 1984. *Another Mother Tongue.* Boston: Beacon Press.

Greenburg, D. 1988. *The Construction of Homosexuality.* Chicago: University of Chicago Press.

Ide, A. F. 1985. *Loving Women: A Study of Lesbianism to 500 CE.* Arlington, Tex.: Liberal Arts Press.

Jeffreys, S. 1985. *The Spinster and Her Enemies.* London: Routledge & Kegan Paul.

Katz, J. 1976. *Gay American History: A Documentary.* New York: Thomas Crowell & Co.

Monter, W. 1981. "Sodomy and Heresy in Early Modern Switzerland." *Journal of Homosexuality* 6:41.

Oaks, R. 1981. "Defining Sodomy in Seventeenth-Century Massachusetts." *Journal of Homosexuality* 6:79.

Robbins, R. 1959. *Encyclopedia of Witchcraft and Demonology.* New York: Crown.

Russell, J. B. 1972. *Witchcraft in the Middle Ages.* Ithaca, N.Y.: Cornell University Press.

Wife Torture in England

FRANCES POWER COBBE

Frances Power Cobbe wrote this article as part of the successful campaign for the Matrimonial Causes Act of 1878, which enabled abused wives to obtain separation orders to keep their husbands away from them. The laws of England and their interpretation by the courts encouraged physical punishment of wives as deriving from a husband's responsibility for his wife's actions. In common law a man had the right "to give his wife moderate correction . . . by domestic chastisement" just as he could his children or apprentices. Common law also recognized his right to restrain his wife physically "to prevent her going into society of which he disapproves, or otherwise disobeying his rightful authority."

The assault on a wife by her husband seems to be surrounded by a certain halo of jocularity which invites people to smile whenever they hear of a case of it (terminating anywhere short of actual murder), and causes the mention of the subject to conduce rather than otherwise to the hilarity of a dinner party. The occult fun thus connected with wife-beating forms by no means indeed the least curious part of the subject. Certainly in view of the state of things revealed by our criminal statistics there is something ominous in the circumstance that "Punch" should have been our national English street-drama for more than two centuries. . . . [In which] it is . . . remarkable that so much of the enjoyment should concentrate about the thwacking of poor Judy, and the flinging of the baby out of the window. . . .

Probably the sense that they must carry with them a good deal of tacit sympathy on the part of other men has something to do in encouraging wife-beaters, just as the fatal notion of the good fellowship of drink has made thousands of sots. . . .

From *Strong-minded Women: And Other Lost Voices from Nineteenth-Century England,* ed. Janet Horowitz Murray. Copyright 1978 Janet Horowitz Murray. Pantheon Books, New York, 1978. Also from *Contemporary Review* (London), April 1878.

The general depreciation of women *as a sex* is bad enough, but in the matter we are considering, the special depreciation of *wives* is more directly responsible for the outrages they endure. The notion that a man's wife is his PROPERTY. . . is the fatal root of incalculable evil and misery. Every brutal-minded man, and many a man who in other relations of life is not brutal, entertains more or less vaguely the notion that his wife is his *thing,* and is ready to ask with indignation (as we read again and again in the police reports), of any one who interferes with his treatment of her, "May I not do what I will *with my own?"* It is even sometimes pleaded on behalf of poor men, that they *possess nothing else* but their wives, and that, consequently, it seems doubly hard to meddle with the exercise of their power in that narrow sphere! . . .

[N]ot only is an offence against a wife condoned as of inferior guilt, but any offence of the wife against her husband is regarded as a sort of *Petty Treason.* . . . Should she be guilty of "nagging" or scolding, or of being a slattern, or of getting intoxicated, she finds usually a short shrift and no favour—and even humane persons talk of her offence as constituting if not a justification for her murder, yet an explanation of it. She is, in short, liable to capital punishment without judge or jury for transgressions which in the case of a man would never be punished at all, or be expiated by a fine of five shillings. . .

[Editors' note: *The preceding text is from* Strong-minded Women; *the text that follows is from Cobbe's original article in* Contemporary Review.]

Nay, in her case there is a readiness even to pardon the omission of the ordinary forms of law as needlessly cumbersome. In no other instance save that of the Wife-beater is excuse made for a man taking the law into his own hands. We are accustomed to accept it as a principle that "lynching" cannot be authorised in a civilised country, and that the first lesson of orderly citizenship is that no man shall be judge, jury, and executioner in his own case. But when a wife's offences are in question this salutary rule is overlooked, and men otherwise just-minded, refer cheerfully to the *circonstance atténuante* of the wife's drunkenness or bad language, as if it not only furnished an excuse for outrage upon her, but made it quite fit and proper for the Queen's peace to be broken and the woman's bones along with it. . . .

Regarding the extent of the evil it is difficult to arrive at a just calculation. Speaking of those cases only which come before the courts—probably, of course, not a third of the whole number—the elements for forming an opinion are the following:

In the Judicial Statistics for England and Wales, issued in 1877 for 1876, we find that of Aggravated Assaults on Women and Children, of the class which since 1853 have been brought under Summary Jurisdiction there were reported,

In 1876	2,737
In 1875	3,106
In 1874	2,841

How many of these were assaults made by husbands on wives there is no means of distinguishing, but, judging from other sources, I should imagine they formed about four-fifths of the whole.

Among the worst cases, when the accused persons were committed for trial or bailed for appearance at Assizes or Sessions (coming under the head of Criminal Proceedings), the classification adopted in the Parliamentary Return does not permit of identifying the cases which concerned women only. Some rough guess on the matter may perhaps be formed from the preponderance of male criminals in all classes of violent crime. Out of sixty-seven persons charged with Murder in 1876, thirty-five were males. Of forty-one charged with Attempt to Murder, thirty-five were males. Of 157 charged with Shooting, Stabbing, etc., 146 were men. Of 232 charged with Manslaughter, 185 were men; and of 1,020 charged with Assault inflicting bodily harm, 857 were men. In short, out of 1,517 persons charged with crimes of cruelty and violence, more than five-sixths were males, and only 235 females. Of course the men's offences include a variety of crimes besides Wife-beating and Wife-torture.

The details of the crimes for which twenty-two men who were capitally convicted in 1876 suffered death are noteworthy on this head (*Criminal Statistics,* p. xxix). Of these:

> Edward Deacon, shoemaker, murdered his wife by cutting her head with a chopper.
> John Thomas Green, painter, shot his wife, with a pistol.
> John Eblethrift, labourer, murdered his wife by stabbing.
> Charles O'Donnell, labourer, murdered his wife by beating.
> Henry Webster, labourer, murdered his wife by cutting her throat.

Besides these, five others murdered women with whom they were living in vicious relations, and three others (including the monster William Fish) murdered children. In all, more than half the convicted persons executed that year were guilty of wife murder—or of what we may term *quasi*-wife-murder. . . .

I have called this paper English *Wife-torture* because I wish to impress my readers with the fact that the familiar term "wife-beating" conveys as remote a notion of the extremity of the cruelty indicated as when candid and ingenuous vivisectors talk of "scratching a newt's tail" when they refer to burning alive, or dissecting out the nerves of living dogs, or torturing ninety cats in the series of experiments.

Wife-*beating* is the more preliminary canter before the race—the preface to the serious matter which is to follow. Sometimes, it is true, there are men of comparatively mild dispositions who are content to go on beating their wives, year after year, giving them occasional black-eyes and bruises, or tearing out a few locks of their hair and spitting in their faces, or bestowing an ugly print of their iron fingers on the woman's soft arm, but not proceeding beyond these minor injuries to anything perilous. . . .

But the unendurable mischief, the discovery of which has driven me to try to call public attention to the whole matter, is this—Wife-*beating* in process of time, and in numberless cases, advances to Wife-*torture,* and the Wife-torture usually ends in Wife-maiming, Wife-blinding, or Wife-murder. A man who has "thrashed" his wife with his fists half-a-dozen times, becomes satiated with such enjoyment as that performance brings, and next time he is angry he kicks her with his hob-nailed shoes. When he has kicked her a few times standing or sitting, he kicks her down and stamps on her stomach, her breast, or her face. If he does not wear clogs or hob-nailed shoes, he takes up some other weapon, a knife, a poker, a hammer, a bottle of vitriol, or a lighted lamp, and strikes her with it, or sets her on fire; and then, and then only, the hapless creature's sufferings are at an end.

I desire specially to avoid making this paper more painful than can be helped, but it is indispensable that some specimens of the tortures to which I refer should be brought before the reader's eye. I shall take them exclusively from cases reported during the last three or four months. Were I to go further back for a year or two it would be easy to find some more "sensational," as, for example, of Michael Copeland, who threw his wife on a blazing fire; of George Ellis, who murdered his wife by pitching her out of a window; of Ashton Keefe, who beat his wife and thrust a box of lighted matches into his little daughter's breast when she was too slow in bringing his beer; and of Charles Bradley, who, according to the report in the *Manchester Examiner,*

> came home, and after locking the door, told his wife he would murder her. He immediately set a large bulldog at her, and the dog, after flying at the upper part of her body, seized hold of the woman's right arm, which she lifted to protect herself, and tore pieces out. The prisoner in the meantime kept striking her in the face, and inciting the brute to worry her. The dog dragged her up and down, biting pieces out of her arms, and the prisoner then got on the sofa and hit and kicked her on the breast.

But the instances of the last three or four months—from September to the end of January—are more than enough to establish all I want to prove; and I beg here to return my thanks for a collection of them, and for many very useful observations and tabulations of them, to Miss A. Shore, who has been good enough to place them at my disposal.

It is needful to bear in mind in reading them, that the reports of such cases which appear in newspapers are by no means always reliable, or calculated to convey the same impressions as the sight of the actual trial. In some of the following instances, also, I have only been able to obtain the first announcement of the offence, without means of checking it by the subsequent proceedings in court. *Per contra,* it should be remembered that if a few of these cases may possibly have been exaggerated or trumped up (as I believe the story of the man pouring Chili vinegar into his wife's eyes proved to have been), there are, for every one of these *published* horrors, at least three or four which *never are reported at all,* and where the poor victim dies quietly of her injuries like a wounded animal, without seeking the mockery of redress offered her by the law.

James Mills cut his wife's throat as she lay in bed. He was quite sober at the time. On a previous occasion he had nearly torn away her left breast.

J. Coleman returned home early in the morning, and, finding his wife asleep, took up a heavy piece of wood and struck her on the head and arm, bruising her arm. On a previous occasion he had fractured her ribs.

John Mills poured out vitriol deliberately, and threw it in his wife's face, because she asked him to give her some of his wages. He had said previously that he would blind her.

James Lawrence, who had been frequently bound over to keep the peace, and who had been supported by his wife's industry for years, struck her on the face with a poker, leaving traces of the most dreadful kind when she appeared in court.

Frederick Knight jumped on the face of his wife (who had only been confined a month) with a pair of boots studded with hobnails.

Richard Mountain beat his wife on the back and mouth, and turned her out of her bed and out of their room one hour after she had been confined.

Alfred Roberts felled his wife to the floor, with a child in her arms; knelt on her, and grasped her throat. She had previously taken out three summonses against him, but [he] had never attended.

John Harris, a shoemaker, at Sheffield, found his wife and children in bed; dragged her out, and, after vainly attempting to force her into the oven, tore off her night-dress and turned her round before the fire "like a piece of beef," while the children stood on the stairs listening to their mother's agonised screams.

Richard Scully knocked in the frontal bone of his wife's forehead.

William White, stonemason, threw a burning paraffin lamp at his wife, and stood quietly watching her enveloped in flames, from the effects of which she died.

William Hussell, a butcher, ran a knife into his wife several times and killed her. He had threatened to do so often before.

Robert Kelly, engine-driver, bit a piece out of his wife's cheek.

William James, an operative boilermaker, stabbed his wife badly in the arm and mouth, observing afterwards, "I am sorry I did not kill both" (his wife and her mother).

Thomas Richards, a smith, threw his wife down a flight of fourteen steps, when she came to entreat him to give her some money for her maintenance. He was living with another woman—the nurse at a hospital where he had been ill.

James Frickett, a ratcatcher. His wife was found dying with broken ribs and cut and bruised face, a walking-stick with blood on it lying by. Frickett remarked, "If I am going to be hanged for you, I love you."

James Styles beat his wife about the head when he met her in the City Road. She had supported him for years by char-work and during the whole time he had been in the habit of beating her, and on one occasion so assaulted her that the sight of one of her eyes was destroyed. He got drunk habitually with the money she earned.

John Harley, a compositor, committed for trial for cutting and wounding his wife with intent to murder.

Joseph Moore, a labourer, committed for trial for causing the death of his wife by striking her with an iron instrument on the head.

George Ralph Smith, oilman, cut his wife, as the doctor expressed it, "to pieces," with a hatchet, in their back parlour. She died afterwards, but he was found Not Guilty, as it was not certain that her death resulted from the wounds.

Alfred Cummins, tailor, struck his wife so as to deprive her of the sight of an eye.

Thomas Paget, laundryman, knocked down his wife in the street and kicked her till she became insensible, because she refused to give him money to get drink.

Alfred Etherington, shoemaker, kicked his wife in a dangerous way, and a week later dragged her out of bed, jumped on her, and struck her. He said he would have her life and the lives of all her children. He gave no money for the support of his family (six children), and he prevented her from keeping the situations she had obtained for their maintenance. She had summoned him six or seven times.

Jeremiah Fitzgerald, a labourer, knocked down his wife and kicked her heavily in the forehead. He had been twice convicted before. The woman appeared in court with her face strapped up.

Patrick Flynn, violently kicked his wife after he had knocked her down, and then kicked a man who interfered to save her. Had already undergone six months' hard labour for assaulting his wife.

Here is a case recorded from personal observation by a magistrate's clerk:

> I attended a dying woman to take her deposition in a drunkard's dwelling. The husband was present in charge of the police. The poor wretched wife lay with many ribs broken, and her shoulder and one arm broken, and her head so smashed that you could scarcely recognise a feature of a woman. She, in her last agony, said that her husband had smashed her with a wooden bed-post. He, blubbering, said, "Yes, it is true, but I was in drink, or would not have done it."

And here is one that has come in while I have been writing:

> At the Blackburn police-court, yesterday, John Charnock was committed for trial on a charge of attempted murder. It was stated that he had fastened his wife's head in a cupboard and kicked her with his iron clogs, and that he had deliberately broken her arm. (3 Feb 1878)

And here another (reported in the *Manchester Courier*, 5 February) so instructive in its details of the motives for Wife-murder, the sort of woman who is murdered, the man who kills, and the sentiment of juries as to what constitutes "provocation" on the part of a wife, that I shall extract it at length:

MANSLAUGHTER AT DUKINFIELD

Thomas Harlow, 39, striker, Dukinfield, was indicted for the manslaughter of his wife, Ellen Harlow, 45 years old, at Dukinfield, on 30 November 1877. The prisoner was committed by the magistrates on the charges of wilful murder, but the grand jury reduced the indictment to that of manslaughter. Mr Marshall prosecuted; and the prisoner, who was undefended by counsel, stated, in his plea, that he had no intention of killing his wife when he struck her.

The prisoner, who was employed in and about Dukinfield, lived with his wife and three children in Waterloo Street, in that town. On the morning of the 30th November the deceased went out hawking as usual, and returned shortly after twelve o'clock. On her return she busied herself in preparing dinner, and the prisoner went out for a short time. In the afternoon the prisoner laid himself down, and slept for two or three hours. About five o'clock the deceased, and a lodger named Margaret Daley, and several others, were sitting in the house, when the prisoner came in and asked his wife for twopence. She replied that she had not twopence, and that she had had trouble enough with being out hawking all day in the rain and hungry. He then began to abuse her, and asked her for something to eat. She gave him some potatoes and bacon; after eating the greater part of which he again began to abuse her. He once more asked her for twopence, and Margaret Daley, seeing there was likely to be a disturbance, gave him the twopence, and told him he had better get a pint of beer. Instead of getting beer, however, he sent a little girl to purchase a quantity of coal, and then recommenced abusing his wife. Shortly afterwards he was heard to exclaim, "There will be a life less tonight, and I will take it." At this time the persons who were sitting in the house when the prisoner came in went out, leaving Harlow, his wife, and their son Thomas, and Daley together. The prisoner had some further altercation with his wife, which ended with him striking her a violent blow under the right ear, felling her to the floor. She died in a few minutes afterwards, the cause of death being concussion of the brain. The prisoner subsequently gave himself into custody, and made a statement attributing his conduct to the provocation his wife had given him.

The jury found the prisoner guilty, and recommended him to mercy *on account of the provocation* he received. Sentence was deferred.

I think I may now safely ask the reader to draw breath after all these horrors, and agree with me that they cannot, *must not,* be allowed to go on unchecked, without some effort to stop them, and save these perishing and miserable creatures. . . . Is it to be borne that we should sit patiently by and allow their lives to be trampled out in agony?

Femicidal Lynching in the United States

COMPILED BY DIANA E. H. RUSSELL

Lynching—"murder committed by a mob of three or more persons"[1]—is inextricably linked in most peoples' minds to the fate of African-American men. While it is certainly true that African-American men were the primary targets of this barbaric practice, it is important to remember that African-American women were also subjected to lynching. Indeed, most people are startled to learn that *white* Americans were also lynched. In her book, *When and Where I Enter* (1984), Paula Giddings maintains that "lynching, always a fixture in the South, had turned more gruesome when, with the end of slavery, the majority of its victims became Black rather than White and the image of Blacks changed from that of children to dangerous animals." More specifically, "between 1840 and 1860 there were three hundred recorded victims hanged or burned by mobs. Of that figure, only 10 percent were Black" (79).

In *Rope and Faggot* (1969), Walter White reports that between 1882 and 1927,[2] 3,513 African-Americans and 1,438 white Americans were lynched—71 percent and 29 percent, respectively. Of these approximately 5,000 lynchings, 92 were women[3]: 76 African-Americans and 16 white Americans (227). Hence African-American women constituted 83 percent of the total number of women lynched, 2 percent of the total number of African-Americans lynched, and 1.5 percent of the total number of people lynched. White provides frequencies for women who were lynched in different states (see table 1). I know of no source that documents the numbers of Latina women lynched. Presumably they were classified as white, as is still the practice of the U.S. Census Bureau.

Since the concept of femicide refers to the misogynist killing of females, and since lynchings of African-Americans by white Americans were chiefly motivated by racism, we cannot assume that every case in which an African-American woman was lynched constitutes a case of femicide. But when the lynching was accompanied by a sexist act—most commonly rape—it is clear that misogyny as well as racism was involved. All five of the lynchings

TABLE 1 Number of Women Lynched in the United States, 1882–1927, by State

State	No. of Lynchings
Mississippi	16
Texas	12
Alabama	9
Arkansas	9
Georgia	8
South Carolina	7
Tennessee	7
Kentucky	5
Louisiana	5
Florida	3
Oklahoma	3
Missouri	2
North Carolina	2
Nebraska	1
Virginia	1
Wyoming	1
TOTAL	91

Note: To his statistical account White added: "Three of the 12 Texas victims were a mother and her two young daughters killed by a mob, in 1918, when they 'threatened a white man.' Thus was white civilization maintained!"
Source: White (1969, 227).

described in the following accounts clearly qualify as cases of racist femicide. The first four segments focus on African-American women, and the final one describes the lynching of a Chicana.

Notes

1. This is the legal definition, according to Giddings (1984, 18).

2. According to White, "Lynchings were not considered sufficiently important for recording prior to 1882, when the *Chicago Tribune* included in its summary of the year's crimes, disasters, and other phenomena the mob murders of that year."

3. The total breakdown of female lynchings by state in table 1 adds up to 91 victims, instead of the 92 referred to by White here (1969, 227).

References

Giddings, Paula. 1984. *When and Where I Enter: The Impact of Black Women on Race and Sex in America.* New York: Bantam Books.

Ginzburg, Ralph. 1962. *100 Years of Lynchings: A Shocking Documentary of Race Violence in America.* New York: Lancer Books.

Secrest, William B. 1967. *Juanita: The Only Woman Lynched in the Gold Rush Days.* Fresno, Calif.: Saga-West Publishing.

White, Walter. 1969. *Rope and Faggot.* New York: Arno Press.

[FEMICIDAL LYNCHINGS OF WOMEN OF COLOR]

GEORGIA—"Southern chivalry" draws no line of sex. An unscrupulous farmer in south Georgia refused to pay a Negro hand wages due him. A few days later the farmer was shot and killed. Not finding the Negro suspected of the murder, mobs began to kill every Negro who could even remotely be connected with the victim and the alleged slayer. One of these was a man named Hayes Turner, whose offence was that he knew the alleged slayer, a not altogether remarkable circumstance, since both men worked for the dead farmer. To Turner's wife, within one month of accouchement, was brought the news of her husband's death. She cried out in her sorrow, pouring maledictions upon the heads of those who had thrust widowhood upon her so abruptly and cruelly.

Word of her threat to swear out warrants for the arrest of her husband's murderers came to them. "We'll teach the damn' nigger wench some sense," was their answer, as they began to seek her. Fearful, her friends secreted the sorrowing woman on an obscure farm, miles away. Sunday morning, with a hot May sun beating down, they found her. Securely they bound her ankles together and, by them, hanged her to a tree. Gasoline and motor oil were thrown upon her dangling clothes; a match wrapped her in sudden flames. Mocking, ribald laughter from her tormentors answered the helpless woman's screams of pain and terror. "Mister, you ought to've heard the nigger wench howl!" a member of the mob boasted to me a few days later as we stood at the place of Mary Turner's death.

The clothes burned from her crisply toasted body, in which, unfortunately, life still lingered, a man stepped towards the woman and, with his knife, ripped open the abdomen in a crude Caesarean operation. Out tumbled the prematurely born child. Two feeble cries it gave—and received for answer the heel of a stalwart man, as life was ground out of the tiny form. Under the tree of death was scooped a shallow hole. The rope about Mary Turner's charred ankles was cut, and swiftly her body tumbled into its grave. Not without a sense of humour or of appropriateness was some member of the mob. An empty whisky-bottle, quart size, was given for headstone. Into its neck was stuck a half-smoked cigar—which had saved the delicate nostrils of one member of the mob from the stench of burning human flesh.

Reprinted from Walter White, *Rope and Faggot* (New York: Alfred A. Knopf, 1929; repr., New York: Arno Press, 1969), 27–29.

NEGRO AND WIFE BURNED

DODDSVILLE, Miss., Feb. 7—Luther Holbert and his wife, negroes, were burned at the stake here to-day by a mob of more than 1,000 persons for the killing of James Eastland, a prominent white planter, and John Carr, a negro, on Wednesday, at the Eastland plantation, two miles from this city.

The burning of Holbert and his wife closes a tragedy which has cost eight lives, has engaged 200 men and two packs of bloodhounds in a four days' chase across four Counties, and has stirred this section of Mississippi almost to frenzy.

Following are the dead: Luther Holbert and wife, negroes, burned at the stake by mob; James Eastland, white, planter, killed by Holbert; John Carr, a negro, killed by Holbert; John Winters, negro, killed by Eastland, three unknown negroes, killed by posses. The killing of Eastland, Carr and Winters occurred Wednesday at Eastland's plantation. Holbert and Winters were in Carr's cabin when Eastland entered and ordered Holbert to leave the plantation. A difficulty ensued, in which it is alleged that Holbert opened fire on Eastland, fatally wounding him and killing Carr. Eastland returned the fire and killed Winters.

When news of the tragedy reached Doddsville a posse was formed and left immediately for Eastland's plantation. Arriving there further shooting occurred, and an unknown negro was killed. Holbert and his wife had fled. Posses were formed at Greenville, Ittaben, Cleveland and other points and the pursuit of Holbert and his wife was begun with horses and bloodhounds. The chase, which was begun Wednesday morning, was continued until last night, when Holbert and wife, worn out from traveling over 100 miles on foot through canebrakes and swamps, were found asleep in a heavy belt of timber three miles east of Sheppardstown and captured. The two negroes were brought to Doddsville and this afternoon were burned at the stake by a large mob in the shadow of the negro church here.

Yesterday two negroes were killed by a posse near Belzoni, Yazoo County. One of the negroes bore a striking resemblance to Holbert, and was mistaken for him by members of the posse.

Eastland was a member of a wealthy Mississippi family, and a reward of $1,200 was offered by relatives for the capture of his slayers. Two brothers of Eastland participated in the chase and capture of the Holberts and both were present when Holbert and his wife were burned.

The dead couple leave a young son.

"Negro and Wife Burned," *New York Press,* 8 February 1904, reprinted in Ralph Ginzburg, *100 Years of Lynchings: A Shocking Documentary of Race Violence in America* (New York: Lancer Books, 1962), 62–63. ©1990 Ralph Ginzburg.

WAS POWERLESS TO AID SISTER WHO WAS RAPED AND LYNCHED

CLOVIS, N.M., Apr. 27—The brother of the young colored girl who was lynched by a mob of white ruffians near Wagner, Okla., a few weeks ago, passed through this town on his way to Mexico. He gave a pathetic account of the lynching to colored citizens here.

The young man's sister was but 17 years old and of respectable parents. Two half-drunken white men walked into their home during the absence of the mother and found the girl dressing, locked themselves into her room and criminally assaulted her. Her screams for help were heard by her brother, who, kicking down the door, went to her rescue. In defending his sister, he shot one of the brutes. The other escaped.

Later in the evening the local authorities, failing to find the brother, arrested the sister, who was taken from jail by a mob at 4 o'clock in the morning and lynched. From his hiding place the brother, who is 21 years old, could hear his sister's cries for help, but he was powerless to aid her.

RAPE, LYNCH NEGRO MOTHER

COLUMBUS, Miss., Dec. 17—Thursday a week ago Cordella Stevenson was found early in the morning hanging to a limb of a tree, without any clothing, dead. She had been hung Wednesday night after a mob had visited her cabin, taken her from her husband and lynched her after they had maltreated her. The body was found about fifty yards north of the Mobile & Ohio R.R., and the thousands and thousands of passengers that came in and out of this city last Thursday morning were horrified at the sight. She was hung there from the night before by a bloodthirsty mob who had gone to her home, snatched her from slumber, and dragged her through the streets without any resistance. They carried her to a far-off spot, did their dirt and then strung her up.

Several months ago the barn of Gabe Frank, white, was burned. The son of Mrs. Stevenson was suspected of the burning. Although Mrs. Stevenson and her husband Arch are regarded as hard-working people, having worked for the same employer eleven years, their son is regarded as shiftless.

"Was Powerless to Aid Sister Who Was Raped and Lynched," *New York Age*, 30 April 1914, reprinted in Ralph Ginzburg, *100 Years of Lynchings: A Shocking Documentary of Race Violence in America* (New York: Lancer Books, 1962), 90–91. © 1990 Ralph Ginzburg.

"Rape, Lynch Negro Mother," *Chicago Defender*, 18 December 1915, reprinted in Ralph Ginzburg, *100 Years of Lynchings: A Shocking Documentary of Race Violence in America* (New York: Lancer Books, 1962), 96–97. ©1990 Ralph Ginzburg.

Mrs. Stevenson was brought to the police station and questioned on the possibility that her son might have set fire to Frank's barn. Mrs. Stevenson said her son had left home several months prior to the burning and she did not know his whereabouts. Convinced of her truthfulness, the police turned her loose and she went home.

Nothing more was thought of the case until Thursday morning. They had gone to bed early, as usual, and heard a knock at the door, according to Arch Stevenson, the woman's husband, who ran all the way in town after the mob had taken his wife. Before he could answer the knock the mob had broken the door down and seized his wife, putting rifles to his head and threatening him if he moved. At the first opportunity he ran 'mid the hail of bullets. After telling his story he left for parts unknown. The mob took the woman about 10 o'clock at night. After that no one knows exactly what happened. The condition of the body showed plainly that she had been mistreated. Sheriff Bell telephoned to Justice of the Peace McKellar to hold an inquest. He was out of town, and didn't return till Thursday night. The body was left hanging in view of the morbid crowd that came to gaze at it till Friday morning, when it was cut down and the inquest held. The jury returned a verdict that she came to death at the hands of persons unknown.

It was the same old verdict that all southern juries return in the cases of this kind. The United States is sending missionaries to teach the heathen, Ford has gone to Europe with his peace party, ministers preach on the good to humanity, but here in the South the same dastardly crimes are committed and no one volunteers to raise his voice against such a crime committed against a member of the race. But retribution comes to all. Belgium robbed the black people of the Congo States of their ivory and rubber and sold for gold the labors of these well-meaning people. If their work was not up to what the Belgians thought it should be, an arm was cut off or some other cruelty imposed. Now Belgium is suffering. The day of reckoning has come. So will it be with this country. As they sow, so shall they reap. Today the business men are trying their hardest to get into South America, and the Latin countries are only going to allow them in under certain conditions. Race discrimination and lynchings will find no upholders there. The people there brand the Americans as lynchers, and it will be hard for the Americans to convince them otherwise.

JUANITA: THE ONLY WOMAN LYNCHED IN THE GOLD RUSH DAYS

"The jury find that the woman, Josefa, is guilty of the murder of Frederick Alexander Augustus Cannon, and that she suffer death in two hours.

Reprinted from William B. Secrest, *Juanita: The Only Woman Lynched in the Gold Rush Days* (Fresno, Calif.: Saga-West Publishing, 1967), 23–26.

"The man Jose is found not guilty, but the jury earnestly request that Judge Rose advise him to leave the town within twenty-four hours. Amos L. Brown, Foreman."

Josefa was stony-faced as several selected guards led her off to a cabin to await her fate. She was allowed to see any of her friends that she chose, as the mob again flocked to the saloons and preparations were made for the execution. Only two hours left now—hours that seemed an eternity to a lynch-mad miner—or hours that passed as fleeting moments to a small Mexican woman as she knelt, making her peace with God.

It was almost over now and too-eager miners began to drift down to the river. The word had been passed that the hanging would take place on the Jersey Bridge, and the early arrivals watched eagerly as a group of men prepared the makeshift gallows. It was a beautiful setting with the roaring, splashing river winding through the shaggy, pine-covered mountains. It didn't seem possible that such an ugly drama could take place amid such surroundings and yet the minutes ticked inevitably by.

So far as is known, no last minute efforts were made to save the doomed Josefa. Except for Doctor Aiken and possibly one or two others, no one had made any significant effort to protest the trial and hanging despite the fact that some substantial men were in town during the whole proceedings. Colonel Weller, according to one historian, refused to attend the trial or intervene in behalf of the woman. David Barstow,[1] an eyewitness to the whole affair, stated that Weller was seated on the speakers' platform throughout the trial and yet he remained strangely silent. Weller was a highly popular orator of the day and it is possible that had he made some effort to avert the tragedy, others would have backed him up. Giving him the benefit of every doubt, it would have taken the highest type of courage to stand up to such a lynch-mad mob and besides, how can you equate two thousand voting miners with one voteless Mexican woman? There were other men in town who were no less prominent than Weller and yet they all remained silent up to the final, damning moment. Actually it is doubtful that anything short of a company of cavalry could have saved Josefa and any efforts to stop the tragedy may well have resulted in more violence.

The scaffold was a simple affair, making use of the overhead beams in the construction. The ends of a heavy timber were fastened to each side of the bridge, about four feet high. The timber was lashed to the bridge with ropes and at a given signal, two men would simultaneously cut the ropes with axes, thus dropping the timber out from under the victim. It was primitive but effective.

Ominously the gong sounded for the final time that day and Josefa was led to the bridge at the lower end of town. Over two thousand men were lining the river banks now and Barstow characterized them as "the hungriest, craziest, wildest mob standing around that ever I saw anywhere." The *Pacific Star* correspondent wrote the final chapter to the drama as he witnessed it:

"At the time appointed for the execution, the prisoner was taken to the gallows, which she approached without the least trepidation. She said, while standing by the gallows, so I was informed, that she had killed the man Cannon, and expected to suffer for it; that the only request she had to make was, that after she had suffered, that her body should be given to her friends, in order that she might be decently interred.[2] This request was promptly complied with (and) she extended her hand to each of the bystanders immediately around her, and bidding each an "adios senor," voluntarily ascended the scaffold, took the rope and adjusted it around her neck with her own hand, releasing her luxuriant hair from beneath it so that it should flow free. Her arms were then pinioned, to which she strongly objected, her clothes tied down, the cap adjusted over her face, and in a moment more the cords which supported the scaffolding had been cut, and she hung suspended between the heavens and the earth." As the body slowly twisted and turned, the crowd quickly dispersed and filed again into the Downieville saloons. It was a little after four o'clock in the afternoon and there was still time for a few more drinks before supper. In the saloons that night was launched the story and the legend of the hanging of Josefa—or Juanita—of Downieville.

As the story of the tragedy fanned out over California, the newspapers of the state were unanimous in condemning the affair. Perhaps the *Sacramento Times and Transcript* spoke for all of California when it said:

"The violent proceedings of an indignant and excited mob, led on by the enemies of the unfortunate woman, are a blot upon the history of the state. Had she committed a crime of really heinous character, a real American would have revolted at such a course as was pursued towards this friendless and unprotected foreigner. We had hoped that the story was fabricated. As it is the perpetrators have shamed themselves and their race."

The inhabitants of Downieville grew increasingly sensitive about the lynching and at least one of the citizens decided that enough was enough. Writing in the *Daily Alta California* for January 29, 1852, he insisted that the lynching was well deserved and that the death of Cannon was nothing less than cold-blooded murder. "The victim in this case," he continued, "was not the first nor the second who had been stabbed by this female . . . the inhabitants (of Downieville) are not the bloodthirsty, diabolical monsters they have been represented; on the contrary, they have heretofore been too mild in their punishment of offenders; and in the case before us, nothing induced them to pursue the course they did, but retributive justice." The letter was signed simply, "Veritas"—the Latin for truth.

Associations are important to the annals of California's Mother Lode country, as they are to most historic localities. One place is famous for its Joaquin Murrieta legends. Another town is known for its associations with Mark Twain or Bret Harte. But there is one town in California with a unique, if somewhat sinister, memory dating back to those early gold rush days. Mention this town to an old-timer in one of the museums or general stores that dot Highway 49 and chances are he'll say, "Downieville? Yeah, that's up north. Yes, sir, back in 1851 they lynched a woman at Downieville."

Notes

1. The historian Bancroft, in his Popular Tribunals, wrote that Weller refused to even attend the trial or to intervene on behalf of Josefa.

2. J. J. McClosky recalled that Josefa was buried behind the old theatre he was managing at the time. Barton's recollection was that Josefa and Cannon were buried side by side in the local graveyard. Later, in the 1870s, the bodies were re-interred when the old graveyard plot was made available for mining. At this time, still according to Barton, Josefa's skull was removed and for some years it was used as a part of the initiation ceremonies of a local secret society.

Women to Burn: Suttee as a Normative Institution

DOROTHY K. STEIN

The practice of burning or burying women alive with their deceased husbands [suttee], even as an expression of an underlying view of women as property, is not as bizarre and exotic a custom as its identification with Hindu India has made it seem. Although Greek visitors to North India wrote accounts of suttee as early as the fourth century B.C., there are accounts of widow sacrifice among Scandinavians, Slavs, Greeks, Egyptians, Chinese, Finns, Maoris, and some American Indians. The practice apparently originated among warriors who probably also elaborated the mythology attached to it. The heroism of the *sati* (the sacrificed woman) was in fact equated with that of the warrior. The connection of suttee with the warrior and ruler (Ksatriya) caste endowed it with a social prestige which it never lost. In the fourteenth to sixteenth centuries, it became usual to make a clean sweep of the women's quarters of a dead ruler before installing his successor. Sometimes even ministers were included, and the total could amount to the burning of several thousand persons, including queens, concubines, and servants of both sexes.[1]

The practice was said to have been forbidden, at least originally, to Brahmans, the highest caste in terms of social rank, but the associations with honor which suttee acquired proved too strong. Eventually, Brahman women were burning as liberally as Ksatriyas, or even in greater numbers as the power and retinues of the princes declined. Quoting the *Calcutta Review* of 1868 Thompson writes:

> In Bengal, at the beginning of the nineteenth or end of the eighteenth century, there are instances of the burning of a score or even two score women with one quite unimportant man. We read of a pyre kept alight for three days while

Reprinted with permission from *Signs: Journal of Women on Culture and Society* 4, no. 2 (1978): 253–68.

relays of widows were fetched from a distance. The dead man was a
(kulin)Brahman, and these women were many of them only nominally his
wives. . . . Few of [the women] ever lived with their husband or even saw him
after marriage, except when they climbed his funeral-pyre.[2]

The Brahman association with suttee was probably responsible for the form
of the ceremony and its assimilation to the scriptural and sacrificial tradition.

The most usual form that suttee took was that of burning the wife alive in or
on the funeral pyre that consumed the husband's body. There were scriptural
rules prohibiting the ceremony while the woman was menstruating (which was
equated with uncleanliness or unchastity), pregnant, or could not be spared from
the care of her young children. In such cases, or when the husband's death
occurred during his absence from home, some women burned themselves along
with an article of clothing or personal effect of the dead man. This "following
after" was forbidden to some castes, including Brahmans. In those castes where
the dead were disposed of by burial rather than cremation, the widow could be
buried alive. Thompson adds:

> Irregularly, it could be by drowning, especially when a woman had escaped
> from the pyre. We have an eye-witness' account of a Brahman in a boat in mid-
> stream in Allahabad superintending the suicide of sixteen women; but I think
> the *Cyclopaidia of India* may have been mistaken in assuming this to have been
> a suttee. Among the lower castes suttee was unusual, but these sometimes
> imitated their betters; and there are instances on record of even Mahomedans
> being burnt and their widows with them.[3]

An occasional mother died on her son's pyre, and this was dubbed the highest form of suttee; once in a while, a sister died with her brother. In the
commonest form of the ceremony, the widow herself, or her eldest son, was
required to light the fire. The widow on her way to the pyre was the object (for
once) of all public attention. She distributed money and jewels to the crowd.
Endowed with the gift of prophecy and the power to curse and bless, she was
immolated amid great fanfare, with great veneration. Since no woman who was
unfaithful to her husband could be burnt, suttee did not make the *sati* virtuous,
but rather proved she had been virtuous all her life. Thus, the widow had but two
choices, a painful but relatively brief and heroic death, or a miserable, obscure,
and humiliating life as a penitent sinner.

It is not hard to see why death might be preferred to widowhood. Prescrip-
tions, often reiterated, for the proper conduct of a widow included instructions
that she should not eat more than one very plain meal a day, that she should perform the most menial tasks, never sleep in a bed, leave the house only to go to
the temple, keep out of sight at festivals (since she was inauspicious to everyone
but her own children), wear nothing but the drabbest clothes, and, of course, no
jewelry. Perhaps most humiliating of all for a high-born lady was having her

head shaved monthly by an untouchable male barber.[4] All this was held to be necessary for the sake of her husband's soul and to keep herself from being reborn as a female animal. In theory, the widow could refuse. In practice, she was under considerable pressure, as a Portuguese chronicler noted: "the mourning finished their relations speak to them, advising them to burn themselves and not to dishonor their generation."[5] Once the widow's commitment was signified by the performance of the appropriate signs and tests, she could not change her mind or risk disgracing the family. The measures taken by family members and officiating priests to prevent this from happening included scaffolds constructed to tilt toward the fire pit, piles designed so that the exits were blocked and the roof collapsed on the woman's head, tying her, weighting her down with firewood and bamboo poles. If all else failed and the woman escaped from the burning pile, she was often dragged back by force, sometimes by her own son.

How could such treatment be rationalized? The orthodox Hindu belief was that the widow was responsible for her husband's predeceasing her, by sin in a previous life if not in the present, for in the normal course of events the wife was expected to die first. A lifetime of austerity was considered scarcely enough to expiate her survival. Suttee, then, was primarily based in the belief that women are by nature sexually unreliable and incapable of leading chaste lives without a husband to control them. Hart tells us that early Tamil (South Indian) literature portrays women as imbued with sacred power that becomes especially dangerous after the deaths of their husbands:

> Sacred power clings to a woman and, as long as it is under control, lends to her life and to that of her husband auspiciousness and sacred correctness. But it is a power which must be kept firmly under control, lest it wreak havoc. Thus women must carefully observe chastity. . . . After the death of her husband, she is especially dangerous and must shave her head, cake it with mud, sleep on a bed of stones, and eat lily seeds instead of rice. . . . If a widow is chaste and young, she is so infected with magic power that she must take her own life.[6]

Only by burning could the widow be sure of "ridding herself of her feminine body." By burning, moreover, she, her husband, her husband's family, her mother's family, and her father's family would be in paradise for 35 million years, no matter how sinful they all had been. In paradise, she rejoined her husband, despite any unwillingness on his part.

Over and beyond these scriptural inducements given, custom conferred prestige on the surviving families in this world as well as the next. For families of high rank and some affluence there were also tangible benefits. When a Hindu girl marries, she is officially transferred from her father's patrilineage to that of her husband; at the same time, her family is relieved of any moral responsibility for her future maintenance. Once widowed, she is of no further value to her in-laws as a potential bearer of sons: indeed, their worst fear is that she should chance to become pregnant, casting a possible shadow on the legitimacy of any previous children. In such a fanatically patrilineal tradition, the widow's death assured guardianship and undisputed influence over her children to her husband's family. It also kept her from enjoying her lifetime rights in her husband's estate.

The Brahman priests and other individuals involved in the actual ceremony also profited:

> Expenses of suttee witnessed by the author at Cuttack, 1824, was, according to the pundit, as follows: "Ghee, 3 rupees; cloth, 1 rupee; woman's new cloth, 2 rupees; wood, 3 rupees; Adawlut pundit received 3 rupees; the woman give one rupee for some purpose; rice, 1 anna; hemp, 4 annas; haldee, one anna; ma-teeanlet, chundun, doop, cocoanut, 1 anna, 1 pice; carrier, 5 annas; musicians, half a rupee; paring nails, 4 annas; cutting wood, 3 annas; total, 15 rupees, 5 annas, 3 pice. Intended shradda [funeral feast] 15 or 20 rupees. Thus 30 rupees (3–4 pounds sterling) was expended. The parties appeared very poor."[7]

Presumably expenses rose with the wealth of the participants. The priest was the recipient of the *sati's* gold ornaments. The crowd received the presents she distributed and, from numerous accounts, found the occasion a festive one. Clearly, any economic advantages disappeared when the family was not wealthy.

The explanation for suttee among the poorer, lower-status castes can be found only in the aspirations indicated by the imitation, sometimes at great cost of those who might originally have benefited from the practice. Although originally an appanage of high rank, by the nineteenth century the practice had spread so far down the social structure that it seemed no caste felt itself too low to aspire to the ceremony. The *Calcutta Review* mentions a group of Nutts having been refused permission to perform a suttee on the grounds of their low social status. A caste breakdown for the year 1823 in Bengal shows that of a total of 576 *satis,* 235 were Brahman, thirty-four Khetries (a respectable, though not aristocratic, caste), fourteen Vaisyas (merchants who traditionally ranked below priests and warriors), and 292 Sudras (traditionally "servants").[8] As to economic status, apart from caste, Mukhopadhyay estimated that in 1825, in one district, twenty-six *satis* were widows of rich men, fifty-two were "middling," and twenty-six were poor, but no standards for these estimations were given. *Satis* of all ages were noted, from eight to over eighty, and Peggs, a hostile observer, has presented tables which include at least one four-year-old.[9]

Within the borders of India, there was great regional variation in the incidence of the practice. By the early nineteenth century, most suttees by far occurred in Bengal, though the practice was increasing in many parts of India. From 1815 to 1824, 6,632 suttees were counted in Bengal, Bombay, and Madras, the three regions directly under British East India Company rule; of these, 5,997 took place in Bengal. An additional 2,137 died in Bengal between 1824 and 1828.[10] These figures are horrifying in their absolute numbers; they also show, however, that suttee was actually engaged in by only a small minority of widows. In Backerganj, in Bengal, for a further example, an estimated 25,000 persons died of cholera alone in 1825; the total number of suttees was sixty-three.[11] The regional variations may have been related to the traditions of the particular castes and sects residing within them, but attempts to account for them in this way have not been completely satisfactory. Mukhopadhyay's examination of the variation from district to district showed no coherent relationship, either with general orthodoxy or particular customs such as *kulin* polygamy. He was reduced to invoking long-established local tradition and a general climate of undervaluation of human life which accompanies the toleration of suicide. But the significance of suttee can best be understood in terms of what the *sati* was valued *for,* the alternatives offered, and the normative place of women in Indian society. It is less important to differentiate the concept of suttee from the practice.

Notes

1. Nicolo dei Conti, in *India in the Fifteenth Century: A Collection of Narratives of Voyages to India,* ed. R. H. Major, Hakluyt Society no. 22 (London: Hakluyt Society, 1857).

2. E. Thompson, *Suttee* (Boston: Houghton Mifflin Co., 1928), p. 36. An unsigned article in the *Calcutta Review* (46 [1868]: 221–26) is taken as an authoritative source by Thompson and other accounts in English. It will be used here mainly to exemplify British attitudes toward suttee at the time it was written.

3. Ibid., p. 39.

4. See, for example, M. Felton, *A Child Widow's Story* (New York: Harcourt, Brace & World, 1966).

5. "Chronicle of Fernato Nuniz," in R. Sewell, *A Forgotten Empire,* 1st Indian ed. (New Delhi: Government of India, 1962), p. 372.

6. G. Hart, "Ancient Tamil Literature: Its Scholarly Past and Future," in *Essays on South India,* ed. B. Stein (Honolulu: University Press of Hawaii, 1975), pp. 43–44.

7. J. Peggs, "The Suttee's Cry to Britain" (1831). Tracts, vol. 694. India Office Library, London. Peggs had been a missionary in Cuttack.

8. Figures from A. Mukhopadhyay, "Suttee as a Social Institution in Bengal," *Bengal Past and Present* (1957): 99–115, esp. p. 109.

9. Peggs.

10. Mukhopadhyay, p. 105.

11. Ibid.

Female Genocide

MARIELOUISE JANSSEN-JURREIT

Better if a daughter is not born, or does not remain alive. If she is born, then it is better if under the earth, if the burial banquet is combined with the birth.
> —Verse of the Uighur

One sex might be favored in the selection. This can lead to a distortion of the sex ratio. A surplus of men would limit the population growth, but possibly increase the general level of aggression in the society.
> —Anne McLaren

The notion that the sexes complement each other harmoniously and that the division of labor between them is natural is a premise of Western social research that is almost taken for granted. It makes phenomena of our past appear to us as ethnological or folklore curiosities rather than as components of behavior that could also gain influence in our present-day civilization. It deals with the custom of female infanticide and the question as to the causes of such behavior.

One of the first important ethnologists of the nineteenth century, the Scotsman John Ferguson MacLennan, regarded female infanticide among primitive peoples to be so widespread a phenomenon that he considered it the cause of exogamy. The surplus of men produced by the killing of female children would automatically lead to women or teenage girls of other tribes being robbed, adopted, or bought.

That newborn children are killed is a universal phenomenon of human society. There is evidence for it among primitive peoples of all continents, but also in the great historical civilizations. Among some peoples it is a reaction to a hostile environment and poor nutritional conditions. Mothers who are still nursing one child and bring another into the world kill the new baby because of a lack of milk for two children. The killing or exposure of the newborn is a question of the survival of the group and a compensation for inadequate techniques of contraception. Whatever the reasons we must not lose sight of the fact that in the majority of societies that practice infanticide, the newborn females are exposed or killed more frequently than the boys and, in many societies, exclusively. Female genocide was practiced even by the rich.

Indeed, naturalization inscriptions as well as Delphic holy inscriptions indicate that, almost exclusively, well-to-do families, and above all, merchants, practiced female genocide.

It is a fact that child exposure and killing of newborns were common in pre-Christian Europe. These paternal acts of terror were justified by the harsh environment and interpreted as necessary, responsible population policy. That such acts repeatedly clarify marital dominance relationships has not been considered by historians. Each act of taking away or killing a newborn broke the mother's inner resistance. Moreover, the female infanticide deprived women of future help in their work and of a possible female ally in their daughter.

In many societies, the change in the sex ratio spread male homosexuality and bachelorhood.

The figures from Greece are informative. For centuries the Greeks lived in fear of overpopulation; in the third and second centuries [B.C.] Greek families had only one or two children. W. W. Tarn, an English historian of antiquity, wrote: "Of some thousand families from Greece who received Milesian citizenship *c.* 228–220, details of 79, with their children, remain: these brought 118 sons and 28 daughters, many being minors; no natural causes can account for these proportions."[1]

Of fourth-century [B.C.] Athens a ratio is mentioned of 87 sons and 44 daughters out of 61 families; the disproportion of the sexes constantly increased.

The ideal family had one or two sons (in case one died in war). Occasionally the sex ratio in Greece shifted to 1:7 in favor of the male population. This does not even allow for the fact that a number of the sons might have emigrated so that in reality the misproportion might have been still larger. "Of 600 families from Delphic inscriptions of the second century [B.C.], just 1 percent reared 2 daughters; the Miletus evidence agrees, and throughout the whole mass of inscriptions, cases of sisters can almost be numbered on one's fingers . . ."[2]

Not only historians but also the majority of ethnologists view female infanticide only as a measure of population policy and not as an expression of male power, arbitrariness, chance disposition, and jealousy. The adaptive value of this female genocide is stressed unilaterally. Researchers who point out the psychological character of female infanticide are rare.

One exception is the American Milton R. Freeman, who comes to the conclusion that the systematic female infanticide among the Netsilik Eskimos had causes other than ecological.[3] A half-dozen prominent Eskimo scholars who have considered this phenomenon contented themselves with the generalization that female infanticide served to balance out the sex ratio; the number of male members of the tribe was so decimated by accidents that this was a sensible measure. Some authors even cite the opinion that years of breast feeding a girl reduces the probability of getting a son who will take care of the parents in their old age. Freeman regards these as "hindsight rationalizations." "In short, my thesis is that, due to the mutually dependent and complementary work roles, it is necessary to point out explicitly the male dominance. The comments by Netsilik informants themselves shed much light on the dominance of the man over the women."

He cites an incident from 1913 which occurred during the visit of a Danish scientist. The latter had contact with a famous hunter with three sons who consistently chose death for his nine daughters. When he heard that a daughter had been born again, he was in the process of spearfishing—one of the hunter's favorite activities—and had made an ample catch. He went to the tent of his wife and this time permitted his daughter to live. Freeman writes: "The father's frame of mind is manifestly significant in the decision of the fate of the female child." He mentions another case from 1918 in which the mother had wished to raise the female child. She said: "I could do nothing; in those days we were afraid of our husbands."

Freeman concludes from his investigations that the father is jealous of the mother, who, in the daughter, is raising a helpmate and a companion, while he has none. "He bears no grudge against the newborn child, but he considers it necessary to assure his dominance over his wife once again: he may even think she played a trick on him."

Although Freeman manages to believe that the advantages of population politics are an unintentional side effect of female infanticide among the Eskimos, like all supporters of functionalistic theories he must define this custom as being adaptive "because it reduces the tension within the decision-making unit of the Netsilik society, namely the household." In other words, the Eskimo man can compensate for his inner tensions by killing his daughters and not hurt the Eskimo mother. Because of her powerlessness in the society her pain is not tension that threatens their life together.

India demonstrates the fact that the systematic killing of female children does not result from environmental stress but is rather the consequence of an excessive male sense of honor. In the Punjab and in Kashmir at the beginning of this century there were castes and tribes in which not one single girl was left alive. A branch of the Sikhs, the Bedees, were known as *koree mar,* or daughter butchers, a tradition passed down for three thousand years. Among other castes, the Rajputs and the Chouhans, the custom is supposed to have existed "since time immemorial."

Three main reasons were cited for female infanticide. The Chouhans were afraid of the high costs of the dowry and festivities for a daughter's wedding. They were too proud to be able to submit to being the father- or son-in-law of anybody at all, and they viewed it as unfortunate to keep a daughter alive. "The last of these three reasons was the most deeply rooted."

In the 1840s, when the Rajah of Mynpoory kept his niece alive, she was probably the first female child who was born and brought up in the citadel of the Chouhans since its construction. Yet when her father and, shortly after, the Rajah, died, this deepened the conviction of the Chouhan community that their deaths were caused by the survival of the little girl.[4]

In Rajputana and in the Jumna in Etawah there was one additional reason. The caste spirit required that a daughter could be promised only to a man of the same or of higher rank. Yet this required so many presents that the fathers would have become beggars. The concept of male honor, according to a British major, presented the Rajputs with a choice of either "sacrificing the happiness of the father or the life of the daughter."

Among the Bedees there was a saying by their caste founder, Dhurm Chand: "If the Bedees remain true to their faith and refrain from lying and strong alcohol, Providence would bless them with male children exclusively."[5]

Midwives of the Bedees killed the child, either by strangling it or by laying it on the cold floor and exposing it to the wind. Or the newborn daughter was killed immediately after birth by stuffing her mouth full of cow dung, or drowning her in cow milk. In Gujarat baby girls were buried alive. Their bodies were laid in a ceramic vessel, the opening of which was covered with a doughy paste. A small pill of opium was given to the child, producing death after several hours. In many cases the mother was condemned to kill her daughter. She smeared her nipples with an opium salve, let the child suck, and waited until it died.

"Even among the mission Indians there exists the custom of killing female children at birth, especially if the couple already possesses several daughters," states a report on the present-day practice of the Waika Indians on the upper Orinoco.[6]

A passage from the *Koran* says: "If an Arab hears that a daughter has been born to him, the sorrow colors his face black; this news strikes him as such an outrageous evil that he shows himself before no one, and it is questionable whether he will keep the daughter born to him to his dishonor or whether he should bury her quickly in the earth."[7]

What is the point of these descriptions of a custom that has long since been conquered? Is anyone seriously willing to claim that in the last third of the twentieth century such practices are still possible?

The answer cannot be an unqualified no. Certainly, it is improbable that female genocide such as that among the higher Indian castes will reoccur in our century. On the other hand, the psychological constellations that made such developments possible are still implanted in our culture: women are the unwanted sex.

Following are several examples of ways in which the tendency of disparaging appraisal of a girl's birth can further survive.

The normal sex ratio of births is 100 girls' births to 105 or 106 boys' births. Because the mortality of the boys due to genetic deficiency was higher than that of the girls until a short time ago even in industrialized countries, the numerical ratio of the two sexes was balanced approximately at the time of sexual maturity; however, it shifted beginning in the twentieth year of life in favor of the woman, so that in all Western societies there is a surplus of women.

Because in the majority of countries the maternal and infant mortality rates have also decreased and women have a higher life expectancy than men, the proportion of women in the world population must be somewhat higher than that of men.

Actually, by the year 1985 the proportion of women is projected to drop from 49.91 percent to 49.78, which means that there will be about 21 million fewer women than men.[8]

The deficiency of women cannot be explained by the opposition of industrialized countries to underdeveloped countries, but there are clear-cut differences between developing countries with a superpatriarchal structure and those in which, due to the culture, fewer attitudes hostile to women exist.

Arabic and Islamic countries have the smallest proportion of women.

Egypt:	49.54 percent
Lebanon:	49.21 percent
Jordan:	49.15 percent
Tunisia:	48.95 percent
Syria:	48.73 percent
Malaysia:	48.17 percent
Libya:	48.00 percent
Iran:	46.92 percent
Kuwait:	43.19 percent

The United Arab Emirates shows the lowest proportion of women in the population, 38.14 percent, which may mean one of two things: either the women are regarded as so insignificant that any census of their numbers is inadequate, or they are consciously decimated by negligent care of female newborns and by inadequate infant and maternal hygiene.

Some countries of South America (Colombia, Ecuador, Cuba, Panama, and Guatemala) and Africa (Central African Republic, Rhodesia, Equatorial Guinea) are also conspicuous for their small proportion of women. India offers an example in which it can be proved that tendencies hostile to women are the causes of regression.

According to Professor Ashish Bose of the Institute of Economic Growth, an organization responsible for demographic inquiry on the status of Indian women: in the year 1901, for every 1,000 men there were 972 women; in the year 1971 there were only 930 women. The infant mortality of girls [in 1971] was 148 out of every 1,000 births; that of boys only 132 out of every 1,000 births. These numbers, which contradict those of Western countries, in which the mortality of boys is far higher than that of girls, are proof that girls in India are given less attention than boys. Physicians believe that females are not nursed or fed as well as males and nearly half the Indian women eat their meals every day after their husbands, fathers, and sons—a custom that leads to great malnutrition of women in the poorer classes.[9]

Some years ago this tradition of the separation of the sexes and the privileged male caused a sensation when it became known that in Biafra, children starved to death first, then women, and last men. Similar reports came from eyewitnesses of the famine in the Sahel Zone.

Still, every shift in the sex ratio in favor of the male population increases the aggression level of a society, as geneticists and biologists have unanimously agreed.[10] Sex selection soon will have great consequences for population politics.

Sex selection would most likely alter infanticide. Some population scientists, statisticians and doctors, have done studies on this subject. In a 1941 study on married couples in the midwestern United States, twice as many men as women preferred a son for an only child.[11] A similar study, which the Gallup Institute conducted in 1947, also showed that men had a much stronger preference than women for a son as the oldest child. In a 1970 poll among unmarried college students, 90 percent of the males questioned and 78 percent of the females wanted a son if they could have only one child.

The same percentage of males who were not students also preferred sons: 70 percent of lower-class women, however, wished for a daughter.

Nor do other statistics brighten the picture: if the first-born was a boy, parents waited on the average three months longer before having the next child. After the birth of a girl, American mothers experienced significantly more emotional disturbances. Pregnant women dreamt twice as often of male babies as female.[12]

These results indicate that, if sex predetermination is possible, the husband will want a son.

Yet, there is a reluctance to practice sex selection; in one recent American survey 46.7 percent were against it, 38.4 percent were for it.[13] Nevertheless, the inclination to determine the sex of the child could be decisively changed. With a simple technique of sex selection motivation to use the method would certainly increase. With a complicated method motivation for sex selection may not increase until after the birth of the first child.

The ideal is the two-child family, the first child a boy, the second a girl. In a one-child or a three-child family, the fact that male children are more often desired would yield a surplus of boys. (In three-child families, for every 100 girls born, 125 boys would be born.)

Sex selection would result in an overwhelming surplus of first-born males. What psychological and social consequences this could have for women has until now hardly been analyzed, although there are an enormous number of studies on the influence of the position in the sibling sequence and the development of only children. The factors of intellectual performance capability, creativity, and neuroticism, according to many studies, are higher in first-borns. Parents usually invest more, not only in the education of sons, but in that of the first-born.

Western scientists may tend to belittle the results of sex selection, but factors such as job development and overall future outlook definitely have an effect on it. Mothers who desire sons need not necessarily value sons more highly but perhaps only hope that they could hold their own better in a world stamped by brutal competition.

Even tensions between political camps could be decisive in producing sons, for soldiers are needed. All countries with a strong patriarchal tradition have to expect a surplus of sons in case the technique of sex selection is not too costly or too complicated. In a patriarchal industrial society like Japan, for example, the consequences are easy to guess. Governments in all overpopulated countries may have an interest in such methods only because a male birth surplus solves population problems in the long run. For all developing countries with imperialist tendencies and a strong patriarchal structure, the male surplus may be so alluring that governments would promote the introduction of chemical preparations for sex predetermination. The motivation of women to take such a remedy would probably be much higher than the motivation to practice contraception, for in all underdeveloped countries the status of the woman is based on how many sons she brings into the world. Still, the consequences of such a change in the sex ratio would not be absolutely positive for women giving birth. Perhaps if females were in demand, their chances to marry would increase, but certainly their chances for liberation would not.

Notes

1. *Hellenistic Civilization,* rev. by W. W. Tarn and G. T. Griffith (Cleveland and New York: Meridian Books, World Publishing Co., 1964), p. 101.

2. Ibid.

3. Milton R. Freeman, "A Social and Ecological Analysis of Systematic Female Infanticide among the Netsilik Eskimo," *American Anthropologist,* vol. 73 (1971).

4. M. N. Das, "Female Infanticide among the Bedees and the Chouhans: Motives and Modes," *Man in India,* vol. 36, no. 4 (1956).

5. Ibid.; cf. also, M. N. Das, "Movement to Suppress the Custom of Female Infanticide in the Punjab and Kashmir," *Man in India,* vol. 37 (1957).

6. Angelina Pollak-Eltz in *Anthropos* (1963–64, 1968–69).

7. Ploss and Bartels, op. cit.

8. Population Division of the Department of Economic and Social Affairs, 1974, UN paper for the international women's conference in Mexico City, June 19–July 1, 1975, E/Conf. 66/3/Add.3.

9. Quoted by WIN (Women's International Network) (Lexington, Mass.: 1975), vol. 1, no. 2, p. 54.

10. Cf. R. Jungk, J. H. Mundt, eds., *Hat die Familie noch eine Zukumft?* (Munich, Vienna and Basel: 1971).

11. Charles F. Westoff and Ronald R. Rindfuss, "Sex Preselection in the United States: Some Implications," *Science*, vol. 184 (1974), p. 633.

12. Sherman, op. cit.

13. Westoff and Rindfuss, op. cit.

Part 2

❖ ❖ ❖

THE PATRIARCHAL HOME:
THE MOST LETHAL PLACE FOR WOMEN

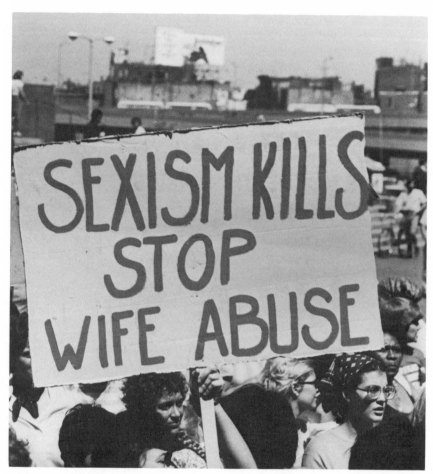

Battered Women Speak-out, Boston, Massachusetts, 1976. Photo Ellen Shub.

Introduction

The selections in part 2 focus on the killing of women in their own home by men with whom they were or are in relationships. It is ironic that the place where women should expect to feel safest—their own home—is the place where they are least safe from lethal sexual violence when they share that home with a man. Also ironic is the fact that it is those men whom women are encouraged to trust and look to for love and protection who pose the greatest risk, be they husbands, lovers, or former husbands or lovers.

The section opens with an excerpt from the poem "Womanslaughter," in which Pat Parker speaks personally about the death of an African-American woman killed by her husband after having been denied police protection. Parker indicts the police and the judicial system for failing to support women in such life-threatening situations.

Parker's personal testament is followed by two academic studies. In "Till Death to Us Part" Margo Wilson and Martin Daly analyze the reasons why men kill intimate female partners and assess the circumstances in which an intimate femicide is most likely to occur. The following article, by Jacquelyn Campbell, is a statistical study of the killings in Dayton, Ohio, over a four-year period. Campbell shows how the threat of female death has been systematically obscured not only by the press but by social scientists, who, like the press, tend to blame the women who are victims of violence.

In a personal account that adds immediacy to some of the issues raised by the above two studies, Rikki Gregory portrays the experience of her friend Mandy with her husband's violence. Like many women living in a violent relationship, Mandy adopted a coping strategy based on denial. This strategy may have enabled her to survive a little longer in the relationship, but it ultimately cost Mandy her life.

The next three pieces address femicide in India. Govind Kelkar links the practice of bride burning, in contemporary Hindu society to the patriarchal family and to the wider economic and political structure of that society, which engenders women's dependency on men. This dependency is exacerbated by traditional marriage patterns. Upon marriage, it is usual for women to leave their family of birth to live with their husband's family, which may be thousands of miles away. This isolation from her first family, together with her dependency on her new family, puts her in a vulnerable position. The author connects this vulnerability to the practice of bride burning in Hindu society. She also explores the protest of bride burning by Hindu women, which counters stereotypical Western views of them as passive.

Govind Kelkar's research-based article is followed by a press report on suttee (widow burning) by Rajendra Bajpai in the *San Francisco Chronicle*. The author reports that the practice of suttee, while condemned by authorities, remains a popular spectacle that draws voyeurs from miles around.

S. H. Venkatramani shifts the focus to another form of femicide, female infanticide. Preference for, and preferential treatment of, male children has a long history in patriarchal societies—in this case, India—in which males in all spheres of life are accorded higher social, political, and economic value than females. In some patriarchal cultures this preference for male children has resulted in the practice of female infanticide. Venkatramani links infanticide with the selective abortion of female embryos. The author's intent is not to imply that abortion is a form of murder but to question whether certain abortions take place as a result of coercion or of choice.

Finally, Karen Stout looks at the alternatives available to women living in unsafe homes and assesses the connections between the extent of intimate femicide and the availability of legal remedies and shelters for women who need them.

Womanslaughter

PAT PARKER

Hello, Hello Death
There was a quiet man
He married a quiet wife
Together, they lived
a quiet life.

Not so, not so
her sisters said,
the truth comes out
as she lies dead.
He beat her.
He accused her
of awful things
and he beat her.
One day she left.

She went to her sister's house
She, too, was a woman alone.
The quiet man came and beat her.
Both women were afraid.

"Hello, Hello Police
I am a woman
and I am afraid.
My husband means to kill me."

Excerpt reprinted from *Crimes against Women,* ed. Diana E. H. Russell and Nicole Van de Ven (Millbrae, Calif.: Les Femmes, 1976), 147–50.

"Lady, there's nothing we can do
until he tries to hurt you.
Go to the judge and he will decree
that your husband leaves you be!"
She found an apartment
with a friend.
She would begin
a new life again.
Interlocutory Divorce Decreeing
the end of the quiet man.

He came to her home
and he beat her.
Both women were afraid.

"Hello, Hello Police
I am a woman alone
and I am afraid.
My ex-husband means to kill me."

"Fear not, Lady
He will be sought."
It was too late,
when he was caught.
One day a quiet man
shot his quiet wife
three times in the back.
He shot her friend as well.
His wife died.

What shall be done with this man?
Is it a murder of first degree?
No, said the men
It is a crime of passion.
He was angry.

Is it a murder of second degree?
Yes, said the men,
but we will not call it that.
We must think of his record.
We will call it manslaughter.
The sentence is the same.
What will we do with this man?
His boss, a white man came.

This is a quiet Black man, he said
He works well for me
The men sent the quiet
Black man to jail.
He went to work in the day.
He went to jail and slept at night.
In one year, he went home.

Sister, I do not understand,
I rage and do not understand.
In Texas, he would be freed.
One Black kills another
One less Black for Texas.

But this is not Texas.
This is California.
The city of angels.
Was his crime so slight?
George Jackson served
years for robbery.
Eldridge Cleaver served
years for rape.
I know of a man in Texas
who is serving 40 years
for possession of marijuana.
Was his crime so slight?
What was his crime?
He only killed his wife.
But a divorce I say.
Not final; they say;
Her things were his
including her life.
Men cannot rape their wives!
Men cannot kill their wives.
They passion them to death.

The three sisters
of Shirley Jones
came and cremated her.
And they were not strong.
Hear me now—
It is almost three years
and I am again strong.
I have gained many sisters.

And if one is beaten,
or raped, or killed,
I will not come in mourning black.
I will not pick the right flowers
I will not celebrate her death
and it will matter not
if she's Black or white—
if she loves women or men.
I will come with my many sisters
and decorate the streets
with the innards of those
brothers-in-womenslaughter.
No more, can I dull my rage
in alcohol and deference
to men's courts.
I will come to my sisters,
not dutiful,
I will come strong.

Till Death Us Do Part

MARGO WILSON AND MARTIN DALY

The revelation of wifely infidelity is a provocation so extreme that a "reasonable man" is apt to respond with lethal violence. This impulse is so strong and so natural that the homicidal cuckold cannot be held fully responsible for his dreadful deed. So says the common law.

Other spousal misbehavior—snoring or burning supper or mismanaging the family finances—cannot be invoked as provocation. Reasonable men do not react violently to their wives' profligacy or stupidity or sloth or insults. In fact, the *only* provocations other than a wife's adultery that are invested with the same power to mitigate a killer's criminal responsibility are physical assaults upon himself or a relative (see, for example, Dressler 1982).

The law of provocation reflects a folk theory of the male mind, for which the apprehension of female infidelity allegedly constitutes a uniquely powerful impetus to violence. This folk theory is not peculiar to Western societies but is extremely widespread. Does it match reality?

PROVOCATION AND THE "REASONABLE MAN"

Despite the contemporary scourges of serial killers, rape-murders, and homicides in the course of robbery, most murdered women are killed by their mates.

A small proportion of the men who kill their wives are found "unfit to stand trial" or "not guilty by reason of insanity." Such men are often deemed to be suf-

Large portions of this chapter have been excerpted with modification from chapter 9 of Martin Daly and Margo Wilson, *Homicide* (Hawthorne, N.Y.: Aldine de Gruyter, 1988). Our research on homicide has been supported by the Harry Frank Guggenheim Foundation, the North Atlantic Treaty Organization, the Natural Sciences and Engineering Research Council of Canada, and the Social Sciences and Humanities Research Council of Canada. This paper was completed while the authors were fellows at the Center for Advanced Study in the Behavioral Sciences, Stanford, Calif.

fering from a psychiatric condition called "morbid jealousy" (Mowat 1966), diagnosed on the basis of an obsessive concern about suspected infidelity and a
tendency to invoke bizarre "evidence" in support of the suspicion. But most men
who kill in a jealous rage are not considered insane. Not only is jealousy
"normal," but so, it seems, is violent jealousy, at least if perpetrated by a man
and in the heat of passion.

The English common law relies heavily upon a conception of the way in
which a "reasonable man" could be expected to behave. This hypothetical creature embodies the judiciary's assumptions about the natural order of marital
relationships and men's passions, assumptions that are laid bare in this legal
scholar's summary characterization: "The judges have gone a considerable way
towards establishing—so far as the law of provocation is concerned—a standard
portrayal of the make-up and reactions of the reasonable man. They say he is not
impotent and he is not normally drunk. He does not lose his self-control on
hearing a mere confession of adultery, but he becomes unbalanced at the sight of
adultery provided, of course, that he is married to the adulteress" (Edwards
1954, 900).

This "reasonable man" may strike the reader as a quaintly English invention, but he is more than that. Solon's law gave the same right to Greek cuckolds, while Roman law excused the homicidal cuckold only if the adultery
occurred in his house. Various such provisions remain in effect in continental
Europe today.

Until 1974, it was the law in Texas that homicide is justified—not a criminal act, and therefore subject to no penalty whatever—"when committed by the
husband upon the person of anyone taken in the act of adultery with the wife,
provided the killing takes place before the parties to the act of adultery have
separated" (Texas Penal Code 1925, article 1220). Elsewhere, this is the
"unwritten law," and cases both in Texas and in other states with analogous
practices based on precedent have considered the justification to extend to lethal
assaults upon the errant wife, the rival, or both. (The factors that are predictive
of the likelihood that a violent cuckold will assault his wife versus his rival have
yet to be elucidated.)

Many other legal traditions quite different from our own address this question of the "victimized" husband's legitimate response in similar fashion. More
than merely entitling the wronged husband to material compensation, adultery is
widely construed to justify his resorting to violence that would in other circumstances be deemed criminal. Among the Melanesian Islanders of Wogeo, for
example, the principal subject of law and morality is adultery, and "the rage of
the husband who has been wronged" is considered predictable and excusable;
the Wogeans say, "he is like a man whose pig has been stolen," only much
angrier (Hogbin 1938, 236–37). Among the Nuer of East Africa, "it is commonly recognized that a man caught in adultery runs a risk of serious injury or
even death at the hands of the woman's husband" (Howell 1954, 156). Having
caught his wife in flagrante delicto, the Yapese cuckold "had the right to kill her

and the adulterer or to burn them in the house" (Muller 1917, 229). Among the Toba-Batak of Sumatra, "the injured husband had the right to kill the man caught in adultery as he would kill a pig in a rice-field" (Vergouwen 1964, 266). In general, the ethnographic record suggests that the violent rages of cuckolds are universally considered predictable and widely considered legitimate.

MALE SEXUAL PROPRIETARINESS

Men exhibit a tendency to think of women as sexual and reproductive "property" that they can own and exchange. To call men sexually "proprietary" is conceptually similar to calling them sexually "jealous" but lacks certain constraining implications of the latter term, such as the sometime connotation of jealousy as excessive or socially undesirable. Proprietariness implies a more encompassing mind-set, referring not just to the emotional force of one's own feelings of entitlement but to a more pervasive attitude toward social relationships. Proprietary entitlements in people have been conceived and institutionalized as identical to proprietary entitlements in land, chattels, and other economic resources. Historically and cross-culturally, the owners of slaves, servants, wives, and children have been entitled to enjoy the benefits of ownership without interference, to modify their property, and to buy and sell, while the property had little or no legal or political status in "its" own right (see, for example, Dobash and Dobash 1979; Russell 1982; Sachs and Wilson 1978).

That men take a proprietary view of female sexuality and reproductive capacity is manifested in various cultural practices (Wilson 1987; Wilson and Daly 1992). Anglo-American law is replete with examples of men's proprietary entitlements over the sexuality and reproductive capacity of wives and daughters. Since before the time of William the Conqueror there has been a continual elaboration of legal devices enabling men to seek monetary redress for the theft and damage of their women's sexuality and reproductive capacity. These torts, all of which have been sexually asymmetrical until very recently, include "loss of consortium," "enticement," "criminal conversation," "alienation of affection," "seduction," and "abduction" (Attenborough 1963; Backhouse 1986; Brett 1955; Sinclair 1987; Wilson and Daly 1992). In all of these tort actions the person entitled to seek redress was the owner of the woman, whose virtue or chastity was fundamental; those holding proprietary entitlements in prostitutes and other women of dubious reputation had no legal cause. Furthermore, the woman's consent did not mitigate the wrong.

Throughout human history and around the world, powerful men have tended to accumulate as many women of fertile age as they could manage and have invested substantial efforts and resources in attempting to sequester them from other men (Betzig 1986). A wide range of "claustration" practices, including veiling, foot-binding, and incarceration in women's quarters, as well as such mechanical and surgical interventions as chastity belts and infibulation, have

been employed by proprietary men in their efforts to retain sexual and reproductive exclusivity (Dickemann 1979, 1981; Hosken 1979). The bride-price paid
in many patrilineal societies by the groom and his family to the bride's father
(see, for example, Comaroff 1980, Borgerhoff Mulder 1988) is really a child-
price that may even be due in installments after each birth. Barrenness is often a
grounds for male-initiated divorce with refund of the bride-price (Stephens
1963). The acquisition of rights to a woman's reproductive capacity entails
rights to the labor and other value of the children she produces and the right to
sire those children. Husbands are almost invariably entitled to exercise control
over their wives' sex lives, and that almost always means retaining sexual access
for themselves. Sexually asymmetrical adultery laws that make sexual intercourse with a married woman an offense against her husband are characteristic
of the indigenous legal codes of all the world's civilizations (Daly, Wilson, and
Weghorst 1982).

Not only have husbands been entitled to exclusive sexual access to their
wives, but they have been entitled to use force to get it. The criminalization of
rape within marriage, and hence the wife's legal entitlement to refuse sex, has
been established only recently (Edwards 1981; Russell 1982). English husbands
have been entitled to place disobedient wives under restraint, and it was not until
1973 that a husband was convicted of kidnapping for restraining a wife intending to leave him for another man (Atkins and Hoggett 1984). The expression
"rule of thumb" derives from the judicial ruling that a husband was entitled to
use only a stick no thicker than his thumb to control an overly independent wife
(Edwards 1985).

HOMICIDE AND SEXUAL PROPRIETARINESS

Granting that men wish to control their wives and are prepared to use force to do
so, the question remains why they kill them. Paradoxical though it may appear,
there is compelling evidence that uxoricide is a manifestation of proprietariness.

Most studies of homicide "motives" have depended upon summary police
files and have been limited by the sparse, special-purpose information recorded
there. The two leading motive categories in Marvin Wolfgang's (1958) trend-
setting study of Philadelphia homicides, for example, were "altercation of relatively trivial origin" and "domestic quarrel." Neither of these category labels
tells us much. "Jealousy" ranked third and was thus the leading substantive issue
on Wolfgang's list, as it has proved to be in many studies.

In Canada, the investigating police file a report on every homicide with the
federal agency Statistics Canada, using a standardized multiple-choice form.
The police are offered a choice of 12 motives, one of which is "jealousy."
Between 1974 and 1983, Canadian police made an attribution of motive for
1,006 out of 1,060 spousal homicides (Daly and Wilson 1988a). Of these, 214

(21.3 percent) were attributed to jealousy: 195 of 812 homicides committed by husbands and 19 of 248 perpetrated by wives. But this is surely a gross underestimate of the role played by jealousy, since the great majority of cases were not linked to any substantive source of conflict: the police attributed 513 cases simply to "argument or quarrel," and another 106 to "anger or hatred." These motive categories reflect detectives' and prosecutors' concern with the question of premeditation versus impulsive reaction, but they tell us nothing about the substance of marital conflict. Any of these cases might have been provoked by the suspicion or discovery of infidelity.

Our claim that the Statistics Canada motive data underestimate the importance of adultery and jealousy in spousal conflict is more than just a conjecture. Catherine Carlson's (1984) study of the spousal homicides investigated by one Ontario police force provides clear evidence on this point. Carlson examined the police files on 36 spousal homicides for which the motive category reported to Statistics Canada was noted in the file. Only four had been labeled "jealousy" cases by the police, and yet sexual proprietariness was clearly relevant to several others. Here, for example, is a statement made to police by an unemployed 53-year-old man who shot his 42-year-old estranged wife:

> I know she was fuckin' around. I had been waiting for approximately five minutes and seen her pull up in a taxi and I drove over and pulled up behind her car. I said "Did you enjoy your weekend?" She said "You're fuckin' right I did. I will have a lot more of them too." I said "Oh no you won't. You have been bullshitting me long enough. I can take no more." I kept asking her if she would come back to me. She told me to get out of her life. I said "No way. If I get out of this it's going to be both of us." (Carlson 1984, 7–8)

In reporting to Statistics Canada, the police classified this case under the motive category "mentally ill, retarded."

In another case classified under "anger or hatred" (the most popular category with this police force, accounting for 11 of the 36 spousal homicides), a 31-year-old man stabbed his 20-year-old common-law wife after a six-month temporary separation. In his statement to police, the accused gave this account of the fatal argument:

> Then she said that since she came back in April she had fucked this other man about ten times. I told her how can you talk love and marriage and you been fucking with this other man. I was really mad. I went to the kitchen and got the knife. I went back to our room and said were you serious when you told me that. She said yes. We fought on the bed, I was stabbing her and her grandfather came up and tried to take the knife out of my hand. I told him to call the cops for me. I don't know why I killed the woman, I loved her. (Carlson 1984, 9)

Police synopses and government statistics are obviously not ideal sources of information on homicide motives. Fortunately, there have been at least a few intensive studies in which the researchers have interviewed the killers themselves about the sources of the conflicts that culminated in spousal homicide. Such studies are unanimous in confirming that male sexual proprietariness constitutes *the* dangerous issue in marriage regardless of whether it is the husband or the wife who is finally slain.

Accused killers are commonly obliged to undergo a psychiatric examination to determine whether they are "fit to stand trial." In 1955, Manfred Guttmacher, the fitness examiner for the city of Baltimore, published a report summarizing his examinations of 31 people who had killed their spouses, 24 men and 7 women. These represented all such killers among 36 consecutive Baltimore cases of intrafamilial homicide, and Guttmacher tabulated what he called "apparent motivational factors" on the basis of his personal interviews with the perpetrators. While the data are presented a little ambiguously (some cases were tabulated under more than one motive), it appears that as many as 25 (81 percent) of the 31 spousal homicides were motivated by sexual proprietariness. Fourteen cases were provoked by the spouse's deserting for a new partner, five by the spouse's "promiscuity," four by "pathological jealousy," one by the discovery of adultery in flagrante delicto, and one by a delusionary suspicion of adultery between the killer's wife and his son-in-law.

A similar report from the Forensic Psychiatry Clinic of the University of Virginia reveals a preponderance of cases of male sexual proprietariness that is even more dramatic than in the Baltimore sample. Showalter, Bonnie, and Roddy (1980) described 17 cases of "killing or seriously wounding" a legal or common-law spouse. Six cases were attributed to psychiatric disorders, but the authors were so impressed with the essential similarity of the remaining 11 that they called their report "The Spousal Homicide Syndrome." All 11 attackers were men, and all professed that they were deeply in love with their victims. Ten of the 11 attacks were precipitated by "an immediate threat of withdrawal," and 8 of the 11 victimized wives had left the offender at least once previously, only to return. Moreover, "in all 11 cases, the victim was engaged in an affair with another man or had led the offender to believe that she was being unfaithful to him. In 10 of the cases, the victim made no attempt to conceal her other relationships" (127). Barnard et al. (1982) reported very similar results in a Florida study.

A Canadian study of convicted spouse killers points again to the overwhelming predominance of male sexual jealousy and proprietariness as motives in spousal homicide. Sociologist Peter Chimbos (1978) interviewed an "availability sample" of 34 spouse killers, 29 men and 5 women. The interviews were conducted at an average interval of three years after the homicide; 30 interviewees were in prison, 4 had recently been released. Seventeen had been legally married to their victims and 17 had been living in common-law relationships. In a finding reminiscent of the Virginia "syndrome," 22 of the 34 couples had previously separated owing to infidelity and had later been reconciled.

The most striking result of Chimbos's study is the near unanimity of the killers in identifying the main source of conflict in their ill-fated marriages. Twenty-nine of the 34 (85 percent) pointed to "sexual matters (affairs and refusals)," 3 blamed "excessive drinking," and 2 professed that there *was* no serious conflict. Remarkably, these few issues exhaust the list. Most of the killers were of low educational and occupational status, but not one pointed to financial problems as the primary source of conflict. Although 28 of the 34 couples had children, no one considered them to be the main source of conflict either. The conflicts were over sexual matters, and that mainly meant adultery.

Unfortunately, Chimbos did not break down the infidelity quarrels according to sex. Nevertheless, it is clear that the wives' adulteries were a far greater bone of contention than the husbands', no matter which party ended up dead. Scattered through the monograph are verbatim quotations from the interviewed killers. Thirteen such quotes from the male offenders included allusions to infidelity, and all 13 were complaints about the faithlessness of the wife. By way of comparison, there were 4 quotes from female killers that made reference to infidelity, but these were not mirror images of the male complaints. All 4 of the women's allusions to adultery concerned their husbands' accusations against themselves; in one of the 4, the accusations were mutual.

Chimbos chose 6 cases for detailed narrative description. Four were committed by men, 2 by women. In every one of these 6 cases—selected, according to the author, to represent the full range of conflicts in the entire sample—the husband angrily accused the wife of adultery before the homicide. In 3 cases, the accusations were mutual.

IF I CAN'T HAVE YOU, NO ONE CAN

Men do not easily let women go. They search out women who have left them, to plead and threaten and sometimes to kill. As one Illinois man told his wife six months before she divorced him and seven months before he killed her in her home with a shotgun, "I swear if you ever leave me, I'll follow you to the ends of the earth and kill you" (*People v. Wood,* 391 N.E. 2d 206).

The estranged wife, hunted down and murdered, is a common item in police files. The converse case of a vengeful murder by a jilted wife is an extreme rarity, the popularity of the theme in fiction notwithstanding. In Canada between 1974 and 1983, 117 of 524 (22 percent) of women slain by their registered-marriage husbands were separated from them as compared to 11 of 118 (9 percent) men slain by their registered-marriage wives. Among these estranged couples the ratio of wife victims to husband victims was 10.6 to 1 (117 versus 11), compared with a ratio of 3.8 to 1 (407 versus 107) for co-residing couples (Wilson 1989). And whereas 43 percent of the 117 homicides by estranged husbands were attributed by the police to "jealousy," only 2 of the 11 by estranged wives were so attributed; the rare case of a woman killing her estranged husband is likely to be a case of self-defense against a man who will not let her be. Wallace (1986) found an even stronger association between estrangement and uxoricide in an Australian study: 98 of 217 women slain by their husbands were separated or in the process thereof, compared with just 3 of 79 men slain by their wives.

The homicides that police and criminologists attribute to "jealousy" include a couple of somewhat different sorts of dramas, which might usefully be distinguished. On the one hand we have what some criminologists have referred to as "love triangles": cases in which there is a known or suspected third party. In other killings, it is not clear that any particular third party was involved or even suspected by the jealous individual, who simply could not abide his partner's terminating the relationship. The jealous party is even more often male in such cases than in triangles. In Detroit in 1972, for example, a man was the jealous party in 30 out of 40 "triangle" murders, and in 17 out of 18 cases where the killer simply would not abide being deserted (Daly, Wilson, and Weghorst 1982).

The distinction between a wife's adultery and her departure illustrates two separable but related considerations underlying male jealousy (Daly and Wilson 1988a; Wilson and Daly 1992). Only the former places the man at risk of cuckoldry and misdirected parental investment in another man's child, but the risks are partly the same: in either case, the man is at risk of losing control of his wife's reproductive capacity (Wilson 1987). And this reproductive strategic commonality between the two sorts of cases evidently imparts a psychological commonality as well: researchers have tended to lump these together as "jealousy" cases is because of the aggressive proprietariness of the husband, who seems to consider adultery and desertion equivalent violations of his rights. The man who hunts down and kills a woman who has left him has surely lapsed into futile spite, acting out his vestigial agenda of dominance to no useful end.

CONJUGAL JEALOUSY AND VIOLENCE AROUND THE WORLD

The phenomena we have been discussing are not peculiar to industrial society. In every society for which we have been able to find a sample of spousal homicides, the story is basically the same: most cases arise out of the husband's jealous, proprietary, violent response to his wife's (real or imagined) infidelity or desertion.

Several monographs have been published, for example, on the topic of homicides among various aboriginal peoples in India. These include the Bison-Horn Maria (Elwin 1950), the Munda (Saran 1974), the Oraon (Saran 1974), and the Bhil (Varma 1978). Rates of lethal violence among these tribal horticulturalists are high, and 99 percent of the killings are committed by men. These homicide samples include 20 cases of Bison-Horn Maria wives killed by their husbands, 3 such Munda cases, 3 Oraon, and 8 Bhil. In each of the four societies, the majority of spousal homicides was precipitated either by the man's suspicion or knowledge of wifely infidelity or by the woman's leaving or rejecting her husband. Moreover, in each of these studies, about 20 percent of the much more numerous male-male homicides were expressly due either to rivalry over a woman or to a man's taking offense at sexual advances made to his daughter or another female relative.

Fallers and Fallers (1960) collated information on 98 consecutive homicide cases (that is, 98 victims) between 1947 and 1954 among the Basoga, a patrilineal, polygynous, horticultural tribe in Uganda. Eight of these were apparently accidents, leaving 90 cases. Forty-two were cases in which a man killed a woman, usually his wife, and some sort of motive was imputed in 32 of these: 10 for adultery, 11 for desertion or for refusing sex, and 11 for a diversity of other motives. An additional 5 male-male cases were clear matters of sexual rivalry. Only 2 women were offenders, one taking the life of a man and one a woman; the latter case was the only one evidently arising out of female sexual jealousy or rivalry, as compared with 26 male jealousy cases. (In polygynous societies, co-wives can be fierce rivals, but they still kill one another far less often than do males.)

Sohier (1959) reviewed court records on 275 homicides leading to convictions between 1948 and 1957 in what was then the Belgian Congo. Many cases were assigned to no particular motive category, but of those with identified motives, 59 were attributable to male jealousy and only one to female jealousy. Sixteen cuckolded husbands killed their adulterous wives or the male adulterer or both. Ten more killed their wives for desertion or for threatening desertion. Three killed an ex-wife after she had obtained a divorce, and 3 more killed an ex-wife's new husband. Another 13 men killed faithless fiancées or mistresses. And so forth. Only 20 spousal cases were not attributed to male jealousy, and their motives were unspecified. The single female jealousy case was one in which a wife killed her husband's mistress.

Are there no exceptions to this dreary record of connubial coercion and violence? Certainly there are societies within which the homicide rate is exceptionally low. But is there even one exotic land in which the men eschew violence, take no proprietary view of their wives' sexuality, and accept consenting extramarital sex as good, clean fun? The short answer is no, although many have sought such a society, and a few have imagined that they found it.

The most popular place to situate the mythical peaceful kingdom is a South Seas island. Margaret Mead, for example, portrayed Samoa in innumerable writings as an idyllic land of free, innocent sexuality and claimed that sexual jealousy was hardly known there.

> Granting that jealousy is undesirable, a festering spot in every personality so afflicted, an ineffective negativistic attitude which is more likely to lose than gain any goal, what are the possibilities if not of eliminating it, at least of

excluding it more and more from human life? Samoa has taken one road, by eliminating strong emotion, high stakes, emphasis upon personality, interest in competition. Such a cultural attitude eliminates many of the attitudes which have afflicted mankind, and perhaps jealousy most importantly of all . . . (Mead 1931, 46)

Derek Freeman finally exploded Mead's myth in 1983, showing that violent responses to adultery and sexual rivalry are exceptionally frequent in Samoa and have long been endemic to the society.

The factual evidence that Margaret Mead's Samoa was a fantasy had long been available. But the facts were ignored. Scholars who should have looked at the data critically wanted to believe in a tropical island where jealousy and violence were unknown. The prevalent ideology in the social sciences combines the premise that conflict is an evil and harmony a good—fair enough as a moral stance, although of dubious relevance to the scientific study of society—with a sort of "naturalistic fallacy" that makes goodness natural and evil artificial. The upshot is that conflict must be explained as the product of some modern, artificial nastiness (capitalism, say, or patriarchy), while the romantic ideal of the "noble savage" is retained, with nobility fantastically construed to mean an absence of all conflictual motives, including sexual possessiveness.

Part of the confusion about the alleged existence of exotic peoples devoid of jealousy derives from a failure to distinguish between societal sanctions and the private use of force. In an influential volume entitled *The Family in Cross-cultural Perspective,* for example, William Stephens (1963) asserted that in 4 societies out of a sample of 39, "there seems to be little if any bar to any sort of non-incestuous adultery" (251). Yet here is one of Stephens's own sources discussing the situation in one of those four societies, namely the Marquesa Islanders: "When a woman undertook to live with a man, she placed herself under his authority. If she cohabited with another man without his permission, she was beaten or, if her husband's jealousy was sufficiently aroused, killed" (Handy 1923, 100). In fact, when one consults Stephens's ethnographic sources, one finds accounts of wife beating as punishment for adultery in every one of the four permissive societies (Daly, Wilson, and Weghorst 1982). What Stephens evidently meant by claiming there was "little if any bar" to adultery was that no criminal sanctions were levied against adulterers by the larger society. Cuckolded husbands took matters into their own hands.

Ford and Beach's classic work *Patterns of Sexual Behavior* (1951) contains an assertion very like Stephens's but even more misleading. These authors claimed to have discovered 7 societies, out of a sample of 139, in which "the customary incest prohibitions appear to be the only major barrier to sexual intercourse outside of mateship. Men and women in these societies are free to engage in sexual liaisons and indeed are expected to do so provided the incest rules are observed" (113). Once again, we can make sense of these assertions only by assuming that Ford and Beach intend "barriers" to refer to legal or quasi-legal sanctions by the larger society. For just as in Stephens's sample, the original ethnographies make it clear that men in every one of the seven societies were apt to respond with extreme violence to their wives' dalliances (Daly, Wilson, and Weghorst 1982). Cuckolded men in these societies sometimes killed their adulterous wives, and they sometimes killed their rivals. If the fear of violent reprisal was not a "major barrier" to "sexual liaisons," it's hard to imagine what would be.

VIOLENCE AS COERCIVE CONTROL

In attempting to exert proprietary rights over the sexuality and reproduction of women, men walk a tightrope. The man who actually kills his wife has usually overstepped the bounds of utility, however utility is conceived. Killing provokes retribution by the criminal justice system or the victim's relatives. At the least, murdered wives are costly to replace.

But killing is just the tip of the iceberg. For every murdered wife, hundreds are beaten, coerced and intimidated. Although homicide probably does not often serve the interests of the perpetrator, it is far from clear that the same can be said of sublethal violence. Men, as we noted earlier, strive to control women, albeit with variable success; women struggle to resist coercion and to maintain their choices. There is brinksmanship and risk of disaster in any such contest, and homicides by spouses of either sex may be considered the slips in this dangerous game.

What we are suggesting is that most spousal homicides are the relatively rare and extreme manifestations of the same basic conflicts that inspire sublethal marital violence on a much larger scale. As in homicide, so too in wife-beating: the predominant issues are adultery, jealousy, and male proprietariness. White-hurst (1971), for example, attended 100 Canadian court cases involving couples in litigation over the husband's use of violence upon the wife. He reported, without quantification, that "at the core of nearly all the cases . . . the husband responded out of frustration at being unable to control the wife, often accusing her of being a whore or of having an affair" (686). Dobash and Dobash (1984) interviewed 109 battered Scottish wives, and asked them to identify the main source of conflict in a "typical" battering incident. Forty-eight of the women pointed to possessiveness and sexual jealousy on the part of the batterer, making this far and away the leading response; arguments over money ranked second (18 women), and the husband's expectations about domestic work ranked third (17 women). A similar interview study of 31 battered American women in hostels and hospitals obtained similar results: "jealousy was the most frequently mentioned topic that led to violent argument, with 52 percent of the women listing it as the main incitement and 94 percent naming it as a frequent cause" (Rounsaville 1978, 21). Battering husbands seldom make themselves available for interview, but when they do, they tell essentially the same story as their victims. Brisson (1983), for example, asked 122 wife-beaters in Denver to name the "topics around which violence occurred." Jealousy topped the list, with alcohol second and money a distant third.

Although wife beating is often inspired by a suspicion of infidelity, it can be the product of a more generalized proprietariness. Battered women commonly report that their husbands object violently to the continuation of old friendships, even with other women, and indeed to the wives' having any social life whatever. In a study of 60 battered wives who sought help at a clinic in rural North Carolina, Hilberman and Munson (1978) reported that the husbands exhibited "morbid jealousy," such that "leaving the house for any reason invariably resulted in accusations of infidelity which culminated in assault" in an astonishing 57 cases (95 percent) (461). Husbands who refuse to let their wives go to the store unescorted may run the risk, in our society, of being considered psychiatric cases. Yet there are many societies in which such constraint and confinement of women are considered normal and laudable (see, for example, Dickemann 1981).

THE EPIDEMIOLOGY OF SPOUSAL HOMICIDE

The above review suggests that the incidences of wife battering and uxoricide are likely to be exacerbated by anything that makes sexually proprietary husbands perceive their wives as likely to betray or quit the marital relationship.

One such factor is the woman's age. Youth makes a woman more attractive to rival men (Symons 1979), as witness the age distributions of pinups and porn stars, the greater likelihood of remarriage the younger a divorcee (for example, Glick and Lin 1987; Sweet and Bumpass 1987), and the fact that rape victimization rates decline rapidly with age beyond the mid-20s (Thornhill and Thornhill 1983). So if spousal homicides represent the tip of the iceberg of coercive violence, then young wives, although in a sense most valued by their husbands, may also be most at risk from them. In Canada, young wives indeed incur the greatest risk of being slain by their husbands (see figure 1) (Daly and Wilson 1988a, 1988b). This finding has recently been replicated in the United States (Mercy and Saltzman 1989). One might suppose that young wives are most at risk simply because they are usually married to young men, who are the most homicidal age-sex class regardless of any relation to the victim (Daly and Wilson 1990); however, young women married to older men are no less at risk (Daly and Wilson 1988a, 1988b).

One might anticipate that demographic and circumstantial factors associated with an elevated risk of divorce will often be associated with an elevated risk of homicide as well, for two reasons. The first is that we consider homicide a sort of "assay" of interpersonal conflict, and divorce is surely another. Moreover, if men assault and kill in circumstances in which they perceive women as likely to desert them, then female-initiated separation and divorce (as well as

FIGURE 1 Age-specific Victimization Rates for Wives Killed by Husbands, Canada, 1974–83 (N = 812 victims)

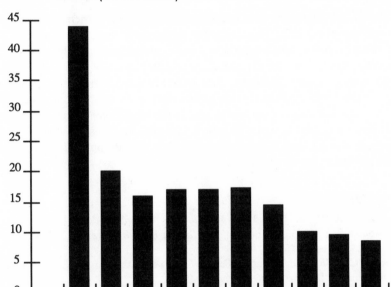

Source: Margo Wilson, "Marital Conflict and Homicide in Evolutionary Perspective," in *Sociobiology and the Social Sciences*, ed. R. W. Bell and N. J. Bell, 45–62 (Lubbock, Texas: Texas Tech University Press, 1989). Reprinted with permission of Texas Tech University Press.

men's divorcing of adulterous wives) are likely to be relatively frequent in the same sorts of circumstances as uxoricides. A large age disparity between husband and wife is one factor associated with enhanced risk of both divorce (Day 1964; Bumpass and Sweet 1972) and homicide (Daly and Wilson 1988a, 1988b; Mercy and Saltzman 1989). A short duration of marriage is another risk factor in wife-killing (Wallace 1986) and in divorce (see, for example, Morgan and Rindfuss 1985; Sweet and Bumpass 1987), but marital duration and age have yet to be adequately separated in statistical analyses of homicides. Children from former unions constitute a potential source of conflict that is definitely associated with increased risk of divorce (Becker, Landes and Michael 1977; White and Booth 1985) and appears to be associated with increased risk of spouse-killing (Daly and Wilson 1988a). De facto unions, as opposed to registered marriages, are relatively prone to dissolution and to homicide (Wilson 1989). These facts indicate that patterns of separation risk and homicide risk are often similar. However, insofar as wife killing is the act of proprietary husbands, its eliciting circumstances are more likely to match those of separations desired and enacted by the wife, and to be distinct from the reasons why men discard wives they no longer value.

Though the motives in wife killing exhibit a dreary consistency across cultures and across centuries—and although the epidemiological patterns of elevated risk to younger women, de facto unions, and so forth, are also robust—it is important to note that the actual rates at which women are slain by husbands are enormously variable. Women in the United States today face a statistical risk of being slain by their husbands that is about five to ten times greater than that faced by their European counterparts, and in the most violent American cities, risk is five times higher again. It may be the case that men have proprietary inclinations toward their wives everywhere, but they do not everywhere feel equally entitled to act upon them.

References

Atkins, S., and B. Hoggett. 1984. *Women and the Law*. Oxford: Blackwell.

Attenborough, F. L. 1963. *The Laws of the Earliest English Kings* [1922]. New York: Russell and Russell.

Backhouse, C. 1986. "The Tort of Seduction: Fathers and Daughters in Nineteenth-Century Canada." *Dalhousie Law Journal* 10:45–80.

Barnard, G. W., H. Vera, M. I. Vera, and G. Newman. 1982. "Till Death Do Us Part: A Study of Spouse Murder." *Bulletin of the American Academy of Psychiatry and Law* 10:271–80.

Becker, G. S., E. M. Landes, and R. T. Michael. 1977. "An Economic Analysis of Marital Instability." *Journal of Political Economy* 85:1141–87.

Betzig, L. L. 1986. *Despotism and Differential Reproduction: A Darwinian View of History*. Hawthorne, N.Y.: Aldine de Gruyter.

Borgerhoff Mulder, M. 1988. "Kipsigis Bridewealth Payments." In *Human Reproductive Behaviour: A Darwinian Perspective*, ed. L. Betzig, M. Borgerhoff Mulder, and P. Turke, 65–82. Cambridge: Cambridge University Press.

Brett, P. 1955. "Consortium and Servitium. A History and Some Proposals." *Australian Law Journal* 29: 321–28, 389–97, 428–34.

Brisson, N. J. 1983. "Battering Husbands: A Survey of Abusive Men." *Victimology* 6:338–44.

Bumpass, L. L., and J. A. Sweet. 1972. "Differentials in Marital Instability." *American Sociological Review* 37:754–66.

Carlson, C. A. 1984. "Intrafamilial Homicide." Unpublished B.Sc. thesis, McMaster University.

Chimbos, P. D. 1978. *Marital Violence: A Study of Interspouse Homicide*. San Francisco: R&E Research Associates.

Comaroff, J. L. 1980. *The Meaning of Marriage Payments*. New York: Academic Press.

Daly, M., and M. Wilson. 1988a. *Homicide*. Hawthorne, N.Y.: Aldine de Gruyter.

_____. 1988b. "Evolutionary Social Psychology and Family Homicide." *Science* 242:519–24.

_____. 1990. "Killing the Competition." *Human Nature* 1:83–109.

_____, and S. J. Weghorst. 1982. "Male Sexual Jealousy." *Ethology and Sociobiology* 3:11–27.

Day, L. H. 1964."Patterns of Divorce in Australia and the United States." *American Sociological Review* 29:509–22.

Dickemann, M. 1979. "The Ecology of Mating Systems in Hypergynous Dowry Societies." *Social Science Information* 18:163–95.

Dickemann, M. 1981. "Paternal Confidence and Dowry Competition: A Biocultural Analysis of Purdah." In *Natural Selection and Social Behavior: Recent Research and New Theory,* ed. R. D. Alexander and D. W. Tinkle. New York: Chiron Press.

Dobash, R. E., and R.P. Dobash. 1979. *Violence against Wives. A Case against the Patriarchy.* New York: Free Press.

_____. 1984. The Nature and Antecedents of Violent Events. *British J. Criminology* 24:269–88.

Dressler, J. 1982. "Rethinking Heat of Passion: A Defense in Search of a Rationale." *Journal of Criminal Law and Criminology* 73:421–70.

Edwards, J. Ll. J. 1954. "Provocation and the Reasonable Man: Another View." *Criminal Law Review* 1954:898–906.

Edwards, S. S. M. 1981. *Female Sexuality and the Law.* Oxford: Martin Robertson.

_____. 1985. "Male Violence against Women: Excusatory and Explanatory Ideologies in Law and Society." In *Gender, Sex and the Law,* ed. S. Edwards, 183–213. London: Croom Helm.

Elwin, V. 1950. *Maria: Murder and Suicide.* 2d ed. Bombay: Oxford University Press.

Fallers, L. A., and M. C. Fallers. 1960. "Homicide and Suicide in Busoga." In *African Homicide and Suicide,* ed. P. Bohannan, 65–93. Princeton N.J.: Princeton University Press.

Ford, C. S., and F. A. Beach. 1951. *Patterns of Sexual Behavior.* New York: Harper & Row.

Freeman, D. 1983. *Margaret Mead and Samoa.* Cambridge Mass.: Harvard University Press.

Glick, P. C., and S.-L. Lin. 1987. "Remarriage after Divorce: Recent Changes and Demographic Variations." *Sociological Perspectives* 30:162–79.

Guttmacher, M. S. 1955. "Criminal Responsibility in Certain Homicide Cases Involving Family Members." In *Psychiatry and the Law,* ed. P. H. Hoch and J. Zubin, 73–96. New York: Grune and Stratton.

Handy, M. J. L. 1923. *Blood Feuds and the Payment of Blood Money in the Middle East.* Beirut: Catholic Press.

Hilberman, E., and K. Munson. 1978. "Sixty Battered Women." *Victomology* 2:460–70.

Hogbin, H. I. 1938. "Social Reaction to Crime: Law and Morals in the Schouten Islands, New Guinea." *Journal of the Anthropological Institute of Great Britain and Ireland.* 68: 223–62.

Hosken, F. P. 1979. *The Hosken Report. Genital and Sexual Mutilation of Females.* Lexington, Mass.: Women's International Network News.

Howell, P. P. 1954. *A Manual of Nuer Law.* London: Oxford University Press.

Mead, M. 1931. *Sex and Temperament.* New York: Morrow.

Mercy, J. A., and L. E. Saltzman. 1989. "Fatal Violence among Spouses in the United States, 1976–1985." *American Journal of Public Health* 79:595–99.

Morgan, S. P., and R. R. Rindfuss. 1985. "Marital Disruption: Structural and Temporal Dimensions." *American Journal of Sociology* 90:1055–77.

Mowat, R. R. 1966. *Morbid Jealousy and Murder. A Psychiatric Study of Morbidly Jealous Murderers at Broadmoor.* London: Tavistock.

Muller, W. 1917. *Yap,* band 2, halbband 1 (HRAF trans.). Hamburg: Friederichsen.

Rounsaville, B. J. 1978. "Theories in Marital Violence: Evidence from a Study of Battered Women." *Victimology: An International Journal* 3:11–31.

Russell, D. E. H. 1982. *Rape in Marriage.* New York: Macmillan.

Sachs, A., and J. H. Wilson. 1978. *Sexism and the Law,* Oxford: Martin Robertson.

Saran, A. B. 1974. *Murder and Suicide among the Munda and the Oraon.* Delhi: National Publishing House.

Showalter, C. R., R. J. Bonnie, and V. Roddy. 1980. "The Spousal-homicide Syndrome." *International J. of Law and Psychiatry* 3:117–41.

Sinclair, M. B. W. 1987. "Seduction and the Myth of the Ideal Woman. *Law and Inequality* 3:33–102.

Sohier, J. 1959. *Essai sur la criminalité dans la province de Léopoldville.* Brussels: J. Duculot.

Stephens, W. N. 1963. *The Family In Cross-cultural Perspective.* New York: Holt, Rinehart and Winston.

Sweet, J. A., and L. L. Bumpass. 1987. *American Families and Households.* New York: Russell Sage Foundation.

Symons, D. 1979. *The Evolution of Human Sexuality.* New York: Oxford University Press.

Thornhill, R., and N. Thornhill N. 1983. "Human Rape: An Evolutionary Analysis." *Ethology and Sociobiology* 4:137–73.

Varma, S. C. 1978. *The Bhil Kills.* Delhi: Kunj Publishing House.

Vergouwen, J. C. 1964. *The Social Organization and Customary Law of the Toba-Batak of Northern Sumatra.* The Hague: Martinus Nijhoff.

Wallace, A. 1986. *Homicide: The Social Reality.* Sydney: New South Wales Bureau of Crime Statistics and Research.

White, L. K., and A. Booth. 1985. "The Quality and Stability of Remarriages: The Role of Stepchildren." *American Sociological Review* 50:689–98.

Whitehurst, R. N. 1971. "Violence Potential in Extramarital Sexual Responses." *Journal of Marriage and the Family* 33:683–91.

Wilson, M. 1987. Impacts of the Uncertainty of Paternity on Family Law. *University of Toronto Faculty of Law Review* 45:216–42.

_____. 1989. "Marital Conflict and Homicide in Evolutionary Perspective." In *Sociobiology and the Social Sciences,* ed. R. W. Bell and N. J. Bell, 45–62. Lubbock, Texas: Texas Tech University Press.

_____, and M. Daly. 1992. "The Man Who Mistook His Wife for a Chattel." In *The Adapted Mind,* ed. J. Barkow, L. Cosmides, and J. Tooby, 243–76. Oxford: Oxford University Press.

Wolfgang, M. E. 1958. *Patterns in Criminal Homicide,* Philadelphia: University of Pennsylvania Press.

"If I Can't Have You, No One Can": Power and Control in Homicide of Female Partners

JACQUELYN C. CAMPBELL

Homicide is the leading cause of death in the United States for African-American women, aged 15–34 (Farley 1986). This fact is seldom cited and almost never analyzed. More research and health care dollars are spent on female infertility, premenstrual syndrome (PMS), and complications of pregnancy than on understanding and preventing one of the primary threats to the health of young women: femicide. While improvements in health care since 1940 have reduced the incidence of female deaths from other causes, the number of homicides has increased for European-American and African-American women (Farley 1986).

African-American men are by far the group most often murdered: 50.6 per 100,000 in 1983. The rate for African-American women is higher than that for European-American men (11.3 versus 8.4), while that for European-American women has stayed consistently the lowest (2.8 per 100,000) (Wilbanks 1986). Even so, an average of 2,746 European-American women were slain each year from 1976 to 1984 (O'Carroll and Mercy 1986). An average of 1,761 African-American women were murdered annually during that time period.

Almost all scholarly attention and concern for the prevention of homicide has focused on men, even though it is clear that homicides involving women (as either victim or perpetrator) have a totally different dynamic (Block 1985; Mercy and Saltzman 1989). Because of the paucity of research into what motivates femicide, and in an effort to compile a body of knowledge that could be useful to those seeking to prevent such killings, I undertook a study of female homicide in a midsized midwestern city in 1980.

BACKGROUND

Dayton, Ohio had a population of almost 200,000 in 1980, with an average per capita income more or less equal to that of most urban Americans. The 1980

99

census revealed an almost equal proportion of African- and European-Americans, with other ethnic groups only marginally represented in the population. Among European-Americans, the single largest cultural group was Appalachian. In 1980, 6 percent of the population was unemployed, close to the national rate. Thirty percent were factory employees, 35 percent worked in government service, and 31 percent were professional, management, or retail employees.

Dayton was close to the median in overall rate of urban homicide from 1968 to 1979. In fact, the 1978 rate of 9.0 per 100,000, including Dayton suburbs, was the same as the national rate (Webster 1979). The patterns of homicide in Dayton in those years were similar to national urban patterns in racial and gender composition, rate fluctuations, and absolute rates (Campbell 1981).

Sources of Data

All homicide cases in the city of Dayton, Ohio, from 1 January 1975 to 31 December 1979 are included in this analysis. The police files of cases involving women as either victim or perpetrator were closely examined. Police reports give more detailed and therefore more accurate information than the aggregate statistics compiled for the U.S. Federal Bureau of Investigation (FBI) *Uniform Crime Reports*. Police files include autopsy information and details that facilitate analysis of the events preceding the homicide. For instance, the police departments code a "motive" for all homicides for the FBI reports. In cases where the perpetrator and victim know each other, the most common motive classification is "argument." Incidents labeled "argument" by the Dayton Police Department for the FBI were as disparate as the following: a dispute over money between neighbors, a confrontation between two barely acquainted young men over athletic prowess, and a fatal wife beating incident that was the last of a series of husband-initiated beatings described in the case file. Thus, analyses using aggregate motive data (such as comparing the percentage of "arguments" with the percentage for other motives, such as robbery) does not take into account underlying and more important issues.

Accuracy is tainted too in aggregate homicide statistics, especially in defining victim-offender relationships. The initial "on the scene" classification often misses prior sexual involvements and/or informal kin relationships common in the inner city. Ex-lovers are often relegated to the acquaintance category, since they do not fit the established nomenclature system. Therefore only a close examination of police records will uncover the relationships hidden within the FBI categories "acquaintance" and "friend." Long-term sexually intimate partner relationships are usually labeled "girlfriend/boyfriend" for FBI reports even when the lovers are in their forties.

In addition to studying police homicide files, I scanned the same five years of Dayton's two major newspapers for all accounts of homicides involving women. I analyzed that data with thematic analysis and descriptive statistics.

Overall Femicide

There were 73 women killed in Dayton from 1975 to 1979, 65 (89 percent) of them by men. Twelve (19 percent) of the 65 were killed by husbands, 5 (8 percent) by boyfriends, and 11 (17 percent) by estranged husbands or boyfriends (see figure 1). Another 7, including 3 young girls, were killed by other male family members (2 sons, 2 fathers, 2 maternal boyfriends, and a nephew). According to statements taken from friends and/or relatives, 5 women (8 percent) were murdered by a former casual sex partner. Eleven (17 percent) were killed by acquaintances and one by a friend. Thus 80 percent of those slain by men knew their killers well. Furthermore, 72 percent of the women were killed at home. This breakdown in relationship category closely parallels patterns documented by national statistics on murdered women (Wilbanks 1986).

CASE ANALYSIS FINDINGS

In-depth analysis of the homicides involving intimate partners, whether married, cohabitating, or otherwise sexually intimate, or partners who had split up, best demonstrates power and control dynamics. Because there were approximately equal numbers of men (28) and women (29) who had killed a spouse, lover, or estranged partner, I was able to make control group comparisons.

FIGURE 1   Femicide (N = 65) by Level of Aquaintance, Dayton, Ohio, 1974–79

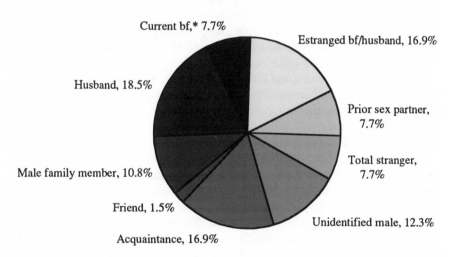

Current bf,* 7.7%

Estranged bf/husband, 16.9%

Husband, 18.5%

Prior sex partner, 7.7%

Male family member, 10.8%

Total stranger, 7.7%

Friend, 1.5%

Unidentified male, 12.3%

Acquaintance, 16.9%

*bf—boyfriend or male partner

Prior Violence

Of the 28 women killed by a husband, boyfriend, or estranged husband or boyfriend, at least 18 (64 percent) were known to have been physically abused by that man prior to the femicide. Abuse was substantiated by a prior arrest record or by witness or family comments made spontaneously to investigating officers. In 1975–79 police did not ask about prior abuse. Since police-documented abuse alone is included in these statistics, they do not account for cases in which the woman concealed her battering or was treated for abuse by hospital emergency staff who did not report the assault to police. Neither do these numbers include cases in which the perpetrator immediately confessed to murder, because police then had no need to get information about past maltreatment for court evidence. In two cases not included in this 64 percent, police had been called to the home for "family violence," but there had been no arrest and no documentation of who was hurting whom in the home. Because of all of this, the figure of 64 percent understates the level of abuse that occurred. As Wilson and Daly (in this volume) and others have shown, woman battering routinely precedes femicide not only in Dayton but everywhere in the world (Counts, Brown, and Campbell 1992; Wallace 1986).

In 15 of the 18 documented prior-abuse cases, the police had made a "family violence" call within the two years leading up to the femicide. In one case the police had been to the home five times. In another, the two-year period preceding the murder included 12 calls made for "family violence" as part of 56 total police visits to that home!

For 19 of the male perpetrators a history of physical brutality beyond that documented in the intimate relationship with their victims was provided by arrest records involving violent crime or by credible witnesses who described the perpetrators as violent toward other persons. One of these men belonged to a motorcycle gang, locally notorious for fighting. In another case, police noted that the homicidal husband had killed a former wife in another state as well but was convicted only of involuntary manslaughter for which he was given probation. These cases contradict the notion of wife abusers as violent only toward their wives. Other research supports the conclusion that the particularly vicious batterer usually has a violent history (Berk et al. 1983).

Most of these men, therefore, were well known to the criminal justice system long before they murdered their intimate partners. The police usually had enough information to predict the extreme danger menacing the female victims. It might be assumed that the women did also, but battered women may not realize the commonality of femicide or may need to minimize their danger in order to not be paralyzed by fear. A police warning could galvanize action on the woman's part, yet in only one instance had any documented attempt been made to warn, let alone protect, her. This "effort" involved advising the eventual victim that the police could not provide sufficient protection from her violent ex-partner. She was told to find a place to hide.

Sadism and Excessive Violence

Four (14 percent) of these 28 cases of intimate-partner femicide involved particularly cruel actions by the perpetrator, suggesting sadism. One man kept his female partner a prisoner for six months as he slowly beat her to death. Police interviews of neighbors indicated that they *knew* she was a prisoner but did not want to interfere in the private business of a man who was notoriously violent. In another case the forensic photographs and autopsy reports showed the woman was first handcuffed and then shot in the temple. None of the cases involving adult women killing men displayed sadistic behavior.

"Excessive violence" is a term introduced in the homicide literature by Voss and Hepburn (1968). They theorized that a single shot or punch or stab can be delivered during a momentary loss of control (such as during an argument), without any intent to kill. Excessive violence, however, demonstrates conscious determination to kill. In 17 (61 percent) of the Dayton intimate-partner cases the man employed excessive violence (shooting or stabbing more than once or beating to death). In one case the woman had been shot by her husband so many times the autopsy report was full of notations of the coroner's exasperation as he tried to figure out which of the wounds were entrances and which were exits. Based on the "excessive violence" test and other evidence of premeditation as interpreted by police, the majority of the intimate-partner femicides showed conscious intent to murder. Women who killed their male intimate partners resorted to excessive violence significantly less frequently than men who committed femicide. Figure 2 presents a contrast between male and female perpetrators in the intimate relationship category, while figure 3 presents the same contrast for victims.

Intoxication

Ten (36 percent) of the male perpetrators intimately related to their victims were intoxicated at the time of the killing, while only four (14.3 percent) of their female victims were intoxicated (figure 3). It should also be noted that although 36 percent of the male and 31 percent of the female perpetrators were intoxicated (figure 2), the majority of perpetrators were *not* intoxicated at the time of the killing. Intoxication cannot be said to explain the majority of these killings (see also Berk et al. 1983).

Motive

Thematic analysis of confessions, police interpretations of interviews and other evidence, and/or witness reports were used to develop motive categories for these homicides. These categories, contrasted by gender, are presented in table 1. The largest number of cases (18, or 64 percent) involved male jealousy. Jealousy of women is a by-product of male attempts to control and possess the

FIGURE 2 Characteristics of Men (N = 29) and Women (N = 28) Who Killed Intimate Partners, Dayton, Ohio, 1974–79

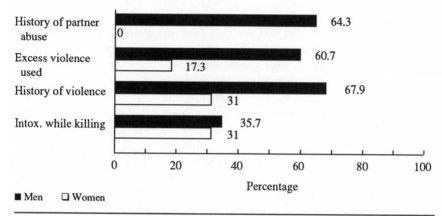

Note: Categories are not mutually exclusive.

FIGURE 3 Characteristics of Men (N = 28) and Women (N = 29) Killed by Intimate Partners, Dayton, Ohio, 1974–79

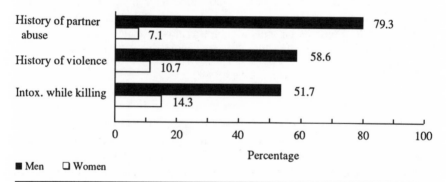

Note: Categories are not mutually exclusive.

women with whom they are (or want to be) intimate. In short, jealousy connotes ownership (Daly, Wilson, and Weghourst 1982). Ironically, in no case in the Dayton femicides did the male perpetrator have direct evidence of the intimate partner's sexual involvement with someone else, evidence that, under patriarchal tradition, renders femicide "excusable" (Greenblat 1985; Lundsgaarde 1977). One man killed his partner when he walked into the house to find her talking on the telephone. He killed her because he was sure she was talking to her boyfriend. Police verified that she had been talking to a relative and that, according to all accounts, she had no boyfriend. Such flimsy jealousy-related

TABLE 1   "Reasons" for Intimate-Partner Femicide
(Men Killing Women), Dayton, Ohio, 1974–79

	% of Cases	No. of Cases
Female jealousy	0.0	0
Victim precipitation	71.0	2
Other	17.9	5
Male dominance	17.9	5
Male jealousy	64.3	18

Note: Categories are not mutually exclusive.

motives for femicide are not unusual based on the Dayton records: one man committed femicide because he did not want his partner to have career aspirations while another man murdered his wife because he resented the attention she gave to her children.

Male dominance issues, while arguably a part of all femicides, were separated into a distinct category to encompass situations such as the one in which the woman refused to get the perpetrator more wine, or another in which the woman declined to give the man her money, or those in which the woman resisted her murderer's sexual advances. With eight such cases (18 percent), male dominance ranked second as a motivating factor in the Dayton femicides.

The third category was originally labeled "victim precipitation." This term has sometimes been used inaccurately to blame victims of violence for their own victimization, but as originally coined, it refers only to violent behavior initiated by the person killed. As defined by Marvin Wolfgang (1957), a victim-precipitated homicide occurs when the victim is the first to show a weapon or strike a blow, creating a situation in which the killing would generally (although not necessarily legally) be interpreted as self-defense. In two (7 percent) of the intimate-partner femicides, the woman first brought out a weapon, an act that led to the man's acquittal on grounds of self-defense. While a mere 7 percent of femicides involved victim precipitation, 79 percent (23 of 29) cases of homicides by then-current or estranged female partners were precipitated by male violence. Homicide data in other cities reveal similar gender-distinct patterns (Curtis 1975; Wolfgang 1957).

While in both instances of female victim-initiated aggression the male perpetrator was acquitted of her death, in only 8 of 23 cases involving male precipitation did the woman escape punishment on the grounds of self-defense. Two of those 8 female perpetrators were acquitted in court trials, and 6 were not charged with any crime. In the majority (12) of the other 15 cases, each woman pled guilty to involuntary manslaughter and was not tried. Patriarchal society's fear of women who kill their men is suggested by those manslaughter charges in spite of clear evidence of initial violence by the victim. Not all sentencing information was contained in the homicide files, but at least 4 of the women pleading guilty to involuntary manslaughter were sentenced to jail. The remaining 3 women in the victim-precipitation category were convicted of voluntary manslaughter by jury trial, and all of them were sentenced to prison terms. During that time period there was no legal precedent for bringing into evidence the effects of the history of battering that was present in all 23 of those cases. These case dispensations underscore the need for expert testimony when battered women kill their abusers to counteract the patriarchal judicial system's proclivity to deny women's need to defend themselves from their husbands (Walker 1988).

The final motive category for femicide, here labeled "other," included unrelated or undiscovered motives and assertions of innocence.

To gain further insight into motive, I examined demographic data. In general, the femicides involved intimate partners from the same race and age group. More occupational information was recorded for the male killers than for their female victims. Twelve of the 24 men who had employment data recorded were unemployed, a much higher rate than the Dayton average, even allowing for the racial composition of the sample (79 percent African-American). Unemployment shatters the traditional masculine provider image, and ensuing self-doubt can increase the need for power and control in other spheres (Goode 1971). The 12 employed men were blue-collar workers, a group that enjoys relatively little control in the workplace. One was a security guard and another a retired police officer, occupations in which power and control are central.

When She Tries to Leave

Men's efforts to reassert power and control was the underlying issue in the estranged-partner homicides. The police reports revealed that, in addition to the 11 women who were already estranged from former partners when killed, one of the wives and one of the "girlfriends" had declared intentions of leaving. In a case not included in my estranged-partner category because it was not officially solved, a woman, her grandmother, and her two children were killed by a fire-bomb. A former boyfriend had expressed anger at her for leaving him, and the police considered him to be the primary suspect. In spite of his failing a lie detector test, the district attorney decided there was not sufficient evidence to charge him.

All 4 of the men killed by ex-partners used violence against their estranged wife just prior to being killed. This violence was motivated apparently by a desire to reclaim ownership (in police terminology, the male was jealous of a new boyfriend or "wanted to get back together"). One particularly illustrative case involved a man who had constantly harassed his ex-wife and returned many times to the house to violently accost her months after the divorce. She eventually bought a gun to protect herself, keeping it in her bedroom. In an account verified by her adolescent children, the ex-husband came again to the house, was let in by one of the children, and chased his ex-wife to the bedroom, where she locked herself in. He broke down the door and moved toward her, even though she had the gun in her hand and warned him she would shoot. He continued to advance toward her. She shot once into the floor but that did not stop him, so she then shot and killed him. This woman was convicted of voluntary manslaughter and sentenced to 20 years in prison. No explanation for this travesty of justice seems plausible, except that judge and jury still believed in the property rights of a man over his wife, 'til death do them part.

In all but 2 of the 15 estranged partner homicides, there had been a documented history of female partner abuse. The battered women's movement also has begun to realize that an abused woman may be most at risk of femicide when she leaves or when it is clear to her husband or partner that she will be leaving for good (Hart 1988).

Two of the men committed suicide immediately after killing their former female partner. These were the only murders followed by suicide among all homicides during this period in Dayton. The pattern of suicide following homicide is specific to men in partner killings (Humphrey, Hudson, and Cosgrove 1981–82; Wallace 1986). Both of the Dayton cases involved extreme violence to the female. The omnipresent importance of maintaining control over a female partner was exemplified in the case of a woman who had divorced her husband because of a long history of abuse. Her ex-husband threatened to kill her, and she had both sought police protection and moved several times to escape him. He located her at her sister's house and killed her in an excessively violent and sadistic way. He also murdered her mother and her sister. His suicide note revealed the cool sanity of his premeditation, asserting that his wife deserved to die for leaving him. Presumably, in his mind, he owned her.

In the second femicide-suicide a young man went on a shooting "spree" after learning his adolescent girlfriend wanted to end the relationship with him. He killed her and randomly shot three other young women, one of whom died. He also killed a man who inadvertently blocked his escape.

WOMEN KILLING MEN

My analysis of the cases of women killing men in the Dayton study was primarily for comparison purposes, so the particulars of these cases will not be presented. But a statistical breakdown is relevant. Thirty-seven percent (43) of the 116 victims of homicides involving women were men killed by women while 56 percent (65) were women killed by men. (The remaining 8 females in the sample were killed by other females; 6 of these were child murders.) Three of the male victims were children.

A total of 11 men (27 percent) were killed by women with whom they had no prior intimate relationship. Out of 70 cases of adult homicide involving female perpetrators, women killing nonrelated males account for 6 percent of the total. In contrast, 43 percent of the femicides were committed by men who knew their victims only slightly or not at all. The most common motive for acquaintance or stranger murders by either sex was robbery, although in only 3 of the convictions involving a female offender was the murder committed by the woman herself. The 5 women who were passive accomplices to murder by being present while their male lovers committed the crime serve to reinforce existing evidence that women seldom initiate murder outside of their families or other intimate relationships. This phenomenon is not unique to the Dayton data and has frequently been explained in terms of lower levels of aggressive behavior for women in general (see, for example, Jason, Flock, and Tyler 1983). However, Gilligan's (1982) research offers an alternative explanation. According to Gilligan, women consider relationships more important than uniform standards in making moral decisions. Thus, men would be more likely than women to use violence because of standards of behavior in a variety of situations (for example, backing down from confrontation is unmanly and thus avoided). Women would kill primarily when personal relationships were involved, as the data supports.

Of more salience to this report was the 67 percent of female perpetrated homicides where the man was a current or estranged husband or boyfriend. Table 2 summarizes these cases. Male victims had beaten their spouses in the past in at least 23 (79 percent) of the cases. In fact, only 3 women in the sample killed husbands, boyfriends, or estranged husbands or boyfriends *without* a history of being battered by that man *and* without his precipitating the killing with a weapon or a blow. Similar findings are being reported in other recent research (Browne 1987; Daly and Wilson 1988; Wilbanks 1983).

Other Findings

Excessive violence and/or sadism also occurred in 70 percent of the 30 femicides outside of family or intimate relationships. Ninety-three percent of these deaths were not preceded by argument, and victim precipitation occurred only once (3 percent). This is in sharp contrast to the 11 cases where women killed men outside of intimate relationships of which there were no instances of excessive violence and 4 cases (36 percent) of eventual self-defense rulings.

Only 5 (8 percent) women were killed by strangers, 4 during a robbery. Eight (12 percent) were killed by unidentified male assailants, and 5 were also raped. These were the only 5 sex murders by strangers in Dayton during this period. Such homicides receive a lot of media attention even though they occur relatively infrequently. A sexual connection generates attention, but the unfortunate consequence of this publicity is that women do not realize they are in more danger from their husbands and boyfriends than from strangers.

Autopsy reports revealed 3 other Dayton victims were sexually assaulted prior to their death by a "casual acquaintance," a "friend," and a previous casual sexual partner. Two of these cases could be categorized as "date rape" that led to femicide. The third involved robbery.

TABLE 2 "Reasons" for Intimate-Partner Homicide
         (Women Killing Men), Dayton, Ohio, 1974–79

	% of Cases	No. of Cases
Female jealousy	6.9	2
Other	13.8	5
Male dominance	17.8	8
Male jealousy	34.5	10
Victim precipitation	79.3	23

Note: Categories are not mutually exclusive.

Police notations revealed that, tragically, 12 children under the age of 15 witnessed the murders or were the first to find the bodies. In many cases, either victim or perpetrator (or both) was a parent of the child witness. There are no interventions for children affected by homicide that automatically occur through the justice system in spite of the documented long-term consequences of anxiety and behavioral problems (Cowles 1988). Because these children are in many cases African-American and poor, they are unlikely to have access to specialized professional help. Prevention of continued violence would include identifying and treating these children as groups highly at risk.

NEWSPAPER ACCOUNTS

Most homicides in Dayton were reported in a few lines in stories buried deep in the paper, giving minimal facts. No differentiation was made—by either the *Dayton Journal Herald* or the *Dayton Daily News*—in space given or type of description between male and female victims. Most of those involved were African-American and poor. Minimizing their deaths suggests that a racist society defines them as worthless and unimportant (Hawkins 1986, 117).

Homicides chosen for extensive newspaper coverage in Dayton revealed a media obsession with the sexual purity of female victims. Young, European-American, ostensibly virginal (at least prior to the crime) murder victims made front-page news complete with photographs, particularly when rape was involved. Young African-American victims, even if sexually abused, rated only a few paragraphs further back. Female victims who were older, sexually active, intoxicated, and/or married (presumably in the category of "used merchandise") rated a few lines in a "news brief" section. Even exceptional brutality or unusual circumstances received only limited coverage.

Obsession with purity also permeated the police homicide records. There was a great deal of information about previous sexual activity of all unmarried female victims (although never the male victims). Diminished culpability was claimed by two men who killed women with unusually active sexual histories.

Their claims were supported by the police, who obtained extensive corroboration for the contention that one victim was a prostitute and that another was "promiscuous," according to her male acquaintances. Mary Daly's (1978) research has linked societal obsession with victim purity with other gynocidal practices, such as foot-binding and genital mutilation.

Subtle blaming of women was apparent in any newspaper report of femicide longer than a few lines. The reporters almost always referred to killings involving intimate partners as being the result of "domestic squabbles," "arguments," or "domestic quarrels." For instance, "domestic trouble" was used to describe the background of the case where the woman was handcuffed before she was shot, while mention of the handcuffing was omitted. "The result of an apparent argument" was used to characterize a premeditated femicide where a man sought out his lover at her place of employment and shot her seven times. Such accounts give the impression that the woman was equally to blame for the murder. History of abuse and female self-defense was similarly hidden. Police tend to initially describe intimate-partner homicides to reporters in those terms, but reporters could ask questions in order to more accurately describe the incident. Halloran (1975) points out that media can "define, give emphasis, amplify, confer status, convey meanings and perspectives, provide labels and stereotypes and indicate approval and disapproval" concerning violence (211). Journalists have participated in obscuring the dynamics of femicide.

DISCUSSION

Formal scholarship too has obscured issues of power and control in homicides involving women. Many analyses collapse men and women into the same categories, such as is done in Jason, Flock, and Tyler's (1983) comparison of primary (family) and secondary homicides and in Chimbos' (1978) analysis of marital homicide.

In addition, the dynamics underlying African-American women's overrepresentation as both victims and perpetrators of intimate-partner homicide has seldom been studied and is therefore poorly understood. In research, the presumed influences of ethnic group membership are often confounded by poverty. Cultural orientation is a term that can be used to represent the combination of ethnicity, residence location and economic status. Cultural orientation (rather than race) influences values, and more analysis and investigation is needed of the relationship between cultural orientation and femicide. One beginning is Lockhart's (1987) research, which suggests there is less wife beating and mutual violence among African-American middle-class couples than among European-American middle-class couples. Also relevant are studies of homicide demonstrating that poverty and crowding have more potent effects on violence than race (Hawkins 1986). However, issues of power and control may be especially salient for a young African-American man when other avenues of achievement and efficacy are blocked and the African-American woman is expected to be all things for him (Wallace 1978). This need for power and control may interact with the needs for status for inner city youth, the models for violent behavior on the streets and in the media, the norm of handgun ownership, the aggressive effects of crack, and the other overwhelming difficulties associated with poverty to create volatile situations conducive to partner battering and femicide.

All women are at risk of femicide, especially from intimate partners and most especially when there has been a history of wife beating and when a woman has decided to leave. This reality has been known by more battered women than scholars in the field of homicide. Battered women often describe their partners telling them, "If I can't have you, no one can." This phrase is coming to be recognized as a particularly dangerous verbal threat indicating extreme female ownership ideation and potential femicide (Stuart and Campbell 1989).

The data presented in this chapter vividly illustrate that property ownership, power, and control are at the core of homicides between partners. The tradition of male ownership of women and male needs for power are played out to horribly violent conclusions. The message of femicide is that many men believe that control of female partners is a perogative they can defend by killing women. This message, and the danger to women, is obscured by most scholarship, media accounts, and the criminal justice system.

Women are most threatened at home and by "loved" ones. The current social myth that family and home are sanctuaries for women as well as men is challenged by feminists. Elizabeth Stanko (1988) is persuasive in her argument that the ideology of the safe home helps to keep women subordinate by making them feel frightened away from that haven. Yet, as we have seen, women in Dayton were much safer away from the "protection" of home and husband.

A recent (1989) *Time* magazine survey of death by guns in one week in the United States echoed the same themes as the homicides analyzed in Dayton. Even the brief one sentence descriptions of the 242 homicides revealed that at least 42 involved men wanting to exert power and control over women. Eleven cases of femicide were followed by suicide of the male partner-killer, one of whom was heard to say just before the murder, "If you're not going to live with me, you're not going to live at all" (*Time* 1989, 35).

References

Berk, R. A., S. F. Berk, D. R. Loseke, and D. Rama. 1983. "Mutual Combat and Other Family Violence Myths." In *The Dark Side of Families,* ed. D. Finkelhor, R. J. Gelles, G. T. Hotaling, and M. A. Straus, 197–212. Beverly Hills: Sage.

Block, C. R. 1985. *Specification of Patterns over Time in Chicago Homicide: Increases and Decreases 1965–1981*. Chicago: Criminal Justice Information Authority.

Browne, A. 1987. *When Battered Women Kill.* New York: Free Press.

Campbell, J. C. 1981. "Misogyny and Homicide of Women." *Advances in Nursing Science* 3, no. 2: 67–85.

Chimbos, P. D. 1978. *Marital Violence: A Study of Interspouse Homicide.* San Francisco: R & E Research Associates.

Counts, D., J. Brown, and J. Campbell. 1992. *Sanctions and Sanctuary: Cultural Influences on the Beating of Wives.* Boulder, Colo.: Westview Press.

Cowles, V. K. 1988. "Personal World Expansion for Survivors of Murder Victims." *Western Journal of Nursing Research* 10, no. 6: 687–99.

Curtis, A. L. 1975. *Criminal Violence.* Lexington, Mass.: D. C. Heath and Co.

Daly, M., and M. Wilson. 1988. *Homicide.* New York: Aldine De Gruyter.

———, and S. Weghorst. 1982. "Male Sexual Jealousy." *Ethology and Sociobiology* 3:11–27.

Daly, M. 1978. *Gyn/Ecology.* Boston: Beacon Press.

Farley, R. 1986. "Homicide Trends in the United States." In *Homicide among Black Americans,* ed. D. F. Hawkins, 13–27. New York: University Press of America.

Gilligan, C. 1982. *In a Different Voice.* Cambridge, Mass.: Harvard University Press.

Goode, W. 1971. "Force and Violence in the Family." *Journal of Marriage and the Family* 33:624–36.

Greenblat, C. S. 1985. " 'Don't Hit Your Wife . . . Unless': Preliminary Findings on Normative Support for the Use of Physical Force by Husbands." *Victimology* 10:221–41.

Halloran, J. D. 1975. "The Mass Media and Violence." *Forensic Science* 5:209–17.

Hart, B. 1988. "Beyond the 'Duty to Warn': A Therapist's 'Duty to Protect' Battered Women and Children." In *Feminist Perspectives on Wife Abuse,* ed. K. Yllö and M. Bograd, 234–48. Beverly Hills: Sage.

Hawkins, D. F. 1986. "Black Homicide: The Adequacy of Existing Research for Devising Prevention Strategies." In *Homicide among Black Americans,* ed. D. F. Hawkins, 211–29. New York: University Press of America.

Humphrey, J. A., R. P. Hudson, and S. Cosgrove. 1981–82. "Women Who Are Murdered: An Analysis of 912 Consecutive Victims." *OMEGA* 12, no. 3:281–88.

Jason, J., J. Flock, and C. W. Tyler. 1983. "A Comparison of Primary and Secondary Homicides in the U.S." *American Journal of Epidemiology* 3:309–19.

Lockhart, L. L. 1987. "A Reexamination of the Effects of Race and Social Class on the Incidence of Marital Violence: A Search for Reliable Differences." *Journal of Marriage and the Family* 49:603–10.

Lundsgaarde, P. H. 1977. *Murder in Space City.* Oxford: Oxford University Press.

Mercy, J. A., and L. E. Saltzman. 1989. "Fatal Violence among Spouses in the United States, 1976–85." *American Journal of Public Health* 79, no. 5 :595–99.

O'Carroll, P. W., and J. A. Mercy. 1986. "Patterns and Recent Trends in Black Homicide." In *Homicide among Black Americans,* ed. D. F. Hawkins, 29–42. New York: University Press of America.

"7 Deadly Days." *Time,* 17 July 1989, 35.

Stanko, E. A. 1988. "Fear of Crime and the Myth of the Safe Home: A Feminist Critique of Criminology." In *Feminist Perspectives on Wife Abuse,* ed. K. Yllö and M. Bograd, 75–89. Beverly Hills: Sage.

Stuart, E. P., and J. C. Campbell. 1989. "Assessment of Patterns of Dangerousness with Battered Women." *Issues in Mental Health Nursing* 10:245–60.

Voss, L. H., and R. J. Hepburn. 1968. "Patterns in Criminal Homicide in Chicago." *Journal of Criminal Law, Criminology and Police Science* 59:499–508.

Walker, L. E. 1988. *Terrifying Love: Why Battered Women Kill and How Society Responds*. New York: Harper & Row.

Wallace, A. 1986. "A Typology of Homicide." In *Homicide: The Social Reality*, ed. A. Wallace, 83–109. New South Wales: Bureau of Crime Statistics and Research.

Wallace, M. 1978. *Black Macho and the Myth of the Superwoman*. New York: Dial Press.

Webster, W. H. 1979. *Uniform Crime Reports*. Washington, D.C.: U.S. Department of Justice.

Wilbanks, W. 1983. "The Female Homicide Offender in Dade County, Florida." *Criminal Justice Review* 8, no. 2: 9–14.

_____. 1986. "Criminal Homicide Offenders in the U.S.: Black vs. White." In *Homicide among Black Americans,* ed. D. F. Hawkins, 43–55. New York: University Press of America.

Wolfgang, M. 1957. "Victim Precipitated Criminal Homicide." *Journal of Criminal Law, Criminology, and Police Science* 48:1–11.

License to Kill

RIKKI GREGORY

On 10 February 1989 at approximately 7:45 P.M. Mandy was stabbed 15 times in her chest and back with a pair of kitchen scissors. One of these wounds went right through her heart. Immediately after these stabbings she was strangled.

Mandy was murdered by her husband. She had left him two weeks previously, and he must have realized that she no longer wanted to be with him. After his arrest he stated that if he couldn't have her, then no one else would.

They had been involved for about nine years. He was away working in Saudi Arabia for about five years; he came then back permanently, and they got married in 1985. Their relationship could not have been easy for Mandy. He was 14 years older than her and was her opposite in personality and character. As Mandy was lively, friendly, and outgoing, he was moody, introverted, and morose. Mandy thought that if she loved him enough he would change and become happy.

In 1986 Mandy had a baby girl. She was very happy; in her words, "over the moon." Shortly after the baby was born the problems between Mandy and her husband got worse. Mandy was very tired, looking after a lively and demanding baby. It was then we began to hear talk of him putting the house on the market and leaving Mandy and the baby.

Soon Mandy became pregnant again. She was depressed and ill throughout the pregnancy. When the baby was born in 1987, things were getting worse. Mandy was very loyal and rarely spoke about what was really going on in her marriage. Apparently it was about then that her husband had started to hit her and again threatened to sell the house and leave her.

It is so obvious now that things were going badly wrong, yet at the time it was so difficult to accept. Mandy's family was worried about her and had been telling her that she was in danger and that she must get away. Unfortunately, it is never that simple.

So there we are—Mandy, who was 28 years old, mother of two young babies, with so much to live for, brutally murdered by the man she had married.

What happened after has been a confirmation of how British society and the legal system treats women and children.

First, the murderer still has parental rights as a father. Although he violently killed the children's mother, he could still dictate where the children went. No one could do anything without his permission. He had all the power. From his prison cell he had arranged an injunction to stop the children from going to stay with Mandy's eldest sister, Jenny. Living with Jenny would have prevented the children from having to go into care. Yet he did not want the children to go to his wife's sister because, as he put it, "she was too opinionated and strong minded." The real reason was that Jenny is a lesbian. She is also my partner of seven years.

Second, Mandy had to have two postmortems. One to establish the cause of death, as if it were not obvious, and another called for by the defense, on the grounds that she could have died of natural causes. Mandy's body was stored for six weeks before the second postmortem. This caused more suffering to her family as it meant that the funeral had to be delayed. It also meant that her body was examined yet again despite the first postmortem, which had established that the cause of death was a stab wound to the heart.

Third, in the meantime, Mandy's children had been taken into care against our wishes. The Social Services handled this tragedy with ignorance, prejudice, and incompetence. They ignored, hindered, and obstructed all of Jenny's attempts to communicate with them about offering the children a home. They then decided, without consulting Mandy's family, to place her children with prospective adoptive foster parents.

We found this out the week of Mandy's funeral. Jenny immediately telephoned the county councillors and to the assistant director (complaints) of the Social Services. She explained what was going on and asked the assistant director why they were supporting the children's father after what he had done and whether they were aware that he had burnt his first wife's house down and that he had an injunction against him to keep him away from his two daughters from that marriage. This was a man with a history of violence, and yet the Social Services put him first and dismissed the children's aunt because she is a lesbian.

The Social Services did not have this information, and it must have had an effect because the decision to place the children with prospective adoptive parents was retracted. They had, however, caused extreme distress on top of the grief and shock to Jenny and some of the family. They had, as is so often the case in domestic murder, viewed the rights of the murderer as paramount.

Mandy loved her children more than anything and would naturally have wanted the best for them, but because the children were so young she had made no legal provision for them. So therefore it is as if she had no rights at all. Mandy's wishes were never considered by the solicitors or the Social Services. *She was treated as if she had never existed.*

Mandy would most definitely have wanted her children to stay and be brought up within her family. They were very nearly adopted by complete strangers. Not only then would they have lost their mother, but they would have also lost the love and support they are going to need from their mother's entire family. They would have been cut further away from their roots and lost their rights to the loving and caring from their mother's closest kin—her two sisters.

The children were made wards of court, and it has cost Mandy's family thousands of pounds to get the children back. They are now with Mandy's other sister, where they belong.

The treatment that Jenny received from the Social Services was despicable. It was very unpleasant and difficult to deal with in that time of great shock and grief.

Due to a technical error by Crown Prosecution Service the murderer was let out on bail just before the May 1989 Bank Holiday weekend. He hung himself in the marital home on the eve of May Day.

In effect, it has never been proven that he murdered Mandy. There are the police's written statements confirming that he admitted the murder, but he was never put on trial. As a result, the inquest could only declare "unlawful killing" of Mandy and "suicide" for him; it also complicates the legality surrounding the estate.

While we acknowledge that he is no longer around to disrupt the children's lives and that they can grow up without fear, lies, and distortions about their mother, it is with the greatest sorrow that we remember Mandy and how she suffered at his hands.

Women and Structural Violence in India

GOVIND KELKAR

> Fifteen women died of burns in this city over a 10-day period between May 24 and June 4 this year. The blaze of deaths aroused public sentiments, but in all but three cases nobody is likely to be punished.[1]

> Bride burning is not a new phenomenon in Delhi. In 1981, the Union Minister of State for Home Affairs had stated in the Parliament that the reported "women burning incidents" in Delhi stood at 394 in 1980.[2]

According to official figures, 332 cases of "accidental" burning were reported in 1982 as against 305 in 1981. These figures show that nearly one woman is being incinerated every day in the capital. But according to various women's organizations an equal number of burning cases go unreported. Many times this is on account of the refusal of the police to register the cases.[3]

The dowry witch-hunt has taken its heaviest toll in the middle-class urban areas, but the burning of women for money and domestic goods in the form of dowry is quite widespread in the slums and rural areas.

Investigations have indicated that although woman-burning is prevalent all over the country, it is most acute in Delhi, Haryana, Punjab, the Western Uttar Pradesh, and the Saurashtra region in Gujarat. In Uttar Pradesh, where I was engaged in a study of rural women's work participation and sex roles, most "dowry deaths" were reported from Thakur and Brahmin caste groups. Both Thakurs and Brahmins are high-caste Hindus and have a recorded history of female infanticide.[4] Over a decade and a half ago, the Gujarat Suicide Enquiry Committee's report noted that 90 percent of all suicide cases were women. Of these, 867 women (as against 302 men) committed suicide due to "family tensions." It was further reported that "particularly in the cases of poorer women, the causes of the tension were often related to dowry."[5]

From *Women's Studies Quarterly* 13, nos. 3 and 4 (Fall–Winter 1985): 16–18. ©1985 by the Feminist Press at CUNY. All rights reserved.

These are more than just crime statistics. They are a manifestation of political malaise in India and malady in the organization of the country's socio-economic system. If we want to understand the nature of structural violence toward women in India today, it is necessary to look at women's subordination in the structure of material production. The issue of peace and women in a Third World society can be studied only in a historical context. I have been struggling to gain a historical perspective on the subject by examining such questions as how the Indian leadership of the Nationalist movement tried to involve women in the freedom struggle and later in the reconstruction of society. To what extent is the family in India responsible for creating and maintaining social structures and ideologies that subordinate women? Clearly, there are structures in place that inherently resist the participation of women in decision making and ideologies created by the sex/gender system that serve to maintain existing power relations and forms of exploitation.

POWER IN THE FAMILY

What is significant to our understanding is that violence runs along lines of power in the sex/gender system. The family, with its division of labor by sex, is the principal institution that underlies the sex/gender system. The violence of woman-burning in the home has to be examined with regard to its systematic relevance. This paper, therefore, intends to include more than just a description of the kinds of violence meted out to women. We need to look at familial authority relations around which dowry violence is organized and at the property relations in which this authority structure is rooted. The subordinate role of women in the family is duplicated in society as a whole. Socioeconomic disparities, such as low wages and poor health care and education for women, have been justified by the assumption that women's employment and physical well being are less important than men's. There is, therefore, a close connection between the family and the organization of the politico-economic system. In other words, the family structure legitimizes the subordination of women in policy making and the organization of the economy.

The Constitution of India declares equality of the sexes, thereby acknowledging that the family should be a basically egalitarian unit, allowing equal rights and free choice to individual family members.[6] In practice, however, the subordination of women to men, of junior to senior, pervades family life in all classes and castes in India. The ideology of subordination is required by the material structure of production. Women are subordinate to, and thereby dependent on, men because men may own land and hold tenancies while women by and large cannot. Customary practices preclude daughters from inheriting land except in the absence of male heirs. It is wrongly argued that women receive their share of patrimony at the time of marriage in the form of dowry.

Despite the Hindu Succession Act, which put daughters on an equal footing with sons in regard to property inheritance, in most of the cases, daughters waive their land rights in favor of their brothers. Otherwise, they would be denounced as "selfish" sisters and would risk alienation or severance from their natal families. (The present discussion deals with Hindu women; the situation of Indian Muslim and Christian women differs in some significant details but is not necessarily any better with respect to law and customs.)

Women marry over long distances and move out of their parental homes to the households of their husbands. Young women are advised that once married they should leave the husbands' houses only after death and that they should bear all pain and humiliation. In order to adjust in the new family, a daughter-in-law has to be on her best behavior at all times. She must be submissive and obedient to her in-laws and demonstrate selflessness about her possessions. Her husband's family receives cash, jewelry, and domestic goods, usually made or bought specially to form a dowry. It is incorrect to regard dowry as a kind of inheritance of the daughter.[7] There are two important points in this regard. First, the dowry is transferred to the bridegroom's *family,* not to the *bride.*[8] The parents-in-law have full control over the distribution of the dowry. Second, land is never given as dowry, as far as I know. In the final analysis, the woman is propertyless for she is unable to generate any wealth from her so-called property. Such arrangements create gender-specific personalities—men tend to value their role as principal contributors to the national economy and breadwinners and supporters of the family, while women are excessively undervalued for their dependence, ignorance of the outside world, and preoccupation with children and household chores. This, I believe, is at the heart of the dowry witch-hunt.

WOMEN'S PROTESTS

It is important to point out that it would be wrong to assume that women in India are passively groaning under an ever-increasing oppression within and outside the family. Women have organized to protest the rapes, the sexual harassments, and the burnings or killings of their sisters. Demonstrations and meetings are organized throughout the country to protest against direct and structural violence against women. For the past few years in Delhi and other major cities in the country, women have led sporadic demonstrations against the husbands, in-laws, lawyers, and police officers involved in the cases of women burned or killed by other means. In early August 1982, thirty women's groups in Delhi jointly organized a protest march against the dowry custom; several hundred women bystanders spontaneously joined.

These demonstrations have acted as checks on husbands and in-laws by exposing the nature of violence or crime against women (usually protracted harassment and battering followed by burning and/or killing) and thereby disallowing the myth of suicide or accidental death. In addition, protestors have pressed for effective implementation of laws protecting women and reorganization of police inquiries into crimes against women. Such organized efforts could not be ignored for long, and the government responded by setting up an anti-dowry police unit in Delhi under the charge of a woman Deputy Commissioner of Police. It is the obligation of the unit to investigate cases of dowry harassment and unnatural deaths of women who have been married six years or less. Strangely enough, the woman officer in charge was recently quoted as follows: "It is very difficult to decide whether a burn case is suicide or murder. In both cases the victim is doused from head to toe in kerosene and severely burnt. We feel that 80 percent of the cases which are brought to our notice are suicides. The husbands and in-laws are certainly culpable because it is their harassment which drives the person to this act."[9]

Notwithstanding, conscious women activists have forged ahead: they have produced skits, plays, and movies on the oppression and exploitation of women; they have launched protests and they have set up women's centers where women in distress can get emotional support and legal aid. Feminist magazines and network bulletins have reported on both the problems of women and women's attempts to alleviate them. Feminist academics have also contributed to this

Protest against dowry system outside municipal corporation offices in Bombay, 1985. India's dowry system has resulted in the burning deaths of thousands of married women. Photo Sue Darlow/Format.

effort. *Towards Equality,* a landmark report, pointed out the national neglect of women and the lack of development programs for women in the fields of employment, health, and education.[10] Feminist researchers have studied women's roles in the protest movements and their participation in the building of the nation. These studies have further pointed out existing inequalities in the socioeconomic and political system, and have demonstrated how women's studies can offer new perspectives toward building an egalitarian social structure within the family and the community.

Women's protests have made the violent crime of woman-burning visible as a serious social problem. By calling attention to the oppression, conflict, and violence hidden behind the portrait of love, support, and nurturance in the family, women have opened a whole new vista. There is a new critical perspective on prevalent ways of thinking about the family. Nevertheless, it would be simplistic to say that we are on the brink of profound change in the social structure toward equality and justice, for I am in agreement with William J. Goode that "we must never underestimate the cunning or the staying power of those in charge."[11]

Besides, a satisfactory theoretical basis is absent in the women's movement in India. No serious attempt has been made to examine the material origins and perpetuation of male supremacy. The family in India has been explained in purely functionalist terms or in terms of the distinctive cultural features of the subcontinent. Social scientists continue to debate whether nuclearization of the joint-family structure is or is not taking place in India.[12] However, research on this topic has not questioned the complex power relations between gender and generation that underlie the family, the ideology and structure of dependence, or the sexual division of labor, all of which strengthen patterns of inequality and the oppression of women and children.

GOVERNMENTAL POLICY

In recent years the family has also emerged as a political issue in India. The government has formulated policies to further strengthen the family, while the women's movement has raised questions about family boundaries. A policy debate on women and the family was initiated in late 1980 in regard to the Sixth Five Year Plan. Planners maintained that the best way to improve women's position would be to improve the condition of the family. Women's organizations pointed out that this women-in-the-family approach would not lead to greater equality in society but to an increased polarization of the sexes. As a result of pressure from women activists and scholars, the planners agreed to incorporate a chapter on "Women and Development" in the Sixth Five Year Plan. The chapter admits that women are "the most vulnerable members of the family" and will continue to be so "for some time in future." It further promises to give "special attention" to the interests of the "vulnerable members." Nevertheless, the Sixth Five Year Plan insists that "the family is the unit for programmes for poverty eradication."

Although the problem of the repression of women in the family was acknowledged, the status of the family as the basic unit of economic development was maintained and constructive analysis was prevented. Such is the nature of the welfare state.[13] Nonetheless, the debate will continue. In many ways, the family plays a repressive role on behalf of the state, and yet at the same time, for most women and men, it is the only place where they have an opportunity for sexual and parental relationships, affection, care, and emotional support.

Notes

1. *Indian Express,* 19 June 1983.

2. Ibid., 20 May 1983.

3. Ibid.

4. Police department document to Inspector General of Police NWP and Oudh, from Secretary to Government of NWP and Oudh, dated 15 October 1892. File No. 1544/VIII 661 A-4 of 1892. State Archives, Lucknow.

5. Kalpana Ram, "Women's Liberation in India" (unpublished paper, June 1980).

6. For a discussion on the Constitutional definition of the family and confusion about the concept, see A. R. Desai, *Urban Family and Family Planning in India,* Chaps. I and II (Bombay: Popular Prakashan, 1980).

7. J. Goody, *Production and Reproduction: A Comparative Study of the Domestic Domain* (Cambridge: Cambridge University Press, 1976). I disagree with Goody in regarding dowry as a means by which daughters inherit in Eurasian societies.

8. "During the drafting of Hindu Code, Dr. Ambedkar had suggested a clear provision laying down that whatever was given as dowry should belong to the daughter. However, this was not pressed or pursued with the result that giving or rather demand for dowry grew so rapidly that even communities which never had this practice started following this." Latika Sarkar, "Legal Aspects of Dowry," *How* 6, no. 3 (March 1983).

9. *Patriot,* New Delhi, 24 June 1983.

10. Government of India, Department of Social Welfare, Ministry of Education and Social Welfare, *Towards Equality: Report of the Committee on the Status of Women in India* (1974).

11. William J. Goode, "Why Men Resist," in *Rethinking the Family: Some Feminist Questions,* edited by Barrie Thorne and Marilyn Yalom (Orient Longman, 1982), p. 132. He compares the position of men with that of other dominant groups and to the complex dialectic of men's control and women's efforts to combat and circumvent it, especially within the relationships of intimacy and mutual dependence in the family.

12. Dhirendra Narain, ed., *Explorations in the Family and Other Essays* (Bombay: Thacker & Co., 1975), see chaps. I and II. See also M. G. Kulkarni, "Family Research in India," in *Sociology in India: Retrospect and Prospect,* edited by P. K. B. Nayar (Delhi: B. R. Pub. Corp., 1982).

13. For a detailed analysis, see Elizabeth Wilson, *Women and Welfare State* (London: Tavistock, 1979).

Thousands Visit Indian Village Where Bride Died by Suttee

RAJENDRA BAJPAI

Huge crowds of Indians defied a government ban yesterday to honor an 18-year-old bride who burned to death on her husband's funeral pyre while calmly holding his head in her lap.

On September 4, Roop Kanwar, a bride of eight months, wore her brocaded wedding sari as she sat on the blazing pyre to commit suttee, the self-immolation seen as the ultimate act of fidelity in ancient India but outlawed for centuries.

The young bride's action turned this desert village in the western state of Rajasthan, 50 miles from Jaipur, into a place of pilgrimage.

Horrified government officials banned ceremonies at the site, barred transportation to the village and arrested the bride's brother-in-law, who had lighted the pyre.

But hundreds of thousands ignored the ban, traveling across the desert on foot or riding camels to join Hindu priests at the site covered by a canopy and perfumed by incense and flowers for the closing of the 13-day mourning period yesterday.

Witnesses said more than 200,000 people came to Deorala yesterday, but the Press Trust of India said the crowd could have numbered as high as 400,000.

Because of the government ban on the rite, few villagers admitted having seen the young woman die in the flames.

Some witnesses said that as flames engulfed the young bride, more than 5,000 villagers chanted "sathi mata ki jai" (mother sathi is immortal).

"She had an aura about her. She was calm as the flames enveloped her," said Rajinder Singh, a 20-year-old student who admitted he saw the suttee.

From the *San Francisco Chronicle*, 17 September 1987. ©*San Francisco Chronicle*. Reprinted by permission.

"When I arrived, half her body had burned. She sat on the funeral pyre with folded hands. There was no sign of panic on her face. She was chanting mantras," he told reporters.

Until two weeks ago, Kanwar was an ordinary village housewife from the Rajput warrior caste. Then on September 4, her husband Man Singh died of gastroenteritis. Within hours, villagers said, she declared she wanted to follow the ancient custom. As the body was brought to the village cremation ground that day, she dressed herself in her bridal finery and sat on the pyre of wood.

Kanwar is the fourth woman to have immolated herself in Deorala in the last 100 years. The last suttee was nearly 70 years ago. There is a temple in that woman's memory near the spot where Kanwar died.

The British banned suttee more than 100 years ago. The Mogul emperors had also declared it illegal in the 17th century.

Female Infanticide: Born to Die

S. H. VENKATRAMANI

A woman should be a lump of clay.

The luckless man loses a horse; the lucky man loses a wife.

Be the mother of a hundred sons.

These proverbs—from Bengal, Punjab, Maharashtra—are still a part of the living folklore which infuses the social customs that dictate the lives of millions of Indians in towns and villages across the country. They are a grim reminder that even in the 20th century—an age in which most of the modern world is awakening to the call of enlightened feminism—India still wallows in the primordial slime of misogyny: man's inhumanity to woman.

In most parts of the country, a woman is still considered a burdensome appendage. She is an economic drain. She must be exploited or dispensed with as a non-person. Because she crushes her family with marriage and dowry expenses she must be raised—from childhood—in financial and physical neglect. Her birth, in many parts of the country is greeted with silence, even sorrow. A boy arrives to the sound of joyous conch shells. Discrimination begins at birth.

Comprehensive studies conducted by UNICEF as well as Indian social scientists reveal an organised pattern of discrimination against young girls and older women in India. Their revelations are startling.

India is the only country in the world where the ratio of women to men has been declining over the years. The sex ratio declined from 972 females per 1,000 males in 1901 to 935 in 1981. And India is one of a handful of countries where female infant mortality exceeds that of the male—notwithstanding the fact that the female child is biologically stronger at birth.

Girl babies are breast-fed less frequently, and for a shorter duration than boy babies. When they grow up, they are provided less nutrition than their

Reprinted with permission from *India Today*, 15 June 1986, 26–33.

brothers. A recent survey of infants, toddlers and pre-schoolers showed that within their combined age groups, 71 percent of females suffered from severe malnutrition, as against 28 percent of the males. A related statistic reveals that boys are taken to hospital for treatment of common diseases in twice the number as girls. Boys do not fall ill more frequently than girls, they are merely provided more health care by parents who value sons more than daughters.

In the widening gender gap in India the female literacy rate—24.88 percent—is barely half that of males—46.74 percent. And the gap continues to widen. In the 6–14 age group, nearly 84 percent of boys are enrolled in schools, as against 54 percent in the case of girls.

It is not a pretty picture. The plight of India's girls aged 15 and under—about 140 million of them—cries out desperately for caring and sensitive attention. They form 20 percent of the nation's population but are denied adequate food and care because their parents are themselves the victims and prisoners of brutal tradition and economic circumstance in which the female shoulders a horrifying responsibility. For her sins, she is burned as an adult bride over dowry demands or, if she is a child bride, condemned to a lifetime of penurious widowhood upon the death of a husband even before her marriage is consummated.

If young girls and older women are denied a living in most parts of India, it is only the next step of this cruel logic that they should be denied life itself. Female infanticide—snuffing out the lives of newborn babies—is ultimately, the catharsis in the tragic drama of female life in this country. The cover story which follows is a graphic and chilling account of the trials and tribulations of families that kill their female infants. It focuses on the Kallars—a community of landless labourers in Tamil Nadu's Madurai district. It may be happening in one state, in one community, but it is a mirror in which all Indians must look and come face to face with the ugliness that surrounds them.

The challenge of developing India into a land of social and economic justice, as Nehru put it, is not just the creation of factories, and machinery and grandiose schemes. "Ultimately," he said, "it is the human being that counts, and if the human being counts, well, he counts more as a child than a grown-up."

Normally, the day should have been one of great rejoicing for 35-year-old Kuppusamy and his 26-year-old wife Chinnammal, both agricultural workers in Chulivechanpatti village in the Usilampatti taluk of Madurai district. It was a May morning of sparkling sunshine and Chinnammal, attractive and slim despite her pregnancy, was in labour inside her mud-and-thatch hut. In a few minutes her second child would be born. Her first, daughter Chellammal, 3, played outside.

The new-born cried lustily as it came into this world. It was a bonny child, fair of complexion, its eyes squinting at the sunlight that filtered in. But when the mother laid eyes on her baby, tears welled up in her eyes. They were not tears of joy.

Chinnammal had seen the sex of the child: a girl. What crossed her mind was not the anticipation of the joys of motherhood but the trials that lay ahead. How could a family of daily-wage agricultural workers belonging to the Kallar group of the Thevar community afford to bring up and marry off two daughters? How could they, when the dowry demanded by bridegrooms was always astronomical? The couple had decided to have a second child only in the desperate hope that it would be a boy. But on this sunny day, the dream lay shattered.

There was only one way out of a lifetime burden of bringing up two daughters. And Kuppusamy decided on what they had to do. That evening he trudged—somewhat unsteadily—into a nearby field, plucked a handful of oleander berries that are known for their lethal poison, and returned home. Chinnammal mashed them into a milky paste and fed her crying infant with the substance. The parents then shut the small door of their hut, sat outside, and waited for the poison to do its work.

Within an hour the baby began to twitch and tremble fitfully. Slowly she started spouting blood through her mouth and nose. The parents heard her whining. A few more minutes, and all was quiet. Chinnammal knew that everything was over. She quietly walked over to her mother's hut close by, dug up a little patch of ground inside, brought and buried the dead baby.

"I killed my child to save it from the lifelong ignominy of being the daughter of a poor family that cannot afford to pay a decent dowry," Chinnammal said, as she sipped water to keep her voice from breaking. "But all the same, it was extremely difficult to steel myself for the act. A mother who has borne a child cannot bear to see it suffer even for a little while, let alone bring herself to kill it. But I had to do it, because my husband and I concluded that it was better to let our child suffer an hour or two and die than suffer throughout life." Kuppusamy, at first reluctant to talk, admitted later during an interview: "I get Rs 13 a day as agricultural wages, on the days that I manage to find work. My wife gets Rs 6 a day. I cannot dream of decently marrying off two daughters. Killing girl babies due to fear of the dowry problem is very common in our Kallar community."

India Today's investigations reveal that over the last 10 to 15 years, female infanticide has come to be increasingly accepted among Madurai district's Kallars (a 2-lakh strong martial subcaste) as the only way out of the dowry problem. Said S. Muthuramalingam, who has a small farm in Paraipatti village: "The practice has grown among the Kallars during the last 10 years, and has become very widespread after 1980." The Kallar group of Madurai district is concentrated in Usilampatti taluk and its 300 villages, and accounts for nearly 80 percent of the taluk's 2.65 lakh population. In a damning confession, Muniamma of Ayodhyapatti village, an agricultural worker, said after some prodding: "There is hardly a poor Kallar family in which a female baby has not been murdered some time or the other during the last 10 years."

Chinnammal was not the only Kallar mother who administered poison to her baby daughter last month. Twenty-five-year-old Chinnakkal of Echampatti village, the wife of a counter clerk, Gopal, in the village cinema theatre, delivered her second baby daughter in the wee hours of May 10 in the Usilampatti government hospital. The mother escaped from the hospital with the new-born baby an hour after childbirth, flouting normal medical advice that a mother should rest a few days in hospital after delivery before getting discharged. Chinnakkal wanted to escape and kill the baby. The entries in the hospital records showed that the mother and daughter had absconded.

But Chinnakkal reported back to the hospital after a week, not with the baby but with her own mother. She came to consult the gynaecologist, Dr. Suthanthiradevi, because her breast milk had clotted. The clotting occurred because there was no baby to breast-feed. When asked by the doctors what had happened to her baby, Chinnakkal explained: "The little one died within four days of birth due to fits and fever." Why hadn't she rushed the baby to the hospital? The answer was barely audible: "I couldn't afford to do that."

Later, under persistent questioning, Chinnakkal gradually revealed the tragic truth: "How can I afford to bring up two daughters in these difficult days?" she asked. "We are a very poor family. Even to bring up my first daughter is going to be an unbearable burden. My husband has not come to see me after I gave birth to my second female child. He must have hated me after knowing it is another daughter. I should let him know that I have done away with the baby."

Dr. Suthanthiradevi said that Chinnakkal and Chinnammal are not exceptions but very much the rule in the Kallar community. She has been practising in Usilampatti for over five years and disclosed that, on an average, 1,200 delivery cases come to the hospital every year. Of these, nearly half deliver female babies. Said Suthanthiradevi: "Over 95 percent of the women who give birth to daughters abscond immediately after the babies are born, and we have recorded this in our registers. We can come to our own conclusions about the motive for absconding."

The statistics are shocking. Nearly 600 female births in the Kallar group are recorded in the Usilampatti government hospital every year, and out of these an estimated 570 babies vanish with their mothers no sooner than they can open their eyes to the world. Hospital sources estimate that nearly 80 percent of these vanishing babies—more than 450—become victims of infanticide.

Besides this, deliveries also occur in primary health centres and in the private nursing homes and maternity hospitals that have mushroomed in the taluk, for which no comprehensive records are available, not to speak of the child births in the village households. Some 20-odd private nursing homes, which admit maternity cases also, have come up in Usilampatti town alone. Said Dr. Sugandhi Natarajan, who runs one of these private nursing homes: "We get about 12 to 15 delivery cases a year even in our small nursing home, and roughly seven of them deliver female children. Almost all of them run away immediately after childbirth, and come to consult us again after a week or 10 days because they invariably have this problem of breast-milk clotting, which has to be corrected with hormone tablets. The female babies inevitably die, and we know how they die. It is very sad but it keeps happening. I have been practising here for five to six years and what happens to female babies is common knowledge in these parts."

In each of the more than 300 Kallar villages in Usilampatti taluk, with populations ranging from 500 to 1,500, 20 to 50 girl babies have been killed in the last five years in the face of the excruciatingly cruel dowry problem. In Chulivechanpatti, which has a population of 300, at least three girl babies have been killed during the last six months. And the parents freely admit to their crime. Apart from Kuppusamy, two other families involved are those of Sivaraj and Oothappa Thevar. And in Paraipatti with a population of 400, a farmer S. Muthuramalingam said in the presence of all the villagers: "Over 50 female babies would have been killed in our village during the last five to seven years."

Going by a rough calculation, nearly 6,000 female babies must have been poisoned to death in Usilampatti taluk in the last decade. Few such deaths are recorded. And births are registered only if the deliveries take place in the hospitals. According to the law, the deaths of these babies under suspicious circumstances should be reported to the village administrative officers and the panchayats or other local bodies. But in most cases, the households keep the information to themselves, although what is happening is common knowledge. As a matter of practice the first child is not killed, even if it is a daughter, but with the second female child there begins a series of killings. Family planning is yet to catch up with the Kallars. It is not that they don't want children. They wish keenly for boys because they can then get dowry. N. Nallasamy, who teaches at the elementary school in Chulivechanpatti, observes: "There is also this widespread belief among the Kallars that if you kill a daughter, your next child will be a son."

The widespread practice of female infanticide is now getting reflected in the changing male-female ratio among the Kallars. Revealed a Madurai district official who did not want to be identified: "Men are now 52 percent of the Kallar population. Ten years ago it was women who were 52 percent."

Many Kallar families realise that they are committing a crime, but they are convinced that, given their difficult circumstances, they are taking the only course open to them. A 26-year-old woman agricultural worker of Mayampatti village, Kanthammal, who killed her second baby daughter immediately after childbirth last year, made no bones about the murder she committed: "How can we poor people rear so many daughters in this painful dowry situation? The village panchayat and the village administrative officer have no right to investigate or interfere in our personal affairs. If I and my husband have the right to have a child, we also have the right to kill it if it happens to be a daughter and we decide we cannot afford it. Outsiders and the Government have no right to poke their noses into this." Her husband, Andi, concurred: "It is impossible to marry off daughters with our uncertain wages."

It is the cruel dowry problem that is the cause of the sad lot of the Kallar women who have to unwillingly poison their own babies and watch them writhe and die. As M. Jeeva, senior coordinator of the privately-run Society for Integrated Rural Development (SIRD) observed: "Female infanticide is only the symptom; it is the dowry problem that is the underlying disease." The dowry demands that parents of marriageable Kallar boys make, bears out what Jeeva said. Said V. Gopal, a small farmer of Chulivechanpatti: "Even if you want to marry your daughter to a poor agricultural worker who does not own even a square inch of agricultural land and who has to lead a hand to mouth existence, you have to give Rs 2,000 cash to the bridegroom and make jewellery worth five sovereigns of gold for your daughter. If the potential bridegroom happens, by chance, to own some land, however meagre the holding, the automatic demand is Rs 10,000 and 10 sovereigns of gold. If a Kallar family wants to celebrate a daughter's marriage in a fairly decent manner, the minimum cost will be something like Rs 30,000 to Rs 40,000, including all the cash and jewellery and marriage expenses. And if your would-be son-in-law has the high socio-economic status of an engineer, lawyer, doctor, or member of Parliament, you have to spend a lakh of rupees and in addition give a kilo of gold."

The dowry system took root among the Kallars after the dam on the Vaigai river brought irrigation water into Usilampatti 25 years ago. With prosperity came increasing dowry demands which today are a part of the Kallars' culture. The case of Mookiah, a daily agricultural labourer of Mayampatti village, is illustrative of what has resulted. Thirty-one-year-old Mookiah's daily income varies from Rs 13 to Rs 15, and it is only on some days in the month that he is able to find work. On the other days he has to make do with a thin gruel to keep body and soul together. But that didn't deter the man and his parents from claiming an exorbitant dowry when his marriage was arranged a few years ago. Another agricultural worker, Maharani, was to be his wife, and her parents were asked to give 10 sovereigns of gold (valued today at roughly Rs 20,000) in return for accepting their daughter into a household with an uncertain income where starvation loomed large.

That wasn't all. Maharani's parents managed to borrow and scrounge enough to get nine sovereigns of gold. Mookiah discovered that he had been cheated of a sovereign and drove his wife out of his house. He recounts: "I sent my wife out when I found that we had got only nine sovereigns instead of the promised 10. I told her that unless she brought that extra sovereign, she could not enter my house. We were separated for two years. Finally she managed to bring one more sovereign and I accepted her."

It is also understandable that this backward Kallar community should have thought of female infanticide as the way out of the strangulating dowry evil. Explains M. Vasudevan, another senior coordinator of SIRD: "These Kallars and Thevars were earlier the warriors for the Chola emperors who ruled parts of Tamil Nadu 10 centuries ago. They are basically a warrior caste and wouldn't hesitate to behead somebody with a scythe. Killing is in their blood." If this explanation is to be believed, it is only logical that when confronted with the blood-sucking dowry evil, these people should opt to kill their new-born girls.

Almost every poor Kallar family would have killed at least one girl baby, and there are families where mothers freely but sorrowfully admit to having killed one baby daughter after another, year after year. Thirty-five-year-old Annammal of Paraipatti village is a daily wage labourer eking out a tough livelihood breaking stones in a quarry. Her 40-year-old husband, Siramai, is an agricultural worker with a small patch of land to call his own. Their first three children were all daughters. Says Annammal, barely controlling her grief: "I had to kill all these three baby daughters because we just could not afford them. Finding a husband for each one of them would have cost a fortune, and we also believed that if we killed a daughter the next child would be a son. But that didn't happen. In spite of killing my three daughters, I again had another four baby daughters in a row. We didn't do anything about them because we didn't know what to do. Then finally I had a son, and lastly again another daughter."

Annammal's case is typical and speaks vividly of the whole phenomenon of killing female babies. As she sits and rubs her blood-shot eyes, mournfully pointing to the spot in her backyard where she buried her first three daughters, she doesn't appear a ruthless, cold-blooded murderer. Rather, she seems an unfortunate and hopeless victim of desperately cruel circumstances. The fact that her daughters are in tattered clothes while her only son is smartly dressed speaks of the whole Kallar culture, in which a son is regarded as a priceless asset and a daughter as a born liability. Her story also illustrates the fact that among the Kallars it is the duty of the mother to kill the unwanted daughter by way of compensation for having failed to give her husband a son.

The Kallar man's cruelty to the woman is terrible. Mookiah of Mayampatti did not condescend to set his eyes on his wife for six months after it turned out that the first child she bore him was a daughter: Vasanthi. Sundayi of Echampatti was driven out of her home last year by her husband Vasu, an Usilampatti-based driver of the Pandyan Roadways Corporation, because she had borne him two daughters. Said she: "I didn't know what to do. My husband said, either kill the two daughters, or bring another Rs 10,000 and 10 more sovereigns of gold from your father. My father had already given five sovereigns and Rs 5,000 at the time of our marriage, and now I am back with my parents because I have been booted out by my husband."

These are the stray instances of Kallar wives refusing to bow to their husbands' wishes. And they suffer for it. The 40-year-old Muthukkaruppan of Paraipatti village drove his 35-year-old wife Nagammal out of their house after she bore him his second daughter because she refused to kill the female children. She stayed away for six months before the family was reunited. And the reunion came about because of the efforts of Muthukkaruppan's father, who gave his son the benefit of his experience in having brought up five daughters. After that Nagammal gave birth to another daughter and two sons. Muthukkaruppan still grumbles about having to look after three daughters with his uncertain daily wage as a stone-cutter, and asks: "Why can't I kill my daughters if I cannot look after them? Why should anybody prevent it?" But that loud questioning withers in the face of Nagammal's maternal dedication.

For all that, the culture of looking down on the woman and the daughter runs very deep in the Kallar blood. In fact, a Kallar husband will not come to the hospital to see his new-born child if it is a daughter. A round of the maternity ward of the Usilampatti hospital last fortnight was revealing in this respect. Rani of Arogyapatti village, who had just got a male child, was ecstatic. And she was talking of spending a week in hospital to make sure there were no problems with her new-born son. She said: "My husband Jayaraman works in a textile mill in Dindigul, and he is rushing to see the child."

On the other hand, 33-year-old Chinnakaruppan of Kattathevanpatti was standing gloomily by his wife Kondaiammal, unable to smile. She had just borne him their seventh child, the sixth daughter. Kondaiammal complained: "I wish the doctor would at least allow us to take the baby away immediately, so that we can kill it. What crime have I committed to be saddled with six daughters?" Santosham of the same village, and Ramakkal of Ayodhyapatti looked equally lost, having just delivered their first baby daughters. And Yellakkal of Doraisamypudur near Kalloothu, who was expecting her third baby (the first was a daughter and the second a son) was very anxious about whether it was going to be a son or a daughter. She gave vent to her fears: "If it is a daughter, my husband Chinniah will surely ask me to kill it, or send me out of the house."

If a Kallar father doesn't force his wife to kill their second daughter, it usually means that the first daughter must have died a natural death. For instance, Rosammal of Chokkadevanpatti delivered her fourth child, a daughter, early in the morning of May 17 and surprisingly the baby is still alive. Her husband Raman, however, explained the mystery: "Our two other daughters died, and we are left only with our son and this baby." If the practice of female infanticide is uniformly prevalent among the Kallars, the gruesome methods used vary. One method of killing a baby is by stuffing a few grains of coarse paddy into its mouth. The infant breathes the grain into its windpipe and chokes to death. But in some cases paddy doesn't work. Annammal's (Paraipatti) is a case in point. She said she had to take recourse to a juicy extract from the *madar* (calotropis gigantea) plant. In some families the husband grows a *madar* plant from the time his wife conceives so he can minister the poison if a daughter is born.

This whole culture of female infanticide is succinctly summed up by a middle-aged woman. Annamayakkal of Singarasapuram: "In our community, if a male child unfortunately dies for some reason, we don't take gruel for a year. It is a great financial loss. And if we fail to kill a daughter, again we skip a meal a day in sorrow, and thus also save some money for her marriage." This basic view of woman as a born liability because of the dowry evil has taken deep root among the Kallars and the Thevars. This, in a state ruled by a chief minister who swears by the greatness of womanhood, in a country that had a woman prime minister for close to two decades, in the age of women's liberation.

"Intimate Femicide": Effect of Legislation and Social Services

KAREN D. STOUT

In the past 15 years, tremendous strides have been made in addressing the needs of female victims of male violence through legislation and direct services, and social workers have become more aware of the dynamics of abusive relationships. However, little attention has been paid to the killing of women by intimate male partners, or "intimate femicide"—the term introduced at the 1976 International Tribunal on Crimes against Women (Russell and Van de Ven 1976) to emphasize that "when women are killed, it is not accidental that they are women" (Russell 1982, 286). This article reports on a study of intimate femicide in the 50 states, focusing on the relationship between services and legislation addressing violence against women and the rate of women killed in the various states.

BACKGROUND

The prevalence and severity of violence against women has been documented by numerous sources. For example, estimates of the proportion of married women in the United States who are beaten at least once in their marriages have ranged from 20–30 percent (Pagelow 1984) to two-thirds (Roy 1982), and Straus, Gelles, and Steinmetz (1980) suggested that 25 percent of married women will be *severely* beaten at least once in their lifetime. Furthermore, violence against women in abusive relations increases in frequency as well as severity over time

From *Affilia* 4, no. 2 (Summer 1989): 21–30. Copyright ©1989 by Sage Publications. Reprinted by permission of Sage Publications, Inc. The data used to analyze the 1980–82 incidence of intimate femicide were made available by the InterUniversity Consortium for Political and Social Research. Data for the *Uniform Crime Reports, 1980–1982: Supplemental Homicide Report* were originally collected by the FBI. Neither the FBI nor the consortium bear any responsibility for the analysis and interpretations in this article.

(Dobash and Dobash 1979; Pagelow 1981) and escalates in severity after an intimate relationship has been severed (U.S. Department of Justice 1980).

The escalation of violence against women can, and all too frequently does, result in their deaths. Each day in this country, an average of four women are killed by male partners. The author's analysis of data from the *Uniform Crime Reports, 1980–1982: Supplemental Homicide Report* (FBI 1984) indicates that from January 1980 through December 1982, 4,189 females aged 16 and over were killed by intimate male partners. All 50 states reported at least one case of intimate femicide during this three-year period. The three-year average frequency of intimate femicide ranged from 1 killing in Vermont to 176 killings in California. Prevalence rates per million women for the same period ranged from 2.6 in Vermont to 14.7 in South Carolina. As Okun (1986, xiv) reported, "Since the founding of America's first battered women's shelter in 1974 through the end of 1983, well over 19,000 Americans have died in incidents of woman abuse or other forms of conjugal violence." Two such victims were Hattie Milo, aged 47, who was shot by her husband, Willie Milo, aged 65, along with her adult daughter ("Police Charge Elgin Man" 1980). Another victim, Sheila Crealey, was found beaten to death with a baseball bat and a belt. Her 24-year-old live-in male lover was arrested for her murder; co-workers noted that she had been beaten before (Cox 1981).

Development of Services

Shelter services that were developed to address the basic needs of battered women and their children have their roots in the women's movement and in the antirape movement (Schechter 1982a, 1982b). These shelters benefit battered women in four ways: They (1) provide safety from immediate danger, (2) allow women time to recover physically and mentally from the abuse, (3) afford women the opportunity to develop a clearer picture of their situation and the options available to them, and (4) introduce battered women to other women who are experiencing similar pain in their lives (Harris 1981).

Since the shelter movement began, many individuals and groups have worked diligently to transform battering from a private matter between an individual man and woman into a public and criminal matter. Through the efforts of the feminist and shelter movements, legislation has been passed in many states to allow a victim of intimate violence to obtain a protection order to remove the batterer from the home, to impose penalties for violating the order by contacting the victim, and to give the police additional power to intervene. As Lerman and Livingston (1983, 2) noted, "The eviction order is possibly the most important form of relief provided by the new legislation. It gives a victim of abuse an enforceable right to be safe in her home, and it establishes that the abuser rather than the victim should bear the burden of finding another residence."

In many states, legislatures have responded by allocating state funds for services to victims of wife/woman beating; defining the physical abuse of a family member as a criminal offense; providing temporary legal injunctions during divorce, separation, and child-custody proceedings; and requiring the reporting and collection of data on family violence.

Many programs for men who batter have also emerged (see "Programs for Men Who Batter" 1980a, 1980b, 1980c). Norberg (1982) cited seven models of treatment used by services for men who batter: (1) peer counseling in all-male groups, (2) intensive therapy addressing the entire family from the onset, (3) services organized by shelters with male-led groups, (4) services organized by shelters with male and female co-leaders, (5) inpatient services in a hospital (a structured court-mandated approach), (6) group therapy with two male therapists organized by a traditional mental health center, and (7) Batterers Anonymous—a self-help model.

The primary aim of shelter services, rape crisis centers, programs for men who batter, and legislative responses is to end violence by men against women. The protection of victims from further beatings or femicide is another critical goal. Social workers have become intimately involved in these programs as providers of services to abusive individuals and couples, and many are advocates of community and legislative changes to eliminate violence against women. However, most social work research continues to focus on intra- and interpersonal factors related to violence in the family. Therefore, social workers need to be alerted to and educated about macro, structural factors that create or maintain an environment that is conducive to violence against women. Accordingly, it is appropriate for social workers to bring the issue of femicide into the professional forum, to begin to examine the problem of men killing women with whom they are intimate, and to struggle with factors that may be associated with this tragic loss of life.

Intimate femicide is unquestionably the most severe form of domestic violence and the victimization of women. Little is known, however, about the impact of legislation and services on this form of victimization. Therefore, the author conducted the study presented here to examine femicide by exploring associations among it, the provision of services, and legislative responses in the 50 states. The two research questions were "Is the prevalence rate of intimate femicide lower in states that have a higher rate of services that address male violence against women?" and "Do states with domestic violence legislation have fewer women killed than states that do not have such legislation?"

METHOD

The study was exploratory, providing information on associations among a number of variables and the prevalence rate of intimate femicide in the states. Given the nature of the topic under review, an experimental, causation design was inappropriate and impossible because of the ethical and legal implications of studying lethality. However, correlational data can provide preliminary information about the strength and direction of associations among variables. The research used archival data; as Colby (1982) noted, the advantage of using secondary analysis for research on women and social change is that one can redefine and refine previous research questions.

The 50 states were the units of analysis, and 1980, 1981, and 1982 were the years under review. All females, aged 16 and older who were killed by an intimate male partner and whose deaths were classified as "murder or non-negligent manslaughter" by the *UCR* (FBI 1984), were scored as the dependent variable; these victims were categorized in the *UCR* as wives, common-law wives, girlfriends, ex-wives, and friends.

Data on intimate femicide were derived from the *Uniform Crime Reports: Supplemental Homicide Report, 1980–1982* (FBI 1984), made available through the InterUniversity Consortium for Political and Social Research in an OSIRIS tape format. The *UCR* was developed in 1929 to provide standardized reports and definitions across jurisdictions (O'Brien 1985). Although the reliability and validity of the data provided in the *UCR* have been criticized, O'Brien found that homicides are well reported. Reliability is also strengthened by the fact that the *UCR* reports rates of victimization rather than of offenses, and, as Wilbanks (1982, 161) stated, it is "far easier to count victims than offenders [since many cases are not cleared]." Data from other sources are presented in table 1.

RESULTS

Availability of Services

This section presents information on the analysis of the research question, Is the prevalence rate of intimate femicide lower in states that have a higher rate of services that address violence by men against women? Three measures were used to assess services that address violence against women in a state: the number of rape crisis centers, the number of shelters for battered women, and the number of programs for men who batter. Each measure was computed to a prevalence rate per million people over age 16. Using Pearson's product-moment correlation coefficient, each service measure was then analyzed to determine its association with the rate of intimate femicide (see table 2).

It was found that two of the three independent variables were statistically significant. The rate of shelters for battered women in a state was negatively correlated with intimate femicide, so that states with a greater number of services had a lower rate of intimate femicide. The availability of rape crisis services was also correlated negatively with intimate femicide. Again, the negative association suggests that those states with a higher rate of services have a lower rate of intimate femicide. The rate of programs for men who batter was not significantly related to the rate of intimate femicide, which may well be a consequence of the restricted range of the services that were available from 1980 to 1982 (19 states had no such services in this period).

TABLE 1 Summary of Independent Variables

Variable	Services and Responses	Data Set
Rate of shelters in a state	Services that provide housing for battered women in a state.	Warrior (1982)
Rate of treatment services for men who batter	Therapeutic services for men who batter, excluding jail or prison services.	"Programs for Men Who Batter" (1986)
Rate of rape crisis centers in a state	24-hour crisis and advocacy services for adult victims of rape.	National Institute of Mental Health (1980)
Legislative responses	1. Civil injunction relief—abuse.	Ross and Barcher (1983)
	2. Temporary injunctions during divorce and separation.	Ross and Barcher (1983)
	3. Physical abuse defined as a crime.	Ross and Barcher (1983)
	4. Arrests without a warrant in domestic violence cases.	Ross and Barcher (1983)
	5. Required reports of domestic violence cases.	Ross and Barcher (1983)
	6. Provide funds or set standards for shelters.	Ross and Barcher (1983)

TABLE 2 Correlation among Selected Service Factors and Intimate Femicide

Services	r	r^2	p
Number of shelters, per million[a]	-.52	.27	.0001
Number of rape crisis centers, per million[b]	-.40	.161	.005
Number of programs for men who batter, per million	.12	.01	NS[c]

Note: Analysis based on data from Warrior (1982). "Programs for Men Who Batter" (1980a, 1980b, 1980c), and National Institute of Mental Health (1980).
[a]Based on analysis of 49 states; Alaska, a statistical outlier, was removed from correlation analysis.
[b]Based on analysis of 48 states; New Mexico and Alaska, statistical outliers, were removed from the correlation analysis.
[c]NS = not significant.

Legislative Factors

Six statutes were examined to assess whether states that had statutory protection for victims of domestic violence had fewer women killed than did states that did not have such statutory protection. Table 3 lists the individual pieces of legislation and the frequency of states with and without legislation (number) and presents the average number of women killed in the states with and without the legislation (mean). As table 3 indicates, the average number of women killed in states that had each of the individual pieces of domestic violence legislation was lower than was the average number of women killed in states that did not have such legislation.

DISCUSSION

The study reported here was an initial step toward delineating factors that are associated with rates of intimate femicide in the United States. It departed from traditional research on homicides in its focus on gender and relationships and in the variables chosen for review.

For practitioners who are activists or advocates for services to victims of abuse, this article presents empirical evidence of a negative association between rape crisis and shelter services in a state and the rate of intimate femicide in a state. Although this author has heard shelter programs accused of being only "Band-Aid" services, the study suggests that the availability of shelters and rape crisis centers in a state is associated with the decreased prevalence of intimate femicide. To date, social workers have not been the leaders in the rape-crisis and shelter movements. It is time for them to begin to explore the premises on which

TABLE 3 Average Number of Intimate Femicides for States with and without Statutes Related to Domestic Violence

Type of Statute	States with Legislation		States with No Legislation	
	Number	Mean	Number	Mean
Civil injunction relief	33	7.36	17	9.59
Temporary injunction relief	25	7.67	25	8.57
Define physical abuse as a criminal offense	20	6.90	30	8.94
Arrest without a warrant	30	7.67	20	8.79
Require data collection and reporting	18	7.19	32	8.64
Provide funds for shelters or set standards	24	7.71	26	8.50

Note: Analysis based on data from Ross and Barcher (1983).

these movements were founded and to review the scholarship, from within and outside the profession, on violence against women. They may find that services for victims of male violence are more than auxiliary.

Practitioners who are concerned about social policy may note that states that passed civil-injunction-relief legislation had fewer women killed on average than did states that did not have such legislation. Such statutes generally provide for a "protection order" that removes the abuser from the home and is often psychologically easier for a battered woman to obtain than going through the criminal courts. This finding may suggest that social workers and others who are involved with victims of violence should strive to obtain immediate and uncomplicated bureaucratic relief for their clients. Furthermore, states that have enacted other forms of domestic violence legislation (funding for shelters, temporary injunction relief, arrests without warrants based on probable cause, and the required reporting and collection of data on family violence) had a lower average number of women killed by male partners than did states that did not have such legislation enacted by 1982. Social workers often seek legislative responses to promote social justice. It appears from these data that legislative responses to domestic violence have been effective in reducing the average number of women killed in a state.

Leaders and line workers in the shelter and rape-crisis-center movements can review these data and feel proud about the work they have done. However, much more must be done to determine and isolate factors that may be associated with services and legislation in a state. Questions to be considered include these: Is the safety of the shelter (the beds, the facility, and the locked doors), or the community organizing that occurred before the shelter was built, the critical factor in reducing the rate of intimate femicide in a state? Are legislative responses associated with the presence of a more liberal, egalitarian attitude toward women in a state? The study presented here provides an empirical foundation that will allow future researchers to explore this problem with more in-depth analyses that will help them move toward predictive modeling. Predictive modeling will allow the assessment of which variables best explain the rate of intimate femicide in a state. Social workers have an obligation to strive to obtain such information so they can maximize the limited human and material resources that are available to deal with domestic violence.

Individual and sociostructural factors that contribute to violence against women are complex and difficult to separate empirically. Tremendous progress has been made in the past 15 years in addressing the prevalence and severity of violence against women. We social workers are now just beginning to explore intimate femicide. We cannot ignore (nor can we allow others to ignore) the woman-slaughter that is occurring in this country. It is hoped that the study presented here has opened the door to discussions of intimate femicide. We must continue to struggle with the many factors that may be associated with this tragic loss of life.

References

Colby, A. 1982. "The Use of Secondary Analysis in the Study of Women and Social Change." *Journal of Social Issues* 38:119–23.

Cox, M. 1981. "Austinite Dies from Battering." *Austin American-Statesman*, 23 April.

Dobash, E., and R. Dobash. 1979. *Violence against Wives: A Case against Patriarchy.* New York: Free Press.

FBI. 1984. *Uniform Crime Reports, 1980–1982: Supplemental Homicide Report.* Ann Arbor, Mich.: InterUniversity Consortium for Political and Social Research.

Harris, B. 1981. "Helping the Abused Jewish Wife or Child. *Sh'ma: A Journal of Jewish Responsibility* 11:145–46.

Lerman, I. G., and F. Livingston. 1983. "State Legislation on Domestic Violence." *Response to Violence in the Family and Sexual Assault* 6, no. 5:1–27.

National Institute of Mental Health. 1980. *National Directory: Rape Prevention and Treatment Sources.* Washington, D.C.: Government Printing Office.

Norberg, C. 1982. *Model Programs: Working with Men Who Batter.* St. Louis, Mo.: Rape and Violence End Now.

_____. 1986. Personal communication, September.

O'Brien, R. M. 1985. *Crime and Victimization Data.* Beverly Hills, Calif.: Sage.

Okun, I. 1986. *Woman Abuse: Facts Replacing Myths.* Albany, N.Y.: State University of New York Press.

Pagelow, R. M. 1981. *Woman-battering: Victims and Their Experiences.* Beverly Hills, Calif.: Sage.

_____. 1984. *Family Violence.* New York: Praeger.

"Police Charge Elgin Man with Murdering Wife, Daughter." 1980. *Austin American-Statesman*, 25 February.

"Programs for Men Who Batter": Part I (1980a), 6–7 April; Part II (1980b), 6–7 May; suppl. (1980c), 3 June. *Response to Violence in the Family and Sexual Assault.*

Ross, S. D., and A. Barcher. 1983. *The Rights of Women.* Toronto: Bantam.

Roy, M., ed. 1982. *The Abusive Partner.* New York: Van Nostrand Reinhold.

Russell, D. E. 1982. *Rape in Marriage.* New York: Macmillan.

_____, and N. Van de Ven, eds. 1976. *Proceedings of the International Tribunal on Crimes against Women.* East Palo Alto, Calif.: Frog in the Well.

Schechter, S. 1982a. *In Honor of the Battered Women's Movement: An Appraisal of Our Work.* Paper presented at the Second National Conference of the National Coalition against Domestic Violence (August).

_____. 1982b. *Woman and Male Violence: The Visions and Struggles of the Battered Women's Movement.* Boston: South End Press.

Straus, M. A., R. J. Gelles, and S. K. Steinmetz. 1980. *Behind Closed Doors: Violence in the American Family.* Garden City, N.Y.: Doubleday.

U.S. Department of Justice. 1980. *Intimate Victims: A Study of Violence among Friends and Relatives.* Washington, D.C.: Government Printing Office.

Warrior, B. 1982. *Battered Women's Directory.* 8th ed. Cambridge, Mass.: Warrior.

Wilbanks, W. 1982. "Murdered Women and Women Who Murder: A Critique of the Literature." In *Judge, Lawyer, Victim, and Thief,* ed. N. Rafter and E. Stanko, 211–32. Boston: Northeastern University Press.

Part 3

❖ ❖ ❖

FEMICIDE AND RACISM

Demonstration, Boston, Massachusetts, 1979, organized by coalition of feminist groups to protest series of femicides in the city's multiracial neighborhoods. Photo ©Tia Cross. All rights reserved.

Introduction

Femicide has no respect for race, culture, age, class, or sexuality. This part of the book focuses on the complex ways in which racism interacts with violence against women and shapes both femicide itself and the ways it is addressed by the local community, the police, the media, and the legal system.

Part 3 opens with Jaime Grant's account of the black community's responses to the murder of 12 young African-American women in Boston, Massachusetts. She exposes the racism in the media coverage, which virtually ignored these killings initially and later depicted the victims in racist stereotypes as runaways or prostitutes. The author also addresses the political response to the killings—the formation of alliances and coalitions among all kinds of women—African-American women and other women of color, white women, feminists and nonfeminists, and lesbians and heterosexual women—and argues for the need for an analysis of the murder of African-American women that acknowledges its racist and sexist dimensions. While the events recorded by Jaime Grant date back to the late 1970s and early 1980s, the issues surrounding the formation of alliances and coalitions among women activists of diverse backgrounds remain significant.

Diana Russell and Candida Ellis focus on the limited response of the police during an investigation of the murder of an unknown number of young African-American women in Atlanta. Next is Diana Russell's account of the rape and murder of Asian women in San Francisco, followed by Russell's description of the kidnapping, sexual torture, and murder of African-American women in Philadelphia. These selections not only document incidents of femicide but illustrate the racism and misogyny that can taint news coverage of the deaths of black and minority ethnic women in the United States.

Evidence of the white culture's lack of concern about the deaths of women of color is pursued by Beverly Singer in her analysis of the impact of femicide on American Indian women. She explores the sensitive question of the murder of American Indian women by American Indian men and traces its source to the genocide, conquest, and colonization of American Indians by Europeans. Like S. H. Venkatramani in part 2, Singer links femicide with imposed fertility control among certain racial and ethnic groups in the United States.

The major theme in part 3 is that an adequate analysis of femicide must take into account the complex ways in which racism and woman hating interact, not just in the phenomenon of femicide but in the responses to it by the police, the judicial system, and the media. Another important theme here is the resistance to femicide displayed by women of color. White feminists, who have tended to subsume women of color into their own struggle, can learn a great deal from these women's older and stronger histories of resistance at grassroots levels.

Who's Killing Us?

JAIME M. GRANT

From January 28 to May 30, 1979, thirteen women, twelve black and one white, were murdered within a two-mile radius of each other in the city of Boston. All but one of the victims were found in predominantly black neighborhoods in the contiguous districts of Roxbury, Dorchester, and the South End. Many of the women were strangled with bare hands or a scarf or cord, some were stabbed, two were burned after they were killed and two were dismembered. Several of the women had been raped just prior to their deaths.

On April 1, statistics showed that already 50 percent more black women had been killed in Boston in 1979 than in all of 1978. On that same date, following the deaths of six black women, 1,500 people took to the streets to mourn the loss of their sisters, daughters, mothers, and friends. The memorial march commenced in Boston's South End at the Harriet Tubman House and paused first at the Wellington Street apartment of Daryal Ann Hargett, the fifth victim, who was found strangled on the floor of her bedroom. When Hargett's aunt, Mrs. Sara Small, stood before the crowd and cried, "Who is killing us?" she posed a question that would reverberate through the city as communities, disparate and diverse, struggled to counter burgeoning violence with action that would ensure the safety of those at risk.

As simple and direct as Mrs. Small's appeal sounded, it reached the various groups in attendance that day on very different levels. To many of the black residents of Roxbury, Dorchester, and the South End, the "us" in Mrs. Small's query meant black women, and in a broader sense, *black people*. Most of them were veterans of the violent desegregation of the Boston public schools in 1974 and of an increasingly brutal relationship with the Boston police force. In the wake of that conflict, they were acutely aware of the overt racist violence of

Reprinted from *Sojourner: The Women's Forum* 13, nos. 10–11 (June and July 1988). Another version of this essay appears in *The Third Wave: Feminist Perspectives on Racism* (Kitchen Table Press, 1992).

which many white Bostonians were easily capable. Against this backdrop, the answer to the "who" in Mrs. Small's question seemed a foregone conclusion: white people—most likely, one or more white men—are killing us.

To the police, walking along the sidelines of the march, directing traffic on foot, or keeping order on horseback, the "who" in Mrs. Small's cry was a series of *perpetrators*. Their experience with street crime made them more inclined to suspect black-on-black violence in these cases, and to question closely those people who were most intimately acquainted with the victims. Throughout the case, the police and Boston Mayor Kevin White's administration would implore the black community's cooperation while emphasizing their firm conviction that the murders were "unrelated." That is, the police strongly suspected that each murder was a singular act of violence by an individual. This was not a case of serial murder, not a "Son-of-Sam" situation, Mayor White asserted over and over again. The "us" to whom Mrs. Small referred was in fact a "them" to the 92 percent white, overwhelmingly male Boston police.

To many of the white feminists who brought up the rear of the march, the "us" to whom Mrs. Small had referred was black *women*. Their grief was focused on the vulnerability of women's lives in a culture in which violence against women was condoned and, at times, glorified. Their experience—as advocates for victims of domestic battering and rape, as activists for women's

Demonstration, Boston, 1979, protesting series of murders of African-American women. Photo Ellen Shub.

safety in neighborhoods across the city—left them inclined to believe that the "who" to which Mrs. Small referred were men, white and/or black, probably men with whom the victims were acquainted. They differed with the police in that they believed the murders were connected and that a sexist denigration of women's lives formed the crux of that connection.

Black feminists scattered in the crowd held yet another point of view. They heard the "us" in Sara Small's cry as black people, specifically *black women,* whose vulnerability was multidimensional in a city infamous for racial violence and where sexist violence was commonplace. Their perception of "who" was not altogether different from the perception of the mainstream black community within whose ranks they stood. They held racism centrally responsible for the conditions that made the unchecked murder of black women easy; and if white men were not themselves carrying out these crimes, as primary brokers of privilege in a white capitalist patriarchy, they remained fundamentally culpable. Their analysis was not unlike that of the white feminists in attendance, as they saw these crimes essentially connected by a cultural ethic that devalued the lives of women. However, black feminists added a critical layer to both anti-racist and white feminist analyses as they perceived that ethic to be steeped in the politics of *both sexism and racism.*

The following chronicles the community responses to the murders of thirteen women in Boston in the early months of 1979; examines the actions and interactions of the Combahee River Collective, CRISIS, and the Coalition for Women's Safety; and explores how the disparate responses to Mrs. Small's impassioned cry of "Who is killing us?" informed the activism of each and all of these groups.

THE COMBAHEE RIVER COLLECTIVE

Barbara Smith was fuming as she stood in the field adjacent to the Stride Rite factory. Fifteen hundred people out to mourn six women's deaths and not a word from the platform addressed sexual violence. A black lesbian feminist and a Roxbury resident, she was not comforted by the anger of men who pledged to "protect their women" through the crisis.

> There were almost entirely male speakers and they were saying things like, "we need to protect our women; women need to stay inside the house." Nothing about sexual politics or sexual violence. It was all about racial crimes. Well, why was it all women being murdered, if the only reason they were being murdered was because of race?

A founding member of the Combahee River Collective, a black feminist collective that had been meeting since 1974, Smith decided then and there that the Collective needed to respond to the murders. She returned to her apartment in Roxbury and began developing a pamphlet that would speak to the fears of black women in Boston.

What I wanted to do was to show that the whole thing wasn't just a racial issue and that violence against women is a pandemic thing. I quoted statistics on rape, etc. I tried to put it in language that would be easily accessible and recognizable to the black community. I typed it up on my little typewriter. I called up, read the pamphlet to [Collective members] over the phone. I started on Sunday; we laid it out that night.

The Combahee River Collective's pamphlet, which would be reproduced 40,000 times in two languages by the close of 1979, was, according to Smith, "the first thing to come out, widely distributed, . . . that was helpful to people about what *to do,* how to feel. . . . It was supportive." Entitled *Six Black Women: Why Did They Die?,* the pamphlet echoed Sara Small's cry of "Who is killing us?" while providing concrete analysis and strategies for survival:

In the black community the murders have often been talked about as solely racial or racist crimes. It's true that the police and media response has been typically racist. It's true that the victims were all black and that black people have always been targets of racist violence in this society, but they were also all women. Our sisters died because they were women just as surely as they died because they were black. . . .

An . . . idea that has been put out in this crisis is that women should stay in the house. . . . [This] punished the innocent and protects the guilty. It also doesn't take into account real life, that we must go to work, get food, pick up the kids. . . . Women should be able to walk outside wherever they please . . . for whatever reason. . . .

WE WILL ONLY HAVE THIS RIGHT WHEN WOMEN JOIN TOGETHER TO DEMAND OUR RIGHTS AS HUMAN BEINGS TO BE FREE OF PHYSICAL ABUSE, TO BE FREE OF FEAR. . . .

What men can do to "protect" us is to check out the ways in which they put down and intimidate women . . . and to tell men they know who mistreat women to stop it and stop it quick. Men who are committed to stopping violence against women should start *seriously* discussing this issue with other men and organizing. . . .

This was followed by a sixteen-point self-protection plan that included safety measures for traveling on foot or by cab, a list of common objects that could be used for self-defense, and emergency numbers. The back page of the pamphlet listed meetings in the community that were forming in response to the crisis, local self-defense classes and safe-houses for women, and anti-violence-against-women programs across the city.

The text of the pamphlet reflected years of consciousness raising as a collective. As early as 1973, Smith and a small core of Boston-based black lesbians had been seeking ways to explore and develop a politic that would illuminate their condition on the margin of white America. Originally part of the National Black Feminist Organization (NBFO), in 1975 the Collective separated from the organization, which was having difficulty sustaining itself nationally. The Combahee River Collective saw itself as taking a more radical position than the national organization, and, according to Smith, "because we were more left, we became an independent group." The core members of the group identified as black lesbian feminists. Smith recalls:

> We met every week at the Cambridge Women's Center. They were open meetings. . . . We did consciousness raising around black women's issues or looked at all issues from a black woman's perspective.
>
> The Collective never would have existed if it had been a multiracial organization. . . . You can't develop the politics. . . .
>
> I've known women of color groups that have existed all over this country and . . . what comes up early on is, is it open to white women? And the fatal mistake at that formative point [is to open it up].
>
> Because the thing is . . . sometimes you need to sit down and talk about what needs to happen here. I've had lovers of all different colors. . . . It doesn't matter who your lover is, you need to sit down and talk . . . and that's what we did.

In the mid-'70s, the Collective concentrated largely on consciousness raising, as women from all over the city came together in an effort to formulate analyses that peeled away at the multilayered texture of oppression bearing on their daily lives. As time went by, they put their developing politics into action. Smith explains that "whenever we saw an issue that impinged on the lives of black women, we tried to relate to it." Prior to the '79 murders, the Collective had been active in support work for Kenneth Edelin, a black doctor at Boston City Hospital who was arrested for manslaughter in the performance of an abortion. They were involved in the case of Ella Ellison, a black woman who was accused of murder because she had been seen in the area in which a homicide had been committed. Collective members picketed with the Third World Workers Coalition to ensure that black laborers would be hired for the construction of a new high school in the black community. Smith recalls:

> I'm a very political person. . . . I was younger then, I had a lot of energy. I wasn't writing then . . . Combahee was my primary political commitment and orientation. That and . . . reproductive-rights stuff, sterilization-abuse stuff, and my teaching. . . .
>
> Whatever was jumping off where race and sex and class intersected. Of course we were involved in Lesbian and Gay stuff, but not more so than everything else. . . . We were involved in a multiplicity of issues.

Smith believes that the kind of political work they had been doing previously made it possible for them to respond effectively to the murders. And while the Collective was not widely known or accepted in the black community, "because we were out lesbians and feminists," the pamphlet drew an overwhelmingly positive community response. It established the Collective as a vital organization in the eyes of both black and feminist groups that were formulating resistance to violence.

At the time, they were killing a black woman almost every week. Almost every time we took it to the printers, it was a different number and instead of whiting it out, y'know, making it all nice and shit, I said to Bev [Smith], we should just mark this out so that people can see the progression, 6–7–8–9. . . .

People really loved the pamphlet. It gave them a little ray of hope. It had information; it had analysis. Somebody was saying black women were important, and we care. And then a whole lot of organizing began to evolve.

Throughout the crisis, the Combahee River Collective's activism was both internal and external to the black community. Internally, the pamphlet was designed to equip women with information and resources, and to communicate the message that black women's lives were valuable. Externally, it was a signal to mainstream institutions that their inadequate coverage and response to the murders was unacceptable. As Smith remarks:

One of the things that most galled people was that, in the beginning, the first reports of the murders had been buried in the back of the *Boston Globe* with the racing reports. It was not news. That was about media! So, okay, you won't highlight this. . . . We had to put out our own stuff.

While the black community paper, the weekly *Bay State Banner,* recorded the details of the crisis on its front pages throughout the year, the *Boston Globe*'s coverage was uneven at best. The January 30 edition of the *Globe* noted the discovery of the bodies of Ricketts and Foye, then unidentified, on page 30 beside the racing forms, in a four-paragraph description entitled, "Two bodies found in trash bag." On January 31, the murder of Gwendolyn Yvette Stinson was noted on page 13 under "Dorchester girl found dead." Additionally, in these few paragraphs, the identities of Foye and Ricketts were revealed and the stabbing death of a woman outside of the Boston area was reported in something of a "p.s." fashion. Caren Prater's death, on February 6, finally warranted a small block on the front page, but what followed was a very confusing article about community outrage and police resources.

Further, the *Globe* added insult to injury when its only "feature" attention to the murders came on February 9, in a scathing column by popular reporter Mike Barnicle, which slammed the black community's criticism of police commitment to the case. Barnicle wrote:

The police are taking an awful beating from the people in the neighborhoods. Everyone seems to think that murders should be solved in minutes, just like on TV. . . .

Part of the problem lies in the fact that the normal flames of tension have been fanned and built into a small bonfire by the politicians. Especially Bill Owens. . . .

Owens would jump out of a building if he thought it would attract media attention. . . . A few nights ago, he was on TV saying that *he thought the mur-*

ders were connected. And if there were only black detectives working on the case, the solution would be almost immediate. . . .

Owens, left to his own devices, could turn *double parking into a crime wave. . . .*

Politicians and murder have never mixed well. And any time you have a politician dabbling in detective work and ending up on TV and in the papers, *you have somebody who is doing business with the devil.* (emphasis mine)

After this, save for a small February 17 article on community response to the murders, the *Globe* remained silent about the crisis until February 21, when Daryal Ann Hargett was found in her apartment. Then, the *Globe* reported the death of the fifth black woman in 30 days inside a small box in the lower left-hand corner of the front page, misspelling Hargett's first name.

Barbara Smith notes that while the local media response was limited, national coverage was worse:

> Even worse than the hostile coverage in the local media was the absolutely nonexistent coverage nationally. There was never a single line in national news magazines, newspapers or network television news. The attitude of the white males who control these means of communication was epitomized in a remark made by a male journalist from the *New York Times* bureau in Boston when asked to attend a press conference concerning the twelfth murder.
>
> "Twelve black women murdered. That's not news. I can call any city in this country and get that statistic."

Mike Barnicle's (and, ultimately, the *Globe*'s) cavalier dismissal of community outrage and of the conviction that the murders were connected exemplified the kind of racist denial that the white establishment maintained throughout the crisis. For Mayor White's police force, the concept of "connection" meant that a single crazed person was committing murder, again and again. For many members of the black community, the concept of connectedness was a broader, but equally palpable, phenomenon. Winston Kendall, chair of the National Conference of Black Lawyers, expressed his sense of this "connection":

> Conditions for black people in the U.S., in Boston, make way for genocide. You have to understand. We control nothing. We don't control our schools; we don't control the factories where we work; we don't control the stores where we spend our money; we don't control the still that produces the liquor that kills us. We control nothing. And if you don't control nothing, if you don't produce nothing, you are helping somebody to control you. This is why it is so convenient for somebody, some person to kill twelve black women. Because whoever they were, they knew fully well that the police department would not get very excited about the deaths of twelve black women. It is a testament to our powerlessness as a people.

The Combahee River Collective would add, "and a testimony to the widespread belief that black women's lives were valueless":

The combined sexism and racism that led the media to ignore the epidemic of murders in Boston is even more blatant when compared to the murders of black children in Atlanta and black men in Buffalo and elsewhere in 1980–81. Some of the same kind of victim-blaming tactics . . . occurred, but at least these murders were seen as newsworthy, even in some cases as a "national tragedy."

The Collective's analysis, that the Boston murders were inextricably bound to the politics of race and sex oppression, was a point of origin for the participation of feminist groups in organizing to stop the violence and provide safety for women in Boston. Working on the crisis from both within and without the black community, the Combahee River Collective would find itself acting as a bridge between nonfeminist community groups like CRISIS and white feminist organizations.

CRISIS

On that rainy April 1 afternoon, when 1,500 people marched to honor the memory of six black women, Marlene Stephens was full of emotion. It was an unbelievable day. Standing amidst her family and friends, she reflected on how it had all come together.

I have six children, and when the murders happened, I had just had my twin granddaughters. So it really hit home. Some of us woke up, got our papers, read about two girls who had been found, maimed, in plastic bags, and wrapped up in a bedspread, right on the street. So we were like—Jesus! The reaction was sort of individual, emotional. But then, almost on a weekly basis another woman, and another woman. . . . So we decided to have a community forum so that people could come talk about it. Some of their fears.

We had the first meeting at the Blackstone Community School. . . . The auditorium was full, there was a lot of anger. One of the women, Mrs. Muse, her daughter had been killed. The white media was saying that these girls were all prostitutes. . . .

From that meeting, some of us thought, okay, what can we do? So we began to meet at the Harriet Tubman House . . . to lay out the plans [for] CRISIS. We also felt that it was important to have a coming together of the community, not to walk in an angry demonstration but to show the families of the women that were killed that we were concerned. Also to show their youthful friends that we were concerned.

CRISIS consisted of a core group of five women, three with whom Mrs. Stephens was well acquainted. These were women who "communicated weekly," women whose lives had become entwined through years of activism in the black community around issues of public housing, health, and education. Marlene Stephens and the members of CRISIS awoke on the morning of the memorial walk and prepared for their first press conference with some anxiety.

The weather was not looking so good, and two recent incidents intensified their concerns about potential violence. According to Stephens:

> We were concerned because before we had the walk, a member of CRISIS was coming home after a gathering in a cab, and she made the mistake of not having the cab wait for her. It was about two A.M., the cab pulled out and two white men in a blue Volkswagen passed her and called her racial names. She just said, "Hey, black is beautiful." They stopped the car as she was trying to get the key in the door. They ran up the stairs and . . . beat her. One kicked her. She finally got in the door and the men ran.

Stephens herself had received racist threats. When she appeared on an edition of "Black News" to elicit support for the march, the taped program had not even concluded when her phone started ringing. She received three calls before the night was over, each threatening violence. She says:

> So that very cold April Sunday—very cold and rainy—I told my kids, look we're gonna walk. If nobody else walks, it'll be all of us. . . .
>
> So we went to the Harriet Tubman House . . . and kind of ad-libbed our way through the press conference and then we came out and I looked and [the place] was filling up! And somebody said, have you seen the folks outside? And I said outside? I couldn't believe it. . . .
>
> Fifteen hundred people walked with us. Fifteen hundred people! We didn't want to walk down to City Hall or to the Commons, we wanted to walk in our own neighborhoods. It was the most moving situation that I've ever been involved in in my life.

For Barbara Smith, of the Combahee River Collective, it was the failure to acknowledge sexist violence as a critical factor in the deaths of six black women that inspired her activism from this day. But for Marlene Stephens, it was the coming together of people in her community and the respectful support of outsiders that cemented her faith in CRISIS' mission and fueled her resistance.

The memorial walk established CRISIS as a vital, grassroots organization in the black community. Their weekly meetings, held at the Harriet Tubman House, brought activists from all over the community together in the sharing of resources, an airing of concerns, and the development of strategies for survival. Stephens recalls that as the organization grew, the grassroots orientation of CRISIS was challenged.

> CRISIS had been started by women of a grassroots perspective. We felt the way to organize was the community and three of us were folks that had worked in the community. We knew where the different services were and . . . that was very important.
>
> But then we had folks that joined us with their own political agenda—a recent graduate of Harvard Medical School along with some sisters who had graduated from Wellesley. . . . They would say, like, "we need to have a political agenda when we go out to tell people what CRISIS is doing."

I said, "Listen! Number one, you need to know the community you're organizing in. You might knock on a door and somebody doesn't want to talk about what you're talking about because they're having some serious problems—they have a kid who is sick. You need to know where the closest health center is and you need to have a contact there."

Stephens's activism, and that of CRISIS, were rooted in the realities of day-to-day life in the black neighborhoods of Boston. If CRISIS spoke most eloquently to the fears and the needs of Roxbury, Dorchester, and South End residents, it was an eloquence that stemmed from the people. Outsiders who endeavored to "improve" on CRISIS' politics, who brought the privilege of private education and an outsider's perspective to their politics, had much to learn from Marlene Stephens and her fellow activists. As Stephens recalls:

We had a meeting at one of the young women's houses. She was very strong and she said, "Y'know, we do everything you say!" So I said, "Whose problem is that? It's yours. If you can't deal with me, you can't organize, because I'm everywhere. In every inner city, you're gonna find me, a woman who's probably raised her children and . . . from dealing with the PTA to . . . that type of thing, has established her ground."

CRISIS' pamphlet, published some time after the Combahee River Collective's work, reflected that established ground. Along with weekly CRISIS meetings, the brochure listed a support group, held on a biweekly basis in the homes of CRISIS members. It explained its Street Rep program, urging people to develop communication networks on a block-by-block basis, including neighborhood watches and telephone trees. Fundraising ideas were elicited to help defray the costs of organizing, and most importantly, to help establish a trust fund for the families and children of the victims. CRISIS invited participation in their public-relations committee, which was designed to counter "media deception" locally and nationwide. Finally, the pamphlet offered a political analysis of the murders:

We of CRISIS are a group of residents of the Black community of Boston who have come together to organize around the immediate crisis: the murders of eleven sisters. . . . Our first goal is to develop a Communications Network throughout the Black community in the interest of safety. The long-term purpose of this Network is to change the conditions that led to these murders in the first place.

It is clear that this society encourages the abuse, rape and murder of women, and that Black women are especially victimized.

It is also clear that no one is going to improve the lot of Black folks in this country but ourselves, and that we can only do this together, not alone. . . .

The CRISIS brochure echoed the conviction of the Combahee River Collective that both racism and sexism were steering forces behind the deaths of black women in Boston. But, in contrast to the Collective's brochure, which called upon *women* to "join together and demand our rights," CRISIS proclaimed that *black people* must "unite or perish." CRISIS' focus came out of a long-standing tradition of black resistance to white supremacy as well as a history of antagonism between white feminists and black women activists. Stephens explains:

> I know I burned some women up here one time because I said I'm not a feminist and I think . . . people should understand what I'm saying. Some people's interpretation of feminism will make a woman of African descent such as myself back away. . . . I've heard feminists say things like, if you have a son over twelve years old, you can't bring him to the meeting. That's bizarre! That's ridiculous! What does that say to the woman who has a son—that she can't come! And maybe she needs to come!

That the implicit, and at times overt, separatism of (some) white feminist organizations is intolerable to black activists is clear in the work of both Stephens and Smith. The Collective's politics, though definitively feminist in contrast to Stephens's, acknowledged the centrality of racist oppression in the lives of black women. In an earlier article, "A Black Feminist Statement," the Collective wrote:

> We reject the stance of . . . separatism because it is not a viable political strategy for us. It leaves out far too much and far too many people, particularly Black men, women, and children. We have a great deal of criticism and loathing for what men have been socialized to be in this society: what they support, how they act, and how they oppress. But we do not have the misguided notion that it is maleness, per se—i.e., their biological maleness—that makes them what they are. As Black women we find any type of biological determinism a particularly dangerous and reactionary basis upon which to build a politic.

However, as black lesbians, members of the Collective were targets of heterosexist oppression within the black community and found support and refuge among some white feminists and lesbians. They did not share Marlene Stephens's faith that the unification of black people would eradicate violence against black women. As black women whose lives were vilified and devalued among black people, they saw coalitions between blacks and white feminists and lesbians as critical to their survival. They saw as essential to the politics of each of these groups a delving into the differences and the shared oppressions that worked on all of their lives. As the crisis intensified, the Collective would find itself in the position of acting as a bridge between blacks and whites, feminists and nonfeminists, heterosexuals and lesbians, as women and men throughout Boston labored to save the lives of black women.

THE COALITION FOR WOMEN'S SAFETY

The white feminists who brought up the rear of the April 1 memorial march had not come as a group. Some had traveled a short distance from their homes, and were moved and alarmed by the words spoken about these women who had lived and died in their midst. Others, from the predominantly white, more affluent communities of Cambridge, Jamaica Plain, and Somerville, were outraged by the statistics that were mounting so rapidly, and dismayed by the lack of attention to the role of sexism in the murders. Many wondered how they fit into the tragedy. As women, they identified along the lines of vulnerability with the black women who had been killed. As feminists, they felt that their politics compelled active resistance. And somewhere, inside the miles and words of that cold April Sunday, came resolve. Soon after, the ad-hoc meetings that had been held at Women, Inc., in Roxbury, crystalized into a formal organization, the Coalition for Women's Safety.

The Coalition brought together women from all over the city: from Jamaica Plain, Somerville, Roxbury, Dorchester, and the South End. Its purpose was, they wrote, to:

> coordinate efforts of various community groups working to end violence against women and to build a citywide network of people committed to solving the problems of racism, sexism, and violence in the city.
>
> We recognize the destructive role that both racism and sexism play in keeping us divided, and we are committed to opposing them, both in our internal process and in our program.

The Coalition saw its mission as that of an educational/outreach organization which supported the work of each of its member groups. For example, Coalition members did the footwork for the massive pamphlet distribution needs of the Combahee River Collective. They worked on the safehouse programs of both the Dorchester and Jamaica Plain Greenlight organizations. The Coalition also initiated its own programs, which included a Women's Safety Month that was publicized through the Massachusetts Transit Authority. Coalition members worked with transit and police officials to develop a crime prevention brochure that advocated women's resistance to violent attacks.

Susan Moir, a representative from Dorchester Greenlight, recalls the emphasis on resistance in the brochure as a major gain in their work with the Boston police. Until this time, all police crime-prevention materials suggested that a woman's best defense against crimes of violence was compliance. Materials produced by this collaborative effort suggested otherwise.

> In the event that you are attacked, there are several natural defenses that will help. As your number one defense, SCREAM. Scratch with your fingernails, bite him if a hand comes near to your mouth. Kick with the point of your shoe . . . or knee him in the groin. If you happen to have a sharp object in your hand, such as keys, try to use it to scratch his face. Screaming may be enough, since it will attract attention, and hopefully scare him off. . . .

Moir remembers the group as one of the most committed, hardworking coalitions of activists with which she had ever been associated. She notes, "It changed the way a lot of us do our work."

Central to that change was the forthright airing of differences among Coalition members who were white, black and Latina, middle class and working class, young and old, lesbian and heterosexual, feminist and nonfeminist. Moir did not see herself as a typical white feminist in the group. Having lived in multiracial neighborhoods in Roxbury and Dorchester most of her life, she perceived her activism as fundamentally different from that of the middle-class white feminists who hailed from predominantly white neighborhoods in Boston. An active socialist, her perception of tensions between herself and other members of the Coalition stemmed more from class differences than race.

> What violence meant was different depending on where you were sitting. In a sense, the [middle-class] outrage about physical violence per se was very elitist. [It] showed a lack of understanding of the breadth of violence in our day-to-day lives. The housing situation in Boston, for instance, is at crisis proportions. People are living in unfinished cellars, ratholes. Lack of decent housing and health care is day-to-day violence.

While Moir's perspective harkens the grassroots focus of CRISIS, for Marlene Stephens, race differences were at the bottom of group tensions.

> There were some . . . serious differences, like for instance, we had a "Take Back the Night" march and many of the black women didn't participate. We talked about it in the beginning; we felt like some of the first marches were really anti-male and we felt like our struggle could not exclude [men]. Also . . . and this still goes on . . . often when white activists are involved, they want to say, "Well, this is the way I feel like it should be done." And we tell them, "Well maybe from your experience, but from our experience, that's not the way it goes."

Barbara Smith's journal entry shows yet another perception of how difference worked against coalition building.

> March 19, 1979—Random thoughts: Violence against us is overwhelming. A sixth woman was murdered last week. Racism from white women and homophobia from Black people is a vice that will choke the Black feminist movement.

Homophobia had surfaced among the members of CRISIS, but Stephens, whose association with Smith had spanned several years, voiced her opposition:

> At [this] CRISIS meeting, men and some of the women were saying that we don't think CRISIS should be associated with lesbians and white feminists, so I said, "Look, now . . . you all don't know anything about me; you don't know if I'm straight or what. Listen, I could go home and sleep with a gorilla—we have some work laid out here to do, our community is in crisis." That's what I said and people . . . just backed off.

The relationship between Smith and Stephens grew out of a mutual respect for the way each woman worked within the black community. Stephens's respect for Smith was critical to combatting homophobic divisiveness and legitimating black feminist activism among her peers. White feminists, however, had a different path to forge in gaining the trust of the black community. Smith wrote of one community meeting:

> The meeting at Harriet Tubman last night was so intense. . . . At one point, a young Black woman made some statements indicating her distrust of the white women there, talked about the bad faith that had occurred in other movements.
>
> This is the major issue. Trust and following through. If white feminists ever needed to have their act together, it's now. I have faith in a lot of women, because I know their politics, their commitments. But it all has got to be proven.

Through their work in the Coalition, white feminists worked hard at gaining that trust. In conjunction with a member group, the Dorchester Youth Alliance, they worked on a video on safety aimed at teenage girls. The Coalition ran workshops for teenage girls and boys on how to respond to violence. The Somerville Women's Center offered rides to women living in high-risk areas and lent space and other resources to those in need of support. In the summer of 1979, the Coalition sponsored a "Run For Women's Safety" to help defray the high cost of organizing for its member group, CRISIS.

Marlene Stephens recalls her twin granddaughters' participation in the "run."

> Aja and Jasmine, from the very beginning, they went to meetings with me. . . . We had a Women's Run and I had people sponsor me to push them. Margo and Sandy, friends of Barbara [Smith]'s, they had two little t-shirts made for them that said "Women's Run." So . . . not only are we activists, we're a family. We all try to keep up with what the others are doing. And I really feel like the basic respect we all have for each other will continue. Out of our pain, we became an extended family.

Susan Moir shares Stephens's feeling that mutual respect laid the foundation for the Coalition's accomplishments. Two years after the crisis, when the Coalition finally dispersed, she remembers: "We even broke up respectfully."

The text of the Coalition's statement at an August "Take Back The Night" rally reflected that respect:

> We should all be inspired by the fact that we have come together tonight—women from all races, ages, different communities and different classes—and marched to show our power, our strength, our unity and determination to end violence against women. We are each other's inspiration. . . .
>
> The losses of the past year have been painful ones. You do not need to be reminded of the slaying of twelve Black women and two white women since January, or of the eight rapes reported in the Allston/Brighton area between December and February. . . .

The legal system which we have been taught to rely on for our safety and justice betrays us constantly. The racist actions by the police force in framing and arresting Black men, as in the case of Willie Sanders [arrested for four of the eight Allston rapes in a police frame-up] does not insure women's safety. Safety does not mean arresting a Black man on very flimsy charges. That only perpetuates the rampant racism of this society. We will not be appeased with unjust arrests. We will not have our demand for safety pitted against a community which has little power in this society. We want to be safe—and safety means preventing rapes, preventing murders and beatings, preventing harassment. It means creating a society in which those actions are not condoned.

Clearly the state cannot be relied upon to provide women's safety. We must do that ourselves. Our efforts of the past year have shown that by unifying our energy, women can build strength, take power, and accomplish victories across race and class lines.

It is a testament to the effective, good-faith organizing that occurred throughout 1979 that 5,000 women were in attendance when the Coalition's statement was read. However, while women of color participated in the march, the protestors were predominantly white. The *Bay State Banner* reported a variety of opinions within the black community about the action, which concluded in the South End's Blackstone Park:

Black marchers and observers held many different opinions about the event, ranging from enthusiasm to refusal to participate. . . .

A member of one group within the Coalition for Women's Safety who attended as an individual said she and others in her organization sensed a strong anti-male bias among the marchers, and that many preferred not to be identified with such a position.

As Black people they also noticed that while many involved with this event are fighting against sexist behavior . . . these same women do not seem as committed to resisting racism. . . .

Betty McKenzie, a Roxbury resident . . . expressed disappointment at the refusal of some Black women to march because they felt "this is a white woman's thing." The issue of women's safety "transcends" these distinctions, she said.

Throughout the crisis, the Coalition for Women's Safety emphasized combatting violence against women with education and grassroots support networks. For the white feminist membership, the multiracial make-up of the Coalition and the analysis of women who identified as black feminists challenged and enriched their conception of feminist activism. Black feminists and nonfeminists, while at times skeptical and conflicted about white feminist analysis and tactics, grew to respect the Coalition's white membership by virtue of hard, honest work. And while divergent replies to Sarah Small's question, "Who is killing us?" prevailed, the conception of "us," among these women, bonded through resistance, gained depth and diversity.

EPILOGUE

By the close of 1979, seven black men had been arrested for the murder of eight of the twelve black women killed. James "Ali" Brown was acquitted in the murder of Yvette Stinson, in a case where an eyewitness testified to his guilt. Brown was gunned down on the street several weeks later. Dennis "Jamal" Porter was convicted for the deaths of Christine Ricketts and Andrea Foye, in a case built entirely on circumstantial evidence. Kenneth Spann was convicted in the murder of Caren Prater despite a woman juror's reply of "Guilty, with reservations."

The arrests did little to calm the fears of the black community or to quell suspicions that there was somehow a stronger connection between the murders. As the case developed, it was learned that many of the victims had known each other. It seemed that a very large percentage of the women were raped and strangled. Of Spann's conviction, Caren Prater's stepmother remarked that it was hard to believe, a black man, killing her daughter. Sara Small expressed the sentiments of many members of the black community when she explained the circumstances surrounding her niece, Daryal's death: Ms. Hargett had been found by her white landlord, who had come by her apartment and seen Hargett lying on her bedroom floor, naked. Thinking that the woman was "sleeping," he closed the door. He returned later, to find her in the same position and once again left her as she was. Finally, returning to his own residence, he felt that perhaps something was "wrong" and returned to Hargett's apartment, accompanied by the police. There, they found her in the same position, strangled. Mrs. Small wondered:

> All the time, the police focused on a hunt for some black man in the community and paid no attention to the landlord's story. He said he kept going back to her apartment because he thought he left his checkbook in there. If I pay you rent, what is your checkbook doin' in my apartment? The whole story seemed thin to me.

None of the community organizations involved in the crisis spent much time or faith on the Boston police or the criminal justice system. Their activism was aimed at compelling the city administration to be more responsive to racist and sexist violence, but their energies were largely focused on equipping those at risk with resources and safety networks. And while none of the community groups definitively solved the mystery of "Who is killing us?", they managed to redefine the terms of the question, bringing a range of potential answers into focus. In doing so, they countered mainstream perceptions of black women as "them," vigorously claiming and honoring their connection to these women whose lives had been extinguished in their midst.

Annihilation by Murder and by the Media:
The Other Atlanta Femicides

DIANA E. H. RUSSELL AND CANDIDA ELLIS

Between late 1978 and 1980, when official attention was focused on the serial killings of the 26 African-American males whose murders are commonly referred to as the "Atlanta Child Murders,"[1] the bodies of 38 girls and women were found in that city.[2] The majority of these victims were young African-Americans, although their ages ranged from 14 to 60, and 4 were white.[3] At the same time that the police in Atlanta were expressing satisfaction that they had found the killer (Wayne Williams) of the 26 murdered African-American males (aged 7 to 27), the 38 femicides remained ignored and unsolved.

Allegations have been made that this figure of 38 is far too low. In 1981 Atlanta mayoral candidate Mildred Glover said of the overlooked female victims: "The potential number is so staggering that it's likely to be the worst problem of unsolved murders in the history of any U.S. city." Including the bodies of all African-American female victims found during this period in the suburbs and in the neighboring counties (as male victims from outlying areas were included in the Atlanta child murders tally) would significantly increase the total. Glover conceded that the numbers were "even greater than epidemic proportions. . . . We need to look at these cases of females, just as we do the males, and see if there's a common thread that may help solve them. . . . It's something that has crossed racial lines," added Glover. "It has caught a lot of us sleeping."[4]

Most of the 38 girls and women had been strangled or stabbed to death; one 15-year-old had been shot. All of them had been killed in suburban De Kalb County, where some of the bodies of the African-American males had been found.

In response to public pressure from African-Americans charging "that the police were not pursuing the killer" of the Atlanta Child Murder victims, a special police task force was organized and the FBI lent assistance to efforts to apprehend the killer(s).[5] No such pressure seems to have been applied to any agency in regard to the female victims. If the special police task force accepted these additional 38 (or more) cases for consideration, its investigation must have been unsuccessful since no killer or killers have been identified, and few people appear to have any knowledge of these atrocities.

The identification of Wayne Williams as the perpetrator in the murders of the 26 African-American males has been criticized by some as a questionable conclusion to a sloppy investigation. Critics claim that the deaths of African-Americans were privately regarded as insignificant by racist authorities. But near-universal apathy over the slaughter of more than 38 mostly African-American females exposes the complicity of both sexism and racism.

Those who previously condemned official indifference to the deaths of young African-American males are united by their present silence with those who hold African-American lives cheap. Because of this solidarity of disinterest, African-American females can be slain with impunity.

Those readers who are antiracist and antisexist can break the shocking silence surrounding these femicides by demanding information about the deaths and by insisting on the kind of thorough investigation that should have instantly followed them. Indifference by the police and the media to this slaughter of women reveals the extent to which racist sexism, or sexist racism, continues to flourish in the United States.

Notes

1. "Mass Murderers from the Past." *San Francisco Chronicle,* 10 June 1985.

2. "The Other Unsolved Atlanta Murders," an article published in the *San Francisco Chronicle,* 15 June 1981, was the only source we could find on these femicides.

3. Ibid.

4. Ibid.

5. "Mass Murderers from the Past." *San Francisco Chronicle,* 10 June 1985.

Femicidal Rapist Targets Asian Women

DIANA E. H. RUSSELL

In 1973 a white serial rapist attacked a number of women in the Nob Hill area of San Francisco. Nicknamed the Nob Hill Rapist, he attacked only Asian women, with the exception of one white woman "who was saved when her screams attracted passers-by."[1] By the time he followed Yoshika Tanaka to the door of her apartment on 27 March 1973, he had already raped another Asian woman in the Nob Hill area and had attempted to rape at least two others.[2]

When Tanaka resisted his attempt to rape her, he stabbed her 15 times and left her for dead. Sex-crime inspectors commented that they "had never known a victim to survive 'such a brutal and vicious attack.' "[3] The following account, written by Keith Powers for the *San Francisco Chronicle,* recounts the details.

> A beautiful Japanese coed remained in critical condition yesterday after surviving a frenzied knife attack by a rapist who has been prowling the Nob Hill neighborhood for two weeks.
>
> Yoshika Tanaka, 19, formerly of Tokyo, a student at San Francisco University, was under intensive care at San Francisco General Hospital for two dozen stab wounds over her upper body and face. . .
>
> The attacker, described as a white man in his mid 20s, used four knives and broke off the blades of two of them in the girl's body, according to Inspectors Chris Sullivan and Don Kennealy.
>
> The officers laboriously pieced together the story of the attack from the girl, who can't speak but was able to communicate through a note and nodded responses to questions.
>
> As a result, the inspectors know of one important identification mark on the attacker—Miss Tanaka said she bit him severely on the tongue when he tried to kiss her. . . .

Selection from "Nob Hill Rapist's Four-Knife Attack" is by Keith Powers. © *San Francisco Chronicle.* Reprinted by permission.

Sullivan and Kennealy have appealed to doctors in the Bay Area to contact the police if they are asked to treat such a wound or hear about treatment being given. . . .

Officers said Miss Tanaka was seized sometime Tuesday afternoon at the door of her ground-floor apartment at 1031 Leavenworth Street.

Inside, she was ordered to undress and when she resisted his sexual assault, the attacker began stabbing her. . . .

The attacker left Miss Tanaka for dead, police said, but she revived and managed to crawl to a neighbor's apartment about 6:30 P.M.

The suspect is described as being white with fair hair, 5 feet 6 inches tall and about 25 years old. In all the attacks he wore dark gloves.[4]

Two weeks later, on 15 April, a 25-year-old married Chinese woman, Guey Yueh, left her job checking hats at the Union Square Hyatt House in San Francisco after her shift ended at midnight.[5] On returning home, Yueh was stabbed to death in the lobby of her apartment building on Pine Street, where she was found by neighbors. They heard Yueh's screams and saw her assailant running away. Presumably it was one of these neighbors who reported the murder to the police. Yueh's husband, also a Hyatt House employee, was at work when the attack occurred.[6]

Yueh had been stabbed above her right wrist and in her heart. The police believed that the so-called Nob Hill rapist had struck again, this time succeeding in killing his victim. The description of his appearance that the neighbors gave to the police was close to the description Tanaka had given them while she was still recovering in San Francisco Hospital. In addition, the methods of both attacks were similar.[7]

On 24 April Yoshiko Tanaka was released from the hospital after "nearly dying of her wounds." She had been stabbed in her heart, liver, spleen, lung, and jugular vein. She still spoke in a hoarse whisper "because of a wound in her throat."[8] Tanaka subsequently picked out John Bunyard's photograph from a set of eight, identifying him less than a month after he had left her for dead.

Bunyard, a delivery truck driver earning $4.40 per hour, was charged with two murders, two rapes, and ten kidnappings, as well as with disarming and stealing the revolvers of two policemen and shooting at officers during his 500-mile flight.[10]

Bunyard's trial over a year later, on 25 May 1974, was transferred to San Bernardino in Southern California on the grounds that the pretrial publicity made it impossible for him to receive a fair trial in San Francisco. Yoshiko Tanaka's testimony was presented to the court in a videotape made before she returned to her homeland in Japan shortly after her release from the hospital. This was only the second time in California that testimony had been given in this form.[11]

Bunyard was found guilty of six felony charges after a two-week trial and was sentenced to 15 years to life in prison.[12] This term was to be served concurrently with two other sentences of 21 years to life for two murders and a variety of other offenses committed during a three-day spree in April 1973 that extended from the San Francisco Bay Area to Lake Tahoe.[13]

The news articles about Bunyard written at the time offered no explanation of what might have motivated him to target Asian women. Instead, a hard-luck story about Bunyard's history of rejection appears, essentially implying a cause-and-effect relationship between rejection by one's family and rape and murder of Asian women.[14]

The newspaper coverage also included interviews with neighbors, all of whom maintained that Bunyard could not possibly have committed such crimes. His next-door neighbor, for example, explained to *San Francisco Chronicle* reporter Kevin Leary that Bunyard "didn't have to rape anyone. . . . He turned down more women than most men pick up."[15] Bunyard's neighbor appears to have subscribed to the common myth that rape is an expression of sexual desire.

More than three years after his sentencing, Bunyard spoke from his cell in Soledad Prison about why men rape and about his long history of incarceration. This account does not support his neighbors' perceptions of him. He became a ward of the California Youth Authority at age seven, and at nine was sent to a reformatory for young offenders. "From then on, he says he can't remember being out of custody more than eight consecutive months."[16]

Bunyard is reported to have told a guard, "Releasing me from prison is like putting a puppy out on a freeway."[17] This description is even less appropriate than his neighbors'. According to the police, "he raped 50 or more women and killed three or four in addition to the two women he was convicted of killing."[18] The police reported that Bunyard perpetrated all these crimes during the six months he was out on parole in 1973. There is no information about whether his victims were predominantly Asian. The articles about him were written at a time when there was far less consciousness than now about racist hate crimes.

Notes

1. "Woman Stabbed to Death–Nob Hill Rapist Feared," *San Francisco Chronicle*, 16 April 1973.

2. Ibid.

3. Keith Powers, "Nob Hill Rapist's Four-Knife Attack," *San Francisco Chronicle*, 29 March 1973.

4. Ibid.

5. "Woman Stabbed to Death."

6. Ibid.

7. Ibid.

8. Charles Petit, " 'Nob Hill' Suspect Charged—Bail Is Set at $1 Million," *San Francisco Chronicle*, 24 April 1973.

9. Ibid.

10. Petit, " 'Nob Hill' Suspect Charged," and Kevin Leary, "The Neighbors Think Rape Suspect Is Innocent," *San Francisco Chronicle*, 24 April 1973.

11. Ibid.

12. "Bunyard Guilty in Nob Hill Case," *San Francisco Chronicle*, 25 May 1974.

13. Ibid.

14. Bruce Benedict, "His Record Goes Back to Kindergarten," *San Francisco Chronicle*, 24 April 1973.

15. Leary, "Neighbors Think."

16. Jim Wood, "He Tells You Why Men Rape," San Francisco Examiner, 25 September 1977.

17. Ibid.

18. Ibid.

Slavery and Femicide

DIANA E. H. RUSSELL

Most people believe that slavery no longer exists in the United States. This is because the term slavery in this country connotes white people owning African-Americans primarily for the purpose of exploiting their labor in the fields. This perception prevails despite the fact that it was also commonplace for white slave owners to rape their female slaves, thereby adding to their slave harvest.

Although cases of this classic form of slavery still find their way into U.S. newspapers from time to time, sexual exploitation has become the primary factor in most instances of slavery today, and females are the primary victims. This practice used to be called white slavery, but feminists renamed it "female sexual slavery" following the publication in 1979 of Kathleen Barry's book, *Female Sexual Slavery*.[1] While nonsexual labor is part of the exploitation in instances of female sexual slavery, the exploitation of females is primarily of a sexual nature, usually entailing forced prostitution. Sometimes these women and girls are purchased; other times they are seduced, manipulated, deceived, or simply kidnapped and held captive. The case described below, based on events reported in *Jet* magazine[2] and the *San Francisco Chronicle*,[3] is reminiscent of the classic form of slavery because the women were all African-Americans and their captor was a white man.

When the police raided a two-story house in North Philadelphia in 1987, they discovered three half-starved, partially naked African-American women in the basement. The women were shackled to a sewer pipe in this secret torture chamber. The police also found 24 pounds of human limbs in a freezer in the kitchen and other body parts in a stewpot and oven. Some of the walls of the house were papered with $1 and $5 bills.

The police had been alerted by a fourth captive, 26-year-old Josephine Rivera, after she managed to escape one night from the fancy car of her captor. She and the other three women—Jacquelyn Atkins, 18, Lisa Thomas, 19, and

Agnes Adams, 24—told the police about being tortured, starved, raped, and beaten during their captivity of up to four months. The women's nourishment had consisted of dog food, bread, and water. They also told the police that two other women had died in captivity, "one electrocuted in a watery pit underneath the cellar's concrete floor, the other killed in a fall."

These women had been lured into this mini-concentration camp by Gary Heidnik, a 43-year-old white man who was a self-ordained bishop in his self-made church—the United Church of the Ministries of God. His kidnap strategy involved "flashing wads of money" while driving around an impoverished neighborhood in a Rolls Royce or a Cadillac. Lisa Thomas reported that she had entered his car willingly "because of his show of wealth." On returning to his house, Thomas recounted that "he handcuffed me to a pipe and said nothing would happen to me if I cooperated."

Gary Heidnik was arrested with 31-year-old Cyril Brown, an African-American man who described Heidnik as his best friend. Both were charged with rape and kidnap, as well as with the murder of the two women who were believed to have been killed in Heidnik's house. The murdered women were identified as 23-year-old Deborah Dudley, "whose body was found in a remote wooded area in New Jersey, and Sandra Lindsay, 24, who authorities said had been butchered and parts of her body left in Heidnik's kitchen."

On 2 July 1988, after "the jury rejected his attorney's argument that Heidnik, a near genius with an IQ of 148, was insane," Heidnik was found guilty of two counts of first-degree murder, kidnapping, and aggravated assault.[4] No mention was made of what happened to his co-arrestee, Cyril Brown.

Prior to his self-appointed role as a bishop, Heidnik had been a nurse and a psychiatric patient, and in 1978 he had been convicted of kidnapping a mentally disabled woman. At the time of his apprehension with Cyril Brown, he was a rich man. Police found documents in his home showing an account worth approximately $500,000. He is reported to have used his money-making talent to turn a $1,500 savings account into more than $550,000 during an 11-year period.

The response of Heidnik's 74-year-old father, Michael Heidnik—described as "a former suburban Cleveland councilman"—to the news of his son's barbaric behavior was that he should be hanged. " 'I'll even pull the rope,' " he is reported to have said.

Despite the efforts of feminists, most people appear to be much less outraged by female sexual slavery than by the classic form of slavery that, although belatedly, many people fought to outlaw. When females are the primary target of abuse, it is apt to be treated as less shocking than when males are targeted. And when the victims are poor and black, the treatment is even more casual or disinterested (as Candida Ellis and I note in "Annihilation by Murder and by the Media: The Other Atlanta Femicides," earlier in part 3). Perhaps by publicizing the savagery acted out by racist misogynists like Heidnik, people can be shaken out of their apathy about the continuing international problem of female sexual slavery.

Notes

1. Kathleen Barry, *Female Sexual Slavery* (Englewood Cliffs, N.J.: Prentice-Hall, 1979).

2. "Black Women Report of Sex, Torture, Murder at Hands of White Philadelphia 'Bishop,' " *Jet*, 13 April 1987.

3. "Grisly Philadelphia Slave Case Ends," *San Francisco Chronicle*, 2 July 1988.

4. Ibid.

American Indian Women Killing:
A Tewa Native Woman's Perspective

BEVERLY R. SINGER

Traditionally, if a man beat his wife, he could expect severe retribution from her family and he would be made to feel ashamed by the community. If he continued, his wife could leave him and not feel like she was a failure as a wife and homemaker. Today we have fallen away from a lot of traditional values and beliefs; a man can beat his wife near death and receive no punishment.

> —Flier from the Sacred Shawl Women's Society
> (Maria N. Powers, 1986)

Silence, born of repression, best describes the state that American Indian women have maintained, until recently, about the violence in our lives. Mostly the silence can be attributed to fear. Since the 1970s there has been some openness and activism around the abuse of Indian women, yet, on the issue of femicide, silence prevails.

Contemporary femicide of American Indian women involves two types: the murders of Indian women by Indian men, and the murder of Indian women by non-Indian men. I will be dealing with the first type here and will argue that the killing of Indian women by Indian men is rooted in the original genocide, conquest, and colonization of American Indians by Europeans and their descendants. The result of that colonization has been the destruction of traditional social patterns and largely egalitarian gender relations (Bonvillain 1989) among the Native peoples. Five hundred years of genocide and colonization has inculcated self-hate, resentment, fear, and violence among American Indians and taught Indian men the new-American styles of male aggression and dominance, including femicide.

There is no comprehensive research on the numbers of Indian women who have been killed in femicidal assaults. Rather, we hear of them largely through word of mouth or randomly in news reporting. For example, we inadvertently discover woman abuse, child abuse, and femicide in the news coverage surrounding an episode of American Indian adolescent suicide. In 1985, on the Wind River Reservation in Wyoming, nine Indian youths killed themselves within an eight-week period. The adoptive mother of one of the suicide victims, 15-year-old Sherry Badhawk, told the *Boston Globe* (1985): "She came from a hard home, they lived gypsy-like always moving around from one place to another. . . . He [her biological father] abused all [five] of the kids . . . and Sherry was worried about her mom." According to subsequent reports, after Sherry's suicide, her natural mother was beaten to death by Sherry's father. The mother's death is primary femicide, and her abused daughter's suicide is a secondary form of femicide.

Stories involving incest, rape, and murder of Indian women are more likely to be reported in American Indian newspapers published by a particular tribe. In the fall of 1979, the *Navajo Times* ran a story indicating that rape was the number-one crime on the Navajo reservation. Femicides and other acts of aggressive violence directed at Indian women are not limited to the reservation, however. Two years ago, a colleague, a teacher in Chicago, mentioned to me that four young Indian women, one of whom she knew as her student, were gang-raped and murdered at separate times within a few weeks of each other. She went on to say that the community had never suspected and were shocked when police informed them that the assailants were young American Indian men.

Aggressive acts of violence coupled with the murder of Indian women off the reservation often go unrecognized in mainstream news reporting. When women of color are killed, little attention is paid to these crimes in the news media and we hardly hear about them in comparison with the femicidal murders of white middle-class women. A woman in Albuquerque, New Mexico, who worked in the coroner's office noted that during 1985–86 at least five American Indian women (mostly Navajo) had been raped and killed and their bodies dumped in the Jemez Mountains about 60 miles northwest of the city. These stories received virtually no news coverage. I had not heard about these murders despite the fact that I was attending the University of New Mexico in Albuquerque at that time.

The Special Initiatives Mental Health Team of the Indian Health Service, a division of the U.S. Public Health Service, recognizes that the problem of murder is a serious one for Indian communities. As stated in a 1988 report, "Although rates fluctuate across [American] Indian communities, between 1981 and 1983, age-adjusted . . . homicide rates for all American Indians were . . . two times higher" than all other groups in the United States (DeBryun, Hymbaugh, and Valdex 1988, 56). Data are limited for American Indian women as a specific group. Some figures for cases of domestic violence and sexual assault are maintained by individual Indian Health Service units on or near reservations. Newer community programs like the Native American Women's Health Education Resource Center in Lake Andes, South Dakota, located on the Yankton Sioux Reservation, have begun compiling their own data. Established in 1985, the center reported in 1989 that 50–70 percent of all murders in South Dakota are family related, of those, approximately 50 percent involve American Indians. The center also reports that there is no domestic violence shelter in their community of 5,000 residents. The nearest shelter to the east is 71 miles away, and to the west, 150 miles away. On 12 September 1991 the center opened a women's shelter despite heavy criticism and racially motivated resistance from the white township of Lake Andes, South Dakota.

Homicide rates in Alaska are higher for all female groups than in all other states except Hawaii. For Alaskan Indian females, the rate is seven times the U.S. white female rate. The researchers Forbes and Van Der Hyde (1988) comment: "Violent death other than suicide is common in Alaska's frontier environment" (44).

These researchers' findings, as well as their references to the "frontier," recall to me the murders of American Indian women during the westward European-American advances through Indian homelands at the end of the nineteenth century. Personal diary accounts of U.S. military men involved in the campaign against Indians are presented in Dee Brown's *Bury My Heart at Wounded Knee* (1979): "There were thirty or forty squaws collected in a hole for protection; they sent out a little girl about six years old with a white flag on a stick; she had not proceeded but a few steps when she was shot and killed. . . . I saw one squaw cut open with an unborn child. . . . I saw one squaw whose privates had been cut out."

The national policy of extermination, coupled with the U.S. use of armed forces in its attempt to eliminate the next generation of American Indians, ensured particularly savage attacks on native women. This original policy of genocide continues in today's society, but in disguised ways. An example is the "nontherapeutic" sterilizations performed on hundreds of young Indian women without their consent by doctors at the Indian Health Service Hospital in Claremore, Oklahoma, in 1975. Approximately 75 percent of the sterilizations performed by the Indian Health Service doctors were a form of population control that the doctors themselves acknowledged (Weyer 1982, 194–200). This forced sterilization of Indian women, while not direct femicide, decimated their bodies' procreative function.

The genocide of American Indians instituted by white male arrogance through historical policy-making and military design has far-reaching effects for contemporary Indian people. Physical survival and cultural survival are at stake. What was a deliberate unconscionable act in history, I suggest, was learned through example by American Indian men whose psychological self-hate made them susceptible to such lessons and who now mirror white men in femicidal behaviors. Indian males committing femicides are engaging in sexist murder and perpetuating a self-inflicted genocide, continuing the unspoken policy of extermination as practiced in the United States against American Indians.

References

Bonvillain, Nancy. 1989. "Gender Relations in Native North America." *American Indian Culture and Research Journal* 13 (2): 1–28.

Boston Globe, 8 October 1985.

Brown, Dee. 1979. *Bury My Heart at Wounded Knee: An Indian History of the American West*. New York: Bantam.

DeBryun, LeMyra, Karen Hymbaugh, and Norma Valdex. 1988. "Helping Communities Address Suicide and Violence: The Special Initiatives Team of the Indian Health Service." *American Indian and Alaska Native Mental Health Research* (journal of the National Center, University of Colorado Health Services Center, Denver, Colo.) 1 (3): 56–65.

Forbes, Norman, and Vincent Van Der Hydge. 1988. "Suicide in Alaska from 1978 to 1985: Updated from State Files." *American Indian and Alaska Native Mental Health Research* 1 (3): 36–55.

Native American Women's Health Education Resource Center. 1990. "Native American Health Education Prevention Program" (a project of the Native American Community Board, Lake Andes, S.D.).

Old Dog Cross, Phyllis. "Sexual Abuse, a New Threat to the Native American Indian Woman: An Overview." *Listening Post: A Periodical of the Mental Health Programs of Indian Heal Services* 6, no. 2 (April 1982): 18.

Powers, Marla N. 1986. *Oglala Women: Myth, Ritual, and Reality*. Chicago: University of Chicago Press.

Weyer, Rex. 1982. *Blood of the Land: The Government and Corporate War against the American Indian Movement*. New York: Random House.

Part 4

❖ ❖ ❖

THE MASS MEDIA, PORNOGRAPHY, AND GORENOGRAPHY

Memorial march for women murdered in spring 1979 in Boston's multiracial neighborhoods, with marchers protesting local media coverage of the murders. Photo Ellen Shub.

Introduction

Feminists have long been critical of media representations of women, particularly in relation to the treatment of violence against women. The readings in part 4 focus on the treatment of femicide, specifically, by the media. The first contributions offer a critical perspective on various aspects of the reporting on femicide; the latter address pornography, a controversial topic among feminists.

Part 4 opens with Sandra McNeill's analysis of the press coverage of a cluster of incidents in the north of England in which husbands killed their wives and then themselves. She identifies the exclusively male perspective that informed the reporting: the male killers were depicted as tragic heroes, dying for love and the cause of family unity, and the female victims were largely ignored.

Deborah Cameron's critique of another media event follows. She writes about the centenary in 1989 of Jack the Ripper, the nineteenth-century English serial killer whose identity was never established. This reading exposes the virtual celebration of the killer as folk hero or legend and the neglect of his female victims.

The next contribution addresses the arrival in the United States of "snuff" films—films depicting the apparently real torture and killing of women as sexual entertainment for men. Beverly LaBelle examines feminist protest against snuff as a form of feminist resistance to femicide. Chris Domingo then offers a historical analysis of the racist and sexist attitudes that consider serial murder, rape-murder, and femicide to be forms of public entertainment. The final selection, by Jane Caputi, like those by LaBelle and Domingo, draws connections between pornography, sexual violence, and femicide. Caputi identifies the sexualization of femicide in snuff pornography and indicts libertarian interests that justify pornography as free speech—a freedom that can be deadly for women.

Woman Killer as Tragic Hero

SANDRA McNEILL

The media reporting of violence against women has been a central issue of concern amongst feminists who are active in working on the problem of male violence in both the United Kingdom and the United States. Other chapters in this book detail feminist campaigns against pornography and women hatred films, and the British media's celebration of the Ripper centenary, for example. This chapter deals with quite a specific point, which forms just one thread of the misogynous web the media weave in their distorted, and often dangerous, portrayal of violence against women—that is, press reporting of a particular crime against women, a man killing his wife and then himself.

It is difficult to make sense of the newspaper reports of these cases if you are simply trying to uncover the facts. As women, we are entitled to reporting that we can understand, and that speaks to our reality. Currently such reports can only be understood by accepting the media's assumption that these events constitute a "tragedy" in which the man, the killer, plays the role of *tragic hero*. I am further concerned that this portrayal of such killers as heroes may encourage others.

In 1986 I was working on a research project on violence against women[1] and as part of the research I monitored the local press treatment of violence against women. The reason for including press monitoring was to further explore the ways our reading about crime, and particularly violence against women, shapes our perceptions of crime and our own safety or lack of it. The papers we were studying were mainly local ones, including the Leeds evening paper, the *Evening Post;* the *Telegraph and Argus,* the Bradford evening paper; and the *Yorkshire Post,* which despite its title is a national quality paper.[2]

In May 1986, there was a spate of men killing their wives and then committing suicide: three cases occurred in one month in Yorkshire. In another case, Peggy Hall and her daughter, Jane Oliewicz, were killed by Peggy's husband, who then committed suicide. When I was filing the press cuttings, I was horrified at the way these murders followed by suicide were reported. Without any in-depth analysis, certain words and phrases, certain assumptions were evident.

First, the murder-suicides were always described as "tragedies," not crime—for example, "Domestic Dispute Blamed in Tragedy" or "Tragic Death of Race Ace Kenny." Second, they were initially described in the local press as "mysteries"—for example, "Moor Gun Death Remains a Mystery."

Actually, there was no mystery about any of these deaths. The men had killed the women—in various ways—and then themselves. What was mystifying was the way they were written up in the newspapers. Some newspapers did not make available the details necessary to make sense of what had happened; others hid the details on inside pages. Readers were supposed to be content to note that a tragedy had occurred.

One significant *detail* that the newspapers ignored or buried was the fact that in every case the woman was leaving the man, or had left, or had asked for a divorce—that is, she was leaving to start a new life, which, at all costs, the man clearly was not going to allow. When this was acknowledged it was from his—the killer's, point of view: "Break-up Couple United in Death." That was how one newspaper heralded the deaths of Jean Whisker and Pam Carter, both buried with the men who murdered them. It was the killers who wanted to be united in death with their wives. What the wives wanted was divorce and a new life away from their husbands.

The newspapers did not report the event as a tragedy *for her*. It was a "tragic couple" or "tragic family." Writing of the spouses being "united in death" evoked romance, like the ending to *Romeo and Juliet*. "But at least they are united in death. . . ."

None of these cases were double suicides. Nor were they accidental. These men would not let go of their wives. These men killed their wives to stop them leaving or living apart from them.

But nowhere in our press were these four killers blamed—not one word of blame for any of them. In the case of Peter Hall it emerged that he had been sexually abusing his stepdaughter, and on being found out, killed his wife, raped and killed his stepdaughter, and then committed suicide. Social Services was blamed for the "Triple Death Tragedy."

So how come no newspaper suggested that these men, these killers, had done anything wrong? Because the man who kills his wife and then himself is seen as, par excellence, the tragic hero.

In the reporting of one of these murders followed by suicide, reference was actually made to Shakespeare's Othello. Before looking at the case in depth, I think it is useful to consider how men view Othello. Here is one (famous) critic: "Before we may be truly stirred by the tragedy of Othello, before we may judge him *worthy* to kill Desdemona, one thing is essential; not a shadow of doubt must remain in our mind that, should Othello remain alone in the world after the death of his lover, he must necessarily and immediately strike *himself* with the same dagger. . . . This . . . is not only a moral necessity, but the absolute condition upon which our sympathy in the tragedy depends."[3] So if any man fulfills this condition, he becomes the hero who is deserving of our sympathy.

In May 1986 Pam Carter was killed by her husband Kenny. He then shot himself. Kenny had been a motorbike racer. This minor claim to fame ensured that the murder-suicide received maximum publicity (front-page headlines) in the two local papers, the *Evening Post* (Leeds) and the *Telegraph and Argus*. It was also reported in the national *Yorkshire Post*.

The story was treated as the tragedy of Kenny Carter, "Speedway Ace." The front page headline in the *Evening Post* was "Speedway Ace and Wife Found Dead," subheaded, "The Pressures on a Sports Star." The inside coverage ran under the headline, "Double Tragedy of Bike Ace."

What was his double tragedy? According to newspaper accounts, it seemed to be that he had killed his wife and himself owing to the pressures of being a bike ace. There were quotes from friends of his, for example: "People do not realise the pressure on riders. I can only think, in Kenny's case, it built up and built up and something happened."[4] This was clearly the angle the *Evening Post* chose to take. Additional information must have been available to them, as more details were given in the *Yorkshire Post*, produced in the same building. But the *Evening Post* was content to list details of Kenny's race successes and failures.

The *Yorkshire Post*, under the headline "Tragedy after Wife "Left" Race Ace," told us that Mrs. Carter had gone to stay with her parents taking the children with her. She had returned to collect her belongings, possibly believing her husband was away.

However, short of switching to a more expensive quality daily newspaper, which women may not usually read, there remained one source of background information—the women's grapevine. Almost at once, someone told me she knew Mrs. Carter's hairdresser, and she said Ken Carter had been beating her up for years and she'd talked of leaving him.

The story from Pam's point of view, which could have been told in the press, was similar to that of the many women who pass through Women's Aid shelters here and elsewhere—woman finally leaves home after years of husband's violence. When he is thought to be out of the house, she goes back to get her belongings. However, in Pam Carter's case, she returned alone, and he was there and he murdered her. However to write that would be to show Kenny as the villain of the piece. And no paper did that.

The next coverage in the local press was of the funeral, focusing on the fact they were being buried together: "Together Again in the Grave" headlined the *Telegraph and Argus*, telling us: "Tragic speedway couple, Kenny Carter and his wife Pam will be buried together." The *Evening Post* followed a similar line but, retaining its emphasis on Kenny as a local star, headlined its reports, "Farewell to Kenny" and "Speedway Fans Pay Tribute to Kenny."

The *Telegraph and Argus* then uncovered another angle, a supposed suspicion on Kenny's part that his wife had a lover. "Kenny's Tragic Jealousy" ran the headline. Friends of Kenny's had revealed Kenny's fears that Pam had a lover, so when Pam walked out, she "sealed her fate." However Pam's friends said she had never been unfaithful.

With this element added in, the case had all the makings of a true tragedy, Othello-style, with Kenny as the tragic hero.

In this version of events, the press was aided by certain comments of the coroner at the inquest, when the final coverage occurred.

The *Evening Post* was clear in its headline: "The Green Devil of Suspicion Kills Two." Clearly, a better angle than pressures on race ace—now Kenny could be seen as *totally* blameless.

The *Yorkshire Post* did not excuse Carter completely but took up the same line; "Jealousy Turned Husband into Killer" ran the headline. "Kenny Carter who could not bear to lose on the track became eaten up with the belief that his wife, Pam, was having an affair. . . . But both Mrs. Carter's father and a close friend told the Halifax inquest that Mr. Carter made a terrible mistake—the mother of his two children was a faithful wife."[5]

Details of the inquest printed in both the *Yorkshire Post* and the *Telegraph and Argus* could have told a different story. But all three papers chose to focus on the jealousy angle, and all three papers ended their reports with the words of the coroner: "Let the couple rest in peace."

The *Telegraph and Argus* headlined, "Jealousy Drove Tragic Kenny to Kill." Well down in the story we learned that

> earlier at the inquest Miss Healy, the close friend mentioned above, said there were rows and Pam could no longer stand Kenny's jealousy and violent temper. Even before they were married, Pam had told her Kenny used to hit her. Pam said she wanted to leave Kenny but he had told her: "You won't leave me. You won't ever leave me, You can't leave me or I'll kill you if you try." Two days before the tragedy Pam took the children and went to live at her parents. Her father went to Carter's house and took away his four shotguns. But on May 21st, the day of the tragedy, Kenny borrowed an automatic shotgun from a friend and bought three boxes of cartridges.[6]

The *Yorkshire Post* gave the clearest details of the murder. Pam entered the hall. "He fired the first three shots at his wife from the top of the stairs. . . . In spite of being hit in the legs, she had tried to run to their Range Rover parked in the gravel courtyard. She fell face down and Mr. Carter had put the gun to her back and pulled the trigger twice more."[7]

But did the *Yorkshire Post* call this "Heroic Wife's Escape Attempt"? It did not. Instead, the report quickly turned to details of Carter's suicide note and the call he made to a friend. So the full horror of Pam's killing was swamped by his declarations of remorse and his love for her and his family.

So there we have it, the reconstruction by the press of a femicide into a Shakespearean tragedy, with the killer starring as tragic hero, a hero of a double tragedy, in fact, as both he and his wife are killed by jealousy. But at least they are "Together Again in the Grave."

Should we be concerned about this? What difference does it make if news-papers report it all from the point of view of the husband-killer and glorify him? I do think how "the facts" are reported affects how we think and act. I am not alone in this; the U.K. government, in particular, has recently taken minute interest in biased reporting. For women, I think this kind of reporting leads to alienation. We can accept such a report on a femicide at its face value, as another mysterious event, but we are left alienated from the woman whose story it is, not understanding what happened to her, her motives and choices cut short. Or else we can shrug, as we so often do, at the biased reporting and rely on the women's grapevine for the truth. This alternative, however, leaves us accepting our marginalized status in the world. So it matters for us women, trying to live our lives and make sense of our lives and the lives around us.

And men must know, after reading these reports, that if they do kill their wives and then themselves, they will be accorded the status of tragic hero.

After May 1986 no man in Yorkshire can be unaware of this.

What if the stories were different. What if they said, even in newspaper-speak: "Wife Brutally Slain by Husband in Premeditated Murder." What if they said he was clearly an inadequate wimp who couldn't live on his own after his wife left him? Or what if he was described as a crazed nutter, or even a worm? The story could then focus on her and her brave attempt to make a new life—cut short.

I think fewer men would do it if they knew that was the sort of coverage it was going to get. I don't know how many fewer. One fewer would be important.

Finally, I think it matters for the women who died: Peggy Hall, Jane Oliewicz, Alison Robertson, Jean Whisker, Pam Carter.

Notes

1. "Women, Violence, and Crime Prevention," a research study commissioned by West Yorkshire Metropolitan County Council. We interviewed all relevant welfare agencies, a sample of lawyers, police, and a representative sample of women. We monitored some court cases and analyzed all local and national press over a one-year period. A report of the study by Jalna Hanmer and Sheila Saunders was published by the University of Bradford in November 1987.

2. Most households in Leeds and Bradford take an evening paper, which gives local as well as some national news. Typically, if there is a major national story, the paper will lead with it, covering local news inside. Otherwise, local news preponderates throughout. Most households also take a morning paper, usually a national tabloid that carries no local news.

The *Yorkshire Post*, a national quality morning paper (circulation 92,629, of which 41,211 in Yorkshire), does feature local news, unlike other quality papers. It is, incidently, the most right-wing of the national quality papers. *The Telegraph and Argus* (Bradford and hinterland, circulation 83,140) gave more details of the Carter case, while the *Yorkshire Evening Post* (Leeds and hinterland, circulation 439,432—called the *Evening Post* in the text, as it is locally and to avoid confusion with the *Yorkshire Post*) concentrated on Kenny as local sports star. This is probably because the Carters lived closer to Bradford, so it would be assumed the readership would be interested in "the details."

3. Stendhal, *Life of Rossini* [1824], trans. R. N. Coe (London: Calder, 1956), 207 (Stendahl's emphasis).

4. *Yorkshire Evening Post*, 22 May 1986.

5. *Yorkshire Evening Post*, 25 July 1986.

6. *Telegraph and Argus*, 25 July 1986.

7. *Yorkshire Post*, 25 July 1986.

"That's Entertainment"?: Jack the Ripper and the Selling of Sexual Violence

DEBORAH CAMERON

The British are famous for their sense of history, their love of pageantry and traditional celebration. And what, after all, could be more traditional, more part of our history than male violence against women? This particular tradition is currently marking a notable centenary which comes around this year. 1988 is the hundredth anniversary of Britain's most illustrious mass sexual killer, the man whom we know by the name "Jack the Ripper"—and the celebrations have already begun, for the pleasure and profit of all concerned. The "Ripperologists," as they laughingly call themselves, are busy getting ready for a massive birthday party. The publishers are churning out various new titles re-examining personalities and events of the case; by the time we get to the actual centenary next autumn we'll be caught up in a flurry of commemorative events, features in the media and Ripper memorabilia (there are plans to sell T-shirts and badges and mugs). What will be glossed over in these mindless festivities—except perhaps by feminists with no sense of fun—is the actual significance of what Jack the Ripper did, and what sexual killers still do a hundred years later.

A TOURIST ATTRACTION

It's worth pointing out that public interest in the Ripper will not begin and end with his centenary year. That will just intensify what already exists, a whole cultural industry founded on "Jack." For a good many years now, the Ripper has been part of what people refer to as "the national heritage." He's a symbol of a vanished Victorian London, a romanticised East End of cobbled streets and gaslight.

Reprinted from *Trouble and Strife,* Spring 1988, 17-19.

This version of history is relentlessly sold both as a tourist attraction and a source of local pride. It appears throughout the country in waxwork museums; in London it confronts you in a dozen different forms. Thus the Trocadero in Piccadilly Circus offers visitors the authentic "Jack the Ripper Experience"; in the East End you can take a guided tour of "Jack the Ripper's London," and finish up with a pint in the Jack the Ripper pub. No-one seems to find this especially offensive (is there a pub in Boston called The Boston Strangler?, or one in Cambridge called the Cambridge Rapist?). Jack the Ripper has been thoroughly sanitised, turned into a folk-hero like Robin Hood. His story is packaged as a bit of harmless fun: only a spoilsport would be tactless enough to point out it is a story of misogyny and sadism.

THE THIN END OF A VERY NASTY WEDGE

If those who market Jack as a quaint London character are guilty of disguising or ignoring his misogyny, others are explicitly fascinated by it, and determined to exploit it for financial profit. For example, a Jack the Ripper computer game has just appeared (the blurb suggests the timing is not a coincidence) which re-enacts the murders in gruesome detail. The images that appear on the player's VDU screen include women with their throats cut and intestines ripped out. And these are not computer graphics or cartoons by the way, they are photographs of models and fairly realistic. This game has been refused a general certificate—it is classifed "18," i.e., for adults only, and is the first computer game to receive this restrictive rating.

It will be interesting to see whether a new genre of "adult" sado-pornographic computer and video games develop in the wake of this pioneering example. If so, Jack the Ripper will have played yet again his insidious role as the bridge between what is considered "entertainment" and what is more clearly perceived as offensive. The thin end, in other words, of a very nasty wedge.

RIPPEROLOGY

Another place where misogyny is rife is in the pseudo-intellectual writings of the so-called "Ripperologists." As I mentioned earlier, the approaching anniversary has inspired a fresh outbreak of "scholarly" publications, studded with such gems as the following observation: "Sex was surely plentiful enough for any man to obtain without murder . . . rape was, in a sense, unnecessary in nineteenth century England."[1] What comes across in this kind of writing, apart from wilful ignorance and complacent male stupidity (for all the Ripperologists I know of are men) is a barely suppressed erotic excitement with the idea of killing for sexual pleasure—and in the case of Jack the Ripper, of *getting away with it.*

The actual history of Jack the Ripper is rather less cosy than the official tourist version and rather less heroic than the Ripperologist fantasy. Let us recall the salient facts of the case and make connections with events in the present.

In the East End of London in 1888, a man whose identity has never been discovered carried out a series of particularly horrible murders.[2] The victims—as far as we know, five in all—were poor working-class women who engaged in prostitution because their earnings from street trade or charitable relief were inadequate to support them (here nothing much has changed!). All the women's bodies were found in a similar condition: hideously mutilated and disemboweled. During what came to be known as "the autumn of terror," London police received letters from a man who claimed to be the killer and signed himself "Jack." One letter contained an account of his motives: "I am down on whores and I shan't quit ripping them till I do get buckled."

The murders were talked about in various ways. Some people saw prostitution itself as the problem, and greater control of women's sexuality as the solution. Others urged the government to clear the East End slums in which, it was felt, the killer's bestial urges flourished. Still others blamed the whole thing on foreigners, or the Jews.

In this welter of misogyny, classism and racism it was left to a few women to make a connection between the acts of the Ripper and the general level of male violence against women. Such violence was part of the everyday experience of women in all classes, communities and conditions, "respectable" and "fallen" alike. Furthermore, this violence was condoned by the same people who could now be heard howling for the blood of the Ripper. As Mrs. Fenwick Miller put it in a letter to the *Daily News* in 1888, "Week by week and month by month, women are kicked, beaten, jumped on until they are crushed, chopped, stabbed, seamed with vitriol, bitten, eviscerated with red-hot pokers and deliberately set on fire—and this sort of outrage, if the woman dies, is called "manslaughter": if she lives, it is a common assault." It's interesting, by the way, that the writings of the Ripperologists never refer explicitly to the kind of feminist protest Mrs. Miller's letter represents—at least one author quotes her directly but without acknowledging his source. That women both analysed and resisted male violence in 1888 is an important fact which has often been concealed: nor is it likely to be mentioned in the anniversary celebrations.

As we can see from Mrs. Miller's remarks, little has altered in the last hundred years. Male violence against women continues to go unpunished, and the kind of murder pioneered by Jack the Ripper has since been repeated at regular intervals. The "Blackout Ripper" of the 1940s, "Jack the Stripper" in the 1960s and the "Yorkshire Ripper" in the 1970s, are only the most notorious examples of men who have set out to continue the Ripper tradition.

A CULTURAL HERO

The word "tradition" is appropriate here, for it is clear that many men have been conscious admirers and imitators of this killer with the status of a cultural hero. During the Yorkshire Ripper case, for example, the police received a tape from a man calling himself "Jack." This man—a hoaxer whose efforts seriously misled the enquiry—quite obviously took his cue from the Whitechapel murders, the details of which he was clearly familiar with. The actual murderer, Peter Sutcliffe, was also familiar with the legend of the Ripper. He used to visit a model of "Jack" in a wax museum in the seaside town of Morecambe (misogyny as tourist attraction once again—and the museum has since installed a model of Sutcliffe!). He also used the same defence of being "down on whores": as he expressed it to his brother, he was "cleaning up the streets." His attitude was as acceptable in 1981 as it had been to Victorian London in 1888.

The Ripper Centenary makes me want to ask, why all the nostalgia for "Jack the Ripper's London"? To all intents and purposes we are living in it still! The sadistic sexual murder of women by men did not disappear with the cobble stones and gas lamps. On the contrary, the attitudes and structures of power which give rise to sexual murder are with us to this day, while the Ripper himself provides a powerful inspiration for appalling acts of violence by men here and now. To propose the centenary of the Jack the Ripper murders as a suitable occasion for national celebration is not only to trivialise past womanslaughter but to rejoice in the continuing violence against us. Such rejoicing is an insult to the memories of those women who have died at the hands of men in the past hundred years. For us who survive, it is a painful reminder of how little society values our lives.

A GROTESQUE ANNIVERSARY

As this grotesque anniversary gets nearer and nearer, we must do what we can to ensure that women's suffering and women's resistance are not just forgotten. Various kinds of protest and direct action are called for. At the very least, feminists should write letters of complaint to those who manufacture and sell "Jack the Ripper" goods (we could start with the video game, see address below). We should also consider disrupting and/or picketing tourist attractions like the Trocadero, as well as any events specially organised for the centenary.

I would also like to see feminists organise our own alternative events, designed to draw attention to what the others try to hide: the prevalence and significance of sexual killing, and more broadly, the way society is permeated with male violence. One of the things I feel strongly is that we should find some way to publicly commemorate the five women who were killed by Jack the Ripper, along with other women who have died at male hands since. Those who glorify the criminal should be forced to remember the victims—and though feminists usually avoid that word *victim*, in the case of sexual murder it is no more than accurate.

Finally, I think that whatever we do, we must be aware, and make others aware, that our resistance to male violence has a context and a history. We are saying what our sisters before us have said: that we condemn male violence in all its forms, and we protest against the attitude which regards sexual murder as a harmless amusement and a cause for celebration.

CAMPAIGNING

STOP PRESS: Since this piece was written, an organised campaign by East London women supported by a local woman councillor has drawn the issue of the Jack the Ripper pub to the public's attention, with the result that the brewery has now agreed to change the name back to the original "Four Bells." This shows that feminist agitation can be effective.

Notes

1. Colin Wilson and Robin Odell, *Jack the Ripper: Summing Up and Verdict,* (New York: Bantam, 1987).

2. Speculations about the identity of the Ripper are an industry in themselves, and range from the idle to the wholly ludicrous. Women may be familiar with the theory that the murders were committed by the Freemasons or by a member of the Royal Family. Liz Frazer and I considered these ideas during the research for our book *The Lust to Kill,* and we did not believe there was much evidence to support any of them. All we know is that "Jack" must have been a man.

Snuff—The Ultimate in Woman Hating

BEVERLY LABELLE

Snuff is the name of a highly publicized movie which purports to show the actual murder and dismemberment of a young woman. It achieved notoriety because of the carnage of its final five-minute sequence.

The film first surfaced in 1975 shortly after the New York City Police Department announced that they had confiscated several "underground" South American pornographic films containing actual murder footage. These films were given the name "snuff" films because the actresses were murdered (snuffed out) in front of the cameras in order to excite the jaded sexual palates of a select pornography audience that requires death rather than mere sex as an aphrodisiac. The curiosity of the regular pornography market was whetted by this police discovery, and the idea of a commercialized "snuff" film was born.

The scenario revolves around a South American cult that is dominated by a man named Satan. All his followers are lovely young women who are willing to rob, beat, and murder at his command. Before joining this select cult, each woman must undergo an initiation of torture in order to seal her commitment to Satan. There is a small amount of rhetoric about killing the rich in revenge for the sufferings of the poor, but this minor theme never achieves prominence and was obviously added in an attempt to justify the violence of the film. The cult also holds some confusing occult beliefs similar to those depicted in Saturday afternoon "horror" films. However, the producer did hope to draw a parallel between Satan's devotees and Charles Manson's "family." The similarities between these two groups are too numerous and too obvious to be mere coincidences. Undoubtedly the image of Charles Manson as a new prototype of sex and violence was deliberately emulated in *Snuff*.

Reprinted from *Take Back the Night: Women on Pornography*, ed. Laura Lederer (William Morrow: New York, 1980), 272–76.

189

The plot is fuzzy, but eventually it becomes clear that the cult is planning a ritual slaughter to avenge both the suffering poor and the demon god of their "religion." The band of mystics proceeds to murder a number of random people, none of whom appear to be members of the elite classes. In one scene a cult member revenges herself upon her ex-lover by castrating him with a razor. The actual cutting is not shown—just scenes of his face contorted by agony. Perhaps the director felt that this scene of a man being destroyed by a woman would be too repellent for his male audience to depict graphically. After that gruesome scene, the blood-crazed devotees prepare for the long-awaited sacrifice of their "perfect victim," an unborn child ready to burst forth from the womb of a beautiful, blond woman (the reincarnation of Sharon Tate, no doubt). First they shoot her wealthy lover, and then they surround the bed where she lies, cowering in fear, with her enormous stomach protruding beneath the satin sheets. The dagger is held high in an invocation to the "powers of evil" and then plunged savagely into her stomach, which explodes with the sounds of gushing blood and gurgling amniotic fluid.

Then silence for a moment before the camera pulls back, and we see the production crew of the film talking about the success of that final scene. A pretty young blond woman who appears to be a production assistant tells the director how sexually aroused she was by the stabbing finale. The attractive director asks her if she would like to go to bed with him and act out her fantasies. They start fumbling around in bed until she realizes that the crew is still filming. She protests and tries to get up. The director picks up a dagger that is lying on the bed and says, "Bitch, now you're going to get what you want." What happens next goes beyond the realm of language. He butchers her slowly, deeply, and thoroughly. The observer's gut revulsion is overwhelming at the amount of blood, chopped-up fingers, flying arms; sawed-off legs, and yet more blood oozing like a river out of her mouth before she dies. But the climax is still at hand. In a moment of undiluted evil, he cuts open her abdomen and brandishes her very insides high above his head in a scream of orgasmic conquest. The End . . . Fade into blackness. There are no credits listed in the final moments of the film.

Snuff was one of the very first pornographic films to elicit strong protest from the feminist sector of the population. It marked the turning point in our consciousness about the meaning behind the countless movies and magazines devoted to the naked female body. *Snuff* forced us to stop turning the other way each time we passed an X-rated movie house. It compelled us to take a long, hard look at the pornography industry. The graphic bloodletting in *Snuff* finally made the misogyny of pornography a major feminist concern.

Across the country wherever the movie appeared, feminists mobilized to protest the showing. In San Diego at the end of September 1977, a feminist noticed *Snuff* playing in a local theater. An impromptu telephone tree notified women from feminist groups, community groups, and church groups, and a meeting was called that night at The Women's Store. There women discussed tactics and decided to picket the movie house the following night. Here is what happened, excerpted from a letter written to *New Woman's Times:*

> About forty women showed up the next night hour before the first showing of the film. We made a circle and walked in front of the theater chanting "Stop *Snuff* Now!" and "This is violence to women." We passed out flyers (which we had printed up that day) to people coming out of the supermarket and other nearby stores. In addition, we were able to get our point across to many people in the city because several TV stations arrived to cover the picket. One of the stations, Channel 8, sensationalized the movie and interviewed the theater owners and moviegoers much longer than they did us; but the other stations gave good balanced coverage which brought home the issue of violence to women.
>
> Two hours after we began picketing, our action was proving successful: no one was entering the theater. We marched for five hours. Before we left the theater we talked with the manager to see if they were going to stop showing *Snuff*. He said they were getting so much publicity that it would be held over for another week. We said we would be back the next night.
>
> When we returned the following night, the movie had been changed. We assume this was a direct result of the community pressure we brought to bear in our ad hoc organizing against *Snuff*. Our last action was a trip to the *San Diego Union,* the city newspaper. We received assurance from the publisher that they would not advertise *Snuff* if it came to another San Diego theater.[1]

Denver, Colorado, was the scene of another *Snuff* protest:

> The women's community of Denver, Colorado protested the attempted showing of *Snuff*. Two of us organized a mass telephone campaign to the theater chain, constantly harassing the owner. We distributed leaflets throughout the community and the neighborhood where the theater was located. Then we made a plea to the Denver district attorney, Dale Tooley, who (because it was near election time) banned the movie and took all the credit for it.
>
> We showed up at the theater before we knew the movie had been banned, prepared to protest the film or interrupt the showing, but we did not have to—our pressure on the D.A. had brought results.[2]

In New York City when *Snuff* was first screened at a movie house off Times Square, it came at a time when there was considerable publicity being given to privately released pornographic films showing actual rape and murder. The films were being offered at private screenings reportedly for prices ranging from $100 to $500 a person.[3] Here *Snuff* attracted daily picketing by feminists, which touched off a lengthy dispute over constitutional rights of freedom of expression. Here is an excerpt from the leaflets which feminists distributed in New York City:

> Why Are We Here? We are opposed to the filming, distribution, and mass marketing of the film *Snuff* currently showing around the clock at the National Theater in New York City. The term "snuff" has been used in the underground film circle to label those pornographic films depicting actual, cold-blooded murder of women. Purportedly a film of this type was produced in Buenos

Aires, Argentina and in this film a real woman was murdered. It is implied in advertisements of the film currently showing that this may be the same film.

Whether or not the death depicted in the current film *Snuff* is real or simulated is not the issue.[4] That sexual violence is presented as sexual entertainment, that the murder and dismemberment of a woman's body is commercial film material is an outrage to our sense of justice as women, as human beings.

Women and other persons of conscience will demonstrate at Manhattan District Attorney Robert Morgenthau's offices to protest his refusal to recognize the clear and present danger of a film in this borough which purports to be a photographic recording of a woman's actual torture and murder.

A telegram signed by many prominent citizens in the arts, the clergy, and social services to petition the removal of this film has received no response from the D.A. Neither has he responded to the continuous demonstrations in front of the National Theater nor the hundreds of phone calls received by numerous city officials.[5]

"Pickets sell tickets," said Allan Shackleton, the man who did the distribution and advertising for *Snuff*. Shackleton told reporters that he was "out to make money, and to be noticed by the motion picture industry." He also said that he had several offers to make sequels to *Snuff*.[6]

Pickets, phone calls, and demonstrations at the district attorney's office in New York City brought no action against the movie, but in other cities around the country, such as Buffalo, Los Angeles, and San Jose, *Snuff* left town early after mobilization of women's groups.

One last series of events in Monticello, New York, is worth reporting. When *Snuff* came to Monticello, a protest was organized by NOW and the local chapter of WAVAW (Women Against Violence Against Women). More than 150 people attended the first performance of the movie. The audience was a mixed group of all ages (the minimum legal age was eighteen for an X-rated film).

Three women, led by Jane Verlaine of Monticello, made a complaint to the police after the first performance, based on the fact that the film's promotion of the murder of women was sexually stimulating. Here are the events that followed this showing of *Snuff*, taken from the daily accounts by *The Times Herald Record*, a Monticello daily newspaper:

THURSDAY, MARCH 11, 1976:

About 40 demonstrators peacefully protested here against the showing of *Snuff*, a motion picture depicting the disembowelment of women. The protestors, including a handful of men, marched in front of the Rialto Theatre. They carried placards including the inscriptions, "Snuff kills women—zap it" . . . Jane Verlaine . . . one of the protest leaders . . . made a complaint to Monticello police after the first performance. The complaint was based on grounds (that) the film's promotion "advertises and advocates murder of women as sexually stimulating." They related portions of the film to police. Sgt. Walter Ramsay, while recording the complaint, said D.A. Emanuel Gellman advised him, "As it stands now, there is no basis for a complaint." Gellman explained that he cannot take action against theatre owner Richard Dames because "there is no place we can go if violence is the only complaint." The only time he can act, he said, is if the complaint is based on pornography. He said he does not believe pornography is involved in this instance.[7]

On Friday, March 12, the women took their complaint to District Attorney Emanuel Gellman, and on Sunday they filed a criminal information. Richard Dames, owner of the theater in question, was charged with second-degree obscenity and ordered to appear in court. Women Against Violence Against Women hired a lawyer, and both sides squared off for a fight.

What followed was a series of delays and court misunderstandings. The defense submitted a motion for dismissal, and the court was adjourned for three weeks; the court required that WAVAW subpoena the film for court viewing. When WAVAW lawyer Andrea Moran did so, the subpoena was quashed the night before the trial. The next day the judge dismissed the case for insufficient evidence: WAVAW did not have a copy of the film. Moran protested this "Catch-22," and the case was appealed. In the meantime ten months passed, but finally in late December 1977, this news clipping appeared in the local paper:

WEDNESDAY, DECEMBER 16, 1977:
County Court Judge Louis B. Scheinman has reversed a Village Court decision and ordered a trial on obscenity charges for theatre owner Richard Dames in connection with the showing of the film *Snuff* in Monticello in March 1976.

The decision was a victory for the feminist group, Women Against Violence Against Women, which has been seeking prosecution on the grounds that the film, which shows the simulated murder and dismemberment of women, is an incitement to acts of violence against women. . . .

Attorney Moran said Tuesday she was very happy with Scheinman's decision, calling it a "real victory for decency."[8]

After this decision the attorney for Richard Dames contacted Andrea Moran. An agreement was made that Dames would publicly apologize to all women for showing Snuff, *and that the women would then drop charges. Following this agreement, Richard Dames disappeared.*

Notes

1. "Letters to the Editor," *New Woman's Times,* 1977, Rochester, New York. (Thanks to Martha Gever for digging out this information.)

2. Ibid.

3. "Film of Violence Snuffed out by Angered Pickets' Protests," *San Diego Union,* September 29, 1977.

4. Women were very concerned about the possible real death of a female in the filming of *Snuff,* but when film distributors denied it was a "real" woman who was murdered, feminists quickly moved to state that the murder of one woman was only the first of many concerns we had about "snuff" films.

5. Leaflet distributed by a New York City *ad hoc* feminist group against *Snuff*. The contact was Leah Fritz, the well-known feminist writer and journalist.

6. "Snuff," *Sister Courage,* April 1976.

7. "Women's Group Picket Showing of Snuff," *The Times Herald Record,* Thursday, March 11, 1976.

8. "Obscenity Trial Ordered in Snuff Film Showing," *The Times Herald Record,* Wednesday, December 17, 1977.

What the White Man Won't Tell Us: Report from the Berkeley Clearinghouse on Femicide

CHRIS DOMINGO

Just after Mother's Day 1991, I was proofreading *Memory and Rage,* the newsletter of the Berkeley Clearinghouse on Femicide. The phone rang. "Chris, another woman's body has been found in the Oakland Estuary. The same place they found the last one. It looks like a serial killer." Angry and sickened, I checked the newspaper reports.

The woman was Leslie Vaile Denevue, a 43-year-old woman and mother of two community college students—murdered and decapitated, her limbless torso disposed of in a sack. Seven months earlier, another woman was similarly killed and was found at the same location in the estuary. The October femicide victim was an unnamed black woman; Denevue, found in May, was white (Harris 1991a).

Here is how a male reporter on a major city newspaper discussed serial murder:

> A serial killer is generally defined by law enforcement officials as a person, usually with psychological motives, who picks successive victims, usually at random, and leaves them mutilated, decapitated, skinned or tortured.
>
> One of Oakland's previous serial killers shot people as they drove on local freeways. Another would stab or beat prostitutes to death, while the third would strangle his victims to death, sometimes after ritualistic sex acts. (Harris 1991a)

Author's note: The writing of this article has truly been a collective process. Many central ideas were hashed out and feedback generously offered in discussions with Chinosole and Angela Davis of the San Francisco State University Women's Studies Department, and with Max Dashu, Melissa Farley, and Rikki Vassall. In addition I am grateful to Candida Ellis, Kathy Kaiser, Naomi Lucks and Helen Vozenilek for their editorial assistance.

Why did this reporter choose not to say what every law enforcement official knows: that serial killers are almost always white men, and that 90 percent of the people they kill are women or girls? What is gained by calling serial murder "random"? The reporter repeatedly used the word *would* instead of *did* or *does*. The word *women* is noticeably absent, replaced by *prostitutes* or *victims*. A killer of unknown gender "picks victims" and then "leaves" them mutilated. Who kills them? Here are the facts, minus the denial and degenderization:

> A serial killer is known by law enforcement officials to be in almost all cases a white man, who kills a series of people, usually women, and leaves them mutilated, decapitated, skinned, and/or tortured.   ⸱
>
>   One of Oakland's previous serial killers strangled women to death, sometimes after molesting or raping them. Another stabbed and beat prostitute women to death, and a third shot people as they drove on local freeways.

How much further we can go in solving a social problem if we start by describing it honestly.

A few days later I attended a friend's college graduation. The keynote speaker, Ramon Cortines, a school district superintendent, addressed the issues of racism and sexism. His basic drift was that "there are still problems, but we've come a long way." He spoke of how women's lives have changed, how women are less constrained by the housewife stereotype that once held sway. Speaking on racial discrimination, he suggested we compare the situation of an African-American person today with that of someone living prior to 1950. "Before 1950," he said, "lynchings of black people were common." The fact is that lynchings still happen, and furthermore, in 1991 women of all races are turning up sexually mutilated, beaten, strangled, every day. I felt angry that this man acknowledged hate violence that has happened in the past but ignored the violence being done to us today.

The public and media reaction to serial killings is quite disturbing. Not only is femicide ignored by mainstream news and discourse, it is joked about and used as grist in the R-rated movie mill. Serial murder is actually *enjoyed*—not only by the woman-haters who commit the murders, as evidenced by the usual presence of semen at the crime scenes—but by a large percentage of the male population, as evidenced by attendance at "slasher" films and the popularity of photographs in which women are victims of violence.

A woman who manages to survive rape is said to face a "second rape" if she brings her attacker to trial or is subjected to voyeuristic interrogation. Similarly, omnipresent messages that trivialize, glamorize, or make jokes about femicide constitute a continuous "psychological murder" of women.

African-American feminist scholar Tracy Gardner (Walker 1980, 75) posits that misogynist cultural representations, and sexist violence itself, are perpetrated by the same white male hegemony that resulted in the thousands of vicious racist lynchings of black men and women that followed the Civil War. "I believe that this obscene, inhuman treatment of black men by white men, has a direct correlation to white men's increasingly obscene and inhuman treatment of women, particularly white women, in pornography and real life. White women, working toward their own strength and identity, their own sexuality, have in a sense become uppity niggers. As the black man threatens the white man's masculinity and power, so now do women."

Simulated violence against women in pornography and "entertainment" and actual violence (which is also sometimes filmed, taped, or photographed) feed on each other. Media presenting rape myths, sexist cartoons, and demeaning photographs magnify existing sexism and provide blueprints for perpetrating sexist violence. Further, femicidal violence in the "entertainment" media would not rake in millions of dollars if it weren't for the fact that women are being murdered daily—black, brown, yellow, and white women—in "real life."

FEMICIDE AS PUBLIC ENTERTAINMENT

> Some males were observed leaving the theatre [after a showing of the film *Snuff* in New York] laughing and saying "Boy, that was a good one."
> —Maxine Sobel (1977–78, 8)

The sexual violence that proliferates in the entertainment media today emerged on a large scale in the 1970s, at the start of the second wave of the women's movement and the campaign to pass the Equal Rights Amendment. During the late 1960s and 1970s, men's magazines and the film industry began making violence sexy and sex violent with the marketing of "slasher" films and an explosion of sexual violence in print.

In an interview with Laura Lederer, editor of *Take Back the Night* (1980), former pornography model Jane Jones observed, "There's been a big change in pornography. The hating way in which women are portrayed has escalated so fast, now you see everything—women being skewered, women being killed" (Lederer 1980, 69).

"Snuff" has been defined as "film which depicts (or purports to depict) the actual torture, mutilation and murder of an actress" (Caputi 1987, 91n). Diana E. H. Russell (1989) has defined hard-core snuff as filmed records of actual killings, and soft-core snuff as those of simulated murders. Snuff photographs and audiotapes are also produced.

In 1976 public femicide was introduced into the United States and Canada with the commercial showing of the movie *Snuff*, distributed by Allan Shackleton of Monarch Releasing Corporation. It was quickly closed down by feminist protests and civil disobedience in several cities (see the preceding contribution in this volume, Beverly LaBelle's "Snuff—The Ultimate in Woman Hating"). Portrayals of femicide as entertainment are widely evident today in the rapid proliferation of soft-core snuff, which has established itself in suburban video stores as "horror," "suspense," and "mystery" films. You might notice that some of the photographs on the covers of these videos are not easily distinguishable from actual atrocities. Some videos claim to "really deliver," just as the prototype *Snuff* did. The line between entertainment-media depictions of femicide and actual murders is becoming increasingly blurred. But there are no widespread protests now, as there were in 1976. The making of hard-core snuff is the commission of a murder. Isn't buying and selling hard-core snuff then complicity to murder?

Since 1976 reports of snuff materials made by serial killers and child abductors have appeared in the news with increasing frequency; the electronic recording of murder is an increasingly common modus operandi of serial killer teams. (Many serial killers also have an immense interest in violent pornography.) The Berkeley Clearinghouse on Femicide files contain documentation on numerous serial murderers of women who filmed their victims as they killed them, including Harvey Glatman (1957), Kenneth Bianchi and Angelo Buono (1978–79), Lawrence Bittaker and Roy Norris (1979), Fred Berre Douglas and Richard Hernandez (1982), and Leonard Lake and his "sidekick" Charles Ng (1985). Ashley Lambey and Daniel T. Depew were arrested for planning to kidnap and "snuff" a young boy (1989). As is typical of serial killers in the United States, nearly all of these snuff killers are white, the exception being Charles Ng (*U.S. News & World Report* 1985; Baraback 1985).

The next phase of misogynist hatred could be filmed and taped femicide—camouflaged by the soft-core snuff now flooding the market—bought and sold with impunity and unnoticed because of our own desensitization and denial. If pornography is "technologically sophisticated traffic in women" (MacKinnon 1989), then snuff by extension is a kind of high-tech lynching.[1] We face the nightmarish possibility that male viewing of films and videos of actual sexist murders could become a "normalized" cultural institution in the United States.

The government is directly implicated in complicity with serial murders for as long as "entertainment" materials indistinguishable from actual murder footage are protected by the First Amendment.

The U.S. Constitution was written when there was no corporate-controlled media, no photography or film, no technology for mass destruction, and no vote for women or African-Americans. Among the dubious benefits offered to women by the Constitution are first and foremost, the right to see your fellow woman degraded and mutilated in "mass" media, including entertainment and advertising, and second, the right to be attacked by a man carrying an assault weapon. Both of these rights are stubbornly guarded, primarily by white men in the businesses of pornography and gun sales who spend millions lobbying and propagandizing to prevent progressive change.

The Bill of Rights is inadequate for a pluralistic society with our present level of technology, let alone for a global community. It is sorely in need of updating.

FEMICIDE IN THE CONTEXT OF WOMEN'S HISTORY

Under 5,000 years of European patriarchal social structure, a small minority of individuals have claimed to "own" most of the earth's land and have invented, inherited, or "gained" control of money, the media, and the "defense industry." People enslave and/or are enslaved and sexually exploited to varying degrees by the enforcement of a racial, gender, and class hierarchy that encourages competition and divisiveness. The hierarchy is enforced psychologically through the use of electronic and other propaganda ("the media") that encourages male violence, female agreeableness, racism, and a generalized obsession with possessing someone in a relationship (Johnson 1991) and "consumer goods." The hierarchy is ultimately enforced through violence. Exploitation, torture, and murder that come down through this structure are, for the most part, distorted or ignored in "mainstream" educational curricula and the "mass" media.

Historian Max Dashu (1991) traces the history of repression and silencing of women through patriarchal violence:

> The silencing originates in the precedent and model for modern femicide. Millions of women were tortured and burned in the European Witch Hunts. This womenslaughter grew from the feudal persecutions of the early middle ages, increased exponentially with the Inquisition's promotion of judicial torture and climaxed between 1400 and 1750. Church and state collaborated in a massive campaign of repression against women, overthrowing such female professions as priestess, healer, herbalist, midwife, counselor, seeress, weather expert, and folk historian. The end result was to engrain a deep, culture-wide subjugation of women, still with us today, which demands internal conformity to patriarchal restrictions.
>
> At the height of this burning Terror, Europeans invaded the Americas and Africa, colonizing, enslaving, and committing genocide on the indigenous peoples. The witch hunters' diabolist ideology, including the demonization of dark-skinned peoples and of all religions other than christianity, were used as rationales for conquest and subjugation. European witch persecution was even exported to places like Massachusetts, Mexico, Colombia, and Peru, where Indian and African women were persecuted for practicing medicine and shamanic religions. All these events are now suppressed and propagandized in Eurocentric education and media.

In the modern era, the vilification of women has passed into a "more purely secular form" (Karlsen 1987, 221). In England, the nineteenth-century suffrage movement coincided with the serial murders perpetrated by Jack the Ripper, a prostitute killer, and his subsequent mythification as a folk hero (see Deborah Cameron's chapter in this book, "That's Entertainment"?: Jack the Ripper and the Selling of Sexual Violence"). In the United States during this time, white racists had begun publicly torturing and killing African-American men and women in extrajudicial mob lynchings. Rape-murders of white women were sometimes used as pretexts for these lynchings.

A RACIST COVER FOR FEMICIDE

Violence against women of all races is never a rare occurrence under white male supremacist rule. Furthermore, white rapists and killers have repeatedly scapegoated black men for their crimes against white women. In Boston in 1989, Charles Stuart committed a carefully premeditated wife-murder, then claimed he and his wife had been attacked in their car by a black man with a gun. When his lie was found out, he committed suicide (Hays 1990; Kennedy 1990). Charles E. Davis did the same thing back in 1920: "Charles E. Davis, prominent [white] Wake County farmer, committed suicide by hanging himself in the city jail today. Davis was arrested on suspicion of having murdered his wife after authorities began to doubt his story that she had been killed by a 'lecherous looking black' " (Ginzburg 1962, 142).

Lynchings of black men, and in one case a black woman (Jennie Steers, accused of poisoning Elizabeth Dolan), followed the murders of at least 24 white women and girls in the United States from December 1899 to May 1937, listed below. Lynchers mutilated, castrated, burned at the stake, shot, hung, and beheaded African-Americans before crowds of cheering whites, sometimes numbering in the thousands. "Confessions" were forced from a few blacks; others refused to confess even under torture (see Diana E. H. Russell's "Femicidal Lynching in the United States" in part 1 of this volume for information on African-American women who were lynched).

In several cases, white men were later proven to be the killers of these white women. For example, in May 1922, Eula Ausley of Texas was found dead from 30 stab wounds. "Shap" Curry, Mose Jones, and John Cornish were mutilated and burned to death for this femicide. Later it was discovered that she was actually murdered by two white men involved in a feud with her family. Following the murder of Annie Mae La Rose, an unnamed black man was lynched and another barely escaped being lynched in New Orleans. Weeks later, her (white) stepfather confessed to the femicide. It is not known who killed the other women of European descent listed below, each of whose terrifying murders was followed by one or more cruel and horrible lynchings. In many cases, though the woman's murderer was not found, the innocence of lynching victims was later established through circumstantial evidence (Ginzburg, throughout).

Eula Ausley	Ruby Hendry
Helen S. Bishop	Ruby Hurst
Mrs. Nellie Williams Brockman	Anza Jaudon
Lola Cannidy	Mrs. Elizabeth Kitchens
Elizabeth Dolan	Annie Mae La Rose
Ida Finklestein	Mrs. Lashbrook
Dower Fountain	Bessie Morrison
Lucy Fryar	Rita Mae Richards

Mrs. Carey Whitfield	Christina Winterstein
Casselle Wilds	Mrs. Younger
Mrs. J. C. Williams	unnamed girl, age 11
Mrs. C. O. Williamson	unnamed school teacher, age 19

In addition to being lynched and killed in race riots (Lerner 1972, 176), African-American women were also no doubt "just murdered" during the post-Civil War years. If murders of black women followed the same pattern as the ongoing rapes of slave women and later domestic workers, most of these femicides were probably interracial—white men killing black women. This is a subject deserving further research.

As I write, the network news presents footage of a stretcher, the body covered with a sheet, being borne away. Two more women students have been found strangled to death in Gainesville, Florida. More wife killings and serial killings will become known to me when I open the Clearinghouse mailbox. If they are not young, white, and middle-class, their murders may go unacknowledged in the malestream media.

The specter of sexist murder presents an enormous challenge to women. First, can we find ways to render ineffective the media propaganda that fans the flames of hatred and snuffs out the flames of outrage? Can we stop the abuse and murder that is diabolically masquerading as "speech"? And finally, can women of all colors share our own thoughts, our fears, and our anger about these terrible deaths among us?

It's time to break the silence about femicide.

Note

1. I coined this phrase a year before Supreme Court Justice Clarence Thomas used it to describe the Senate hearings on sexual harassment charges made against him.

References

"Are Serial Killers on the Rise?" 1985. *U.S. News & World Report,* 9 September.

Baraback, Mark. 1985. "Mass Killer Lake Reportedly Linked Ng to S. F. Crimes." *San Francisco Chronicle,* 22 October.

Berkeley Clearinghouse on Femicide. Research files: hate crimes, serial murder, snuff. P.O. Box 12342 Berkeley, Calif. 94701-3342.

Caputi, Jane. 1987. *The Age of Sex Crime.* Bowling Green, Ohio: Bowling Green State University Popular Press.

_____, and Diana Russell. 1990. "Killed for a Cause." *Sojourner: The Women's Forum,* January, 7.

Dashu, Max. 1991. Personal correspondence, 19 August.

Davis, Angela. 1983. *Women, Race, and Class.* New York: Random House.

Fimrite, Peter. 1990. "Fear of Killer Stalks East Bay Women." *San Francisco Chronicle*, 22 November.

Giddings, Paula. 1984. *When and Where I Enter: The Impact of Black Women on Race and Sex in America*. New York: Bantam Books.

Ginzburg, Ralph. 1962. *100 Years of Lynchings*. New York: Lancer Books.

Harris, Harry. 1991a. "Murders Shock the City." *Oakland Tribune*, 16 May.

_____. 1991b. "Murder Victim IDd as Former Oakland Teacher." *Oakland Tribune*, 17 May.

Hays, Constance L. 1990. "Husband of Slain Boston Women Becomes a Suspect, Then a Suicide." *New York Times*, 5 January.

Hazelwood, Robert, and John Douglas. 1980. "The Lust Murderer." *FBI Law Enforcement Bulletin* 49, no. 4.

Johnson, Sonia. 1991. *The Ship that Sailed into the Living Room*. Estancia, N.M.: Wildfire Books.

Karlsen, Carol F. 1987. *The Devil in the Shape of a Woman*. New York: Random House.

Kennedy, Dana. 1990. "Silence Shrouds Massachusetts Murder Case." *San Francisco Chronicle*, 1 April.

Lederer, Laura. 1980. "Then and Now: An Interview with a Former Pornography Model." In *Take Back the Night*, ed. Laura Lederer, 57–70. New York: William Morrow and Co.

Lerner, Gerda. 1972. "The Memphis Riot, 1865." In *Black Women in White America*, ed. Gerda Lerner, 173–79. New York: Vintage.

MacKinnon, Catherine. 1989. *Toward a Feminist Theory of the State*. Cambridge: Harvard University Press.

Sobel, Maxine. 1977–78. "SNUFF: The Logical Conclusion." *New Women's Times* 3:8.

Walker, Alice. 1980. "Porn at Home." *Ms.*, February.

Advertising Femicide: Lethal Violence against Women in Pornography and Gorenography

JANE CAPUTI

The neighborhood I grew up in had very few girls my age. When we were 12 and 11, my sister Margaret and I hung out with my cousin Billy, who lived one block over, and his boy friends. This was Long Island in the mid-1960s, and there were still some spots of undeveloped land. So we had a "fort" (the boys' word), a hollowed-out place among the vines and bushes on a hill, where we would all congregate. One day when Margaret and I walked into the fort, there was a new addition: large, glossy, colored pictures of naked women with their legs spread, hung on the vines and brambles. This itself was bad enough. But the boys also had burned out the vaginas and nipples with cigarettes. Sex and violence, all together, all at once. Very soon after, the boys started attacking us regularly, throwing us to the ground, calling us sluts and cunts and, as they put it, "depantsing" us. There never was any doubt in my mind that the attacks on us were connected to the pornography. That moment in the fort when I first faced those pictures precursed the boys' intentions and prepared me, as it had them, for my assigned role in this new ritual of patriarchal sexual initiation.

Drawing upon such experiences of our own, the testimony of other women, the examination of actual pornography, as well as social scientific studies, many feminists (Barry 1979; Brownmiller 1975; Dworkin 1981; Griffin 1981; Lederer 1980; Russell 1984, 123–32; Russell 1988) have demonstrated the intimate relationship of pornography and sexual violence, manifested in a multiplicity of ways, including:

1. In many cases, pornography actually *is* sexual violence, a document of actual degradation, rape, torture, and even murder (as in the snuff film).
2. Pornography is used manipulatively to undermine women and children's capacity to avoid or resist abuse (Russell 1984, 123–32; Lanning and Burgess 1989).

3. Pornography causes sexual violence through its capacities to normalize that violence, give ideas to receptive male viewers, and break down some men's personal and social inhibitions against behaving in a violent manner (Russell 1988).

Violence against women and children in the United States is frequently spoken of in terms of an "epidemic," with abuses including rape, incest, sexual harassment, battering, and, increasingly, murder. Each year in the United States around 1,500 women are counted as being murdered by their husbands and lovers (FBI 1987, 11). Each year an uncounted number of women are killed by strangers or disappear never to be found; many of these are serial killings—or what law enforcement officials term "recreational murder," a form of murder that has increased dramatically in the past two decades (Ressler, Burgess, and Douglas 1988, 2–3). In an FBI study of 36 serial sex killers, pornography was determined to be the primary "sexual interest" of 81 percent of them (Ressler, Burgess, and Douglas 1988, 24).

The connection between pornography and serial sex murder received intense national attention when the notorious Ted Bundy, just before his execution, openly claimed a link between his near-lifelong use of pornography and his evolution into a serial killer (Lamar 1989). Many commentators discredit his statements, saying that Bundy was merely trying to absolve himself in his eleventh hour by blaming society.[1] A *New Yorker* editorial (1989) was typical. After pooh poohing the "deadly dangers of nude centerfolds, X-rated movies, and bottom-rack periodicals," it averred with utter certainty that neither "Ted Bundy [n]or anyone else understood what made him commit and repeat the crimes he confessed to" (23). A feminist analysis, of course, would not accept the equation that to recognize the responsibility of social institutions for femicide is to absolve the murderer. Rather, it would point to the intimate connection between Bundy and his society, naming Bundy as that society's product and henchman. Moreover, although many men expediently throw up their hands, claiming Bundy and his ilk to be a complete mystery to them, that same feminist analysis can state quite clearly why Bundy did what he did.

As Kate Millett (1970) noted in her classic work *Sexual Politics:*

> We are not accustomed to associate patriarchy with force. So perfect is its system of socialization, so complete the general assent to its values, so long and so universally has it prevailed in human society, that it scarcely seems to require violent implementation. Customarily, we view its brutalities in the past as exotic or "primitive" custom. Those of the present are regarded as the product of individual deviance, confined to pathological or exceptional behavior, and without general import. And yet . . . control in patriarchal society would be imperfect, even inoperable, unless it had the rule of force to rely upon, both in emergencies and as an ever-present instrument of intimidation. (59–60)

Femicide, like that perpetrated by Ted Bundy, is not some inexplicable phenomenon or the domain only of the mysterious deviant. On the contrary, femicide is an extreme expression of patriarchal "force." It, like that other form of sexual violence, rape (Griffin 1982; Brownmiller 1975; Russell 1975), is a social expression of sexual politics, an institutionalized and ritual enactment of male domination, and a form of terror that functions to maintain the power of the patriarchal order. Femicide, moreover, is not only a socially necessary act; it also is experienced as pleasurable and erotic—by those men who enact it as well as by those who variously represent it and contemplate it.

Recognizing femicide to be a fundamental need of the masculinist state, we can survey its various forms across time and place as well as the different methods through which it was legitimated and propagated. For example, the torture and killing of women as witches for three centuries was institutionalized by both church and state and was incited through sacred writings—papal bulls and church-backed torture texts, such as the *Malleus Maleficarum* (1486)—as well as through elite and popular art depicting naked women engaged in sex with each other and with "the devil" (Caputi 1987) and "graphic etchings and woodcuts showing varieties of tortures, drownings, and burnings of women" (Sjöö and Mor 1987, 309). Sjöö and Mor continue: "Some feminists might feel these popular press images were the snuff films and *Penthouse* magazines of their day. They purported to be on-the-spot depictions of tortures and burnings, with naked and half-naked female bodies screaming and writhing in endless postures of agony, surrounded by well-dressed male judges, religious accusers, "prickers," and other righteous gentlemen of the time. There is no doubt that

Demonstrator, before joining antipornography protest against a Playboy read-in in Berkeley, California, 1991. Photo Diana E. H. Russell.

these mass-printed images fueled a mass-paranoia against women, against witches; they also mark the beginnings, in the West, of pornography as popular entertainment" (309).

As the apparatus upholding the witch-craze collapsed by the mid-eighteenth century, a new mode of femicide (beyond the ongoing murder of wives) was needed—a mode with a new manner of execution, a new type of perpetrator, and a new form of propaganda. That new mode is the explicitly eroticized murder, a form first heralded in the early nineteenth century by the writings of the Marquis de Sade, the father of contemporary pornography (Dworkin 1981) and first philosopher of sexual murder (Cameron and Frazer 1987); it then was first culturally meaningfully enacted by an unknown man, nicknamed "Jack the Ripper," who killed and mutilated five prostitutes in London in 1888. At that time, Sade's views were not yet common currency, there was no cultural understanding of the category "sex murder," and since the Ripper did not rape his victims, his crimes were at first quite incomprehensible to the populace. Yet soon, with the help of Freud and Krafft-Ebing, the Ripper's knife was understood as a substitute for the penis and the "murderous act and subsequent mutilation of the corpse . . . [as] equivalents for the sexual act" (Krafft-Ebing 1965, 59).

By the late twentieth century, the names of both Sade and the Ripper have become household words, sexual killings are an hourly occurrence (in both fact and fiction), and it is commonly accepted that murder and mutilation can be sexual acts. The official story is that sex murder is a crime, an atrocity, yet as Dworkin (1989) notes, if you make a record of the sex murder, as in a snuff film, the film is legally understood as "speech" (310). Correspondingly, if you simulate a woman's stabbing death it can be rapturously applauded as cinematic genius (the shower scene in Alfred Hitchcock's *Psycho)* or it can be hailed as a seductive sculptural masterpiece (Alberto Giacommetti's *Woman with Her Throat Cut).* Though modern femicide is officially disowned, only covertly propagated, and nominally illegal,[2] its artistic and entertainment value would suggest that it, like the witch-craze, is ultimately sponsored by the masculinist state. Because femicide is a need, not an option, in the maintenance of patriarchal dominance, the state, albeit covertly, must endorse femicide and recruit agents to enforce its rule. As previously mentioned, the witch killings were incited and legitimated by sacred texts and images; so too is modern femicide—by the vehemently defended and protected "free speech" of pornography.

Like many other feminists, I make a distinction between pornography and erotica. Erotica is nonsexist sexual depictions, admittedly difficult to imagine in a society where eroticism is so closely intertwined with unequal gender roles and sexual objectification. Nevertheless, all sexual representation is not, as the right wing would have it, by definition pornographic. Rather, pornography is *sexually explicit sexist propaganda.* Andrea Dworkin and Catharine MacKinnon (1988) define pornography as the "graphic sexually explicit subordination of women through pictures and/or words that also includes one or more of the following: (i) women are presented dehumanized as sexual objects, things, or commodities; or (ii) women are presented as sexual objects who enjoy pain or humiliation; or (iii) women are presented as sexual objects who experience sexual pleasure in being raped; or (iv) women are presented as sexual objects tied up or cut up or mutilated or bruised or physically hurt; or (v) women are presented in postures or positions of sexual submission, servility, or display; or (vi) women's body parts—including but not limited to vaginas, breasts, or buttocks—are exhibited such that women are reduced to those parts; or (vii) women are presented as whores by nature; or (viii) women are presented being penetrated by objects or animals; or (ix) women are presented in scenes of degradation, injury, torture, shown as filthy or inferior, bleeding, bruised, or hurt in a context that makes these conditions sexual" (36). Helen Longino (1980) defines pornography as "sexually explicit material that represents or describes degrading or abusive sexual behavior so as to endorse and/or recommend the behavior as described" (44).

These two definitions highlight the factors that link pornography to femicidal actions: (1) its construction of a worldview that legitimates and enables sexual murder via its systematic eroticization of violence and objectification and derogation of women; and (2) the function of such imagery in endorsing or recommending, essentially *advertising,* violence against women. I will first survey some examples of femicidal imagery found in pornographic as well as mainstream materials and then offer a theoretical comparison of advertising and pornography.

PROMOTING THE ACT

To promote their act, they [the heavy metal group W.A.S.P.] have used a picture of a bloodied, half-naked woman chained to a torture rack. Past performances have included the simulated attack and torture of a woman. Reportedly, in the act lead singer Blackie Lawless wore between his legs a codpiece adorned with a circular saw blade. He pretended to beat a woman who was naked except for a G-string and a black hood over her head, and as fake blood cascaded from under the hood, he seemed to attack her with the blade. In another version of the act, he pretended to slit her throat.

—Tipper Gore (1987, 51–52)

Comic-book reader surveys show a young (ages 13–29) and almost entirely male readership. John Davis, a major distributor, comments: "The readers are teen-aged boys, so what you have is a lot of repressed anger. They're going through puberty, and they like to see characters act out their aggressions. The companies respond to what the readers want." Noting that a recent issue of "Green Arrow" depicts a crucified stripper—graphic enough in its execution that many would consider it pornography—he remarks, "They do like to see the characters sliced and diced."

—Joe Queenan (1989, 34)

Using women in situations where they are killed or sexually attacked . . . . [is simply] a genre convention . . . like using violins when people look at each other.

—Brian De Palma, quoted in Pally (1984, 17)

One large law enforcement agency now has in its possession a new film reportedly made in a foreign country that looks extremely realistic. The death scene shows a nude woman lifted several feet off the ground by ropes tied to her wrists. While suspended, her intestines are ripped out through her vagina and she then hangs there bleeding to death while another woman dances underneath her, drinking some of the blood that flows out. Whether or not this is a real snuff film, it is important to keep in mind the kind of sadistic personality that will be buying copies of this film.

—Robert Morneau and Robert Rockwell (1980, 213)

As the above selections indicate, a continuum of materials—from the actual snuff film through boys' comic books—enacts, legitimates, sexualizes, propagates, and promotes the act of femicide. In her contribution in part 6 of this volume ("The Rampage against *Penthouse*"), Melissa Farley describes femicidal imagery found in the top-floor pornography of *Penthouse*. Clearly, the threat of femicide also pervades the basement level—the captivity, bondage and torture materials. An example of this is *Cunt Torture,* a film clip shown in a Times Square adult store in the early 1980s in which a woman, tied to a tree, struggles and cries out while knives, guns, and other objects are forced into her vagina; clearly, she would have to actually be killed on camera to more explicitly suggest femicide.

Of course, actually torturing and killing women on camera is the essence of the "snuff" film, where the porous border between femicidal reality and pornography completely disappears. In making a snuff film, the pornographer must arrange the murder of a woman (or in some cases a child or a man); hence, pornography becomes sexual murder. Concomitantly, a number of sex killers record their slaughters by taking photographs or making audio- and videotapes; hence, sex murder becomes pornography. For example, the murderers Charles Ng and Leonard Lake made extensive videotapes of the atrocities they committed as a team in their Calaveras, California, home, what one commentator describes as "snuff videos that combine violent sex with vivid scenes of actual murders committed on camera" (Norris 1988, 148). While snuff films are kept underground and command very high rental fees (reportedly a few thousand dollars for an individual screening), simulated snuff is available in every mainstream video store for just a couple of dollars.[3]

There, one can find numerous, frequently obscure, erotic videos, in the horror, thriller, suspense, action, and adult sections, whose cover descriptions indicate femicidal themes. In November 1989 I viewed a number of these and will describe two of them here, one from the "horror" section and one from the "adult." Each was "soft-core" porn (no male nudity and only simulated sex) but sexually explicit to the extent that there was a great deal of full female nudity (in long or medium shot), a variety of sexual situations, and "lesbian" themes. Significantly, there was little difference between the video housed in the horror section and the one placed in the adult section.

In the "horror" film, *Obsession: A Taste for Fear* (1989), a serial killer hires models to pose in bondage scenes. We see him (dressed as a woman) bind and gag naked women, threaten them with knives, and then begin the knife attack; moreover, the killer makes snuff videodiscs of his efforts, which are then shown over and over as a snuff film within a pseudo-snuff film.

MacKinnon (1987) writes: "Men, permitted to put words (and other things) in women's mouths, create scenes in which women desperately want to be bound, battered, tortured, humiliated, and killed" (148). The "adult" film, *Sugar Cookies* (no date), enacts precisely that scenario. It opens as a sadistic porn film producer plays a game with one of his female stars. He is fully dressed; she is completely naked. He has her fetch and load his gun and then presses the gun into her vulva and supposedly makes her come. Next, he tells her that if she obeys him it will enable her to prove to him how much she loves him, which she is most eager to do. He has her lie down, commands her to open her eyes—because "I want you to see this"—and points the gun into her mouth. She is totally acquiescent and offers no protest at any time. After rambling about love, freedom and creativity, he then shoots her through her open mouth. Later he goes to fuck the murdered woman's "lesbian lover." The scenes of their simulated sex are intercut with scenes of the autopsy being performed on the body of the dead woman, including images of a knife slicing the corpse and a doctor's gloved hand lifting internal organs from her body and displaying them for the camera—overtly necrophilic images that none too subtly recall the fixations of the actual snuff film.

This is just a sampling of the material that is available in mainstream video stores. Yet equally disturbing femicidal imagery also can be found in a less likely place. An erotic 1989 calendar issued by a group called "Leather Women" in San Francisco features 12 different photographs of women engaged in sexual acts or displaying different sexual fetishes. I would not count all of the images as pornographic, but one in particular stood out. It showed two faceless women. One, wearing a black skirt and fishnet stockings, was on her hands and knees. The other, in leather pants, held a large knife to her vulva. Here, we find lesbian women identifying with the sexuality of "Jack the Ripper."

Monica Sjöö and Barbara Mor (1987) aver: "Every attempt to escape from sexuality transforms itself into prurience. Nowhere has sex been so debased—and pornography so profitable—as in the realms of Christendom" (291). Moreover, where sex and women are debased, violence frequently is exalted. For nearly seven decades, depictions of sexual acts were taboo in traditional cinema; thus filmmakers often resorted to violence in order to "represent passion" (Slade 1984, 150). However, the self-censorship of the film industry does not completely explain the popularity of such substitutions, for they did not disappear with changing social attitudes. Rather, since the 1960s, along with franker screen sex, there has been ever more graphic and passionate screen violence, culminating in what an anonymous wag in the film industry dubbed "gorenography"—those features, such as slasher films, that specialize in sensationalized and fetishized scenes of violence.

Gorenography is a useful term because it so unmistakably signals the sexual significance of violence. Social scientific studies reveal that purely violent descriptions "devoid of sexual content" (a man cutting a woman with a knife and beating her into unconsciousness) stimulate sexual arousal in a significant number (about 10 percent) of male subjects (Malamuth, Check, and Briere 1986; Malamuth 1985). This certainly helps to explain why filmmakers substituted violence for sex. As MacKinnon (1983) has noted, under male supremacy sex and violence are "mutually definitive" (650) and "acts of dominance and submission, up to and including violence, are experienced as sexually arousing, as sex itself" (1987, 6). This equation of sex and violence is the essence of gorenography, and I will use the term here to refer to those materials that, although not sexually explicit enough to qualify as pornography (that is, not enough close-up nudity or graphic sexual acts), nonetheless are like pornography (as I have defined it here) in that they present violence, domination, torture, and murder in a context that makes these acts sexual.

Elsewhere (Caputi 1987) I have extensively discussed novels and films that focus upon sex killers—elaborate accounts that are classified not as pornography but as "horror" or "thriller" stories. These materials provide a veritable *Kama Sutra* of ways to "do it" to a woman when "it" is not sex but murder. For example, a 1978 novel, Steven Whitney's *Singled Out,* features a compellingly handsome man who picks up women in single's bars, takes them home for sex, and then murders them in increasingly grotesque modes. He stabs one in the abdomen when she has an orgasm and disembowels another with an icepick through her vagina; he cuts another's heart out of her body on Valentine's Day and crucifies a Christian cult member in a Manhattan cathedral. Comparable gorenographic films include *The Tool Box Murders* (dir. Dennis Donnelly, 1978), *Friday the 13th* (dir. Sean Cunningham, 1980) and its sequels, and *Pieces* (dir. J. P. Simon, 1983), which fetishizes dismemberment.

These are generally "exploitation" products, deliberately catering to (and conditioning) a prurient interest in murder and mutilation. Yet such themes proliferate in sensationally popular and/or critically acclaimed products as well. Mickey Spillane's books have sold over 40 million copies (Cawelti 1976, 183). One of his most successful was his first, *I, the Jury* (1947), a novel that introduced his detective hero, Mike Hammer, as well as one of his recurrent themes—"violence as orgasm" (Cawelti 1976, 185). In this story, Hammer's one-armed war buddy has been viciously murdered—shot in the stomach and then psychologically tormented. Mike vows vengeance and sets out to find the killer. By the time he figures it all out, he is engaged to the blonde-bombshell murderer. They haven't had sex yet; Mike wanted to wait until they were married. But now Charlotte tries to forestall him by offering her body. As he chants the details of her violences, she gives no reply to his accusations but slowly strips. Finally, she is almost nude and Mike is winding down his litany:

> No, Charlotte, I'm the jury now, and the judge, and I have a promise to keep. Beautiful as you are, and as much as I almost loved you, I sentence you to death. *(Her thumbs hooked in the fragile silk of the panties and pulled them down. She stepped out of them as delicately as one coming from a bathtub. She was completely naked now. A sun-tanned goddess giving herself to her lover, with arms outstretched she walked toward me. Lightly, her tongue ran over her lips, making them glisten with passion. The smell of her was like an exhilarating perfume. Slowly, a sigh escaped her, making the hemispheres of her breasts quiver. She leaned forward to kiss me, her arms going out to encircle my neck.)*

Immune to her charms, Mike calmly puts a bullet into her "belly." He then looks behind his head and notices that there is a gun on the table; her arms weren't really going out to embrace him, but to grab the gun and shoot him.

> When I heard her fall I turned around. Her eyes had pain in them now, the pain preceding death.
>> Pain and unbelief.
>> "How c-could you," she gasped.
>> I only had a moment before talking to a corpse, but I got it in.
>> "It was easy," I said. (245–46)

The trappings of this scene are highly eroticized and approximate the conventions of a sex scene: the two are "in love"; the woman seductively strips. Moreover, Hammer's penetration of Charlotte's "lower belly" with a bullet from his cocked and ready gun is a thin substitute for intercourse; the pornographic violence of this scene is the only sexual consummation between the two lovers. Cawelti (1976) proposes that Spillane's readers prefer him over straight sadistic pornography because of the "sentimental feelings" that render Hammer's "orgiastic sadism . . . acceptable and cathartic for a mass audience"(188). *I, the Jury,* one of the most popular American novels ever, represents women as unconscionably vicious, and femicide as heroic, erotic, justified, and "easy."

A cinematic equivalent of Spillane's literary femicide can be found in *Psycho* (dir. Alfred Hitchcock, 1960). Once again, the woman who has been elaborately set up as the object of male desire is not fucked (in the genital sense) but is, instead, pornographically murdered. "Sex-symbol" Janet Leigh, who has been showcased in bra and slip a number of times in the film, strips (off camera) and enters a shower. She clearly is enjoying the sensuality of the water when the killer invades to slash her to death with a large knife. This is, as critic Raymond Durgnat (1978) avowed, a peculiarly "pornographic murder" (499), "too erotic not to enjoy, but too grisly to enjoy" (503). *Psycho*'s innovative coupling of a sensual scene, meant to sexually arouse the viewer (Rothman 1982), with a violent, symbolically orgasmic attack has been endlessly repeated and has emerged as the signature convention of the contemporary "slasher film" (Maslin 1982; Donnerstein, Linz, and Penrod 1987); it can even be noted in such mainstream films as *Prizzi's Honor* (dir. John Huston, 1985) and *Harlem Nights* (dir. Eddie Murphy, 1989).

Psycho's shower scene is what one critic called "probably the most echoed scene in all of film history" (Clover 1987, 224). It is impossible to imagine the masculinist cinema producing and then endlessly echoing a scene in which a man is sexually slashed to death. Woman as murder victim is built into the very genre system; as Brian De Palma whined: "I'm always attacked for having an erotic, sexist approach—chopping up women, putting women in peril. I'm making suspense movies! What else is going to happen to them?" (Mills 1983, 9). Things can only "happen to" women in the femicidal grammar. We also can note with great irony just whom De Palma claims is being attacked.

Similarly, the so-called Grandaddy of Gore (Loder 1984), director Herschell Gordon Lewis, who has achieved cult status for his 1960s gore movies featuring mutilations and disembowelments of women as well as the fondling of inner organs, claims: "Yes, we mutilated women, but we didn't degrade them. Nor was there any applause for the people who did it. I mutilated women in our pictures because I felt it was better box office. If that group of fanatics [Women Against Pornography] would promise to go see a movie if I disemboweled a man, I'd do it" (Loder 1984, 21) But, of course, a woman routinely disemboweling a man would be bad box office, not inherently exciting or energizing to the "audience"; it would constitute grossly incorrect usage, for in the pornographic grammar, as MacKinnon (1982) puts it, "Man fucks woman; subject verb object" (541).

Slasher films, the descendants of Hitchcock and Lewis films, emerged as a powerful genre in the mid-1970s—at about the same time that public awareness of snuff films emerged. Also beginning in the mid-1970s, and continuing into the present day, was a marked trend to use snufflike scenes in mainstream advertising, particularly advertising aimed at women so that we too will internalize the femicidal view of ourselves. Women are shown suffocated under plastic bags, run over by cars, or buried under the sand in order to sell such products as boots, perfume, stockings, and shoes (Caputi 1987).

Mainstream advertising also communicates femicidal ideology when it borrows the pornographic convention of showing a woman visually dismembered and reduced to a body part. For example, a mid-1980s ad for a Christian Dior perfume, "Choc Clair," depicts a woman's severed head horizontally arranged on the floor. The "Coed Killer," necrophile, decapitator, and mutilator, Edmund Kemper once told *Front Page Detective:* "What do you think when you see a pretty girl walking down the street. One side of me says, 'Wow, what an attractive chick. I'd like to talk to her, date her.' The other side of me says. 'I wonder how her head would look on a stick' " (Von Beroldingen 1974, 29). The fantasies of Edmund Kemper and Christian Dior apparently are not so disparate.

A not atypical 1980s ad for Yves Saint Laurent stockings shows a pair of high-heeled legs, cut off at the waist, spread and waving in the air, connoting a dismemberment and necrophilic rape. The intent and meaning of all such symbolic dismemberments can best be understood by listening to an actual sex killer describe the meanings of his actions: "Then I cut her throat so she would not scream . . . at this time I wanted to cut her body so she would not look like a person and destroy her so she would not exist. I began to cut on her body. I remember cutting her breasts off. After this, all I remember is that I kept cutting on her body. . . . I did not rape the girl. I only wanted to destroy her" (Hazelwood and Douglas 1980, 21).

I would not argue that advertisements such as these directly incite men to violence against women. Nevertheless, by glamorizing and normalizing images of female dismemberment, gorenographic ads like these parallel the actions of actual sex killers, reflecting, normalizing, and legitimating violence against women. They endorse, recommend and advertise not only shoes, stockings, and makeup but, simultaneously, misogyny and abuse. Indeed, pornographic and gorenographic images work much the way that advertisements do, inviting the viewer to imagine herself or himself in that magical tableau, to perhaps even try in real life what is depicted. In the concluding portion of this essay, I will explore further the convergence of advertising and pornography.

EDUCATING THE CONSUMER

> People learn from advertising. They learn about the products that are available to them, and they learn how they can better their lives.
> —Courtland Bovée and William Arens (1986, 10)

> He told me he had seen whores just like me in [three pornographic films mentioned by name], and told me he knew how to do it to whores like me. He knew what whores like me wanted. . . . After he finished raping me, he started beating me with his gun all over. Then he said, "You were in that movie. You were in that movie. You know you wanted me to kill you after this rape just like [specific pornography film] did."
> —Interview with rape victim, in Silbert and Pines (1984, 865)

Feminists have long claimed that pornography is a form of propaganda, that it peddles a view of women as objects, commodities, things to be owned, used, and consumed, and pushes companion beliefs, including: all women are whores and it is acceptable to do anything you want to whores; sexual violence is normal and acceptable; women deserve and want to be raped; women deserve and want to be killed, etc. Working from that position, and drawing upon social scientific research from the past decade, sociologist Diana E. H. Russell (1988) has suggested a theoretical model demonstrating the ways that pornography can cause rape. She proposes that "pornography (1) predisposes some men to want to rape women or intensifies the predisposition in other men already so predisposed; (2) undermines some men's internal inhibitions against acting out their rape desires; and (3) undermines some men's social inhibitions against the acting out" (41).

Russell's model rests upon two aspects of pornography particularly relevant to my discussion here: its construction of a worldview that encourages and normalizes violence against women; and its ability to create desires. While mainstream academics generally ignore or dispute pornography's power in these areas, an increasing amount of scholarship explores the ways that advertising performs precisely these functions. In a review essay (1987) on various contemporary forms of propaganda (pornography is ignored), Garth Jowett finds in three recent scholarly works (Marchand 1985; Pope 1983; Schudson 1984) incontrovertible evidence that advertising is "organized consumer propaganda" that not only promotes the acquisition of objects but shapes public consciousness, leading "to the formation of specific, widely held cultural beliefs within the general population" (112–13). One analyst under review, Michael Schudson (1984), argues that advertising serves to "articulate some of the operative values of American capitalism" (219) and suggests that it is analogous to socialist-realist art, dramatizing the ideals and values of the system more effectively than purely realistic depictions. Schudson insightfully designates advertising as "capitalist realism" (209–33). Jowett remarks: "Advertising therefore has a symbolic and cultural utility that transcends the mere selling of merchandise; like the socialist-realist art it emulates, advertising serves as a constant reminder of the cultural and economic basis of our society" (1987, 111). Correspondingly, we might consider pornography to be a sort of "patriarchal realism"—not the utopian sexual fantasy or "pornotopia" described by Stephen Marcus (1964, 269), but an arena where cockocratic (Daly 1984, 206)—that is, unequal, sado-masochistic, and ultimately femicidal—relations between men and "idealized women" are nakedly and ceaselessly enacted. Paraphrasing Garrett, we can understand such patriarchal realism to serve as a constant reminder, reinforcement, and reconstitution of the *sexually oppressive* basis of "our" society.

Not only does pornography, like consumer advertising, effectively promote dominant worldviews, but of critical concern is its ability to create desires and/or stimulate previously unarticulated desires. Many who would scoff at the notion that pornography can create desires would not hesitate to impute that power to advertising. One of the earliest and most influential critics of advertising was John Kenneth Galbraith (1976). In *The Affluent Society* (1958) he avers: "[The] central function [of modern advertising] is to create desires—to bring into being wants that previously did not exist" (129). This is precisely the power of pornography that Russell (1989) terms its "role in predisposing some men to want to rape." One way it does this is to teach men "who were not previously aroused by depictions of rape to become so after repeatedly associating arousing portrayals of female nudity with rape" (51).

Femicidal pornography and gorenography use a similar tactic: repetitively associating the conventions of arousal (female nudity, couples' lovemaking) with mutilation and murder. The covers of such "true crime" publications as *Front Page Detective* regularly feature "prefemicidal" scenes: skimpily clad women in bondage and held at knife point or gunpoint by a threatening, often masked man. Similarly, slasher films regularly "contain explicit scenes of violence in which the victims are nearly always female, and the films often juxtapose a violent scene with a sensual or erotic scene (e.g., a woman masturbating in the bath is suddenly and brutally attacked)" (Donnerstein, Linz, and Penrod 1989, 125). It requires no great leap of imagination to realize that such messages about murder and mutilation, endlessly reiterated, can induce sexual arousal to where none had existed before. Russell (1989) pointedly writes: "There is no good scientific reason to assume that people cannot develop new ideas or desires from the media. Would billions of dollars be spent on advertising or propaganda if it had no effect?" (53). Even if one denied the power of advertising to create desires (as, for self-serving reasons, many advertisers of cigarettes and alcohol do), certainly we can recognize its effect on previously existing ones, its power to "reinforce those desires, give them life, embodiment, and provide them with a permanence they might not otherwise attain" (Schudson 1984, 238). Pornography, like advertising, reinforces and normalizes femicidal desires, inflaming the consumer and instructing him in potential ways to embody his desires and act out his fantasies.

FANTASIZING FEMICIDE

> He [Bundy] told me that long before there was a need to kill there were juvenile fantasies fed by photos of women in skin magazines, suntan oil advertisements, or jiggly starlets on talk shows. He was fascinated by the sight of women's bodies on provocative display.
>
> —Steven Michaud (Michaud and Aynesworth 1983, 117)

> Many serial killers found an outlet for their vivid sexual fantasies in pornography. [Edmund] Kemper [the "Coed Killer"] scoured detective magazines for pictures of corpses and frequented "snuff" movies in which intercourse is a prelude to murder. "That didn't make me mean," he says. "It just fueled the fire."
>
> —Mark Starr (1984, 105)

As I noted earlier, in one systematic study involving interviews with 36 sex killers, pornography ranked as their highest sexual interest, topping even masturbation. Those same researchers, Ressler, Burgess, and Douglas (1988), also found that sexually violent fantasy plays an extremely powerful role in the development of the individual sex killer: "When questioned about the murders themselves and about their preparation for the murders, the murderers identified the importance of fantasy to the rapes and murders. . . . These cognitive acts gradually lead to the conscious planning and justification for murderous acts" (43). They further note that the role of fantasy in sadistic murder is increasingly being recognized; some researchers (MacCullough et al. 1983) suggest that sadistic acts and fantasy are linked and that fantasy drives behavior. Although pornography in its essence is "sexual reality" (MacKinnon 1987, 149), it simultaneously is material designed to stimulate the viewer's fantasies—a factor highly praised by many of its supporters (for example, Gagnon 1977, 357). Nevertheless, Ressler, Burgess, and Douglas did not probe the relation between the killers' regular use of pornography and the importance or content of their personal fantasies. This is a serious omission and greatly needs to be addressed in further research.

Like pornography, advertising also deals expressly in the manufacture of fantasy: "It does not claim to picture reality as it is but reality as it should be—life and lives worth emulating" (Schudson 1984, 215). Historian Roland Marchand (1985) speaks to the importance of fantasy tableaus in advertising imagery and the ways that ordinary individuals incorporate advertising's "visual clichés" into their personal daydreams and, he implies, into their behaviors. He cites psychologist Jerome Singer, who "asserts that daydreaming and fantasizing represent part of the thinking upon which behavior is based. Daydreams, he argues, represent rehearsals and 'trial actions' for practical future activity" (235). Marchand further comments: "To the extent that individual daydreams are shaped by an available vocabulary of familiar images, the clichés of popular art of an era, particularly if they are dramatically and repeatedly paraded before the public eye, may induce individuals to recapitulate in their own fantasies some aspects of the shared daydreams of the society" (235). Pornography and gorenography also are forms of popular art; like advertising, they too deal in the stimulation of the viewers' fantasies and in endlessly reiterated visual clichés (domination, rape, torture, murder), providing tableaux to be incorporated into personal daydreams, recipes to be followed, scripts to be enacted.

For example, in June 1985 a Marin County banker, Leslie Arthur Byrd, murdered a 19-year-old prostitute, Cynthia L. Engstrom. He first gagged and bound her and then drowned her in his bathtub. At his trial, former prostitute Erica Merle Clarke testified that Byrd had asked her if she would participate with him in a plot to drown a bound woman. As she related to the court, he told her: "I want you to see the look of fear in her eyes just before she is killed." She recalled that Byrd had told her that he had seen "pornographic 'snuff films' . . . of women being 'murdered live.' " Not especially interested in the "bloody ones," his favorite was of a woman being drowned in a hot tub (Ingram 1985). That film obviously fed his fantasies and gave him a script to enact in his own snuff scenario.

In October 1988, 19-year-old Sharon Gregory was murdered in Greenfield, Massachusetts, when 18-year-old Mark Branch stabbed her over 50 times. Branch, at the time, was undergoing psychological because of his obsession with slasher films; he particularly identified with "Jason," the murderer in the *Friday the 13th* series. When his home was searched, police found over 75 slasher videos and 64 similar books, 3 knives, a machete, and three hockey goalie masks just like the ones worn by his gorenographic role model Jason (Simurda 1988, 28).

In Japan, in 1989, there were a series of highly publicized crimes in which men and teenaged boys murdered and then dismembered young girls. When police searched the apartment of Tsutomo Miyasaki, a 26-year old printer who confessed to the murders of four girls, they found thousands of pornographic videos and comic books, called *manga*. One extremely popular type of manga is entitled "Lolita" and features pornographic stories of young girls and men (Hughes 1989). In the previous section, I argued that femicidal pornography/gorenography works to sexualize murder for some men and create in them a desire to kill. While I cannot say for sure that the snuff films Byrd watched, the slasher films Branch was obsessed with, or the pornographic videotapes and manga that so gripped Miyasaki, transformed previously unmotivated men into sex killers, we can at least say that these materials obviously helped to shape the fantasies of each killer and to determine the form the femicide would take.

In sum, much of what malestream thought takes for granted about the powers of advertising—that it can create and inflame desires, construct world views, insinuate itself into personal fantasies, and significantly influence behaviors—should be applied to an understanding of the ways that pornography affects violence against women. Ironically, an apologist for pornography also drew a comparison between it and advertising. When queried by *Playboy* regarding Ted Bundy's aspersions on pornography, Irwin Stotzky, a professor of criminal law at the University of Miami, averred: "The argument that looking at pornography will lead to violence is like saying alcohol advertisements will lead to heroin addiction. The Supreme Court has looked at pornography and, so far, none of the Justices has gone out and murdered" (Playboy Forum 1989, 49–50). This is a strangely illogical statement in a number of ways. First of all, the fact that femicidal pornography does not cause *all* viewers to go out and kill cannot be taken as proof that it never has this effect on some of them. Moreover, although alcohol advertising assuredly does not lead to heroin addiction, its effects on alcoholics and potential alcoholics cannot be so easily dismissed.

One thoughtful commentator on contemporary advertising, Michael Schudson (1984), writes:

> Some advertising promotes dangerous products or promotes potentially dangerous products to groups unlikely to be able to use them wisely. Liquor advertising to the young or to the heavy drinker, if it is effective even in the slightest, is socially costly and morally questionable. The advertising and

marketing of infant formula in Third World countries where poverty and ignorance guarantee widespread abuse of the product is a grotesque case of the
pursuit of profit gone berserk. It is the kind of savagery that people of some
future generations may look back on as we look back to slavery, witch burning,
or infanticide. (239–40)

Similarly, the glamorous and eroticized enactments of violence against
women in pornography and gorenography should be recognized as normalizing,
legitimating, creating desires for, lowering inhibitions against, and providing
imitable scripts for femicide. This is, indeed, the kind of civilized "savagery"
that so marks the modern masculinist world. Indeed, that very savagery makes it
a bit ironic to speak here of future generations, for the *same* pornographic mind
that uses a knife as a substitute penis and experiences sexual ecstasy over a dead
and mutilated female body is operative in the development and proliferation of
an even more lethal phallic weapon—nuclear bombs (Caputi 1987, 188–97;
Caputi 1991; Russell 1989). Moreover, the aim of those weapons is to achieve
"orgasm" via another sort of femicide—the murder of "Mother Earth."

Witch burning and slavery generally were not perceived as atrocities when
they were at their height. On the contrary, those persecutions were defended by
the highest authorities and the most sacred writings (from papal bulls to the
Constitution). So, too, femicide today is not understood as patriarchal terrorism
but dismissed as inexplicable deviance; correspondingly, pornography is

Feminist guerilla action
organized by the
Preying Mantis Brigade in
Santa Cruz, California, 1980.
Photo Nikki Craft.

defended as "free speech." Yet if the planet does survive, some future generations indubitably will look back and see pornography and its effects as very much a sexually political atrocity. Along with slavery, witch burning, and infanticide, future generations also will see femicide.

Notes

1. This was not a "deathbed" theme for Bundy. When he was first arrested in 1978 and throughout the 1980s, he repeatedly told interviewers that pornography (soft- and hard-core) as well as true crime images and stories had fed his fantasies, given him ideas, and taught him a way of viewing women that encouraged his development into a sex killer (Michaud and Aynesworth 1983).

2. When men kill women they "own"—wives and lovers—they often have been treated leniently. Police, community, and judiciary also respond with apathy and lenience when killers prey upon prostitute women (Caputi 1989). Jack Hampton, a Texas judge who gave a lighter sentence to a convicted murderer because the victims were homosexuals, proudly told the *Dallas Times Herald*, "I put prostitutes and gays at about the same level. And I'd be hard put to give somebody life for killing a prostitute." Judge Hampton has been cleared of all charges of bias (Belkin 1989).

3. Along with a friend, I went to several Oakland and San Francisco adult bookstores to see what types of femicidal materials were available. While there was bondage and torture material, there was virtually nothing focusing upon the killing of women. Femicidal porn, like child porn, is largely taboo and is available primarily under the counter or through mail-order. The proprietors happily encouraged us to go to mainstream video stores to find woman-killing material and to leave them alone.

References

Barry, Kathleen. 1979. *Female Sexual Slavery*. New York: Avon Books.

Belkin, Lisa. 1989. "Judge in Texas Is Cleared of Bias in Remarks about Homosexuals." *New York Times,* 2 November.

Bovée, Courtland L., and William F. Arens. 1986. *Contemporary Advertising*. 2d ed. Homewood, Ill.: Richard R. Irwin.

Brownmiller, Susan. 1975. *Against Our Will: Men, Women, and Rape*. New York: Simon and Schuster.

Cameron, Deborah, and Elizabeth Frazer. 1987. *The Lust to Kill: A Feminist Investigation of Sexual Murder*. New York: New York University Press.

Caputi, Jane. 1987. *The Age of Sex Crime*. Bowling Green, Ohio: Bowling Green State University Popular Press.

_____. 1989. "The Sexual Politics of Murder." *Gender & Society* 3, no. 4:437–56.

_____. 1991. "The Metaphors of Radiation: Or, Why a Beautiful Woman Is Like a Nuclear Power Plant." *Women's Studies International Forum* 14, no. 5:423:42.

Cawelti, John G. 1976. *Adventure, Mystery, and Romance: Formula Stories as Art and Popular Culture*. Chicago: University of Chicago Press.

Clover, Carol J. 1987. "Her Body, Himself: Gender in the Slasher Film." *Representations* 20 (Fall): 187–228.

Daly, Mary. 1984. *Pure Lust: Elemental Feminist Philosophy*. Boston: Beacon Press.

Donnerstein, Edward, Daniel Linz, and Steven Penrod. 1987. *The Question of Pornography: Research Findings and Policy Implications*. New York: Free Press.

Durgnat, Raymons. 1978. "Inside Norman Bates." In *Great Film Directors: A Critical Anthology*, ed. Leo Braudy and Morris Dickstein. New York: Oxford University Press, 499–503.

Dworkin, Andrea. 1981. *Pornography: Men Possessing Women*. New York: E. P. Dutton.

_____. 1989. *Letters from a War Zone: Writings 1976–1989*. New York: E. P. Dutton.

_____, and Catharine A. MacKinnon. 1988. *Pornography and Civil Rights: A New Day for Women's Equality*. Minneapolis: Organizing against Pornography.

Gagnon, J. H. 1977. *Human Sexualities*. Glenview, Ill.: Scott, Foresman.

Galbraith, John Kenneth. 1976. *The Affluent Society* [1958]. 3d ed. Boston: Houghton Mifflin.

Gore, Tipper (Mary Elizabeth). 1987. *Raising PG Kids in an X-Rated Society*. Nashville: Abingdon Press.

Griffin, Susan. 1981. *Pornography and Silence: Culture's Revenge against Nature*. New York: Harper & Row.

_____. 1982. "The Politics of Rape" [1971]. In *Made from This Earth: An Anthology of Writings*, 39–58. New York: Harper & Row.

Hazelwood, Robert R., and John E. Douglas. 1980. "The Lust Murderer." *FBI Law Enforcement Bulletin* 49 (April): 18–22.

Hughes, Beth. 1989. "Japan Frets at Kidporn Popularity: Experts See Link to Series of Slayings of Young Girls." *San Francisco Examiner*, 28 August.

Ingram, Erik. 1985. "Ex-Hooker Talks of Banker's Death Plot." *San Francisco Chronicle*, 4 September.

Jowett, Garth. 1987. "Propaganda and Communication: The Re-emergence of a Research Tradition." *Journal of Communication* 37 (Winter): 97–115.

Krafft-Ebing, Richard von. 1965. *Psychopathia Sexualis [1906]*, 12th Germ. ed., trans. Franklin S. Klaf. New York: Stein and Day.

Lamar, Jacob. V. 1989. "I Deserve Punishment." *Time*, 6 February, 34.

Lanning, Kenneth V., and Ann Wolpert Burgess. 1989. "Child Pornography and Sex Rings." In *Pornography: Research Advances and Policy Considerations*, ed. Dolf Zillmann and Jennings Bryant, 235–55. Hillsdale, N.J.: Lawrence Erlbaum Associates.

Lederer, Laura. 1980. *Take Back the Night*. New York: Morrow.

Loder, Kurt. 1984. "Night Creatures." *Rolling Stone* 19 July–2 August, 99.

Longino, Helen. 1980. "What Is Pornography." In Lederer, *Take Back the Night*, 40–54.

MacCullough, M. J., P. R. Snowden, P. J. W. Wood, and H. E. Mills. 1983. "Sadistic Fantasy, Sadistic Behaviors and Offending." *British Journal of Psychiatry* 143:20–29.

MacKinnon, Catharine A. 1983. "Feminism, Marxism, Method, and the State: Toward Feminist Jurisprudence." *Signs: Journal of Women in Culture and Society* 8 (Summer 1983): 635–58.

_____. 1987. *Feminism Unmodified: Discourses on Life and Law*. Cambridge, Mass.: Harvard University Press.

Malamuth, Neil. 1985. Testimony before the Attorney General's Commission on Pornography hearings, Houston, Texas. Unpublished transcript, 68–110.

_____, J. V. P. Check, and J. Briere. 1986. "Sexual Arousal in Response to Aggression: Ideological, Aggressive and Sexual Correlates." *Journal of Personality and Social Psychology* 50:330–40.

Marchand, Roland. 1985. *Advertising the American Dream: Making Way for Modernity 1920–1940*. Berkeley: University of California Press.

Marcus, Stephen. 1964. *The Other Victorians*. New York: Basic.

Maslin, Janet. 1982. "Bloodbaths Debase Movies and Audiences." *New York Times*, 11 November.

Michaud, Stephen G., and Hugh Aynesworth. 1983. *The Only Living Witness*. New York: Linden Press/Simon and Schuster.

Millett, Kate. 1970. *Sexual Politics*. New York: Ballantine.

Mills, Michael. 1983. "Brian De Palma." *Moviegoer*, 12 December, 8–13.

Morneau, Robert H., and Robert R. Rockwell. 1980. *Sex, Motivation, and the Criminal Offender*. Springfield, Ill.: Charles Thomas.

New Yorker. 1989. Editorial. 27, February, 23–24.

Norris, Joel. 1988. *Serial Killers: The Growing Menace*. New York: Dolphin/Doubleday.

Pally, Marcia. 1984. "Double Trouble." *Film Comment*, October, 12–17.

Playboy Forum. 1989. "Ted Bundy's Original Amateur Hour." *Playboy*, June, 49–50.

Pope, Daniel. 1983. *The Making of Modern Advertising*. New York: Basic Books.

Queen, Joe. 1989. "Drawing on the Dark Side." *New York Times*, 30 April, 32–34, 79, 86.

Ressler, Robert K., Ann W. Burgess, and John E. Douglas. 1988. *Sexual Homicide: Patterns and Motives*. Lexington, Mass.: Lexington Books/D. C. Heath and Co.

Rothman, William. 1982. *Hitchcock—The Murderous Gaze*. Cambridge, Mass.: Harvard University Press.

Russell, Diana E. H. 1975. *The Politics of Rape: the Victim's Perspective*. New York: Stein and Day.

_____. 1984. *Sexual Exploitation: Rape, Child Sexual Abuse, and Workplace Harassment*. Beverly Hills: Sage.

_____. 1988. "Pornography and Rape: A Causal Model." *Political Psychology* 9: 41–73.

_____, ed. 1989. *Exposing Nuclear Phallacies*. New York: Pergamon Press (Athene Series).

Schudson, Michael. 1984. *Advertising: The Uneasy Persuasion: Its Dubious Impact on American Society*. New York: Basic.

Silbert, Mimi H., and Ayala M. Pines. 1984. "Pornography and Sexual Abuse of Women." *Sex Roles* 10:861–68.

Simurda, Stephen J. 1988. "75 Horror Films Found in Slay Suspect's Home." *Boston Globe*, 9 December.

Sjöö, Monica, and Barbara Mor. 1987. *The Great Cosmic Mother: Rediscovering the Religion of the Earth*. San Francisco: Harper & Row.

Slade, Joseph. 1984. "Violence in the Hard-Core Pornographic Film: A Historical Survey." *Journal of Communication* 34, no.3:148–63.

Spillane, Mickey. [1947]. *I, the Jury*. New York: New American Library, 1975.

Starr, Mark. 1984. "The Random Killers." *Newsweek*, 26 November, 100–106.

Von Beroldingen, Marj. 1974. "I Was the Hunter and They Were the Victims." *Front Page Detective*, March, 24–29.

Whitney, Steven. 1978. *Singled Out*. New York: Morrow.

Part 5

FEMICIDE AND TRAVESTIES OF JUSTICE

Women picketing the British government's Home Office, London, 1991, in support of women convicted for the murder of their violent husbands. Photo Pam Isherwood/ Format.

Introduction

Part 5 addresses the response to femicide by the judicial system. Each contribution takes specific instances of femicide as a starting point and, in tracing the legal response, constructs a critique of its inadequacy and its misogyny. Collectively, the selections compose a comprehensive critique of man-made law and legal practice in England and the United States.

Jill Radford analyzes two instances of femicide, occurring within a year of each other in a small town in southern England, to demonstrate how the law shifts responsibility from the male killer to the woman killed by permitting the defenses of "diminished responsibility" and "provocation." She shows how such legal defenses not only succeed in reducing the killer's sentence but in putting the woman on trial—reconstructing her through male eyes, trying her by male norms, finding her wanting by male standards, and ultimately blaming her for her own death.

Sue Lees's study of murder trials in the United Kingdom makes similar points about the use of the defense of provocation and the systematic way the law adopts woman-blaming strategies to deny a man's responsibility when he knows the woman he has killed. She further shows that this strategy is rarely accepted in the unusual circumstances of a woman killing a man, even when the evidence for provocation is much clearer. In England, such cases have led feminists to demand a new defense of "self-preservation." It would allow women who kill after years of sexual violence and abuse a viable defense against a charge of premeditated murder, with its mandatory sentence of life imprisonment (Kelly, Radford, and Mavolwane 1991).

Lucy Bland analyzes the trial of serial killer Peter Sutcliffe. What seemed to be on trial was less the killer than men and masculinity. At the heart of the tense

225

trial were the questions, is he a dangerous beast, a man of diminished responsibility, a messenger of God, or, as the judge surprisingly suggested, simply a man?

Diana Russell discusses the attempted murder and subsequent suicide of Fay Stender, a well-known California attorney, feminist, and former activist in the U.S. prison reform movement. In a moving and personal account, the author attempts to unravel the complex political dimensions of the attack and links it with Fay Stender's involvement in prison reform and antiracist work. As a woman who was a feminist and a lesbian, Fay Stender was clearly a woman who could be blamed. Russell suggests that her gender may be central to understanding the motivation for the attack on her life.

Reference

Kelly, Liz, Jill Radford, and Sibusiso Mavolwane. 1991. "Women Who Kill." *Rights of Women Bulletin* (London). Spring, 52–54.

Retrospect on a Trial

JILL RADFORD

I wasn't too happy about moving to Winchester. I found it smug and narrow, and I was lonely. After a while I was amazed to discover that this conservative little town had a Women's Liberation group, which I immediately joined. It was there I met Mary Bristow who, over the next seven years, became not only a close and valued friend but, for me, the acceptable face of Winchester itself.

At first sight, I was rather in awe of Mary. She was magnificent-looking: dramatically tall—maybe six foot three in her bare feet—with all the conventional female virtues of beauty, grace and dignity. Added to that she possessed many virtues that the Winchester mentality would regard as manly—independence, vitality, an uncompromising regard for her own sensibilities, and an enormous measure of self-confidence.

As I got to know her better, I realised she was merely a woman who had achieved her own autonomy. She was almost blatantly happy; happy with herself, happy in her work, happy in her friends.

She had no sense of personal ambition. She had worked at the library since she came down from university and she had no burning desire to work anywhere else. She had her own home, she was well-known, well-liked, and Winchester fitted her exactly as a custom-made glove.

We shared many things. We were both mad about Jane Austen, we canvassed for the Labour Party together, and we joined CND and the Winchester Anti-Nazi League.

In my work as a criminologist, Mary was always enormously helpful. When Winchester Crown Court tried the notorious Asher case last year, and Gordon Asher received a suspended six months' sentence for killing his wife in a fit of petty jealousy, Mary was rocked by the aftermath of fear and dismay expressed

---

Reprinted from *New Society*, 12 September 1982, 42–48.

by the ordinary women of Winchester. It was typical of Mary that she helped me write an article about the case and the significance, for women, of its outcome. Three months after we finished the work, Mary Bristow was herself killed by a proprietorial young man to whom she did not wish to belong.

HOW MARY WAS KILLED

On the night of 29 October 1981, Mary was clubbed with a meat tenderiser, smothered with a pillow, and strangled. On the morning of the following day, Peter Wood was charged with her murder and sent for trial at Winchester Crown Court.

I don't think I had ever spoken to Peter Wood. I registered him as a fitness-freak, and was vaguely aware that in the dim and distant past he had been Mary's lover. But in the years I knew her I found him a rather boring young man who hung around Mary and Mary's home. She was kind to him as she was kind to everybody, but he did grow in nuisance-value, even Mary had to admit that.

He had a habit of turning up on her doorstep with nowhere to go, no job and no money, and Mary would grit her teeth again and give him house-room. There usually was a lodger at Mary's, somebody with a temporary accommodation problem; she had the space, and she was not someone to slam a door in any-body's face.

She did lose patience with Peter Wood, though. One time she refused to let him in and he broke in. Another time she was so desperate she called the police to evict him, but they refused to be involved. Once, too, she hit on the idea of putting all his belongings out in the street, so he would have to go away.

But there was no shaking him off. He haunted her, and pestered her until some of us—but never Mary—came to the conclusion that he was dangerous. We knew, for instance, that a couple of weeks before she died, she had discovered that Wood had broken into her house, bored holes in her bedroom ceiling, and taken to spying on her from the loft. She had been livid, she told us, and made Wood understand that this truly was the last straw.

We knew, too, that ten days before her death, the ground floor of Mary's house had been gutted by fire; that Wood had been in the house at the time; and that the police had taken several statements from him in connection with it. We knew the incident had frightened Mary very much. I remember one of the last times I saw her; when she was doing her Friday-night stint at a local bar—she thought bar-maiding was great fun—she put her hands over all the ashtrays before emptying them to make quite, quite sure they couldn't start a fire.

Many of us took it for granted that we would be called upon to testify to the nature of Mary's relationship with Wood at the trial. We assumed wrongly. It seemed to us, as the trial proceeded, that it was not Peter Wood on trial at all, but Mary Bristow, and that her defence was disallowed.

Wood's trial opened on 14 June 1982, and lasted for four days. It was heard by Judge Bristow—who was pleased to point out from the outset that he was not related to Mary—with Mr. Simon Tuckey acting for the Crown, instructed by Mr. Philip Melsh of the Director of Public Prosecution's office, and Mr. Patrick Back defending. Wood pleaded not guilty to murder, but guilty of manslaughter on the grounds of diminished responsibility and provocation, according to the provisions of the Homicide Act 1957.

At first I have to grant that the proceedings almost resembled a murder trial. Wood admitted that he had habitually spied on Mary, and that on the night he killed her, he had watched her go out with a man friend and had got into her house to await her homecoming. Suggestions that he might have broken in through a top window using an otherwise unexplained ladder, were unpursued, as were so many details of the events. But it is clear that Wood watched Mary from the privacy of her own hall when she came home with her friend, kissed him goodnight, and came alone into her home.

Wood claimed that he then sneaked out of the back door, came round to the front door, knocked, and was admitted by Mary. The prosecution was content with Wood's claim that he and Mary then made love and his statement that he had admitted to her that he was in the house when she came home. He said she was "livid" again and that he had selected this inappropriate moment to demand that Mary favour him with a monogamous relationship. When she refused, he decided to kill her.

According to his account, he then went to the kitchen to get a meat tenderiser, thereafter to the spare room for a pair of socks and a pillow. He put the tenderiser into the socks, went into Mary's bedroom and hit her over the head with the tenderiser. When she struggled, he throttled her and put the pillow over her face.

For myself and for all of Mary's friends this was grotesque news. For those of us who could believe she was dead at all, remained the hope that she died peacefully, that maybe he had killed her as she slept, and she never knew of his brutality. Nevertheless, it struck us as very odd that all parties to the case went to such pains to negate the facts of Wood's violence.

The judge deemed it unnecessary for the jury to be shown autopsy photographs of the extent of Mary's injuries. But we saw them. Sitting in the front row of the gallery, waiting in the corridor outside the courtroom, it was impossible not to see them, as the various gentlemen of the court passed them from hand to hand for their own edification. They seemed to want us to see.

Thereafter the killing was referred to in euphemisms—"the incident," "the events in question," and "the tragedy of that night."

PUTTING THE VICTIM ON TRIAL

The curious thing about the defence of manslaughter to a murder charge is that, since there is no injured party available as a chief prosecution witness, the prosecution's case is based primarily on the statements made by the defendant to the police. Similarly, the case for the defence relies on the one eye-witness, the accused. The case for Wood's defence was not different in tone from the prose-cution's case.

Certainly there was little at issue between them. It seemed that the only way out of this deadlock was to put Mary Bristow on trial, at which they were ably aided and abetted by the British gutter press. "Savage Killing of a Women's Lib Lover," the *Sun* headlined. "Milady's Link with Free-Love Killer," said the *News of the World*. And the *Star* excelled itself with "Kinky Secret Life of Beauty at Library," sub-titled "Mary's sex games turned jealous lover into killer," and accompanied by a photograph of a naked woman captioned "Victim Mary . . . enjoyed kinky sex games"—which, needless to say, was not a picture of Mary at all. There was nothing we could do about it. "The dead," our lawyer assured us, "cannot be defamed."

No doubt entirely secure in that knowledge, Wood's counsel proceeded with a relentless assassination of Mary's character, unchecked by any consideration of truth, logic or common decency. Mary's real qualities—her kindness, her concern for others, her strong feminist principles, her independence, her intelli-gence, her popularity, her political commitments—and even her age and her height, were used as sticks to beat her with.

Describing the relationship between Mary Bristow and Peter Wood, Patrick Back, defending, stated:

> There was between him and Mary Bristow what you may think of as a very strange relationship, in which a gifted and older woman took him in hand, and sought to fashion him into something she thought superior, but which his birth and background did not really design him to be. The six-year-old relationship was a Pygmalion or *My Fair Lady* situation in reverse. Mary had a brilliant intellect and an IQ of 182. She took the part of a female Professor Higgins, and he that of a male Eliza Doolittle. She was also middle-class, and as sometimes happens with very clever people she was in a state of rebellion against the morality favoured by that class. She regarded marriage as, at any rate, some-thing not for her. I suppose she thought of it as something that would restrict her freedom. She was a devotee of many causes. The Women's Liberation Movement, pro-abortion and CND demonstrations.

With such cant and insidious innuendo, Back hoped to take responsibility for Mary's death away from Peter Wood and cast it squarely upon Mary herself.

"Her rejection of him, perhaps in a rather nasty way," he said, "must have been like a stab in the body." In other words, she was "asking for it."

Provocation, in law means

> some act or series of acts done by the deceased which would cause in any rea-sonable person, and did cause in the accused, a sudden and temporary loss of self-control, rendering him so subject to passion as to make him not for the moment master of his mind. The sufficiency of the provocation shall be left to the determination of the jury, which shall take into account everything both said and done according to the effect which, in their opinion, it would have on a *reasonable man* [Homicide Act of 1957].

In this case, the alleged provocation was simply Mary's disinclination to enter into an exclusive sexual relationship with Peter Wood. And it was, according to Winchester Crown Court, enough. Thus, any reasonable man might be provoked into killing a woman if she has the temerity to refuse to marry him.

The second defence entered by Wood's defence counsel was that of diminished responsibility. In law, this means (according to the Homicide Act) that the defence must show that the accused was "suffering from such abnormality of mind (whether arising from a condition of arrested or retarded development of mind, or any inherent causes or induced by disease or injury) as might substantially impair his mental responsibility for his acts and omissions, in doing or being a party to the killing."

The Mental Health Act 1959 contributes a more comprehensive and enlightened definition of mental disorder: "Mental illness, arrested or incomplete development of mind, psychotic disorder, and any other disorder or disability of the mind." And the sixth (1979) edition of Smith and Keenan's *English Law* says: "A killing arising from drink or drugs is not covered, because the condition is self-induced. And jealousy, hate or rage are not covered because they are ordinary human frailties which the defendant is expected to control."

Psychiatrists appearing for the prosecution and defence were in almost total accord about Wood's state of mind before the murder. They had not, of course, actually met him at this stage, but they were happy to take his word as gospel. He was "depressed," they agreed, because of his own admission that he had been "drinking heavily" and was currently out of work.

These facts might have been easily ascertained at any time in the past five years from less expert witnesses: any Winchester bar person, for instance, or a member of the Department of Employment. However, the psychiatrists agreed that the cause of Peter Wood's stressful life was Mary Bristow's determination to live her own life in preference to one prescribed by Wood.

Both psychiatrists agreed, too, that when they met Wood after the murder he was not then, in their opinion, suffering from depression—because the cause of his stress (Mary) had been removed. This was enough to persuade the jury to accept a plea of diminished responsibility—implying again that, if a woman's life-style, independence and refusal to be ruled by a man is stressful to him, she is deemed to be responsible for any violent reaction on his part.

In his summing-up, the judge endorsed the view that Mary brought her death upon herself.

"Mary Bristow," he said,

with an IQ of 182, was a rebel from her middle-class background. She was unorthodox in her relationships, so proving that the cleverest people aren't always very wise. Those who engage in sexual relationships should realise that sex is one of the deepest and most powerful human emotions, and if you're playing with sex you're playing with fire. And it might be, members of the jury, that the conventions which surround sex, which some people think are "old hat," are there to prevent people if possible from burning themselves.

In drawing a distinction for the jury between murder and manslaughter, he explained, "Murder involves wickedness, manslaughter does not necessarily involve wickedness, as when out-of-their-depth and totally-unable-to-cope people do things which are totally foreign to their nature. There is a difference between a villain shooting a policeman, and a husband killing his wife or lover at a stage when they can no longer cope."

Effectively the jury were thus instructed that it is reasonable for a man to kill a woman he has slept with on a regular basis, if that woman behaves in a way which frustrates him. Such an idea not only denies women an equal status in law, it also denies them the status of persons. And the jury accepted it.

The implications of the manslaughter verdict are obvious. If women are more intelligent, stronger and more independent than the men they associate with, and if they refuse to be governed by those inadequate men, they are deemed in law to be responsible for their own deaths. Female strength and independence are construed as wilful acts of provocation which diminish men's responsibility for their violence. On this basis, Peter Wood will probably be free in 18 months' time.

I left Winchester after the trial. I doubt I shall ever live there again. The Women's Liberation group that had supported us all for seven years gradually disintegrated. It no longer exists. It is good to hear that a new women's group now meets.

The Case of the Yorkshire Ripper: Mad, Bad, Beast or Male?

LUCY BLAND

Now, stealing fearful or chaperoned through the shadowed streets
Night, in Leeds, in November, is *fifteen hours long*
We know only, that each man, or group of men on these streets
Is an enemy, or if not the enemy waiting for us.
Not our *personal* enemy, then one walking at large, unshadowed, free
While we the survivors
Pinned down under artificial light in our fragile homes
Feel the pressure of dread in the darkness nudging the panes,
Thin as our skin—and hear the voices:
"No woman is safe." (It is the police this time)
"No woman should go out after dark—" then in a whisper:
"but we men can."
The voices ride in on the wind
That butts against the walls—
(Walls vulnerable as our skulls)—
"No woman is safe"—
The voices climb in as draughts through the cracks—
"Women"—(it is all men speaking now)
Fear the dark, stay at home
We cannot answer for the consequences
If you get on buses;
Leave *us* the hunting paths in the city jungle—
Be good: be stupid: never, never be free.

Reprinted from *Causes for Concern*, ed. Paul Gordon and Phil Scraton, 186–209 (London: Penguin, 1984). Many thanks to Jill Radford for her collaboration on an earlier version of this paper; to Victoria Greenwood, Maureen McNeil, and Angela McRobbie for their helpful comments and Victoria's invaluable newspaper cuttings; and to Jean Keir for her legal knowledge.

And we remember
The woman, who was, or could have been.
Our sister, student, colleague, friend, neighbour
Ordinary, admirable, easy to like, tired
Who got off a bus, and for whom there was no going home
And we, we the women who as yet survive, we say:
"We have waited a long time for anger.
But we are angry now
For each and every betrayal of trust.
For each and every degradation, the greater and the less
For each and every evil done to women
And all are remembered: and all are written down—
We are coming to claim our justice
That is justice for us all
For our blood cries out, and unnumbered women cry out
Through our voices, and our time has come, and *we are coming*

Yes, *we are coming.*

—From "Poem for Jacqueline Hill"[1]

On the evening of 2 January 1981 a man was arrested in Sheffield for the possession of false car number plates. He was subsequently charged with the murder of thirteen women and the attempted murder of another seven. Two police officers, during their routine check of stolen car registration plates as part of an anti-vice patrol, had succeeded, by chance, in apprehending the man unsuccessfully sought for five and a half years by an investigation of 250 detectives, costing £4 million of public money. The two policemen had caught the man known as the "Yorkshire Ripper." His name was Peter Sutcliffe.

The Yorkshire Ripper murders began in October 1975 in Leeds with the brutal killing of Wilma McCann. The mode of attack and the subsequent rituals concerning the arrangement of the victim's body and clothing became a familiar pattern, known to the police as the Ripper's "mark." The Ripper approached his victims from behind, and hit them several times with full force over the head, usually with a hammer. Then he stabbed and slashed his victims, often numerous times, mainly across the breasts and abdomen, with a knife or a sharpened Philips-type screwdriver. It appears that stabbing would often continue after the death of the victim. He frequently left the body ritually posed with clothing pulled up to reveal the breasts and abdomen.

Although Wilma McCann was the first of the Ripper's murdered victims, his attacks had begun at an earlier date. Attacks on Anna Rogulskyi and Olive Smelt, in July and August 1975 respectively, in the form of several extremely violent blows to the head, were recognized by the police in summer 1977 as the work of the Ripper. Central to the police hesitancy in identifying these attacks as Ripper attacks was the fact that neither woman was a prostitute, although the police and media were quick to label them "women of loose morals." Olive Smelt subsequently became terrified of going out at night and her marriage nearly broke down because, as she put it, she grew to fear "all men."

It was subsequently revealed, in early 1981, on his own admission, that Peter Sutcliffe had attempted to murder two prostitutes back in 1969. However, these women remain anonymous and he has not been charged with their assault. His second murdered victim, Emily Jackson, was killed in January 1976, also in Leeds. She received numerous blows to the head, followed by fifty-two stabbings from a sharpened screwdriver. On her thigh was the print of a size 7 Dunlop boot, the first of many small clues to the killer's identity. In May 1976 Marcella Claxton narrowly survived what was only much later recognized to be another Ripper attack. The Ripper's third murder took place in February 1977, again in Leeds, with the killing of Irene Richardson. Her murder was followed in April by that of Patricia Atkinson. This time the Ripper had changed his procedure in two respects. Until Patricia's death, all his victims were attacked in the open; Patricia was killed in her own flat. Prior to Patricia's murder, the killings had all occurred in Leeds; this murder took place in Bradford. It forcibly struck home that it was not simply women in Leeds but all women in the north of England who were at risk from the Ripper's murderous attacks.

Two months later, this time again in Leeds, the Ripper killed Jayne MacDonald. The shock of having to identify his daughter's mutilated body left Jayne's father paralysed, soon to die. Until Jayne's murder the Ripper's victims were all thought to have been prostitutes. The label "Yorkshire Ripper," coined by the press, reflected the initial belief that this mass murderer, like his predecessor "Jack," was intent on the extermination of prostitutes. With the killing of Jayne came the public recognition that all women, prostitutes or otherwise, were the Ripper's potential prey. (Though many women had felt for some time that stepping outside their front doors after dark, for whatever purpose, entailed the risk of death.) The actions of the Ripper placed a tight curfew on *all* women; a curfew reinforced by police advice to women. Increasingly, the streets became emptier as terror accompanied the Ripper's campaign of murder. This put even more at risk those women who chose not to be intimidated by the Ripper, or whose life circumstances gave them no choice.

With Jayne's death came press and police horror that the Ripper had made an "error" in his killing of an "innocent, perfectly respectable" victim. By implication prostitutes were deemed non-innocent, non-respectable victims, who had brought death upon themselves by virtue of their trade—an occupational hazard. According to Beattie (*The Yorkshire Ripper Story,* p. 42): "For the first time the Ripper saga became national news . . . at last the police started getting the cooperation they needed." *The Times* (25 May 1981) was later to comment: "The police do deserve a measure of sympathy over the overwhelming task they faced, the major problem during the early years being apathy over the killing of prostitutes."

Two weeks after the murder of Jayne MacDonald, the Ripper struck again. This time his victim, Maureen Long, survived, despite serious injury. His next victim, Jean Jordan, was not so fortunate. She was murdered in Manchester on 1 October 1977, but her body was not found for a number of days. Once discovered, it was clear that her killer had returned eight days later, and attacked again. In this second attack he had stabbed her many times and had also attempted to sever her head from her body with a hacksaw. Her bag contained a clue to the Ripper's identity, a new £5 note, issued by a bank to various employers in Yorkshire two days before the attack. It was believed to have been given to her by her attacker in payment for her services as a prostitute. The police tried to trace the source of the £5 note and Peter Sutcliffe was one of the many men they interviewed. In fact he had received the note in his pay packet. As in the case of eight subsequent interviews with the police, the Ripper's true identity remained concealed. He was to kill a further seven times.

In December, the Ripper attempted to murder Marilyn Moore. Despite severe injury she survived, retaining the memory of what subsequently proved to be a fairly accurate description of her attacker: a dark-haired man with a "Jason King" type moustache. His next victim, Yvonne Pearson, murdered in Bradford on 21 January 1978, lay undiscovered until 27 March. As with Jean Jordan, the murderer had returned to the body in the intervening period. Unlike the Ripper's previous victims, neither Yvonne nor Jean was stabbed to death. Yvonne's death came with the force of the blow to her head. While she lay dead but undiscovered, the Ripper killed again, this time in Huddersfield. On 31 January Helen Rytka was struck over the head five times and then stabbed repeatedly. During Sutcliffe's trial in May 1981 it was revealed that she was the one victim with whom the Ripper had had sexual intercourse. Intercourse took place after she had been struck on the head. She was probably dead at the time.

In February 1978 the publishers of the *Yorkshire Post* and *Evening Post* offered a reward of £5,000 for information leading to the Ripper's arrest: the West Yorkshire Police Authority raised this figure to £10,000. Rita Rytka, Helen's twin sister, made a TV appeal to the Ripper to give himself up. *After* the discovery of Helen's body but *before* the discovery of Yvonne's body, the "Ripper squad" received the first of three letters from a man calling himself "Jack the Ripper." On the arrest of Sutcliffe in January 1981, these letters, and the subsequent tape sent by "Jack," were revealed as hoaxes. At the time, however, the police, particularly George Oldfield, who had been heading the Ripper squad since June 1977, took the letters and tape (received in June 1979) to be genuine. (Oldfield took on the "hunt" for the Ripper as a personal vendetta—man against man. "Jack," in his personal address to Oldfield on the tape, reinforced this tendency.) Part of the reason for the belief in the letters' authenticity lay with certain details in the first letter concerning the murder of Joan Harrison. Joan had been killed in Preston in November 1975, by a single blow to the head. She had not been stabbed. Her attacker had had sexual intercourse with her and his remaining semen revealed him to be of the rare blood group B (only 6 per cent of the population are of this group). At the time her murder was not linked with the murder of Wilma McCann. Although Joan was a prostitute, like Wilma and many of the Ripper's subsequent victims, the nature of her attack was qualitatively different. There was no stabbing and it was thought to involve a "sexual motive" (which the Ripper murders were believed not to entail). Sutcliffe has vehemently denied that he killed Joan Harrison. However, by the time of the first letter's arrival, her death was being treated as a possible Ripper murder, although this had not been publicly discussed. That the author of the "Ripper" letter knew of this connection confirmed his authenticity as far as many of the police were concerned. It was an authenticity reinforced with the arrival of the third letter the following year in which saliva traces on the envelope revealed him to be of the same blood group as Joan's killer. However, as the *New Statesman* (12 September 1980) was to point out, the belief that the letters contained information that only the killer could possess, such as the connection made with Joan Harrison's murder, was unfounded. Short accounts in the *Daily Mirror* and the *Yorkshire Evening Post* already had mentioned a possible link with the murder in Preston. Further, whether or not the author of the letters and tape was the killer of Joan, the evidence at the time did not confirm that he had committed the *other* murders. On the contrary, as the same *New Statesman* article was to indicate, the first letter's "boast" that the police had not acknowledged the full death-toll—eight (including Joan) and not seven—omitted to mention information which would have been known to the "genuine" Ripper. This was that another murder had occurred, of Yvonne Pearson, as yet undiscovered. Most of the police apparently failed to register "Jack's" error. Their discovery of Yvonne's body did not lead to a reassessment of the letter's authenticity, but to a police poster in Bradford which read: "The next victim may be innocent" (see *Spare Rib*, 88, 1979).

In May, with the murder of Vera Millward, the Ripper killed for the second time in Manchester. For the rest of the year there were no more Ripper attacks. In March 1979 the third "Jack the Ripper" letter was received. The second had been sent to the *Daily Mirror* soon after the first. The third letter was followed by the murder of Josephine Whitacker in Halifax. Of twenty-five stabbings, three were in her vagina. At the time this aspect of the murder was not revealed. What concerned the press, the police and certain sections of the public was that for the second time the Ripper had killed an "innocent" victim, for Josephine Whitacker was not a prostitute. After her murder, Oldfield called a press conference and declared: "The girl is perfectly respectable, similar to Jayne MacDonald" (Beattie, p. 73). To claim that the Ripper had killed "by mistake" was no longer very convincing to anyone. Certainly "Jack" himself in his first letter had claimed to have killed Jayne in error. He had said: "About the MacDonald lassie, I didn't know she was decent and I'm sorry I changed my routine that night." But the murder of Jo Whitacker, and all subsequent Ripper attacks, took place outside red-light areas. Slowly the police and media were having to admit that the Ripper might kill *any* woman, *anywhere*. As the *Daily Mirror* (7 April

1979) phrased it, quoting Oldfield: "The next victim could be anyone's wife, daughter or girlfriend"—apparently a woman could only be seen in terms of her relationship to a man.

Women readers of the *Sunday Mirror* (15 April 1979) were told that they should answer five crucial questions forming a "Checklist for Survival." These included a clear warning not to be complacent—Do you think you are safe because you are not a good-time girl?"; a warning not to precipitate an attack—"Do you go out alone at night, even to walk just a few yards?"; and a warning not to let their toleration of sex be known—"Do you make any secret of the fact that when talking to a man you don't mind having sex?"

Two months later Oldfield received a tape from the man calling himself "Jack." In a Geordie accent, identified as Wearside, the tape mocked the inability of Oldfield and "his boys" to catch him. During a press conference, at which Oldfield played the tape, a Fleet Street journalist suggested that it was time to call in Scotland Yard. The immediate response of Dick Holland (one of the Ripper squad) was "Why should we call them in? They haven't caught their own Ripper yet." Oldfield's belief in the authenticity of the letters and the tapes formed the basis of subsequent police strategy in the Ripper hunt. However, according to Beattie (p. 77) the tape and letters were never universally accepted as genuine. Certain detectives had their doubts, as did senior officers of the Northumbria Police, expressed in a top-secret report sent soon after the tape's arrival. Jack Lewis, a linguist, also stated that he and his colleagues thought that the tape was a hoax. He argued that: "His accent is so individualistic that the man would have been brought to police attention if he were living . . . anywhere but Wearside" (Beattie, p. 97). Nevertheless, between June 1979 and June 1981 the police set up a special telephone number which callers could dial to hear the tape. In all, 878,796 calls were made.

On 2 September 1979 Barbara Leach was murdered in Bradford. Feminists responded to the murder with a rally and a march through Bradford to speak out against violence against women and to commemorate all the victims of the Ripper. In their press release to the local media they stated:

> We mourn for all victims of the Ripper and all women victims of murder, rape, assault and battering by men. The attacks of the Ripper are an extreme example of the sort of attacks that are made on women all the time. The police are telling women to stay in at night. Why should women stay in at night, when they have done nothing? We should have a curfew on men, and the right to defend ourselves so that all women can walk at night without fear. (Reprinted in *FAST*, no. 3)

Police responded by interviewing all first-year students at Bradford University, as Barbara Leach had been a student there. The students who had come to university a month after Barbara's murder were mostly about fourteen when the Ripper attacks had started, and they were mainly from other parts of the country. The West Yorkshire police and the Leeds-based advertising agency of Poulter and Associates Ltd, jointly set up Project R. Designers, photographers and distributors gave their services free. Newsagents gave away two million copies of a four-page news-sheet which profiled the murders and carried samples of the handwriting from the three "Ripper" letters, and a transcript of the tape. Plastered on 6,000 hoardings in more than six hundred towns and villages were the words: "The Ripper would like you to ignore this. The man next to you may have killed twelve women." The tape was broadcast several times a day on radio and TV. The police also played it over loudspeakers at Leeds United football ground, but it was drowned with chants from the fans of "You'll never catch the Ripper. 12 nil! 12 nil!"

The public were urged to maintain constant vigilance. Tragically they were being directed to listen and look for the wrong signs. Public response was immense. In the first six weeks of Project R the police received more than 18,000 calls, leaving them with 17,000 suspects. The police were unable to cope, and the project was discontinued. By late January 1980, the posters had come down and the taped voice was no longer broadcast (Beattie).

However, although they were not able to catch the Ripper, the police did manage to arrest eleven women picketing a cinema showing "Violation of the Bitch." Further, Yallop (*Deliver Us from Evil*) claims that in 1979-80, while prostitutes were being used as live bait in Bradford, officers sat in a car and watched one woman being attacked without helping or calling help. Apparently they were there only to collect car numbers. It was left to the English Collective of Prostitutes to challenge the police definition of prostitutes as "deserving" parties to the crime in their statement to the Metropolitan Commissioner, David McNee, in January 1980. The Collective stated: "To the Ripper and to the police, prostitutes are not decent, we are not innocent victims. What are we guilty of to deserve such a death? 70 per cent of prostitute women in this country are mothers fighting to make ends meet and feed our children. But because we refuse poverty for ourselves and our children we are treated as criminals. In the eyes of the police we deserve what we get, even death."

The next Ripper attack was apparently more than a year later, the attempted murder of Theresa Sykes in Huddersfield. However, Sutcliffe has admitted to two attacks in the intervening period, attacks which at the time were not associated with the Ripper. These were the strangulation of Margo Walls in August 1980 and the attempted murder of Dr. Uphadya Bandara, also with a garotte.

Less than a week after the attempt to kill Theresa, he murdered Jacqueline Hill in Leeds. There was public concern at the initial police treatment of the case. A student had found her handbag and, on the discovery that it was bloodstained, the police had been contacted. The student who had rung the police commented: "All the way throughout the conversation, we kept saying they [the police] ought to check whether Jacqueline Hill was in her flat or whether she was still out, but they just didn't want to bother . . . they treated it as lost property" (quoted in Beattie, p. 94). After Jacqueline's murder, much of the press demanded the calling in of Scotland Yard. Ronald Gregory (West Yorkshire

Chief Constable) refused, but presented a compromise. This was the creation of a new "super squad," a "think-tank" of senior police officers drawn from other forces and headed by Jim Hobson. The demotion of Oldfield was seen as an implicit criticism of his handling of the case.

On hearing that the Ripper had struck again, the football fans' response was repeated at Elland Road football ground with the chant "Ripper 13, police 0!" (*Daily Mail,* 27 November 1980). On 27 November 1980, BBC 2's "Newsnight" carried a seven-minute item in which some of the Ripper's surviving victims and the families of victims spoke of their hatred and grief directly to the murderer "out there somewhere" in the television audience. In a letter to the *Guardian* (1 December 1980) the Hebden Bridge Women's Group (West Yorkshire) suggested that rather than suffering the danger of going out with a male escort, as the police and media were suggesting, "women should 'escort' each other by, for example, setting up car pools (where cars are available), or approaching each other at bus stops and stations and offering to walk together. Local areas ought to provide self-defence classes for women. Men could support women by keeping out of their way, not approaching them if they don't know them and not walking closely behind women."

On a decision taken at a conference on "Sexual Violence against Women," many feminists, in the name of "Angry Women," took various forms of action on 11 and 12 December all over Britain. Sex and porn shops were picketed, walls were fly-posted and spray-painted, cinema queues were leafleted, public meetings were held, interviews and articles were given to national and local media and self-defence groups were set up (see *Spare Rib,* no. 103, February 1981). Police told the press, "these women are dangerous," and there were fifty arrests (see Anna Coote and Beatrix Campbell, *Sweet Freedom,* p. 205).

On 2 January 1981, a man arrested in a routine anti-vice procedure of the Sheffield police admitted to being the "Yorkshire Ripper." As John Alderson, Chief Constable of Devon and Cornwall had predicted three weeks earlier on radio, the suspect in the Ripper murders was found by an alert, uniformed police patrol (*Guardian,* 6 January 1981). The Ripper squad's immediate response was public jubilation and declaration of its imminent disbanding. At a press conference on 4 January, the day before the accused's preliminary hearing in court, Ronald Gregory announced, "I can tell you we are absolutely delighted with developments at this stage." But the response of some was concern that the defendant's trial could only be prejudiced by such a public display of euphoria (see for example, the Editorial and J. Sweeney's letter in the *Guardian,* 7 January 1981).

THE LEGAL PROCESSING OF SERIOUS CRIME

When the police arrest a suspect and charge him/her with an offence, the suspect is brought to a magistrates' court for a preliminary hearing. In cases of serious crime, the magistrates' court must decide whether or not the evidence justifies committing the accused to a crown court, known as the committal proceedings. If the charge is upheld, as is usually the case, the accused is either granted bail or remanded in custody. Police write a report based on inquiries, and it is sent either to a prosecuting solicitor, or, in serious cases, including all cases of murder, to the Director of Public Prosecutions (the DPP). The DPP is a government official, responsible to the Attorney-General. The DPP's office instigates prosecutions and the Attorney-General may act as prosecutor in important cases. The DPP advises the police as to whether or not to proceed with the case. If the decision is to proceed, the accused, now a defendant, is committed to a crown court for trial on indictment.

If the indictment is one of murder, unlawful homicide with malice aforethought needs to be established. Malice aforethought consists of intention, on the part of the accused, to kill or cause grievous bodily harm to another human being. Malice aforethought does not imply either premeditation or ill will. The general rule is that the accused's motives, good or bad, are irrelevant to his/her liability. However, the concept of criminal responsibility, central to our criminal law, *is* relevant to the question of liability.

The concept of criminal responsibility rests on the assumption that *mens rea* (literally "guilty mind"—a criminal intention or knowledge that an act is wrong) is an essential element in crime. It is a necessary element in liability, which has to be established *before* a verdict. To determine whether the accused did or did not have the guilty intention to do wrong, the law presumes that we normally intend the natural consequences of our actions (Wootton, *Crime and Penal Policy*). Thus liability to conviction for serious crimes depends on the offender both having committed a forbidden act and having done so with a certain will.

Since a conviction of murder requires the prior establishment of *mens rea,* homicide is not punishable as murder if it is done unintentionally, accidentally, by mistake or while suffering from certain forms of mental abnormality. There are various possible defences, unique to a charge of murder, which reduce the charge to one of manslaughter. These consist of a plea of diminished responsibility, of provocation (leading the accused to lose self-control) and of the accused having acted in pursuance of a suicide pact.

In relation to the plea of diminished responsibility, section 2 of the 1957 Homicide Act stipulates that: "Where a person kills or is a party to the killing of another, he shall not be convicted of murder if he was suffering from such abnormality of mind (whether arising from a condition of arrested or retarded development of mind or any innocent causes or induced by disease or injury), as substantially impaired his mental responsibility for his acts and omissions in doing or being party to the killing."

Thus to establish diminished responsibility, the defence has the burden of proving three elements: (1) that the accused was suffering "abnormality of mind" at the time of the killing: (2) that the abnormality of mind resulted from one of the specified causes; and (3) that the abnormality of mind must have substantially impaired the accused's mental responsibility. From the viewpoint of the accused, the possibility of getting a murder charge reduced to section 2 manslaughter has the possible advantage over a verdict of insanity or of murder in that a homicide conviction involving insanity carries automatic committal for an indefinite period to Broadmoor or a similar institution, while in a conviction of murder, a sentence of life imprisonment is mandatory. A verdict of diminished responsibility, however, like any verdict of manslaughter, can be dealt with in a number of ways ranging from absolute discharge to an order under the 1959 Mental Health Act, confining the accused to a special hospital, through to life imprisonment. The sentence is at the discretion of the judge.

If the accused decides to plead not guilty to a charge of murder but guilty to a charge of manslaughter by reason of diminished responsibility, it is open to the defence counsel (if prepared to accept this plea) to approach the prosecution in the hope of persuading him/her to accept this plea and thus to change the charge. If agreement is reached between prosecution and defence as to this plea, it is then at the discretion of the trial judge at the crown court as to whether the plea is accepted (thereby curtailing the trial to a trial without jury consisting of the presentation of the uncontested prosecution case of diminished responsibility, followed by the judge's sentence) or rejected (thereby necessitating a trial by jury in which the defence has to persuade the jury of the accused's diminished responsibility, thus shifting the burden of proof from the prosecution to the defence).

THE TRIAL OF PETER SUTCLIFFE

On Wednesday 29 April 1981 Peter Sutcliffe appeared in court before Judge Boreham. Due to the extreme seriousness of the case, the Attorney-General, Sir Michael Havers, had chosen to act as prosecutor. During the period in which Peter Sutcliffe had been in custody, a bargain had been struck between the defence and the prosecution. Sir Michael accepted the accused's plea of not guilty to murder but guilty to the manslaughter of thirteen women on the grounds of diminished responsibility. Sutcliffe also pleaded guilty to the attempted murder of another seven women. The prosecution and defence anticipated a brief trial, lasting a maximum of two days, in which the prosecution, backed by psychiatric evidence, would present an uncontested plea of diminished responsibility and the judge would subsequently pass sentence.

They had not reckoned on Judge Boreham. The judge rejected the bargain between the prosecution and defence and demanded a trial by jury, with the prosecution upholding the charge of murder. Sir Michael had argued that his pre-trial "very severe cross-examination" of the psychiatrists had convinced him that Sutcliffe was suffering from paranoid schizophrenia. Boreham had repeatedly asked Sir Michael for the *factual* basis to the plea—the supporting evidence. Sir Michael's inability to reply prompted Boreham to insist that a jury must decide Sutcliffe's state of mind.

This meant that the Attorney-General, having apparently been convinced of Sutcliffe's madness, now had to convince the jury of Sutcliffe's sanity. Sir Michael's enforced switch of positions showed in stark relief the hypocrisy of the system of plea bargaining.

The trial by jury of Peter Sutcliffe opened at the Old Bailey on 5 May 1981. It ran until 22 May, with a jury of six women and six men. Sir Michael Havers and Harry Ognall, QC, prosecuted, and Chadwin defended.

The case was set up in terms of whether Peter Sutcliffe was a lunatic or a liar; whether the doctors were correct in believing that he was a paranoid schizophrenic who felt he had a "divine mission" to kill prostitutes, or whether he "was a clever, callous murderer who had tried to feign insanity" (*Guardian*, 6 May 1981).

To back his argument that Sutcliffe was a liar, feigning insanity, Sir Michael initially pointed to three different kinds of evidence: first, that Sutcliffe had never mentioned the "divine mission" during his hours of police interrogation; second, that while in custody, one prison officer had heard Sutcliffe plan to feign madness, while Sutcliffe had told another prison officer how amusing it was that the doctors thought him mad; third, that the last six women killed by Sutcliffe were not prostitutes but "absolutely respectable" women, thus refuting Sutcliffe's claim of a "divine mission" to kill prostitutes only.

As the trial proceeded, however, the evidence which the prosecution chose to emphasize noticeably shifted. The prosecution held on to the first and third points of the above evidence as "proof" of Sutcliffe's sanity, but it "lost" to the defence over the interpretation of what Sutcliffe had said or been heard to say by prison officers. The defence read from the prison report that Sutcliffe, as well as being "amused" that doctors thought him mad, had *also* said that the doctors thought there was something wrong with him because he heard God's voice; to which he had asked why he should be thought mad because of this. This represented momentarily a "win" for the defence, as it appeared to show a madman thinking himself to be sane. When the psychiatrist, Dr. Milne, insisted that premeditation and deliberation were not inconsistent with schizophrenia, the prosecution also partly abandoned its argument over examples of Sutcliffe's "calculating" rational thought (such as Sutcliffe choosing not to kill women in his car because it would be too noisy and would leave evidence).

The prosecution, however, developed two further arguments to substantiate its claim that Sutcliffe was not suffering from diminished responsibility: first, that Sutcliffe's killings were "understandable" in terms of rational, reasonable *motives;* second, that there was a sexual component to six of the attacks. The latter contradicted the divine-mission argument (that Sutcliffe had killed only on God's order to rid the world of prostitutes) *and* offered a reason *for* the attacks (sexual gratification).

In the course of the trial, the psychiatrists' diagnosis was ridiculed by the prosecutor, Ognall. On the one hand the psychiatrists' "reading" of symptoms was reduced to their being "taken in" by the lying Sutcliffe. In the case of the psychiatrist, Dr. MacCulloch, psychiatric expertise was blatantly challenged. MacCulloch had omitted to read the interviews with Sutcliffe conducted by the police. Sir Michael commented: "What sort of an expert is that who forms a view without knowing all the facts . . . ?" On the other hand, Sutcliffe's "creation" of a divine mission was taken as being a direct response to the doctor's prompting. In his summing up, Judge Boreham pointed out that the factual basis of the doctors' opinion was under challenge (reflecting a long history of legal discourse refusing to take doctors' opinions as "facts"). The jury, by a majority of ten to two agreed with the prosecution that this "factual basis" was absent and they convicted Sutcliffe as guilty of murder and not manslaughter.

One disturbing aspect of the trial was the way in which the prosecution developed its argument that Sutcliffe's killings were "understandable" in terms of rational motive and motivation. As I have indicated already, the law presumes that normally we intend the consequences of our actions and that where an unlawful act has been committed, the accused's *motives* are irrelevant to his/her liability. However, in challenging a plea of diminished responsibility, the establishment of understandable motive and motivation acts as a means for the prosecution to demonstrate *rational* intention to kill, and thus the existence of *mens rea*. As the Sutcliffe trial proceeded, the prosecution increasingly took this tack. Further, the defence, including the psychiatrists called by the defence, converged with the prosecution in a "common-sense" understanding of the motive to kill prostitutes. As I shall demonstrate, they also agreed on the role of Peter Sutcliffe's wife, Sonia. This proved possible despite their different objectives and, in the case of the psychiatrists, a fundamentally different language of explanation.

The defence, in attempting to establish diminished responsibility, had to establish both that the accused was suffering an "abnormality of mind" and that he was *so affected at the time of the killings.* The establishment of the latter is not possible within the terms of psychiatry, since psychiatry involves the diagnosis of states of mind, but is incapable of determining the causes of acts—in this case, whether or not paranoid schizophrenia accounted for the killings. The language of psychiatry, with its stress on the determining power of the unconscious, fundamentally conflicts with the law's stress on conscious intention as revealed in the acts themselves (see Roger Smith, *Trial by Medicine,* for an account of this conflict as revealed in nineteenth-century trials). Judge Boreham, in his summing up, for example, directed the jury to look at *actions,* for "actions speak louder than words very often" (*Guardian,* 22 May 1981). The notion of "diminished responsibility" is a muddled compromise which straddles the two modes of explanation.

Nevertheless, in the case of Sutcliffe, as in many other cases of male violence against women, the language of law and psychiatry met in a common "understanding" of Sutcliffe's acts, in terms of *female precipitation.* Both the prosecution and the defence, despite different objectives (the one to establish Sutcliffe's "reason," the other to establish his "diminished responsibility"), took the actions of certain women in Sutcliffe's life as the key to understanding and explaining his behaviour. A focus on woman-as-precipitator got around the problem of whether or not the (male) actor was responsible for his actions. In effect, both the prosecution and the defence placed the blame and the responsibility for the Ripper murders on women. For the prosecution, Sutcliffe was responsible for his actions in the sense of having *rationally* responded to the behaviour of certain women. These were: a prostitute who "cheated" him of £5, his wife Sonia and, to a certain extent, his mother. The fact that these women had acted to precipitate his behaviour, however, effectively *removed* his responsibility. For the defence, Sutcliffe was not responsible for his actions because he was acting under the delusion of experiencing a "divine mission." To the psychiatrists, this mission was "understandable" in terms of the behaviour of certain women (again the cheating "prostitute," Sonia and his mother). In effect, these women were pointed to as the precipitators if not the cause of the Ripper's actions. It appeared that it was not so much Sutcliffe but these women who were on trial.

Sir Michael Havers made his views on prostitutes clear from the outset. In his introductory speech he remarked of Sutcliffe's victims: "Some were prostitutes, but perhaps the saddest part of the case is that some were not. The last six attacks were on totally respectable women." Members of women's organizations, including the English Collective of Prostitutes, accused Havers of "condoning the murder of prostitutes." They objected angrily to his prostitute/"respectable woman" distinction. Women demonstrated outside the Old Bailey with placards which read:

Women are not responsible for men's crimes

70 percent of prostitutes are mothers

Prostitutes are innocent OK

23 kids are motherless

Prostitutes have families too

Attorney-General condoning the murder of prostitutes

In his distinction between "prostitutes" and "respectable women," Sir Michael Havers was drawing on an "understanding" and a morality which predated the trial. This was, as Joan Smith ("Getting Away with Murder") put it, a view of the Ripper's motives as "not entirely reprehensible." From the time of Jayne MacDonald's murder, the media and the police consistently made the distinction between the Ripper's "innocent," "respectable" victims and the "others"; the "unrespectable, " guilty prostitutes and "loose women." On 26 October 1979, four years after the killing of Wilma McCann, the *London Evening News* had reported an "anniversary plea to the Ripper"—a statement by West Yorkshire's Acting Assistant Chief Constable, Jim Hobson. He had said: "He has made it clear that he hates prostitutes. Many people do. We, as a police force, will continue to arrest prostitutes. But the Ripper is now killing innocent girls." Addressing the killer directly he had added, "You have made your point. Give yourself up before another innocent woman dies" (quoted by Joan Smith). It almost sounds like an address to a small boy who has gone just "a bit too far" in his naughtiness.

The prosecution, the defence and Sutcliffe all agreed that back in 1969 a prostitute who had tricked him out of £5 change from a £10 note and then a week later, in front of Sutcliffe, shared the joke with her mates in the pub at his expense, had so humiliated Sutcliffe that it formed the basis for his subsequent hatred of all prostitutes. Before he told the story of a divine mission to the psychiatrists, Sutcliffe had told the police in January, just after his arrest, that he had killed after being humiliated by a prostitute. In his cross-examination of the psychiatrists, Ognall, for the prosecution, presented this story as the basis for a "perfectly sensible reason for harbouring a grudge against prostitutes" (*Guardian*, 16 May 1981), providing "a perfectly common-sense motive . . ." (*Guardian*, 19 May 1981). As Sir Michael Havers put it in his closing speech: "Was this not a classic case of provocation? . . . God hasn't told him to hate prostitutes or kill them. It was a reaction which, you may think, was not altogether surprising, the reaction of a man who had been fleeced and humiliated . . . the sort of loss of control which you don't have to be mad for a moment to suffer (*Guardian*, 20 May 1981).

This should be compared with, say, a suggestion that the "provocation" of a shopkeeper shortchanging a man, prompted the man to hate and kill all shopkeepers! For the sake of £5, then, thirteen women died. The defence, too, pointed to the "cheating" prostitute as an "explanation" for Sutcliffe's hatred of prostitutes. Although by the time of his trial Sutcliffe was arguing that it was the divine mission which had led to his killing of prostitutes, of course it was prostitutes who were still to blame. For had not God, no less, told him that prostitutes "were responsible for all the trouble?" Thus the prosecution, the defence and Sutcliffe, supported by the media and the police, all shared a common morality that killing prostitutes "made sense."

Sonia, Sutcliffe's wife, was also viewed as a key precipitator to the killings. Her "neurotic" behaviour was described at length in the psychiatrists' reports and eagerly taken up by the media. She was labelled temperamental, difficult, over-excited, highly strung and unstable. She was allegedly so obsessed with cleanliness that she refused to allow Sutcliffe to wear his shoes in the house and she spent hours cleaning specks from the carpet. Sonia, it was claimed, sometimes pulled out the TV plug when Sutcliffe was waiting for his tea, and when he wanted to read a newspaper she would shout and swipe at him. It was further claimed that Sonia would not let Sutcliffe help himself from the fridge. Dr. Milne told the court, "Sutcliffe's version of his wife's behaviour accounts for his aggressive behaviour towards many women." Despite the qualification here that it was *Sutcliffe's version* of Sonia's behaviour, the accounts of this behaviour were presented by the doctors and taken up by the media as factual truth. The *Daily Express* (7 May 1981), for example, carried the headline "Henpecked Ripper," and all papers gave long details of Sonia's "difficult" behaviour. However, whether or not Sonia did behave as Sutcliffe claimed, the *relevance* of the details of this behaviour is hard to grasp. Nevertheless, both the prosecution and the defence took Sonia's behaviour as crucial to their "explanation" and "understanding" of the Sutcliffe murders. Sutcliffe had claimed that prior to his marriage, Sonia's affair with another man had prompted him to seek out a prostitute. This was the woman who had allegedly "cheated" him of £5. The general acceptance of this story added to the implication that Sonia was a key precipitator to the subsequent string of horrendous events. In his closing speech Sir Michael Havers argued that if the jury did not accept Sutcliffe's story of hearing God's voice, there were various alternatives. Either Sutcliffe was a liar and "a cold, calculating killer . . . or is it because he was having a rough time after his marriage? Was his wife, also because of her own illness, poor soul, behaving impossibly so that he dreaded going home?" (*Guardian,* 20 May 1981).

In addition to the claim that Sutcliffe's killings were "understandable" in terms of rational motive, the prosecution also developed the argument that his killings had a sexual component.

The psychiatrists were initially adamant that a sexual component was absent. Dr. Milne stated that he had looked carefully for such a factor but had found that both Sutcliffe and Sonia considered their sex life to be "entirely satisfactory." Sutcliffe had denied feeling sexual excitement during the killings and he had sex with only one of his victims. This illustrates the psychiatrists' narrow notion of the "sexual," namely pleasure (presumably orgasm) from penetration. The prosecution, in an attempt to discredit the claim of a divine mission, broadened the notion of what a "sexual" killing could entail (rather uneasily, I would suggest, since although it proved the crucial means of discrediting the psychiatrists, it was not taken up by either the prosecution or the judge in their summing-up).

To attempt to illustrate that the killings had a sexual component, the prosecution drew both on certain remarks from Sutcliffe and on his actual behaviour. Sir Michael Havers referred to Sutcliffe's comment to the police that having killed Emily Jackson, he pulled her bra up and her pants down, to "satisfy some sort of sexual revenge on her." In almost every case, Sutcliffe removed his victims' clothing before stabbing them. He said that he did this so that when they were found "they would look as cheap as they are." With Sutcliffe in the witness-box, Sir Michael Havers also pointed out that he had frequently stabbed his victims in the breasts and had stabbed one in the vagina. "Was this sexual gratification?" he asked Sutcliffe. Further, if he so hated prostitutes, how was it that Sutcliffe had sex with one (Helen Rytka)? "God didn't tell you to put your penis in that girl's vagina," Sir Michael insisted. In Ognall's cross-examination of the psychiatrists, he repeated the question of whether the stabbing of Jo Whitacker three times in the vagina could be anything but sexual. Dr. Milne initially suggested that it could have been accidental (!), but was forced to admit that it could *only* be sexual, as also the nail scratches around Margarita Wall's vagina. Ognall named six of Sutcliffe's victims as having been killed for sexual reasons and Dr. Milne was forced to admit that this evidence substantially challenged the claim of a divine mission. The psychiatrists' case effectively was lost at this point in the trial.

Given that the trial of Sutcliffe turned out to be more a trial of prostitutes, of Sonia and of psychiatry, would it have been better if Judge Boreham had accepted the plea of diminished responsibility, thereby curtailing the length of the trial? Sutcliffe may or may not be a paranoid schizophrenic; I do not and cannot know. I would argue, however, that the greatest cause for concern in the conduct of the trial was not the ultimate verdict, but the means by which that verdict was arrived at. Nevertheless, the trial served an important purpose. It prompted further inquiry into the police handling of the Ripper case and as *The Times* (23 May 1981) has argued, it acted as a public catharsis, an exorcism. Further, as Wendy Hollway has pointed out: "Sutcliffe's trial demonstrated men's collaboration with other men in the oppression of women. As the mouth-pieces for legal, psychiatric and journalistic discourses, men collaborated in reproducing a view of the world which masks men's violence against women."

As I have suggested, this masking took the form of placing blame squarely on women.

THE WIDER ISSUES OF THE RIPPER CASE

In addition to the conduct of the trial and its shifting of the blame on to women, there are a number of other serious causes for concern in the handling of the Ripper case. These include: the disturbing nature of the police investigation; the widespread operation of the "Ripper myth"; the avoidance of discussion of the wider context within which the possibility of Sutcliffe's murders is nurtured and supported.

The Police Handling of the Ripper Case

The Ripper investigation was the largest criminal investigation ever conducted in Britain. During the trial it was revealed that the police had interviewed Peter Sutcliffe as many as nine times without suspecting him, although each time he was seen as a known potential suspect or in circumstances directly related to the Ripper case. Even before the trial, however, there was widespread public disquiet over the police handling of the Ripper case. This reached a crescendo immediately after the trial. The faith which the police placed in the authenticity of the Ripper tape and letters was referred to as "the £1 million blunder . . . the most costly blunder ever made by British police" (*Daily Mirror*, 23 May 1981); a document on suspects, circulated secretly, had listed as the fifth point for elimination: "If his accent is dissimilar to a north-eastern (Geordie) accent."

Media criticism was widespread. Michael Nally of the *Observer* (24 May 1981) was not untypical in commenting: "Senior officers are happy to attribute the Ripper's conviction to 'good coppering.' They are less eager, understandably, to acknowledge that he might have got away with murder because some officers were not up to the job. . . ."

The Ripper squad admitted that Sutcliffe had never been a prime suspect. One detective had named him as such, but that detective's report to his superiors was shelved. Sutcliffe's name appeared approximately fifty times on police computer checks on cars in red-light areas. He had been cautioned in 1969 for hitting a woman over the head in Chapeltown, Bradford (where several of the Ripper murders subsequently took place). In the same year he had been fined for "going equipped for theft" (although he admitted in court that he had been about to use the hammer to attack another woman). Also there were other pieces of evidence such as Sutcliffe's size 7 Dunlop boot.

Ronald Gregory, the Chief Constable of West Yorkshire responded feebly to the criticisms with the plea that of course we have the advantage of hindsight. He stated: "If we had known this investigation was going to reach such proportions we would have used a computer from the beginning. But when we looked at the possibility, we were some years into the inquiry and it would have been pointless" (quoted in Beattie, 144).

In response to MPs' demands, the Home Office set up an inquiry into the police investigation of the Ripper case. In the report of its findings, its main criticisms were, predictably, the acceptance that the author of the tape and letters was the Ripper, and the non-use of a computer in compiling and collating the mass of information. However, what has unsurprisingly been omitted in this criticism of the police is any unease with the specific ways in which police sexism shaped the "hunt." As I have already said, Yallop claims that women were used as bait by the police. Further, the urging of women off the streets, the aggression shown to women's protests, the implication that it was a battle of male giants (police v. Ripper), acted both to terrorize women still further and to place even more at risk those women wishing or needing, for whatever reason, to walk along the streets at night.

Debunking the Ripper Myth

There is another important criticism to be made of the police handling of the case which the inquiry, also unsurprisingly, never mentioned. This was its wholesale adoption of the romanticized myth of the Ripper. The myth of Jack the Ripper is enormously powerful. It absolves men of responsibility but it also titillates men. There is even a pub named Jack the Ripper; no doubt a "Yorkshire Ripper" pub is soon to come. The Ripper myth, fuelled by modern imagery in film and fiction, involves the lone vigilante (whether policeman or "mad killer," Clint Eastwood as "Dirty Harry" or de Niro in Scorcese's *Taxi Driver*) waging war single-handedly on society's "moral decay." To the police the "Yorkshire

Ripper" was a twentieth-century version of Jack, a tortured, lonely, prostitute-hating man, engaged in a deadly (but oh-so-thrilling) "war of wits." Oldfield was the self-styled St. George, out to slay the Dragon. Women were mere pawns in a men's game. As Joan Smith points out, the Ripper myth predisposed police to accept any confirmation of that myth, and the letters and tape did precisely that. The police were certain that they would "know" the Ripper if and when they interviewed him, yet his very ordinariness had fooled them nine times. (Sutcliffe claims that he hated the name "Yorkshire Ripper." According to Beattie he referred to the killings as the acts of the "Head-banger.")

The media also was central to the perpetration of the myth. The major public criticism of the media's reportage of the Sutcliffe case has been its condemnation of "blood-money" or "cheque-book" journalism (and here newspapers were acting in breach of past Press Council declarations). The voyeurism of such media reports detracts from and thereby degrades the victims' suffering, while at the same time feeding on the horror of the crimes. Newspapers play an active role in creating "media events" out of such attacks. However, there has been no wide public objection to the media's role in myth-making. As Joan Smith points out, even with the arrest and trial of Sutcliffe and the revelation of, in most respects, his male *normality,* the media desperately searched for possible unique and aberrant qualities in Sutcliffe. Beattie, for example, himself a journalist, played up Sutcliffe's ghoulish past, his exploits in the graveyard and his obsession with death. After all to Beattie "it seemed inconceivable that the monster which had been hunted so long . . . should turn out to be that ordinary-looking man" (p. 107). However, as Colin Wilson has pointed out, in his *Encyclopedia of Murder:* "Belief in the abnormality of the murderer is a part of the delusion of normality on which society is based. The murderer is different from other human beings in degree, not in kind" (quoted in the *Guardian,* 23 May 1981).

To understand the Ripper, many people identified him not as simply an exceptional, aberrant case, but as sub-human, a beast, a monster. Sutcliffe himself used these terms. He told the police, for example, that the names of all his victims were "all in my brain, reminding me of the beast I am," and in reference to reading about Jayne MacDonald's father dying, he said, "I realized what a monster I was." Beattie's bestseller is sprinkled liberally with references to Sutcliffe as an animal, a fiend, a monster. For example he writes: "like the marauding animal he was, he needed a fresh killing" (p. 90). On BBC 2's "Newsnight" programme (27 November 1980) Jayne MacDonald's mother, speaking out to the killer, remarked, "you are not a man, you are a beast." The law, however, does not punish or "treat" animals and monsters. In punishing Sutcliffe, the law presumes he is a man who is responsible for his actions. Had he been judged to have "diminished responsibility" and thus to be in need of "treatment," the argument would have still held. Sutcliffe cannot be understood and "explained away" by denying that he is a human male. The myth of this murderer as a beast or monster was and is necessary to men in particular if they are to *distance* themselves from him and separate this form of violence towards women from other forms of male-female relationships.

The Normality of Male Violence and Misogyny

Male violence towards women is endemic to our society. The Metropolitan Police recorded 12,505 attacks on women in London in 1981. Joan Smith comments: "Most authorities agree that such attacks are under-reported by a factor of around four, suggesting that 50,000 women suffer attack yearly in the capital city alone."

The media and the trial's glaring focus on certain "women in Sutcliffe's life," deflected attention away from other far more pertinent factors. As the testimonies of his mates reveal, Sutcliffe, rather than being the loner of the Ripper myth, was a man who was regularly immersed in a normal male culture of drinking, prostitution and violence. According to the *Daily Mirror* (23 May 1981), he went regularly to strip joints and, at eighteen, became a regular kerb-crawler in red-light districts. The same article comments that although he claimed to hate pornography, that also was a lie. He regularly read pornographic magazines. Many of his drinking mates accompanied him on his kerb-crawl "jaunts." Trevor Birdsall, for example, had been with him the night he attacked Olive Smelt. According to Birdsall, Sutcliffe had left the car for twenty minutes. Although the "coincidence" of facts (location, time) revealed next day in the press must have been apparent to Birdsall, he did nothing. The *normality* of male violence towards women is such that Birdsall could comment, on another Sutcliffe attack: "He had a sock and I think there was a small brick or stone in it . . . I think [he said] he hit her on the head . . . But Peter never showed any hostility to prostitutes and there was nothing unusual in his attitude towards them" (*New Standard*, 7 May 1981).

Sutcliffe's brother, Carl, stated, "Looking back I realize he always loathed prostitutes." However, Carl reveals that his brother's hatred, as we well know but the Ripper myth denies, was not only of prostitutes. When Sutcliffe used terms like " 'filthy slags' . . . 'disgusting' or 'dirty cows' . . . he could be talking about any woman he thought a bit loose" (quoted in Beattie).

This distinction between women—as asexual and pure, or sexual, desired and hated—is centrally rooted within "common-sense" notions of women. The traditional "virgin/whore" dichotomy operates as a means of "policing" women's sexuality, but the control of these categories—including the infinitely expansive category of "loose woman"—resides with the male arbiter or labeller (in this case a murderer!) and thus any woman is at risk. In a new account of the "Yorkshire Ripper" case, *Un Homme nommé Zapolski*, Nicole Ward Jouve backs up the argument that it was precisely Sutcliffe's normality, including his participation in normal male culture, which was crucial to his remaining free for so long. According to Anne Corbett, in her discussion of the book, Ward Jouve notes that: ". . . he had just a few minor excesses which seemed normal to his friends and workmates—like jumping on coffins when a gravedigger and playing at being the Incredible Hulk and roughing up one or two prostitutes. That did not make him either the pathetic victim of circumstances nor the monster the police sought. It actually made him . . . an admirable exponent of social values."

The wider context that makes possible brutal killings such as Sutcliffe's is one of widespread misogyny and a culture which encourages and supports a male sexuality based on violence and aggression towards women. Despite the defence's denial of a "sexual motive" to Sutcliffe's killings and the prosecution's unease with the suggestion, the Sutcliffe killings centrally implicate Sutcliffe's sexuality in particular and male sexuality and masculinity in general. Far from "deviating from the norm," Sutcliffe was an exaggeration of it. Violence and aggression form central components of male sexuality as it is socially constructed. (This is *not,* however, an argument for the biological or evolutionary inevitability of male aggression.)

Common speech, ideas about women's sexuality and numerous visual images, from adverts to pornography and "sex and violence" films, all act to bolster a masculinity involving violence towards women. Taken together they create and support a climate in which such violence is normalized. The reaction on the football terraces to what was seen as a "contest" between the "Ripper" and the police illustrates both this prevalent misogyny and the construction of the "Ripper hunt" as a popular (male) sport—with, as I've argued already, women as pawns.

As Hilary Rose and others in their letter to *The Times* (3 December 1980) commented: " 'The Ripper' only makes public and unavoidable that which, as a whole, society tries to avoid thinking about, namely the high level of violence against women, whether within the home or on the streets."

This article has attempted to demonstrate, through the case of the "Yorkshire Ripper," that throughout society—in the courts, the medical profession, the media, the police, the football terraces—there runs the common thread of misogyny. As a part of this misogyny, women are blamed for male violence towards them thereby absolving men of the responsibility. It is time that men's role in perpetuating that violence was faced head on. Women have been scapegoated for too long as *victims* of male violence, as the supposed *precipitators* of their violence, and as the cause—the persistent image of "Eve the temptress."

Note

1. "Poem for Jacqueline Hill" was written by a woman in Leeds (available in full from WAVAW, Corner Bookshop, 162 Woodhouse Lane, Leeds).

Womanslaughter: A License to Kill? The Killing of Jane Asher

JILL RADFORD

The Ashers' marriage had problems. At least that was how it was portrayed by Gordon Asher. In particular he stated that he did not like the attitudes his wife, Jane Asher, held towards other men. He claimed to have "had it out with her many times." In the course of these arguments he admitted to hitting Jane but he could not remember how many times. Jane's voice is silent. We know that Gordon Asher left her and went to live with his mother. We also know that Jane had affairs with other men. After a while they were reconciled. Gordon Asher claimed that this happened after he had sensed that she was short of money.

On 22 September 1980, Jane and Gordon Asher went together to a party. In his account of the events, he claimed that she danced with another man during the party and then he was unable to find her for about half an hour. There is no account from Jane. On finding Jane he demanded to know where she had been. She said repeatedly that she had been "nowhere" and he called her a "bloody liar." He continued to interrogate her in the bathroom of the house. Then, he says, that as she started to move away he grabbed her round the neck. He stated: "The next thing I knew she slid down the wall to the ground." Another guest at the party, however, said that Gordon Asher pinned his wife to the wall by her throat and shouted at her. He said that her face was a funny colour and she was not crying. Soon after this another guest saw Jane lying on the floor and, thinking that he had intruded on a scene of intimacy, closed the door. Later Asher was seen leaving the house carrying his wife. A guest said that she "looked as if she'd been knocked cold, like he'd clocked her one." For some reason this had given rise to some amusement amongst the guests. Jane Asher, it appears, was

---

Reprinted from *Causes for Concern*, ed. Paul Gordon and Phil Scraton, 210–27 (London: Penguin, 1984).

dead. Gordon Asher drove six miles with his wife's body in the car, "hoping she'd wake up." When she didn't he buried her in a chalk pit. He was arrested a week later and the naked body of his wife was recovered.

Gordon Asher was charged with murder. The trial opened in June 1981 and was heard before Justice Mars-Jones at Winchester Crown Court. In court Asher was portrayed as a model husband and father, his wife as a "two-timing flirt." Asher was acquitted of murder by a jury of three women and nine men, and convicted of manslaughter. Justice Mars-Jones passed a six months' suspended prison sentence, allowing him to walk free from the court.

After leaving the court, Asher is quoted as having said, "It is marvellous; I am a really happy man," adding that if he married again it would have to be "someone very special" (*Hampshire Chronicle,* 12 June 1981).

DOMESTIC KILLING: THE LEGAL FRAMEWORK

With the exception of rape, a husband can be prosecuted for all offences against the person: murder, manslaughter, attempted murder, wounding or other acts endangering life and all forms of assault—on his wife. In terms of its formal provisions, however, the legal system until recently has treated wife assault as different from other forms of violent crime. For example, it was excluded from the scheme, initiated in 1964, through which victims of violent crime could claim compensation from the Criminal Injuries Compensation Board. The guidelines state: "where the victim who suffers injuries and the offender who inflicted them were living together as members of the same family, no compensation will be payable. For the purposes of this paragraph where a man and woman were living together as man and wife they will be treated as if they were married to one another" (*The Criminal Injuries Compensation Board Scheme* 1964, Paragraph 7).

In October 1979 the law was amended to allow "battered" women and their children to claim compensation provided that the injury justified compensation of at least £500. The explanation for the original exclusion of wife assault from the provisions was, perversely, the large number of claims that *could* be brought and that public interest is not concerned with violence in the home.

The legal processing of violent crime between spouses is in theory the same as other violent crime. It may be initiated by a report to the police by a victim or witness. The police then make inquiries, a suspect is charged with an offence and brought to court. If it is considered to be a "serious" matter, the suspect is committed to the crown court for trial. The trial is an adversary process in which both the prosecution and defence are entitled to present their cases. They call witnesses, cross-examine each other's witnesses and summarize their case. The judge then sums up the case and a jury is expected to reach a verdict, consistent with the "facts" as presented to the court, of either "guilty" or "not guilty." If the verdict is not guilty, then the defendant is acquitted. If it is a guilty verdict, the defendant is convicted. Following a conviction defence counsel mitigates, that is, presents details of any extenuating circumstances and any points in the defendant's favour. The judge should take these points into consideration in deciding on an appropriate sentence. The sentence is passed on the basis of a wide discretion which judges possess within the law. Discretion dominates every stage of the process—from the decision to act on reports in the first place to the appropriate punishment for the crime at the final stages.

Following an attack, the whole process of referral, investigation and examination is dependent on the choices and decisions of a range of individuals. The person attacked or witnessing an attack decides whether or not to report the attack to the police. The police use discretion in deciding whether or not to record a report which they receive. Matters deemed by them either to be "trivial" or "not police matters" are not recorded. Their judgment also shapes the investigation and the enthusiasm with which it is carried out. Following the apprehension of a suspect the police again use discretion in deciding whether to issue an informal warning or to arrest. If a person is arrested the police alone decide whether to issue a formal caution or to charge the suspect with a criminal offence. From the evidence which they have, the police decide on the most appropriate charge. For example, an attack by a man on a woman could result in charges ranging from assault to attempted murder. This depends on the police evaluation and judgment of the seriousness of the attack. Often such decisions are informed by prejudices with regard to marital violence. The decision in serious cases may be referred to the Director of Public Prosecutions or to solicitors acting for the police. When the case comes to court the magistrates, or the jury in a crown court, make a judgment on the facts before them. In relation to fatal attacks, the charge brought initially may be murder, but a jury has the right to find the defendant guilty of a lesser offence, manslaughter, if they decide that it is warranted in the circumstances.

Murder is defined as: ". . . unlawful homicide with malice aforethought, the death occurring within one year and one day of the act alleged to have caused it. Malice aforethought means an intention to kill or cause grievous bodily harm to another human being, whether the person killed or not. Thus D is guilty of murder, if he shoots at A intending to cause A grievous bodily harm but in fact kills B" (Newton 1977, p. 171).

There are special defences which are unique to charges of murder. These are diminished responsibility and "provocation sufficient to cause a reasonable man to lose control of himself and do what the defendant did."

Diminished responsibility is a defence only to a charge of murder. Section 2 of the Homicide Act 1957 provides that if a person charged with murder "was suffering from such an abnormality of mind . . . as substantially impaired his mental responsibility for his acts and omissions in doing or being a party to the killing," then he or she is guilty of manslaughter rather than murder. Manslaughter verdicts are also found in the following circumstances:

(a) when the defendant escapes conviction for murder solely because of his plea of diminished responsibility, provocation or suicide pact;

(b) where the defendant commits an unlawful act likely to cause another person some harm and which results in another's death;

(c) where the defendant, without malice aforethought but intentionally or with gross negligence, fails to perform certain duties which then cause the death of someone else.

To get a conviction on a murder charge, the prosecution has to prove to the jury, beyond reasonable doubt, that the defendant intended to kill or cause grievous bodily harm. In his or her summing up, the judge may provide guidance to the jury regarding the application of these laws. Table 1, giving the outcome of homicide cases, shows the extent to which manslaughter verdicts are reached in cases where the original charge was murder.

The verdicts of murder or manslaughter are of crucial importance to sentencing. If a murder verdict is brought the judge has no discretion, as life imprisonment is the mandatory sentence for murder. If a manslaughter verdict is reached the judge, in contrast, has a wide discretion in law; the sentence may range from a maximum of life imprisonment (there is no legal minimum) to

TABLE 1 Suspects Indicted for Homicide by Outcome of Proceedings

	1978	1979	1980
Indicted for			
Murder	439	491	368
Manslaughter	78	87	74
Total	517	578	442
Convicted of			
Murder	138	166	113
Manslaughter	273	298	249
Total	411	464	362
Not convicted			
Acquitted on all counts	70	72	51
Convicted of lesser offence	31	33	20
Not guilty due to insanity	—	3	1
Unfit to plead	2	3	2
Not tried[a]	1	2	4
Infanticide	2	—	2
Total	106	113	80

Source: *Criminal Statistics 1980*, Table 4.7. England and Wales.

a. This usually implies the suspect has been dealt with for some other serious offence.

non-custodial sentences. The prosecution has no right of appeal, although it is possible for defendants to apply for leave of appeal against a sentence. Table 2 gives an indication of how this discretion has been used in recent years.

If in its formal provision the criminal law is intended to give protection to all people, independent of their social status, its practical operation has given rise to considerable criticism with regards to violence against women who are married to their attacker. The *Report of the Select Committee on Violence in Marriage* concluded: "If the criminal law of assault could be more uniformly applied to domestic assaults there seems little doubt it would give more protection to the battered wife" (House of Commons 1974–75, p. xvi).

The social process through which an incident of assault is transformed from an act of private terrorism by a man towards a woman with whom he is in a "relationship" to an officially recognized crime of violence is complex and uncertain. Initially it involves a decision on the part of the injured woman to make a report to the police. Many women, fearing further violence as reprisal, the break-up of the family home and perhaps homelessness and poverty on the one hand or humiliation and embarrassment by the police or courts on the other, choose to say nothing. The level of hidden violence in family life remains unknown. Jane Asher had been hit by Gordon Asher before the fatal party. Her response to this violence remains unknown. Assuming a woman does call for police assistance, whether the attack surfaces in court depends on the attitudes of the police to domestic violence as an issue of police concern and their evaluation of the specific incident.

TABLE 2 Sentences for Murder and Manslaughter

	1978	1979	1980
Murder			
Life imprisonment	138	166	113
Manslaughter			
Life imprisonment	18	29	12
over 10 years	4	0	1
4–10 years	59	71	65
4 years or under	99	97	91
Borstal or detention centre	6	4	4
Restriction order	21	24	25
Hospital order	5	10	7
Probation	32	31	28
Suspended sentence	23	22	16
Other	6	10	—
Total	273	298	249

Source: *Criminal Statistics 1980*, Table 4.8. England and Wales.

The reluctance of police to intervene in "domestic violence" is now well known as a result of Women's Aid's vigorous campaigning on this issue. Anna Coote and Tess Gill state:

> If your husband made a violent attack on someone in the street in front of witnesses, he would probably be arrested by the police and charged with a criminal offence. But if he did the same to you in your own home, the police would be most unlikely to take the same action against him. If they did decide to arrest and prosecute him for a criminal offence and he pleaded guilty in court, he would probably be fined or "bound over" to keep the peace and sent home. . . . If he denied the charge a date would be fixed some weeks ahead for his case to be heard. In the meantime he would probably be allowed home on bail free to carry out further assaults or intimidation . . . so you can't look to police for protection under the criminal law. (1979, p. 9)

The evidence given by the police largely endorses this criticism:

> Whilst such problems take up considerable time . . . in the majority of cases the role of the police is a negative one. We are, after all, dealing with persons "bound in marriage" and it is important for a host of reasons to maintain the unity of the spouses. (Association of Chief Police Officers of England and Wales and Northern Ireland, Evidence to the Select Committee on Violence in Marriage, *Minutes of Evidence,* in House of Commons, ii, 1974–75, p. 366)

According to the police, the maintenance of the marriage bond should be preserved at almost any cost, including criminal violence. As the official police attitude towards domestic violence is hesitant, it comes as no surprise that their actual practice is characterized by inactive non-interventionism. The 1976 Select Committee on Violence in Marriage recommended that "Chief constables should review their policies about the police approach to domestic violence" (p. xvi). Despite new powers under the Domestic Violence and Matrimonial Proceedings Act 1976 (which came into force in June 1977) and the Domestic Proceedings and Magistrates Courts Act 1978 (which came into force in April 1979) police practice appears little changed: "On the whole, they [the police] still regard domestic violence as different from—less serious than—other forms of violence, and consider the procedure laid down in the new law a waste of time. They often need persuading to use their powers of arrest at all" (Coote and Gill 1979, p. 16).

THE ASHER CASE AT COURT

In the Asher case, although Gordon Asher admitted to having hit his wife in the past, there is nothing to suggest that she made any official complaint to the police. Police intervention was only initiated after she was killed. Asher was arrested in September 1980 for the murder of his wife. Yet during the time from his arrest until his trial in June 1981, with the exception of the weekend during the trial itself, he was allowed to be free, on bail. That men charged with the murder of their wives be allowed out on bail is, I suggest, quite wrong and is a further indication of the trivializing of violence against women within the legal system.

In court both prosecution and defence counsel portrayed Gordon Asher as a model husband and his wife as a lying, two-timing flirt. In focusing the trial on Jane's behaviour, it appears that counsel and later the judge considered that she had acted in such a way as to provoke violence and so contributed towards her own death. In court Mr. Paul Chad, QC, acting for the *prosecution,* said, "Mr. Asher was clearly a model husband devoted to his children." Yet Jane was portrayed quite differently: "His wife enjoyed the company of her lover and took another one. After a while he sensed she was short of money. . . . A husband had his uses and on 22 September last year they were reconciled. He wanted it for the sake of the children and she wanted it not for a roof over her head and the money, but the freedom to enjoy herself elsewhere" (*Hampshire Chronicle,* 5 June 1981).

"Freedom" it is assumed by prosecuting counsel, is something no wife has any right to expect. The prosecution counsel was criticized by the judge, who said in his summing up to the jury:

> You may well be forgiven for thinking that he [i.e., Mr. Chadd] was addressing you on behalf of the defence. . . . You may think that the prosecution has not been put or not put properly. That is for you to consider. . . . I have felt an unwarranted burden has been put on me because I have to make up to some extent for the failure of Mr. Chadd. . . . Our court system is adversary [*sic*] where both counsel for the prosecution and defence pursue their cases with rigour and fairness. In this trial you have not had the advantage of hearing from Mr. Chadd how he puts his case for either murder or manslaughter. (*Hampshire Chronicle,* 12 June 1981)

This is a serious and unusual criticism of prosecution counsel. It was clearly deserved and has frightening implications for all women. The strength of the ideology of male control of women is such, that in a case where a man went to the extreme of killing a woman in enforcing "his right" of possession and control, the prosecution failed to make an effective case against him.

Throughout the case the male voice was dominant and the woman's voice silent. Male perceptions of marriage and the perfect husband went unchallenged. The view of marriage which prevailed was one where a wife had to account for her time and movements to her husband. Asher's concern with his wife's where-abouts for thirty minutes during the party was deemed perfectly proper. It was seen to be understandable that he should be jealous and could expect her to stay with him, little more than a possession. Jane did not conform to the male expectations of "innocent victim"—chastity and loyal wifeliness—and because of this her actions were portrayed as contributing to her death. Although the judge was highly critical of the performance of prosecuting counsel, he appeared to give support to the traditional male double standards of morality. First, in his summing up he directed the jury towards a manslaughter verdict: "The judge said there were three verdicts open to the jury: guilty of murder, not guilty of murder but guilty of manslaughter, and not guilty. 'You may think the latter is rather an academic choice. . . . I imagine you will wait for a long time before you return a verdict of murder in this case' " (*Hampshire Chronicle,* 12 June 1981).

Second, Asher received a suspended sentence for killing his wife, which appeared an implicit endorsement of the use of violence in this case. In passing sentence the judge remarked: "Asher had a positively good character. He was obviously admired by Jane's relatives and their mutual friends. They have all spoken of him as a model husband. Asher was not a violent man and had never been known to raise a hand against his wife. Jane's relatives bore him no grudge although they knew he was responsible for her death." (Quoted in *Hampshire Chronicle,* 12 June 1981).

Clearly Asher's sentence and the judge's reasoning behind it represent a major cause for concern. It apparently condoned the use of male violence for the social control of women in close relationships. Its implications for women are frightening. For any woman who breaches her husband's expectations concerning her behaviour could seemingly be killed with impunity. In that sense, the marriage licence becomes a licence to kill. The implications for men in Winchester were too clear. Following a public expression (*Sun,* 22 June 1981) of anger over the case, the Winchester Women's Liberation Group had women coming to them saying that their husbands had said to them part in threat, part as jest—"It's easier than divorce" and "If I kill you I can get away with it."

WOMANSLAUGHTER: THE WIDER IMPLICATIONS

The criminal law cannot cope with violence against women, either within or outside the home, for the roots of male violence are embedded deep within masculinity as constructed in a male-dominated or patriarchal society. The freeing of Gordon Asher constitutes a dangerous move towards the decriminalizing of violence in the home and even of wife-slaughter. The terrorizing and killing of women in their own homes, where they are told they are secure, by their own husbands and lovers, whom they are taught to trust and look to for protection, must not be included in the category of crimes for which decriminalization can be advocated.

One argument for decriminalization turns on some notion of "victim precipitation"—that the victim "was asking for it" or in some way provoked or contributed to it. In this argument women are held, as in rape cases, to be responsible for male violence committed against them. Kathleen Barry notes the pertinence of the rape paradigm in which ". . . the victim of sexual assault is held responsible for her own victimization . . . [this leads] to the rationalization and acceptance of other forms of enslavement, where the woman is presumed to have 'chosen' her fate, to embrace it passively or to have courted it perversely through rash or unchaste behaviour" (Barry 1979, p. 33).

The Asher case demonstrates clearly the contradictions facing a society which claims to abhor, yet tolerates violent crime. Crimes of violence, we are frequently told by politicians, police chiefs and other right-thinking men are anathema to civilized society. Considerable measures are "reluctantly" resorted to in order to free society from violent criminals. The Prevention of Terrorism Act, for example, curtails our civil liberties, but we are informed that it is necessary to rid society of the menace posed by the "men of violence."

Examination of the official crime statistics, however, demonstrates that homicide (a collective category which includes murder, manslaughter—and womanslaughter—and infanticide) is in fact largely a family matter (see table 3). Thus formulated, there is insufficient evidence to determine the extent to which "domestic" or "family" violence is in fact male violence, or that homicide is in fact woman-killing (or feminicide). It cannot be without significance, however, that a new table appeared in the 1979 and 1980 Home Office statistics (see table 4).

TABLE 3 Offences Currently Recorded as Homicide by Relation of Victim to Principal Suspect

	1979		1980	
	No.	%	No.	%
Relation				
Spouse, cohabitant or former spouse/cohab.	131	24	111	20
Lover or former lover	25	5	18	3
Parent, son, daughter	91	16	65	11
Other family	12	2	25	4
Friend	116	21	102	18
Other associate	27	5	36	6
Sub-total	402	73	357	63
No Relation				
Police officer (victim)	1	<.5	1	<.5
Victim of terrorism	1	<.5	4	<.5
Other stranger	106	19	159	28
No suspect	41	7	43	8
Total	551	100	564	100

Source: *Criminal Statistics*, 1980.

TABLE 4 Serious Offences between Spouses Recorded by the Police

		Total	Victim Wife	Victim Husband	% in Which Men Are Violent to Women
Murder, manslaughter, attempted murder, threat to murder	1979	200	163	37	81
	1980	172	144	28	84
Wounding, acts endangering life, and serious assault	1979	5,721	5,236	485	91.9
	1980	5,850	5,354	496	91.5
Totals	1979	5,921	5,399	522	91.2
	1980	6,022	5,498	524	91.6

This table has not appeared since 1980 and was published only for 1979 and 1980. It demonstrates that in relation to serious offences of violence, it is men who are overwhelmingly the aggressors. This is the evidence, as defined by the police, regarding "serious offences." There are no equivalent figures available for less serious offences, which anyway would be unreliable due to the "dark" figure of hidden crime masked by the victims' reluctance to call the police and the police attitude to domestic violence. However, it can be seen that in relation to serious or very serious assaults, it is men—men as husbands—who disproportionately feature as society's violent men and it is their wives who are their victims.

Given that major claims are made for a clamp-down on violent crime, and that the highest proportion of violent crime occurs in a "domestic" context where men as husbands are overwhelmingly the aggressor—how can the suspended sentence awarded to Asher be defended?

In the British legal system, judicial discretion in sentencing (with the exception of murder and treason, which carry mandatory life imprisonment and death sentences respectively) is very broad. Judges, in determining sentences, make reference to an eclectic mixture of different, even incompatible penal philosophies—retribution (punishment), individual deterrence, general deterrence, rehabilitation and protection of the community. In part, sentencing disparities may be explained by their differential commitments to the differing ideologies and their assumed appropriateness to different offenders and offences informed by their differing definitions of seriousness.

Feminists have found the question of sentencing for offences of violence against women difficult. We are in danger of having our anger towards male violence appropriated by the forces of reaction—"the hang 'em and flog 'em brigade." We must demand a penal system which accepts that violence against women is serious crime, but without allowing ourselves to be used as part of a repressive law-and-order campaign. Our difficulty is the centrality of the crime and punishment issue to the working of the social order—a fact long recognized by the fascist right.

It is only by analysing existing philosophies and dispelling a few myths that it becomes possible to look towards a constructive policy.

The Myth of Deterrent Sentencing

At neither an individual nor a general level is deterrence effective, except to the extent that imprisonment does temporarily remove the offender from circulation. On a longer-term basis there is no evidence that those sentenced to imprisonment have a lower re-conviction rate than those sentenced to non-custodial measures—or even, as reported in "self-report" studies, in respect of those who are never caught or convicted of offences. (In self-report studies, random samples of the population are interviewed about their law-breaking activities in confidence.) At a general level, exemplary sentences (those which are much higher than is average for a certain type of offence) are not followed by any reduction in that type of offence. As an example, in the past exemplary sentences have been given and publicized in relation to football violence or "mugging" without any noticeable reduction in those crimes. Stan Cohen concludes: "There is no evidence that the rate of crime rises or falls with such changes in penal policy as the intensity of punishment" (1979, p. 26).

The Rehabilitative Myth

In the post-war period a philosophy of reform or rehabilitation was popular in liberal penal thinking. Disturbed by what they saw as the negative nature of punishment, liberal penologists identified reform through "treatment" or "corrective training" as the aim of the penal system. Innovations in the prison regimes and in non-custodial measures were introduced to secure this end. Again, research, including that undertaken by the Home Office itself, has demonstrated the ineffectiveness in terms of subsequent conviction rates. In 1979, the May Report on the Prison System reflected official disenchantment with the rehabilitative ethic.

A closely related philosophy remains current amongst many involved with domestic violence. Erin Pizzey, for example, suggests that the criminal law is inappropriate for matters of domestic violence. She advocates a forward-looking approach concerned with the welfare of those concerned rather than a retrospective blame-apportioning criminal law. Her context is that of "wife-battering" rather than "woman-slaughter," which is the issue here. It has been suggested that in the Asher case it was the judge's concern for the well-being of the "survivors" that in part prompted the suspended sentence. This individualistic welfare philosophy may have some legitimate claim as a humane approach, but it is also, on many levels, problematic. In non-fatal cases there is no evidence to show that leniency deters subsequent attacks. In terms of justice, a lenient sentence is taken to indicate that the court does not view the offence as a serious matter. In terms of attacks on women, lenient sentencing of male offenders gives substance to the feminist claim that the law is made by, and for, men. It is the freeing of wife-killers which issues the licence to kill. Clearly lenient sentencing of violent men overlooks the welfare of women in the wider community.

Towards a Feminist Analysis

It is accepted here that the criminal law cannot resolve the problem of male violence in the home. Neither should the advocacy of the use of criminal law inhibit the development of measures to support the battered wife, like, for example, the development of crisis shelters fought for by Women's Aid groups. Violence against women in "domestic situations" should be defined as criminal violence and punished as such. With the failure of the rehabilitation ethic, the only legitimate response to unacceptable forms of behaviour is to have confidence in that definition and punish accordingly. This raises the basic question of what forms of social action or behaviour should be defined as unacceptable. Feminists argue that any behaviour which threatens the freedom, well-being and dignity of women is unacceptable. This is not a demand for sexist privilege. The same definition should be applied to the male population. Thus all crimes of violence against the person should be defined as such and punished consistently. Punishing the aggressor is a clear statement of recognition of an offender's responsibility for his (and I mean "his") actions. Furthermore it is a statement of society's condemnation of violent behaviour.

While part of a "back-to-justice" philosophy this is not part of any repressive law-and-order campaign. Its starting point is a reappraisal of the dominant values held and institutionalized in our society. At a time when shoplifters are imprisoned for small thefts, when sentences of imprisonment are passed on those who "moonlight" in an effort to stretch state welfare payments to cover the cost of living and wife-killers are allowed to go free, it is surely appropriate to question judicial values and priorities.

In the short term, what is needed is consistent application of the criminal law in punishing crimes of violence against the person. In the longer term, we should look forward to an ending of violence against women through radical changes in the male-dominated culture which encourages fantasy, and accepts and trivializes the reality of violence against women.

In the following comment from Stan Cohen, "violence" could be substituted for "crime."

It is of course possible to isolate the factors which have something to do with conventionally defined crime . . . overcrowding, slums, poverty, racism, deprivation, degrading education, unhappy family life—but eradication of such conditions should not have to depend on their supposed association with crime . . . crime is connected not just with these evils but to society's most cherished values, such as individualism, competitiveness and masculinity. (1979, p. 28)

In looking to mend male violence against women, it is to the last of these three values that attention should be directed. Masculinity in a patriarchal society serves to maintain and reproduce power over women. Andrea Dworkin notes: "The first rule of masculinity is that whatever he is women are not" (1981, p. 50). The bases of male power have shifted and changed at different times in patriarchal history but its roots have remained in the male monopoly of economic, political, legal and educational resources. Underlying all, and surfacing at times when these socio-economic monopolies are threatened, is male violence, male superior strength and the culturally acquired capacity to transform that strength into violence. "As women gain greater independence, so men use more sexual violence to maintain their position of male power over women. Sexual harassment at work undermines our confidence, rape and sexual assault keep us off the streets, sexual abuse in the family cripples our lives and teaches us our place in the world" (*Report on Sexual Violence Conference*, Leeds, November 1980, quoted in *Spare Rib*, 103, February 1981; also quoted in Campbell and Coote 1982).

The women who pose the greatest threat to masculinity are those who assert or appear to assert independence. Any assertion of independence from or resistance to male control may incite or "provoke" male violence. In the streets it is "manless" women who receive most abuse and aggression; at work it is those women who resist male attention-seeking strategies, or what Dale Spender refers to as "ego massage," who experience most harassment; in the home it is women who in any way appear to challenge or threaten male patriarchal or autocratic rule who are most likely to be threatened, beaten and killed; in pornography it is the humiliation and degradation of the "liberated" lady which provides a popular "turn-on" for men (e.g., the film *Visiting Hours*, which celebrated the brutalization of a feminist woman). In patriarchal society, male violence is an all-pervasive feature of women's lives. This is not to assume a biological explanation of male supremacy but to assert that violence is central to the construction of masculinity under patriarchy. As Dworkin argues, in the process of becoming men boys are socialized into a commitment to violence: "Men develop a strong sense of loyalty to violence; men come to terms with violence because it is a prime component of male identity. Institutionalized in sports, the military, acculturated sexuality, the history and mythology of heroism, it is taught to boys until they become its advocates—men, not women" (1981, p. 51).

Given the centrality of violence to masculinity in patriarchal society, any challenge to male violence requires a transformation or rejection of that masculinity. All celebrations of masculinity constitute a denial of humanity and a degradation of women. All forms of male aggression—the sale of toy guns, violent sports, the sale of arms and threats of nuclear war—must be defined as inhumane. All assaults on the freedom and dignity of women, from the routine harassment of women in the streets, on public transport and at work and the sexist cracks of the television comedian, to degrading pornographic magazines and films, must likewise be condemned.

> You dictate our lives
> You dictate our needs
> You have filled our heads with fear
> But together we're strong and clear
> We have kept our anger in
> We who don't are seen as men
> We are judged by your law
> Your law is made for men.
>
> —From Ova, untitled tape released in 1976

References

Barry, Kathleen. 1979. *Female Sexual Slavery*. New York: Avon Books.

Campbell, Beatrix, and Anna Coote. 1982. *Sweet Freedom: The Struggle for Women's Liberation*. London: Pan Books.

Cohen, Stan. 1979. *Crime and Punishment*. London: Radical Alternatives to Prison.

Coote, Anna, and Tess Gill. 1979. *Battered Women and the New Law*. London: National Council of Civil Liberties.

Criminal Injuries Compensation Board Scheme. 1964. London: Her Majesty's Stationery Office.

Criminal Statistics. London: Her Majesty's Stationery Office, 1980.

Dworkin, Andrea. 1981. *Pornography: Men Possessing Women*. London: Women's Press.

Hampshire Chronicle, 5 June 1981.

Hampshire Chronicle, 12 June 1981.

House of Commons. 1974–75. *Report on the Select Committee on Violence in Marriage*. 553.

Newton, C. R. *Principles of Law*. London: Sweet and Maxwell, 1979.

Naggers, Whores, and Libbers: Provoking Men to Kill

SUE LEES

> An Meanwhile rest of t'Sutcliffes
> spent up their Fleet Street brass
> an put the boot in Sonia
> 'Job's all down to t'lass
>
> 'Our Pete were nivver a nutter,
> E'd allus a smile on t'face
> that Sonia nagged im rotten
> till a killed ooors in er place.
>
> 'Cos that's the rub wi women,
> they push us blokes too far
> till us can't be eld responsible
> for being what we are
>
> —Blake Morrison, "The Ballad of the Yorkshire Ripper," 1987
> (Sonia is Peter Sutcliffe's wife)

This chapter focuses on the way the defense of provocation in homicide trials serves to perpetuate the condoning of male violence. In rape trials it is often argued that women "precipitate" the rape by arousing the man's desire and then withdrawing consent (Lees 1989). Similar allegations of precipitation are more blatantly embedded in the defense of provocation in murder trials. Here the assumption is that the woman, usually a wife or lover, drives a man to take temporary leave of his rationality and kill her.

The study is based on an analysis of 1980s press reports and attendance at homicide trials. A free-lance journalist, Caryll Faraldi, gave invaluable help for three months. Between September 1987 and September 1988, we attended selected murder trials at the Old Bailey, the Central Criminal Court in London, and collected newspaper cuttings of murder trials that had taken place since

1986. In these cases provocation was accepted as a defense solely on the evidence given by the accused or his friends, who clearly had an interest in maligning the victim's character. The prosecution can demand evidence "in rebuttal" of allegations, but in practice this rarely occurs. If the defense of provocation is accepted, a manslaughter verdict ensues and the judge has complete discretion in sentencing (usually between three and six years). Some men can literally "get away with murder" and walk free from the court. Usually, sentences are between three and six years. For murder the sentence is mandatory life imprisonment.

No such license to kill is given to women who stand trial for male murder since the basis of the defense rests on the idea that a "reasonable man" can be provoked into killing by insubordination on the part of a woman. In other words, the woman provokes her own death. Even if a woman is raped or has been beaten up, a defense of provocation is rarely upheld. Most murderers are known to their victims. According to the 1986 British Home Office statistics, 70 percent of the victims of homicide were acquainted with the suspects, 22 percent were not acquainted, and in 8 percent of cases there was no suspect. This means that in only about one case in five is the attacker a stranger. One important component of this "bond" between attacker and victim is that a substantial proportion of murders are of women by their husbands or lovers. In 1986, 61.6 percent of all British homicides with a woman victim were women killed by their husbands, lovers, or former lovers. It is not the stranger you lock out of your house at night but the men locked in with their wives who are most likely to murder. In Britain the proportion of family homicides involving women as victims has been difficult to estimate, as the Home Office statistics have only recently given a breakdown for murder in terms of the relationship between the murderer and the victim. Statistics recently became available from the Home Office documenting defendants' relationships with the victims (see table 1). It is not only when the victim is the opposite sex that a relationship is relevant. A significant number of homicides committed by men with male victims are triggered by a sexual relationship in which possessiveness is a factor. Often the victim is the ex–wife or girlfriend's new lover, or a man who has intervened to protect the wife or girlfriend from violence.

Women kill far less frequently than men: the ratio of men killing women to women killing men is about 8:1. (In 1986–87, 31 women killed men, and 209 men killed women.) The group most prone to becoming homicide victims is young men. The overwhelming proportion of them are killed by other men—89.6 percent in 1986–87 (285 of the 318 men were killed by male assailants)—and 116 of them knew their assailant. Therefore, *male friends or acquaintances accounted for 40.7 percent of males suspected of killing men.* Only 18 women killed other women. Men's violence leads not only to the death of women—lovers and wives in particular—but also to the death of their male friends and acquaintances. In case after case the most frequent remark recorded

TABLE 1 Offenses Recorded as Homicide, by Relationship of Victim to Principal Suspect and Sex of Victim and Suspect (England and Wales, 1986)[a]

Relationship of Victim to Principal Suspect	Sex of Victim	Sex of Suspect			
		Male	Female	No Suspect	Total
Victim acquainted with suspect					
Son or daughter	Male	17	8	—	25
	Female	9	7	—	16
Parent	Male	9	—	—	9
	Female	3	2	—	5
Spouse[b]	Male	—	12	—	12
	Female	109	—	—	109
Other family	Male	11	—	—	11
	Female	6	2	—	8
Lover or former lover[c]	Male	19	4	—	23
	Female	13	1	—	14
Friend or acquaintance	Male	116	6	—	122
	Female	36	6	—	42
Other associate	Male	14	—	—	14
	Female	6	—	—	6
Total	Male	186	30	—	216
	Female	182	18	—	200
Victim not acquainted with suspect	Male	99	1	2[d]	102
	Female	27	—	—	27
No suspect	Male	—	—	32	32
	Female	—	—	20	20
Total		506	50	54	610

a. As of 1 June 1987.
b. Spouse, cohabitant, or former spouse or cohabitant.
c. Includes spouse's lover or lover's spouse or other associate.
d. Attributed to acts of terrorism.

by male defendants is, "If I can't have her, no one else can." The jealous husband kills either the wife or her alleged lover. In some cases the allegations of infidelity are completely unfounded.

The press gives wide coverage to killers like Denis Nillsen, a homosexual civil servant who strangled to death 16 young men between 1978 and 1983, and

Peter Sutcliffe, the "Yorkshire Ripper" who murdered 13 women and attempted to murder another 7, and keeps us up-to-date with every development of the Myra Hindley case (the notorious "Moors Murderer" who in the 1960s, with Ian Brady, tortured and murdered children on the Yorkshire moors), but it rarely mentions the murderers who are known to their victims. This leads to a conception that the typical murderer is a psychopathic killer.

A jury has to decide between five alternative verdicts in British murder trials, a choice that can be somewhat confusing. First, the defendant can be found guilty of murder, which carries a mandatory life sentence. Second, he can be found not guilty: he did not do it, or he did it accidentally. Third, he can be found not guilty on the grounds of self-defense. Fourth, he can be found not guilty of murder but guilty of manslaughter on the grounds of provocation or, fifth, on the grounds of diminished responsibility. A defense counsel does not necessarily confine himself to arguing only one of these alternatives. If the defendant pleads "not guilty" to murder (on the grounds for example that there is doubt whether he in fact knifed the victim or whether the victim fell on the weapon), the defense counsel can suggest alternative verdicts to the jury: that the defendant acted in self-defense, was provoked, or even was not guilty at all. It is often quite difficult for a defense counsel to present several grounds for defense simultaneously. The complexity of the alternatives is often too much for juries to contend with, resulting in some bizarre verdicts. For example, in the case of *McDonald v. The Crown* (1985) a young woman charged with the murder of her lover, who had been the subject of previous violence from him, was heard by two witnesses to say, "I've knifed him, I've knifed him," and they gave evidence that she held the murder weapon in her hand and saw the defendant coming towards her with a look in his eye that he had had before when he had attacked her. But the jury found her not guilty of murder rather than not guilty on the grounds of self-defense.

WHAT CONSTITUTES PROVOCATION?

The Homicide Act of 1957 amended the law in Britain so that one category of homicide carried the death sentence and all others carried a mandatory sentence of life imprisonment. The death penalty was suspended for murder in 1965 and abolished five years later. All murders were then made punishable by life imprisonment. Under sections 2 and 3 of the act, the grounds for extenuating circumstances were widened by introducing the ground of diminished responsibility, by which murder could be commuted to manslaughter (section 2) and by widening the defense of provocation (section 3). There are problems with both these categories. In this article I will be concentrating on the defense of provocation. This is not to say that the concept of diminished responsibility, which rests on psychiatric advice, is not also used in such a way as to condone male violence. For example, I have seen a diagnosis of depression accepted as evidence for diminished responsibility when there was no evidence that the defendant was undergoing any kind of treatment or suffering any significant symptoms and he had written in his diary that he planned to kill his wife and children by setting fire to them. Diminished responsibility seems to be put forward when the offense is particularly brutal or shocking and when children are involved.

The defense of provocation is based on the premise that the behavior of the victim precipitates his or her own death to some lesser or greater extent. Before 1965, only limited types of conduct were sufficient to constitute provocation: physical violence or detection of a spouse in the act of adultery was almost invariably required in order to bring a case of provocation. The House of Lords stated in *Holmes v. DPP* (1946) that, save in circumstances of a most extreme and exceptional nature, a confession of adultery by one spouse to the other could not constitute sufficient provocation to justify a verdict of manslaughter if the injured spouse killed his spouse or the adulterer (Cross and Jones 1984). Section 3 of the Homicide Act changed this and provided for a manslaughter verdict on the grounds of provocation when there is evidence of a sudden and temporary loss of self-control:

> Where on a charge of murder there is evidence on which the jury can find that the person charged was provoked (whether by things done or by things said or by both together) to lose his self control, the question whether provocation was enough to make a *reasonable man* do as he did shall be left to be determined by the jury; and in determining that question, the jury shall take into account everything both done and said according to the effect which in their opinion, it would have on a reasonable man.
>
> Juries must therefore take into account
> 1. the events which have happened ("anything done or said (or a combination of acts and words) will suffice")
> 2. the relevant characteristics of the defendant which may result in loss of self control. (Cross and Jones 1984)

The difficulty with these guidelines is that both the jury's view of the events that happened and the relevant characteristics of the defendant is ambiguous. As Dr. Susan Edwards comments, "Whilst provocation might well appear as a relatively clear legal category bound by rules and procedures, what precise forms of action, behavior, mannerisms, speech and situation, and relevant characteristics a jury may consider constitutes provocation, is both arbitrary and ambiguous" (1985, 138).

The concept of provocation is, as Atkins and Hoggett, writers of a legal textbook, succinctly put it, "the most insidious concept of all to emerge from cruelty cases" (1984, 129). It is based on three very questionable assumptions. The first is that a reasonable man, rather than by controlling his emotions, can be provoked into murder by insubordinate behavior—infidelity, bad housekeeping, withdrawal of sexual services, and even nagging. In divorce cases provocation is unlikely to be used to legitimate a husband's use of force to make his wife obey orders. Yet in murder cases it is very much in use. The law provides a legitimation for men to behave violently in the face of insubordination or marriage breakdown. The focus of the trial shifts from the defendant to the victim. If it can be successfully alleged that the victim was unrespectful, unfaithful, unconventional, or negligent in her wifely duties, then provocation is usually accepted. Second, the idea that women can be similarly provoked even when they have been beaten up or raped is rarely entertained. This would be a "license to kill" rapists and wife batterers. Third, although the main distinction between murder and manslaughter revolves around whether the killing is premeditated or not ("Malice aforethought," or intention to kill, is murder, but if someone kills by accident or through negligence or is provoked, it is manslaughter), in practice, a defense of provocation on the basis of "loss of self-control," as we shall see, often overrules evidence of premeditation.

In murder verdicts the judge has no discretion and life imprisonment is mandatory. In manslaughter verdicts, by contrast, the judge has wide discretion. Sentences range from a maximum of life imprisonment to absolute discharge. Provocation has therefore functioned as grounds for the commutation of murder to manslaughter, with the result that judges have allowed men who killed their wives or lovers to walk free from court. That this tendency has recently increased is suggested by the fact that the number of life sentences for murder dropped from 169 in 1979 to 114 in 1984, in spite of an increase in the number of homicides from 546 to 563 during the same period. It is, however, difficult to know exactly how long the sentences for manslaughter based on provocation are. Statistics collected by the Bedford College Legal Research Unit show the distribution of sentences in the years 1957–68 as follows: "7 discharged, 7 probation or an unspecified sentence. Prison sentences of between 3 to 6 years for half the remainder" (Ashworth 1975, 76–79). More recent statistics are not available, but the pattern in the cases cited below is sentences in the region of three to six years (a third of which with good behavior is remitted).

THE DEFENSE OF PROVOCATION

The double standard is evident in the grounds for provocation that are considered legitimate; even more progressive judges define them in a sexist way. The hypothetical example judges use to describe provocation is of the soldier returning home, either from action in the Falklands or Northern Ireland, to find his wife in flagrante delicto—in bed with her lover—so when he goes "out of his senses" he kills her. (On the other hand, if a woman is raped and kills her rapist, doing so may be regarded as revenge, which is grounds for a murder conviction.) To allege infidelity in presenting a defense of provocation is crucial.

Mumtaz Baig and Pamela Megginson

A comparison of two cases, heard at the Old Bailey—Mumtaz Baig, a man who killed his wife, and that of Pamela Megginson, a woman who killed her lover—illustrates the way the law excuses the man but blames the woman even when the facts suggest greater intentionality on the part of the man. In September 1987 I attended the case of Mumtaz Baig, who was charged with murdering his wife Rohila by strangling her with a piece of rope that he said she used for tying up a rubber plant. This was refuted by Rohila's sister, a witness for the prosecution, who in her evidence said that she had frequently visited her sister and that her sister had used knitting wool to tie up the plant.

They had married in 1980. Mr. Baig had left and returned to Pakistan shortly before the birth of their second son in 1982 following what he described as arguments with his in-laws. His pregnant wife had returned to her parents after her husband had beat her up. He admitted hitting her but described it as "not hard—I swear I was never violent towards her." Nonetheless she obtained a transfer of the house to her name and a legal separation. Between 1982 and 1986 his only contact with the family was to send birthday and Christmas cards. In January 1986 he returned to England and later that year Mrs. Baig made it clear that she wanted a divorce. He killed her in December. His defense—of provocation—rested on his unsupported allegation that she had been unfaithful with a friend of his called Ibrahim. In his evidence he stated that after making love on the day of her death, he had asked why she looked so happy and she had said to him, "I have a friendship with Ibrahim. You're doing well, but he has a really big thing." Ibrahim was called to the witness-box and vehemently refuted these allegations. He maintained that he had never been alone with Mrs. Baig, let alone had a sexual relationship with her. The unlikelihood of any woman, let alone a devout Muslim, making this comment was not raised, nor was the horror with which her family would have reacted to such an allegation. As Baig's English was poor all his written statements were translated, and he had an interpreter in court. He did, however, use colloquial English idioms, but not quite correctly, as in, "I was not in my senses," which sounded as if it might not have been his own phrase. In his evidence, on the other hand, he also stated quite blatantly, "Because she wanted to take away the children, I intended to kill her."

The contradiction between these two positions was not taken up. The defense counsel, in summing up, asked, "Is there any evidence that he was anything but a gentle husband and father?" With good reason, he was confident that the evidence of his violence, his four-year absence, his own admission that he intended to murder his wife, and his failure to contribute anything to the household would be disregarded. The prosecution did comment weakly that "you've only heard one side of the story. No one knows what Rohila Baig would have said." But this did not prevent the jury from finding him *not guilty* of murder on the grounds of provocation. He was sentenced to six years for manslaughter.

Compare this with the case of Pamela Megginson, aged 61, who in September 1983 killed her 79-year-old, self-made millionaire lover, whom she had lived with for the past 13 years. He was rendering her homeless by taking another lover. In evidence, she said the only thing that had excited him sexually was hitting her, and although she had not wanted sex on the night in question, she had agreed to try in order to persuade him to change his mind. After he hit her she lost control and hit him over the head with a champagne bottle, which killed him. She pleaded not guilty of murder but guilty of manslaughter on the grounds of provocation. She was, however, found guilty of murder and given a mandatory life sentence.

In both cases the victim was planning to break up the relationship, though in the Baig case it had really ended five years before. Nonetheless, the jury in the Baig case took the view that the man was provoked by his wife's desire to continue to live on her own with the children. The lack of corroboration to his allegations of her infidelity and the absurdity of his description of their bedtime talk made no difference. Nor indeed did the evidence that he had contributed little if anything to the marriage, had been violent in the past, and had by his own admission intended to kill her lead the jury to reject his plea of provocation. With remission he could be released within four years, little redress for a cold blooded, premeditated murder of a defenseless and innocent woman.

In the Megginson case, though the evidence appeared to point to an unpremeditated, unintentional, and accidental death occurring in the course of sexual sadomasochistic activity initiated by the victim, the jury found her guilty of murder. Neither the context of the actual killing nor the threat of the loss of her home and relationship was regarded as grounds for provocation. The alleged infidelity of a woman, even if uncorroborated, is accepted as grounds for provocation for a man, but a man's infidelity is no grounds. The very wording of the law excludes a woman.

In one of the few summaries made of murder trials (occurring between 1957 and 1962), criminologists Terence Morris and Louis Blom Cooper conclude that "one factor emerges very clearly from these homicide cases and that is that the area of heterosexual relationships is one exceptionally fraught with potential violence whether within marriage or outside it" (1964, 322).

The close relations between love and hate, the intense feelings of possessiveness and passion raised by close relationships are widely accepted. What is, however, less accepted is that the possessiveness that leads to violence is almost always male and is widely condoned not merely by the populace but by the law and its enforcement agencies. Criminologists have failed to investigate male possessiveness and to question the acceptability of male violence in the family.

According to the 1986 statistics, 109 wives and only 12 husbands were recorded as victims of homicides in which the chief suspect was their spouse. Studies indicate that femicides are the tip of the iceberg of male violence against women. Female violence, when it occurs, is often a response to years of wife battering and mental cruelty.

REVIEW OF CASES WHERE PROVOCATION WAS USED AS A DEFENSE

The following cases in which provocation was used as a defense for murder illustrate the way the law encourages male possessiveness even to the point of condoning murder. In all these cases the relationship between the defendant and the victim had been under strain or it was alleged that infidelity had occurred. Corroboration for the allegations was not considered necessary.

In 1981 Winchester Crown Court acquitted Gordon Asher of the murder of his wife Jane the previous September on the grounds that, while he was a model husband, she was a "two-timing flirt." Mr. Justice Mars-Jones passed a six-month sentence suspended for two years for manslaughter, allowing Asher to walk free from court. In June 1982 Peter Wood was brought to court for the murder of Mary Bristow, a librarian whom he had clubbed to death with a meat tenderizer, smothered with a pillow, and strangled. In the far distant past he had been Mary's lover, and for a time a lodger in her house. Some years back she ended the relationship, but Wood had continued to pester her. He was found not guilty of murder and sentenced to six years for manslaughter—he was released after four years. In March 1985 Peter Hogg was charged with having murdered his wife in 1976 and disposing of her body in the Lake District. He was acquitted of murder and received a three year sentence for manslaughter, described by trial judge Pigot as "the least possible sentence I can give." Hogg was in fact released in June 1986 after having served 15 months of his sentence. In October 1985 Nicholas Boyce was tried for the murder of his wife. He had dismembered the body in the bath, cooked parts of it to disguise them, and dumped them in plastic bags in several parts of London. He was acquitted of murder and sentenced to six years for manslaughter. In February 1989 he was released on parole. He had served little more than three years of his sentence. In May 1987 Leslie Taylor, aged 36, stood trial at Aylesburgh Crown Court for knifing his wife to death after he discovered she had been kissing another man at a wedding reception. He was found not guilty of murder and sentenced to six years for manslaughter on the grounds of provocation. In January 1989 Stephen Midlane strangled and cut up his wife but did not even need to stand trial: a defense of manslaughter on the grounds of provocation was accepted.

It is the derisory nature of these sentences by comparison with those for other crimes, such as those involving property, that is surely the problem. Violence against women and children is not taken seriously by the courts. It is clear that the submissions of mitigating circumstances in these cases accepted by the courts would have little parallel in any case of murder or serious assault other than those committed by men against women.

A more detailed look at some of these cases provides ample illustration of this discrimination.

Stephen Midlane

In January 1989 Stephen Midlane, aged 30, was charged with strangling and cutting up his wife Sandra, aged 23, by whom he had two children. Officers toiled for weeks looking for her remains on an Essex rubbish tip and found everything except one leg. Stephen Midlane was not even charged with murder.

The Crown Prosecution Service accepted his plea of guilty to manslaughter of Sandra and attempted murder of the couple's two sons, aged 4 and 5. Judge Neil Denison sentenced him to five years (which, with full remission, amounts to only three years). In mitigation, the defense claimed that Sandra had been unfaithful and that he attacked her in the middle of an argument over her infidelity, accidentally hitting the vagus nerve on her neck. The manslaughter plea ensured that a number of critical statements made to detectives by friends and family were never put before the judge. These statements outlined the breakdown of the marriage because of incompatibility, the increasing use of violence by Midlane against Sandra and her hospital treatment for broken bones at the Charing Cross Hospital, their separation and her determination to divorce, and his threats of further violence—in all, a picture indicating premeditation for the attack, a picture very different from that given by the defense. Debby Jennings, aged 24, Sandra's closest friend, when interviewed by Terry Kirkby of the *Independent* (20 January 1989), said: "I told police how she was scared that Stephen was going to kill her. He had begun to beat her up in the last few months, and had started breaking into her flat late at night and demanding to stay. She told me that he had once tried to strangle her and had once tied her up. Two weeks before he killed Sandra he hit her so badly her jaw was fractured. That was how she was identified from her remains on the tip."

Peter Hogg

The case of Peter Hogg was given wide coverage in the press. His past record as a war hero was given prominence, as was indeed his wife's alleged promiscuity. The *Times* (9 March 1985) reported her to have had "a reputation for promiscuity which stretched back to her teenage years although her marriage in 1963 appeared to have a calming effect. It was not long before she began to show an interest in the friends of her husband." It is not suggested that they also might have shown an interest in her. When her husband, an airline pilot, was abroad flying she was said to spend hours on the phone running up bills which he had to pay. In October 1976 Mrs. Hogg went for a week's holiday with her lover, Mr. Graham Ryan, a banker she had been seeing since 1973. When she returned, Hogg said, "I just lost control and grabbed her throat with both hands and squeezed until she stopped screaming."

During the night he dragged the body outside, put it in the boot of the car, and put into action an intricate plan to dispose of the body. He rang the head of the public school where his son was a pupil, put a concrete bar in the car, and drove to the school, saying he was spending the night there. Instead, he drove with a rubber dinghy to the Lake District, dumped the body, and then drove back to Taunton. He spread the story that his wife had walked out, reported her missing to the police, and filed for a divorce, which was granted in October 1977. Hogg's derisory 15 months in prison was justified on the basis of his wife's alleged infidelity. On his release Hogg said, "*Locking me up didn't achieve a thing.* What had happened had happened, nothing could put the clock back, nothing could bring my wife back."

Nicholas Boyce

In the Nicholas Boyce case at the Old Bailey, murder was commuted to manslaughter through a combination of arguments involving provocation and unintended consequences. The jury apparently accepted that Nicholas Boyce had been the subject of, to quote his defense counsel, "a nonstop form of humiliation and degradation which drained every bit of self respect from a grown man. He used to sneak home terrified of his life [*sic*]." Counsel continued that Boyce had been subjected to a regime of "rules" by his wife Christabel that had included no sexual relations; he was not even allowed in the marital bed, irrespective of whether his wife was there at the time. He could not even take a bath at home. Add to this the constant abuse and accusations allegedly screamed at Boyce by his wife, and is it surprising that "he finally broke down in circumstances in which an ordinary man might also have done" (judge's summing-up)?

Disregarding the justifiability of the allegations, two important assumptions underlie this statement: (1) there are limits to the degree of "nagging" that a man can take and murder is a reasonable response to this behavior—rather than walking out or perhaps listening to the reasons why a woman is "nagging"; and (2) the ordinary man cannot be expected to put up with insubordination on the part of his wife, particularly if it involves withdrawal of marital relations. The fact that Christabel wanted him to leave after years of an unsatisfactory marriage is not considered relevant by the recorder, who in his judgment said:

> I will deal with you on the basis that you were provoked, you lost self control, and that a man of reasonable self control might have been similarly provoked and might have done what you did. Not only did you kill her but you came to your senses and took meticulous steps to ensure her death would never be discovered (is this a mitigating circumstance?). You got rid of her body, you cleaned up the flat the best you could. You cut her up and boiled her skin and bones. You bagged up the pieces and over the next two days, disposed of her body. Later to your credit you gave yourself up.

The judge expresses the opinion that "a man of reasonable self control could calmly cut up his wife." One would have expected such evidence to be brought forward to show Boyce's insanity and lack of responsibility for his actions. Instead, it is used as evidence of his sanity and his wife's provocation. As the defense counsel, Mr. Michael Wolkind, put it: "Boyce took a job as a cleaner to satisfy his nagging wife's demands." In actual fact, at the age of 37 Boyce had never had a steady job and Christabel had been the sole breadwinner for two years when her husband's postgraduate grant ran out. She had worked full-time at Bethnal Green Hospital as well as taking the main responsibility for looking after the two children. Mr. Wolkind went on: "She constantly bullied him and remorselessly ground him down until he finally snapped and strangled her with an electric flex. What he wanted, all he ever wanted was some peace and time to spend with his children" (court transcript).

There are two further disturbing aspects of this case. First, the tone of the comments made by the recorder of London, Sir James Miskin. His description of Boyce's "coming to his senses," disposing of the body meticulously, and giving himself up suggests approval of Boyce's actions rather than condemnation. The failure to condemn Boyce's action was thrown into interesting relief by Miskin's comments at a later trial of a group of black teenagers who raped two white women in Brixton: he remarked that the defendants' actions revealed "man's inhumanity to woman" (see Benn [1986]). Second, the whole trial revolved around the assumed character of the victim, which opened the door for all sorts of unverifiable allegations. Journalist Maureen Cleave, writing in the *London Standard* after the trial, reported that Christabel had moved to Lavenham with the two children but had agreed to spend Christmas with her husband. She had written to her aunt, however, saying she feared Boyce was planning to kill her. She reported that two close friends of Christabel, who had asked to give evidence at the Old Bailey but were never called, had a different story:

> They would have told the court how worried they had been about Christabel, how they begged her to spend Christmas with them, how their telephone conversations with her would end abruptly when apparently Nicholas came into the room; how she was frightened; how she had brought her few possessions to them in a box for safe keeping because he had begun to break things that were special to her, beginning with her watch; how he had been reading books about criminal law. (Smith 1989, 5)

Leslie Taylor

Leslie Taylor, aged 36, appeared at Aylesbury Crown Court charged with knifing his wife to death after he discovered she had been kissing another man at a wedding reception. He had spent the night drinking and then went to his mother-in-law's in Islington, where his wife had gone, and stabbed her eight times in front of their 12-year-old son. He claimed his wife had been unfaithful to him during the previous two years of their 16-year-marriage. He said he had "felt totally humiliated at what she had done in front of my family" and "could not sleep," so after phoning his wife to say he was coming, he took a knife round to the house. Normally this would imply intention, but a manslaughter verdict ensued, on the grounds of provocation, with a six-year sentence.

Gordon Reid

When a husband argues that he still loves his wife and makes no allegations about her, he is likely to be treated much more harshly, even if his wife did not die in the attack. Consider the case, heard at the Old Bailey, of Gordon Reid, who was found not guilty of attempted murder but guilty of wounding and causing grievous bodily harm to his co-habitee, and the mother of his three children, Irene May Reid on 28 July 1987. Believing his wife was having an affair, he got drunk and, armed with two knives, stabbed her in the upper part of her abdomen and then stabbed himself. She drew the knife out of him and was taken to the hospital, where she remained for a fortnight and then made a complete recovery. He spent three days in the hospital, where he said to the police, "How is she? We've been married for 20 years. The last three months she's been getting screwed by some bloke. I wanted her and myself to die" (court transcript). The defense counsel said that he still cared for his wife and wished to stay with her. She wanted him to leave. He said, "I wanted to hurt her and myself because I'd allowed it to happen. I still love her. I admit everything."

Judge Justice Henry accepted that Reid's attack was unpremeditated and happened during a period of stress and emotion. He took into account that Reid's wife had made a full recovery and that he was contrite. The judge then said: "The sentence to be passed is to deter others and the least sentence that one can pass is 5 years imprisonment."

Two questions arise from this sentence. If the attack was unpremeditated, is it not contradictory for a judge to pass a sentence to deter others? Second, if Reid had argued that she was a "two-timing bitch," is it not likely that he would have been treated much less harshly?

CAN WOMEN USE THE DEFENSE OF PROVOCATION?

What seems to be clear in the way provocation is used as a defense is that it is acceptable as a defense for men but rarely for women. A successful defense based on provocation depends on evidence of:

1. A sudden and temporary loss of control
2. An action that immediately follows the provoking act
3. A reasonable relationship between provocation and retaliation

It is the acceptability of male violence as a response to any form of insubordination from the woman that is at the core of the acceptance of such a plea. When a woman is attacked by a man, on the other hand, and attacks him back, the argument of provocation is rarely accepted. The mitigating defense based on provocation is quite distinct in law from the justification of self-defense. Provocation is based on a sudden loss of self-control in circumstances where the accused does not entertain a reasonable or, generally speaking, any kind of belief that his life is in danger. A woman who is attacked is presumably scared for her life, so she can only use self-defense, not provocation; however, this plea too is invariably unacceptable. Bel Mooney, in an article in the *Times* entitled "Has the Woman the Right to Fight Back?" reports the following case of *R v. Maguire,* heard before Judge Stanley Price at York Crown Court on 17 July 1981, as follows:

On the night in question the victim started to walk home after securing her pony and missing the last bus. The accused, aged 24, was being driven home when he saw her walking along a lane. After being dropped off at home, he ran back over one mile and confronted the girl, pretending to be a policeman. He dragged her into a field and told her he was going to kill her. The "victim," although clearly terrified, managed to pull out a small sheath knife which she used to cut open bales of hay and "stuck it into the defendant's neck." The jury found him guilty of threatening to kill her. The judge, who felt that the defendant had already been punished enough, in passing a twelve month suspended prison sentence remarked: "This young lady inflicted a very considerable punishment on you."

The judge, in other words, allowed a man guilty of an appalling attack—of attempted murder—to go free because his victim protected herself. Iqbal Begum, who was found guilty of murdering her husband with a five-foot metal bar, told the police, "I didn't know what I was doing, but he wanted two of the children to be killed and I said, 'Don't let the children get killed.' " Owing to the absence of an interpreter, the court misunderstood Mrs. Begum to have made a plea of "guilty" when she in fact said "mistake," which sounds like "guilty" in Urdu. The plea of provocation was rejected, and she was sentenced to life imprisonment. After demonstrations and protests from women's groups, she was given a retrial and her sentence was reduced to four years, still disgracefully long in view of the circumstances.

Two trials we attended provide some grounds for optimism.

Janet Clugstone

The case of Janet Clugstone in September 1987 was described as "a beacon of hope for victims of rape"(*Guardian*, 6 October 1981) when she was found not guilty of murdering her rapist, Stephen Cophen, on the grounds that she had acted in self-defense. The case was heard by a judge (now deceased) known to be progressive, Judge John Hazan. The facts of the case were as follows.

In October 1986 Mrs. Clugstone, aged 38, met Stephen Cophen, aged 24, on her way to a discotheque. The night ended at 2 A.M. in a friend's flat where the electricity had been disconnected; she alleged that she had been forced to enter it and that he raped and buggered her repeatedly. Mrs. Clugstone could not cry out because her larynx had been removed owing to cancer. She found an open penknife on the floor and stabbed Cophen with one wound that killed him. She then gave herself up to the police. Her account was supported by medical and forensic evidence and by a woman police constable, who described it as the worst case of sexual abuse and degradation she had ever encountered. The transcripts of the trial reveal several significant differences from cases in which the defendants are male.

First, in summing up Judge Hazan bent over backwards to emphasize that "the issue is not to blacken the character of a man who isn't here to speak for himself." He documented corroboration for the allegations with great care, showing how they were supported by witnesses, evidence of previous criminal offenses, and medical and forensic evidence.

Second, the questions of whether Janet Clugstone acted in self-defense or for revenge rested on whether or not Cophen had withdrawn his penis at the time of the attack rather than on whether repeat rape was a terrifying, life-threatening experience. To quote Judge Hazan's directions to the jury:

> The question is did she kill him after he'd withdrawn, kill him in reasonable self defence to stop him raping and assaulting her? In lawful self defence you should acquit. If she's not telling the truth—why isn't she? Is she a lady killing a young man in circumstances she's unwilling to reveal after he's withdrawn in revenge for the rape? *That is not a lawful killing.* She should then be found guilty of murder—an unprovoked and unlawful killing with intent to cause death or serious injury.

It is penetration that is all important in assessing her motivation—not whether she was terrified for her life, humiliated, and pushed "beyond her senses" but simply whether or not she killed him when he was penetrating her. This absurd distinction obscures what is the reality of rape as experienced by the victim.

Third, much of the trial was concerned with assessing whether or not Janet Clugstone was a "decent woman." In the middle of the most sensitive cross examination about the details of the rape, she was asked, "Have you had sex with other West Indians?"

In a rape trial this question would have been disallowed on the grounds that questions relating to the past sexual history of the victim can only be raised at the discretion of the judge.[1] (See section 2 of the Sexual Offenses [Amendment] Act of 1976.) The prosecution counsel should certainly have objected to the following question, too. Janet Clugstone was asked by the defense counsel, "Do you get on well with West Indians and other races on the council estate where you live?" Judge Hazan ended by warning that his verdict should not be seen as a charter for victims of serious crime to kill their attackers.

Trevor Virgo

The importance of contesting irrelevant probes into the reputation of women subjected to violence emerges graphically from the testimony of the main prosecution witness Julia Wolton, in the case of Trevor Virgo, whose attack on her resulted in the miscarriage and death of her unborn child. After having to recount the appalling details of Virgo's attack on her—he forced her to undress in the snow near a motorway—Julia Wolton was subjected to the following cross-examination by the defense counsel:

> DC: You're quite a lot older than the Defendant—you have had wider experience than him?

JW: Yes.
DC: Wider sexual experience than him?
JW: Is this relevant?
JUDGE: Very good question.
JW: I think you are trying to stereotype me.

JUDGE (to DC): Has her previous sexual experience any relevance to the attack?
DC: I'm trying to put the whole picture.

Julia Wolton was perfectly right; the defense was trying to stereotype her. This is the most common ploy that is used to discredit women subjected to male violence. Evidence that this ploy is common practice not only in England but elsewhere comes from an Australian study of women who had killed co-habitees or husbands. In all but three cases the women had been assaulted by the men in the past, in some cases beaten up over a period of 20 years. Thirteen out of 16 women interviewed said they had killed their husbands or co-habitees to protect themselves from physical assault. In court the image of the women presented was of a cold-blooded and premeditating murderer rather than of a woman provoked beyond endurance by a man's violence. Research into battered women indicates, on the other hand, that women who have lived for years in a battering relationship reach a point where they reasonably believe that if they do not kill their husbands they will be killed. Bacon and Lansdowne (1982) concluded:

> The images of women as victims, neurotics and provocateurs, and the ideology of privacy which surrounds the institutions of sexuality and the family, play a role in perpetuating the domination and violence experienced by these women. The same ideologies and myths pervade the criminal justice system and prevented the actual circumstances of these homicides emerging in the court process which judge and sentenced them. (97)

Conclusions

This study of the use of "provocation" as a defense in cases where wives are on trial for the murder of their husbands are treated quite differently from husbands murdering their wives or children. It is almost permissible and by definition "reasonable" for a husband to kill his wife (or even his children) for insubordination. Similarly, a man is more readily excused for killing his wife's lover than a woman for killing a rapist after an attack.

The acts of men and women are subject to a different set of legal expectations and standards. As we have seen in most cases where provocation is alleged by men, it is the character of the victim, if a woman, rather than the defendant that is up for trial. When the victim is a man, allegations about his sexual infidelity would just not be taken seriously, and it is doubtful whether they would even be raised. As we saw in the Clugstone case, care is taken not to align his character. In the far more typical cases where the victim is a woman, her reputation, particularly her sexual reputation, is regarded as crucial to the questions of the defendant's guilt.[2] If infidelity is alleged, let alone proved, provocation is usually allowed. As a friend watching the Boyce trial commented, *"Christabel was on trial, not Nick."* Since the victim is not there to tell her side, the defendant can give an account that is unchallengeable.

In theory, the prosecution counsel can call witnesses to counter the defense, but in practice this is rarely done. Part of the problem lies in the assumption that the crown counsel's role is one of impartiality and that it should not be concerned with defending the victim. In the Boyce trial both the police and the prosecution counsel seem to have been taken by surprise that a defense based on provocation was brought. They thought the evidence suggested premeditation. Another factor may be the reluctance of the prosecutor to dig up the history of a marriage.

It is time for the prosecution counsel to become more concerned about the victim and to call for evidence from witnesses. In the United States, Canada, and Australia the prosecution is insisting that evidence in rebuttal should be brought when allegations about a murdered victim are made. The main distinction between murder and manslaughter revolves around whether the killing is premeditated or not. "Malice aforethought," or intention to kill, is murder. If someone kills by accident or through negligence, or is provoked, then it is manslaughter. However, we have seen that there was clear evidence in a number of the cases cited above that the murder was planned and therefore intentional. In practice, if allegations about the woman victim are accepted, evidence of prior intention is disregarded. In both the Baig and the Boyce cases there was evidence of prior intention. However, in cases of women who kill, any evidence of prior intention precludes arguing self-defense.

THE CONDONING OF MALE VIOLENCE

Case studies allow us to make a detailed investigation of empirical reality. We then can see how the court ascribes specific roles to men and women that are used as evidence of whether the crime is "reasonable." The defense of provocation reflects the defendant's relationship to the social world. As Mary Eaton (1983) states: "Should this relationship follow an acceptable pattern it will be used to show that the defendant is not really a criminal since the social identity in question is basically conformist. Criminal activity will be presented as a temporary aberration" (389). If the victim's behavior is considered unconventional, on the other hand, this is presented as grounds for provocation, and it is the defendant who is presented as reacting to intolerable pressure. The victim is then presented as the real culprit in having pushed the man to violence. Sexist concepts about the nature of men and women's roles in the family, and about the acceptability of male violence as a reaction to any behavior deemed to be insubordinate to male authority, legitimize the violence they purport to protect women from.

The problem is not so much with the individual behavior of judges as with the system, which serves to entitle men to behave violently in close relationships.[3] There are three ways in which this condoning operates.

First, judges frequently sympathize with the male assailant. Judge Pickles, for example, in a TV interview in 1989 referred to the "Jekyll and Hyde" within all men. He regretted that sometimes "he had to send a man down" but paradoxically claimed that he was basically "pro women."

Such sympathy for the murderer even extends to cases where the wife has not been unfaithful, contemplating divorce, or allegedly failing in her wifely duties. In one case a man who killed his wife 21 years earlier was discovered only after he bragged to his second wife that he had committed the "perfect" murder. He had hit his first wife twice with a heavy stool and then pushed her downstairs after a furious argument over his passionate affair with the woman who became his second wife. Judge Igor, QC, summing up, said, "He has lived his life with the appalling threat of exposure to the world and to his adored sons. In one sense he has served a life sentence in prison in his own mind, trapped by his own fears."

The defense counsel must have assumed that the jury would be sympathetic to the idea that the defendant had suffered and therefore did not deserve to be punished again. The fact that he murdered his first wife cold-bloodedly in order to marry his second wife is not considered sufficiently important to preclude such a plea for clemency. It is inconceivable that such a plea would have been put forward in a case where a woman had killed her husband in order to marry someone else. In this case the defendant was acquitted of murder, found guilty of manslaughter, and sentenced to only six years.

During the last few years women killers of men who had subjected them to persistent violence have successfully pleaded cumulative provocation, though the defense may not be allowed if a woman is seen to be acting in revenge. In many of these cases self-defense would seem to be the more relevant plea, which if successful would result in a "not guilty" verdict rather than a conviction for manslaughter. This is unacceptable on the grounds that it would give some justification to women to kill their husbands.

A second way in which violence is condoned is by discounting anger as an acceptable response to frustration on the part of a woman. In law it does not appear that a "reasonable" woman can be driven "beyond her senses" and remain "reasonable" unless she is suffering from premenstrual tension (PMT) and is "at the mercy of her hormones." This fits in with the idea that nonconformity in women is due to biological imbalance rather than rational choice.

PREMENSTRUAL TENSION: THREE CASES

In line with the idea of women offenders as neurotics dominated by their ovaries or as Katherine Dalton (1971) put it, "at the mercy of their raging hormones," the only foolproof mitigating circumstances that have been used by women convicted of murder relate to postnatal depression and premenstrual tension, epitomizing the tendency to treat female conforming behavior as healthy and nonconforming behavior as sick or mad. In 1981, for example, Mrs. Kristina English killed her lover by driving her car at him after he had told her that he was going out with another woman. She claimed that something had snapped when he had made a *V* sign at her. Medical and psychiatric evidence diagnosed her as suffering from PMT on the basis of PMT pointers: following pregnancy she had suffered from postnatal depression; she had been sterilized; and she had not eaten for some hours before the event. It is alleged that failure to eat in PMT sufferers produces hypoglycemia, which causes a predisposition to aggressive behavior. Her plea of diminished responsibility was accepted. She was banned from driving for a year and given a one year conditional discharge (see Luckhaus 1986). As Barbara Amiel argued in the *Times:* "The courts did not give her a reduced sentence because her boyfriend was a cad . . . she was conditionally discharged because she convinced the court that PMT had led to diminished responsibility—even though she had threatened to run the boyfriend over earlier in the day, which might have been taken as evidence of premeditation."

More recently in March 1987 Miss Linda Hewlett, aged 31, walked free out of the Old Bailey after being convicted of attempted murder. The judge had given her three years probation for stabbing her sleeping lover whom she had become reconciled with after a short separation. Mr. Justice Leonard's reasons for the sentence were that Hewlett had become depressed after the birth of her twins, and that she had become irritated by her lover's lack of interest in her obstetric complications. "I could not face another day of him saying, "Have you done the vacuuming, have you dusted?" The judge accepted that Hewlett was suffering from postnatal depression heightened by PMT.

Third, in April 1988 Anne Reynolds, a 19-year-old girl who had killed her 61-year-old mother with a hammer and had been found guilty of murder and sentenced to youth custody at Northampton Crown Court, won her appeal on the grounds that PMT and postnatal depression had impaired her sense of responsibility. The appeal judges, Lord Justice Stocker, Mr. Justice French, and Mr. Justice McKinnon, substituted a verdict of manslaughter through diminished responsibility and put her on probation for two years with a condition that she seek psychiatric treatment.

A woman is therefore deemed either to be suffering from diminished responsibility—which means she is then confined, usually for an indefinite period to a mental hospital—or to be suffering from PMT, or to be acting in revenge and to be guilty of murder. This implies that, unlike a man, she cannot be "provoked" into violence and remain a reasonable person in the way a man can by asserting that he was acting "beyond his senses" but has now returned to his senses. Clearly the whole basis for a provocation defense is entirely spurious and should be abolished.

Lastly, this condonation is reflected in the lack of understanding about the predicament of victims of violence. Bochnak, in her study of women subjected to male violence in the family, found judges often fail to understand what living under the threat of attack involves. As one of the trial judges commented: "Given your domestic troubles, which as I find were present but are not to be accepted in their entirety, *the law itself is not without remedy and was not without remedy to you. There are friends: there are relations: there are community and Church and other avenues of advice: there are policemen, there are Chamber Magistrates: there are solicitors: there are means of protection in the community"* (Bochnak 1981, italics in original).

The concept of provocation embodies the idea that murder is precipitated by the victim, that, in effect, the victim is to blame for her death. The arguments used in court by the prosecution reflect a strong gender bias that discriminates against women and allows some malicious and violent murderers to be lightly punished.

The reluctance of the judiciary to adequately protect women is part of the general condoning of male violence in marriage. As far back as 1962 one judge commented on the danger of wives using provocation too often as mitigation. Justice Thesiger at the Essex Assizes, in finding Kenneth Burrell not guilty of murder but guilty of manslaughter on the grounds of provocation by his wife, who was in bed with a lover when her husband killed her, commented: "The accused undoubtedly had very severe provocation but on the other hand the large number of divorces do indicate that this sort of situation, though not quite in such a dramatic form is apt to arise and it would be a terrible thing if all people who commit misconduct while their husbands are away were subjected to a violent attack like this."

Criminologists have been no more enlightened than the judiciary. The main textbook on homicide cases, Terence Morris and Louis Blom Cooper's *A Calendar of Murder*, reflects sexist attitudes. For example, in their summary chapter they state:

> Few people, it might be argued, die simply because they have been careless, promiscuous, avaricious or vain. And while it is relatively easy to say that a man has lost his belongings through his own fault, it is much more difficult to say that a man has lost his life through his own fault. For one of the most permanent qualities attributed to the victims of murder is that of innocence. Even a cursory reading of the thumbnail sketches of homicide printed in this book will show that this is often misplaced generosity, for some of the victims might well have been capable of killing either by provocation in words or deeds, or by incessant nagging that they clearly precipitated their own death. (322)

Nagging, according to these criminologists, is a quite reasonable provocation to murder. In other words, women have only themselves to blame for male violence. Prostitutes, and even young girls, are also "asking for it," as they suggest on the next page: "While understandably, little sympathy attaches in the public mind to the prostitute victim of homicide, the same is not true of other victims of sexual murders particularly when they are young. . . . While little girls cannot be classed directly with adult prostitutes by no means all of them are lacking in sexual curiosity. . . . It is invariably a drive they dimly perceive but one which may draw them into situations where they may become victims of crime" (323).

In France the defense of *crime passionnel* was abolished in 1977 following feminist opposition. As long as the accused had been able to prove his spouse's adultery, he had stood a good chance of being convicted only of manslaughter. In England it does not even appear to be necessary to prove adultery; simple allegations are sufficient. It is time the discriminatory workings of the judiciary were laid bare and contested.

Notes

1. The Heilbron Advisory Group on the Law on Rape recommended that reference should only be made to the woman's sexual experience at the discretion of the judge. The judge should be satisfied

(a) that this evidence relates to behavior on the part of the complainant that was strikingly similar to her alleged behavior on the occasion of, or in relation to, events immediately preceding or following the alleged offense; and

(b) that the degree of relevance of that evidence to issues in the trial is such that it would be unfair to the accused to exclude it.

Zsuzsanna Adler, in her study of 81 rape cases heard at the Old Bailey, found that in the 50 contested cases, 5 failed to go ahead and application to introduce evidence of the woman's previous sexual experience was made in 18 of the remainder (40 percent), 75 percent of which were successful (see Adler 1987). Judith Roland (1985) describes the weight given to woman's sexual history by juries in America.

2. Several feminist criminologists have pointed out the significance of the woman's reputation to the outcome of cases (see *Respectable Women and the Law; Sociological Quarterly* 23 Spring [1982]: 221–34).

3. In a court system that is so predominantly male (of the 339 circuit judges authorized to try murders only 10 were female in 1986, and only 3 out of 77 women were high court judges), the definition of the law is based on what the "reasonable" man would do, sexist biases and prejudices prevail.

References

Adler, Z. 1987. *Rape on Trial*. London: Routledge.

Ashworth, A. J. 1975. "Sentencing in Provocation Cases." *Criminal Law Review* 1:3–46.

Atkins, S. and B. Hoggett. *Women and the Law*. Oxford: Blackwell, 1984.

Bacon, W., and R. Lansdowne. 1982. "Women Who Kill Husbands: The Battered Wife on Trial." In *Family Violence in Australia*, ed. C. O'Donnell and J. Craney. Melbourne: Longman Cheshire.

Benn, M. 1986. "Comment on Boyce Trial." *Rights of Women Unit Newsletter*, January.

Bochnak E. 1986. *Women's Self-defense Cases: Theory and Practice.* Melbourne: Mitchie Co.

Cross, R., and P. Jones. 1984. *Introduction to Criminal Law.* London: Butterworths.

Dalton, K. 1983. "The Menstrual Cycle" [1971]. In Eaten (1983).

Eaten, M. 1983. "Mitigating Circumstances: Familiar Rhetoric." *International Journal of Law* 11:285–400.

Edwards, S. 1986. *Gender, Sex, and the Law.* London: Croom Helm.

_____. 1986. In *Women on Trial*, ed. S. Edwards, 175–76. Manchester: Manchester University Press.

_____. 1987. " 'Provoking Her Own Demise': From Common Assault to Homicide." In *Women, Violence, and Social Control*, ed. J. Hanmer and M. Maynard. London: Macmillan.

Kruttschnitt, C. 1982. "Respectable Women and the Law." *Sociological Quarterly* 23 (Spring): 221–34.

Lees, S. 1989. "Rape on Trial." *New Statesman and Society*, 23 November and 1 December.

Lever, L. A. 1986. "No-one Speaks for the Dead." Thames documentary (August).

Luckhaus, Linda A. 1986. "Plea for PMT in the Criminal Law." In Edwards (1986).

Mooney, B. 1981. "Has the Woman the Right to Fight Back?" (London) *Times*, 21 July.

Morris, T., and L. Blom Cooper. 1964. *A Calendar of Murder.* London: Michael Joseph.

Morrison, Blake. 1987. "The Ballad of the Yorkshire Ripper." London: Chatto and Windus.

Smith, J. *Mysogynies.* London: Faber & Faber, 1989.

Fay Stender and the Politics of Murder

DIANA E. H. RUSSELL

> It's hard to accept the idea that, in the mind of some would-be assassin, pulling out [of the prison movement] just before she burned out is a sin punishable by the kind of lunatic brutality visited on her in the middle of the night in her own home.
>
> —Austin Scott, *Los Angeles Times,* 5 June 1979

I have written about the death of Fay Stender, a well-known California attorney, because I was very deeply affected by it. In part this was because I knew her. And her lover—who was present when she was shot—was a close friend of mine. In addition, Stender lived in my neighborhood, and I happened to be visiting her at her home only 24 hours before she was shot. As a feminist and former leftist, I also identified with her. Consequently, I found the attempt to kill her for political reasons particularly horrifying.

This is one of the cases in this book in which a man's attempt to murder a woman was unsuccessful. Rape researchers also study attempted rape, and for the same reasons, attempted femicides are a fitting subject for this volume. First, I will describe the attack on Stender, and then explain why her story is included in an anthology about femicide. Finally, I will explain why I consider this attack to be a case of attempted femicide—that is, why I believe misogyny to have been relevant in the attempt to assassinate her.

THE ATTACK

In the early hours of Memorial Day in 1979, Fay Stender was shot six times at point-blank range in her Berkeley home by a man later identified as 27-year-old

This is a revised version of an article published in *On the Issues* 18 (Spring 1991). I am indebted to Peter Collier and David Horowitz for their well-researched, informative article, "Requiem for a Radical," *New West,* March 1981, to Joan Morris (pseudonym) for reviewing the accuracy of this article and lending me news clippings about Fay Stender, and to Candida Ellis and *On the Issues* for editorial assistance.

ex-convict Edward Brooks. One .38-caliber bullet hit Fay's head, narrowly missing her brain. Three other bullets struck her in the abdomen and chest, damaging her spinal cord and right lung. The remaining two bullets fractured bones in her arms, causing nerve damage there. When Brooks ran from Stender's home, he "left her for dead" (Williamson [*SFC*] 1980).[1] Stender was 47 years old at the time, a feminist, the mother of two children, Neal and Oriane, and had recently separated from her attorney husband Marvin.

Stender was on the critical list for the next few days, and in the intensive-care unit at a Berkeley hospital for two to three weeks. When she was discharged, she was permanently paralyzed from her waist down. From that point on, Stender was always in pain, physically and psychically. Since she regarded Brooks "as a gun whose trigger had been pulled by others" (Collier and Horowitz 1981, 145), she was haunted by the constant fear that one of these others would return to complete Brooks's bungled effort to bestow on her—a Jew—"the final solution."

Unable to endure profound disillusionment and relentless physical pain, Stender herself eventually completed Brooks's attempt to terminate her life. " 'I'm just living for this [Brooks's] trial,' she told friends. 'I want to see him put away' " (Collier and Horowitz 1981). Three months after Brooks was sentenced to 17 years in state prison for attempted murder, an overflowing congregation of grieving family, friends, and acquaintances attended Stender's funeral on 28 May 1980—a year to the day after Brooks forced his way into her home and shot her.

Stender died in Hong Kong from a drug overdose. She had fled there in an effort to quell her terror of another assassination attempt. But with the diminution of this terror, Stender's grief, disillusionment, and anger came to the fore. Try as she might, she was unable to obliterate these feelings and the state of profound despair that accompanied them. She killed herself after less than two months in the country she had chosen for self-banishment, half a world away from her Berkeley home.

Edward Brooks had used a woman to gain entrance to Stender's home. Believing her to be in distress, Stender's 20-year-old son Neal opened the door. Brooks—armed with a gun—then stepped forward and demanded to speak to Stender.[2]

"Please don't hurt us," pleaded Neal.

"Get moving," Brooks insisted, "or I'll blow your fucking head off."

Neal led Brooks upstairs to the bedroom where his mother sleepily answered his knock.

"There's a man with a gun who wants to talk to you," warned Neal. Seeing two women in the bed, Brooks asked Stender to identify herself. He then ordered her to sit down at the desk.

"Have you ever betrayed anyone?" Brooks asked Stender. She denied that she had.

"Don't you feel you betrayed George Jackson?" Once again, Stender denied that she had. Brooks then ordered her to write the following statement:

"I, Fay Stender, admit I betrayed George Jackson and the prison movement when they needed me most."

Before he was gunned down in a prison escape attempt, Jackson had been a charismatic political radical, and author of the much acclaimed best-seller, *Soledad Brother* (1970), a passionate and eloquent account of his prison experiences and revolutionary politics (Williamson [*SFC*] 1979). He had also been a longtime client of Stender.

After starting to write this coerced confession, Stender protested. "This isn't true. I'm just writing this because you're holding a gun to my head." But she completed the "confession' when Brooks threateningly waved his gun at her.

After pocketing the statement, Brooks requested money. Neal and "Joan Morris"—a pseudonym for the other woman trapped by Brooks in Stender's bedroom—gave him the few dollars they had with them, while Stender told him her money was downstairs in the kitchen. Brooks ordered Neal to tie Morris's hands together. Next, he forced Neal to lie face down on the bed, tied his hands behind his back, then followed Stender down to the kitchen. There she started to give him the $40 she had stashed away in a drawer, but Brooks suddenly raised his gun and, from a distance of only two feet, shot her six times.

Responding to Stender's screams, Neal ran downstairs, his hands still tied behind him. He found his mother lying on the floor, soaked in blood. "I'm dying," she sobbed. How intensely she later came to wish that this had been true.

THE ARREST

Because Stender's would-be murderer did not know her, and because of the note he had forced her to write, police started their search for suspects in the Black Guerrilla Family (Collier and Horowitz 1981, 142). The members of this militant African-American prison group that George Jackson had cofounded regarded him "as a martyred saint" (142).

On 8 June Brooks was arrested in San Francisco for possession of marijuana. A gun found in his possession by the police was later determined by ballistic tests to be the weapon used to shoot Stender. But Brooks was released before the test was conducted. A few days after his release, Brooks was apprehended with five other men—four of them (including Brooks) ex-felons on parole from California prisons—for the armed robbery of a Berkeley Wells Fargo Bank (Williamson [*SFC*] 1979). Brooks's apprehension for these other criminal activities greatly assisted the police in their efforts to identify Stender's assailant because of the incriminating evidence found in his possession.

On 19 June 1979, Edward Brooks was charged in court with attempting to murder Fay Stender.

BROOKS AND THE BLACK GUERRILLA FAMILY

It was not only Fay Stender who believed that Brooks was a gun whose trigger had been pulled by others. Most law enforcement authorities believed—and still do believe—that he was a member of this all-male group of prisoners and ex-prisoners formerly known as the Black Family but transformed by Jackson into the Black Guerrilla Family (Isabel [OT] 1983). Jackson had hoped to replace "the criminal mentality" of the group members with a "revolutionary conscious-ness" (Reiterman and Martinez [SFE] 1979).

Brooks, however, steadfastly denied that he had any connection with the Black Guerrilla Family. He said that he admired George Jackson but had never met him (Isabel [OT] 1983). During the trial, Thomas Broome, Brooks's attor-ney, did not allow his client to testify. According to Peter Collier and David Horowitz, "Broome did not want Brooks to reveal his feelings about George Jackson, 'which was something he was really into and that would have hurt his case' " (1981, 145).

Nonetheless, less than two months after Brooks's attempt to assassinate Fay Stender, *Berkeley Barb* reporter Bill Wallace expressed skepticism about Brooks's affiliation with the BGF (1979, 3). In part this skepticism was based on what Wallace considered to be the unreliability of the sources, often referred to in vague terms such as "law enforcement experts" or "prison authorities." But because there was so much fear of the BGF, sources claiming knowledge of Brooks's membership may have insisted on anonymity. In addition, since secrecy about BGF membership was one of that group's rules, Brooks's denial of participation cannot be taken at face value.

Now, more than 10 years later, the weight of the evidence at my disposal[3] indicates that Brooks was a member of the BGF.

For example, the *San Francisco Examiner* claims to have obtained a 22-page BGF document drafted at San Quentin in 1974 (Reiterman and Martinez [SFE] 1979), stating, "Our support has been destroyed by the vultures who call themselves movement lawyers, with the help from their patron saint Huey P. Newton. We call upon the most Honorable Magistrates [of the BGF revolution-ary court] to render the people a just verdict by exposing and punishing those responsible for such atrocious crimes [against] the revolution." Although Sten-der was not mentioned by name in this document, she was almost certainly one of the attorneys the authors had in mind; Stender left the movement in 1973 and this BGF document was written in 1974.

In their 1979 article about the attack on Stender, *San Francisco Examiner* reporters Tim Reiterman and Don Martinez cited "official prison sources" as reporting that "Stender was one of a half-dozen lawyers named on BGF 'death warrants' issued several years ago, about the time [i.e., 1973] that Stender was dropping her emphasis on prison law."[4]

Less than a month after Stender was shot, Charles Garry, a well-known, longtime Black Panther attorney with whom Stender had practiced law for

nearly a decade, said that he had been informed by the Department of Corrections in Sacramento that he was also on an assassination hit list, as was attorney
Salle Seamen Soladay. Both had also been very active in the prison reform
movement (*SFC* 1979).

Since police protection was provided for Soladay and Garry, the authorities
evidently took this hit list very seriously (Williamson [*SFC*] 1979; *SFC* 1979).
While many on the left would likely mistrust information that comes from the
Department of Corrections, Soladay and Garry took it seriously. The two attorneys were described as "staying in a constant state of preparedness against the
chance that they may be the next assassin's target," and Soladay "left the Bay
area temporarily" because she felt so threatened (Wallace [*BB*] 1979).

Reporters Collier and Horowitz write that a week after Stender was shot,
Fleeta Drumgo—one of the Soledad Brothers who had been acquitted of murder
after George Jackson's death—appeared in Garry's law offices (1981, 142). "He
said he was a member of the Black Guerrilla Family, that he had known of the
BGF's plans to shoot Fay two weeks before the event and that he was willing to
sell information. He reappeared on several occasions, sometimes wearing a gun
in his belt, and named a former prisonmate of Brooks as head of the BGF and
the man who had ordered the shooting" (145). One month before Brooks's trial
began in January 1980, Drumgo was shot dead on an Oakland street (145).

Of course, Drumgo could have manufactured his story in an effort to exploit
Garry's fears and extort money from him. On the other hand, consistent with
Drumgo's story is the fact that Stender's daughter Oriane had bumped into him a
few days before her mother was shot, and "he had told her someone was looking
for her mother" (Collier and Horowitz 1981, 142). In addition, Stender's mother
"received a death threat in the mail, signed by the BGF" (142).

At the time of the attempted murder of Stender, prison officials apparently
considered the BGF to have become "a loose-knit 'gang' with little of its initial
political impetus" (Williamson [*SFC*] 1980). By 1989 this group was described
in the *San Francisco Chronicle* as having completely lost its political dimen-
sion, having become instead "active in drug dealing, commercial burglary rings,
contract murders, armed robbery gangs and forgery" (Congbalay and Chung
[*SFC*] 1989).

In March 1984, almost five years after Brooks shot Stender, he was stabbed
nine times and killed by two Folsom Prison inmates. His murder allegedly
occurred "during a fight between factions of the Black Guerrilla Family prison
group" (*SFC* 1984). According to another source, "officials believe he lost his
life because he dropped out of the Black Guerrilla Family" (*DJ* 1987).

As I write these words, Tyrone Robinson, who claimed membership in the
BGF, is on trial for the 1989 murder of Huey Newton. An altercation about
drugs was reported to have been involved in this homicide, as well as Robinson's desire "to ingratiate himself with [BGF] group leaders" (Congbalay and
Chung [*SFC*] 1989). "Telling authorities about his affiliation broke one of
the group's strict rules and put his life in jeopardy," one unnamed source told

Congbalay and Chung. His admitting his BGF membership to the police is considered a particularly grave betrayal, and those who do so "can expect other members to go after them—and kill" (Congbalay and Chung [*SFC*] 1989).

STENDER'S ALLEGED BETRAYAL OF JACKSON

Why did the BGF feel that Stender had betrayed George Jackson and the prison movement when they needed her most?

The irony of this accusation is "almost beyond belief"—as reporter Austin Scott pointed out ([*LAT*] 1979)—since it was Stender who first brought Jackson to public attention. She conceived the idea of Jackson authoring a book to bring his plight to the attention of the public, and she was responsible for finding a publisher for what became an influential, passionate, and moving best-seller, *Soledad Brother*. As Jackson's attorney, she was doing everything in her power to get him out of prison through legal channels before he was killed in 1971.

Many of Jackson's letters to Stender are included in *Soledad Brother*. In some, he expressed great fondness and respect for her. "You are a very intelligent, sensitive, and wonderful person," he wrote on 5 March 1970. In April of the same year: "You are positively my favorite person." Then on 28 July 1970: "You're like no one I've ever met from across the tracks. I do think a very great deal of you. . . ." He ended this letter, "Fondly and Always," adding that he loved her.

Stender was so dedicated and active in the prison reform movement that Austin Scott described her as having been "nearly consumed" by it from 1969 to 1973 ([*LAT*] 1979). In 1971 she formed the Prison Law Project, which visited prisons, investigated charges of mistreatment, insisted on access to inmates, filed suits, talked to legislators, and tried in every way possible to arouse public concern about what she considered to be the unjust and oppressive treatment of prisoners—particularly those who were African-American. Indeed, like many leftists at that time, Stender considered all prisoners to be political prisoners, no matter what had caused their incarceration.

According to Scott, "For a few years in the very early 1970s, the Bay Area had the largest, best organized and best financed prison reform movement in the nation" ([*LAT*] 1979). At one point Stender received more than 100 letters a day from prisoners throughout the state seeking her assistance.

One source, who prefers to remain anonymous, maintains that Stender was seen as deserving death because she had refused to supply George Jackson with a gun. Jackson believed that so armed, he would have been able to escape and initiate a revolution. According to Collier and Horowitz:

> Because she had opposed Jackson's suicidal plans, it was whispered on the prison movement's paranoid grapevine that she was a "sellout" and possibly even a police agent. She made her decision to leave the case when she received an envelope in the mail one day and opened it to find a razor blade . . . . When

Jackson asked to see Fay late in June [1971], the person who relayed the message noted that her face was torn with fear. "I'm not going in there alone," Fay said. "I'll take another lawyer with me." (1981, 134)

In 1973 Stender had to close the Prison Law Project for lack of funds and because, "after four years of doing nothing else . . . it was just too painful" (Scott [*LAT*] 1979). The pain included extreme disappointment in the behavior of some of the men she had helped. Attorney Doron Weinberg told Collier and Horowitz about one of Stender's clients for whom she had won parole. "Within a month he supposedly threw his girlfriend out the window. She knew the man well, and he had hurt the woman badly" (1981, 136). Although Stender was appalled by his behavior, she continued to defend him, so his parole was not revoked. This provided him with the opportunity to kill someone else (136).

BECOMING A FEMINIST

After closing the Prison Law Project in 1974, Stender opened up a private law practice. During subsequent years, she became a feminist, increasingly involved in thinking, writing, and organizing on feminist issues. Among other things, she helped to found California Women Lawyers. She also represented Jane Scherr, longtime live-in companion and parent of two children with Max Scherr, founder of the *Berkeley Barb*, in a palimony case. When they separated, Max refused Jane's claim for a share of the property. Having taken a strong feminist stand on this case, Stender felt stabbed in the back by former leftist friends who failed to support Jane, and ended up concluding that "the left betrayed me" (Collier and Horowitz 1981, 139). Although the often virulent sexism of many male leftists is a common experience for feminists, for Stender this meant the loss of the community "that had been her main professional support" (139).

Stender's questioning of herself, her life, and her sexuality opened her up to a lesbian relationship with attorney Joan Morris. This relationship was so important to her that after a lot of soul-searching and turmoil, she decided to initiate a separation from Marvin—her husband of 25 years. But her relationship with Morris was cut short by Brooks's bullets. In the suicide note she sent to her lover from Hong Kong, she wrote: "Know that I tried and at times with you almost thought I might make it, but—I couldn't—every moment of it hurt overwhelmingly—too deep, too pervasively—way beyond acupuncture or psychotherapy" (Collier and Horowitz 1981, 147).

REACTIONS TO THE ATTACK ON STENDER

A great deal of fear was engendered by the attack on Stender. As *Berkeley Barb* reporter Bill Wallace stated several weeks afterward: "The atmosphere of fear created by the shooting remains impenetrably thick" (1979, 3). Wallace quoted a local prison movement activist as saying, "I'm glad that you're the one doing this story and not me—I want nothing to do with it!" Likewise, several of my friends expressed anxiety on my behalf simply because of the short article I was writing about Stender's murder for a little-known feminist publication. Many people refused to even talk about the case. One lawyer is reported to have said, "Who's going to want to take a chance getting involved in a field of law where you can get murdered just because you piss somebody off?" (Wallace [*BB*] 1979, 15).

At Brooks's trial, which I attended almost every day, at least half the court seats were filled by Brooks's supporters. They sat together on one side while Stender's supporters sat on the other. The tension and hostility between the groups was often palpable. I have never ceased to be shocked and bewildered by the fact that Brooks's dastardly act was able to garner so much support.

My early attempts to understand this horror story in all its complexity produced only the most cynical and bitter "insights." For example, I felt that Stender's experience showed that it was foolish—indeed dangerous—to try to work for radical change. That those who do so can never enough—incurring criticism, being treated as "the enemy" by some of these critics, and becoming the target of accumulated hatred and frustration while the real enemies are ignored. It seemed to be a warning to inactive but politically progressive people not to try to help solve some of the inequities in society, because if they do so, they might be in danger when they stop. And for those already in the struggle who haven't become too well known or hadn't been recognized as too valuable to the movement, the message seemed to be, quit and be safe.

Not surprisingly, I was not the only one to respond in this way. For example, Ezra Hendon, a friend and former colleague of Stender in the Prison Law Project, said that Stender's death "marked the end of an era in my life, and I think the end of an era, period. Her conviction that you could be committed to a political goal, work for it and be brilliant in its service—in a clean way—that's over for me. I don't know about the others, but I can't have that belief anymore" (Collier and Horowitz 1981, 147).

"I guess it would be easy to say," Hendon continued, "that Fay played with fire, and people who play with fire get burned. But it should count for something that she wanted to be a force for good in the world, that she was a brilliant, remarkable woman who dedicated her life to others and to making the world a better place" (147). Noting that Hendon's eyes began to tear as he tried to make sense of Stender's murder/suicide, Collier and Horowitz expressed their own deep disillusionment by concluding, "Like others, his mourning is not merely for a lost friend but for a lost cause as well" (147). These reactions mirrored that of Stender herself.

> "I should never have gotten into prison work," she told a friend. "This is what happens." And, even more despairingly: "I would never again make the mistake of doing something for somebody else's benefit." The ironies of her life gnawed at her. "I structured my whole existence around trying to do something about

racism. I moved my family to a neighborhood where my children would have friends of all races. I passed up other opportunities so I could work with prisoners. Now this. It's too much to bear." (Collier and Horowitz 1981, 142–44).

While appreciating the despair Stender and others felt, my own initial disillusionment and conclusion that I might as well devote myself to self-interest came to feel intolerable and incompatible with feminist principles. I was also aware that my privileged position makes it possible for me to weigh the pros and cons of making a commitment to social change instead of feathering my nest. This privilege is one of the inequities that some less privileged people, like Brooks, respond to with rage—in his case, murderous rage.

WHY THE ATTACK ON FAY IS FEMICIDAL

Aside from the political motivation evident in the assassination plot—albeit twisted and outrageously unjust—I believe that sexism was another aspect of Brooks's and the BGF's political motivation in attacking Fay Stender.[5]

For a start, I don't believe it was mere coincidence that a woman was the first and only person on the BGF's hit list to be physically attacked, and that the most prominent radical woman attorney involved in the prison movement was the one to be riddled with bullets. I believe that Stender was probably not only shot for pulling out of the prison movement, but because she was a *woman* who did so.

Austin Scott described the way Stender was treated in the prison reform movement after she had left it. "She was ridiculed and threatened by those who disagreed with her position, abused and pulled in far too many directions by far too many inmates who saw her as their one desperate chance to get out." Many of them, continued Scott, "smuggled pleading letters out of their prisons up and down the state to her" ([*LAT*] 1979). Reporters Reiterman and Martinez quote a San Quentin convict as pointing out that "for everyone she helped, there were two or three others who wanted her help but couldn't get it" ([*SFE*] 1979).

The picture that emerges is one of hundreds of needy, dependent men—needy and dependent because of their incarcerated status—relying on Stender for assistance. It was assistance with life versus death, freedom versus incarceration issues that they wanted. Yet sometimes after Stender had succeeded in winning the release of a client, he spurned her.

For example, she was extremely hurt by Black Panther Huey Newton's treatment of her after she had worked so hard to get him out of prison. Roberta Brooks, a friend of Stender, told journalists Horowitz and Collier that "She told me that she and Huey had been very close, and then when she saw him at a party after he was released on the basis of her appeal, he didn't even speak to her. Her attitude was, 'Jesus Christ, I sacrificed spending weekends with my family to go down there to San Luis Obispo to deal with his case, and then I see him in a room and he doesn't speak to me' " (Collier and Horowitz 1981, 139–40).

Brooks also told Collier and Horowitz that from her discussions with Stender, "it was clear that her feminism drew in part on the time she'd spent representing men in prison." Stender felt that "they ripped her off on some level" (139).

Because Stender felt used and abused by some of the male prisoners whom she had helped or tried to help, some of whom had been very significant in her emotional and professional life, because she felt exhausted and depleted by the extreme demands of the work, discouraged by the declining funds and public support for the Prison Law Project, and appalled by what some of the men she helped to free did with their freedom, Stender decided to withdraw.

It is not uncommon for needy, dependent, misogynist men to kill their wives, lovers, and girlfriends for walking out on them against their wishes. Perhaps Stender's walking out on the male prisoners tapped into this kind of rage against a woman who finally dared to put her own interests before theirs.

Interestingly, "there were signs as early as 1977 that Stender was concerned about her safety." For example, according to Reiterman and Martinez, she and her husband "changed their phone number several times and wouldn't give it out to some friends" ([*SFE*] 1979). Stender also apparently had "window vents in her house designed so that no one could climb through the openings." She even told the *San Francisco Examiner* in June 1978 "that many people were unhappy that she quit prison reform work, that some believed she had betrayed the prison movement, that threats had been made against her and that she wouldn't be surprised if someone took a shot at her" (Reiterman and Martinez [*SFE*] 1979).

As a college professor for more than 20 years, I have frequently experienced a phenomenon that many of my female colleagues have also observed, particularly those who are feminists. Many students feel free to make demands on me—some of which are quite outrageous—that I am convinced they would not so readily make on a male professor. One student—an excellent women's studies major, I'm sorry to say—asked me to move my 35-student class to another building so that someone who wasn't enrolled in the course could attend it for 20 minutes out of the 75-minute period. When I refuse to accommodate such requests, the response is often that I am being unreasonable, authoritarian, or mean. That is, I am perceived and experienced as "the bad mother."

Other feminist professors have described such experiences to illustrate how sexism operates in the classroom. But such responses are not confined to academic settings. It is a common experience of women in powerful roles no matter what their profession—lawyer, politician, businesswoman, doctor, therapist, employer, minister, even landlady. We are expected to give more than men to our clients/patients/employees/congregations/tenants, to be more accessible to them, to be more willing to listen to and to accommodate their personal problems.

Furthermore, the reaction of females and males to not getting what they want is also often very different. Males are much more inclined than females to violently act out their dissatisfactions, disappointments, and anger.

This phenomenon may be relevant to an understanding of what happened to Stender. Because she was a woman—one whom the prisoners initially saw as a good mother figure who passionately wanted to free them no matter what they had done—she became the object of the expectations, hopes, demands, and dreams of many of her clients and would-be clients. When she couldn't or wouldn't fulfill these wishes—for example, the request to supply a gun to George Jackson—she came to be seen as a betrayer and a bad mother.

I am not maintaining that men in authority are not subject to some of these same dynamics. I *am* suggesting that these dynamics operate much more strongly with women in positions of authority than with men in such positions. And I *am* arguing that the misogynist attitudes and behavior of many men, whether in authority or subject to it, are often unleashed when women don't give them what they want, what they feel entitled to, or what they believe they were promised—whether we are talking about sex, or wifely "duties" such as dinner being prepared on time, or efforts to release them from prison.

When people who are perceived as inferior (e.g., women) frustrate hopes and expectations of those who perceive themselves as superior (e.g., men), this evokes a very different reaction than when such frustrations are caused—in actuality or in perception—by people who are perceived as superior or equal (e.g., other men). And the more violence-prone the frustrated men are, the more this form of sexism will be expressed violently—including femicidally, as in Stender's case.

Marvin Stender said of Fay: "She loved Jackson; she had said to friends that, outside her own family, he and Newton were the only people she had ever been willing to die for" (Collier and Horowitz 1981, 134). She said this at the height of her commitment and belief in them and in what they and she were doing, not after all the psychic wounds she was subjected to prior to the savaging of her body and her soul with bullets.

Yes, betrayal is what Stender's story is about. Not the betrayal of George Jackson, but the betrayal of Fay Stender, woman.

Notes

1. The following newspapers will usually be abbreviated in this chapter: *LAT* for *Los Angeles Times; SFC* for *San Francisco Chronicle; OT* for *Oakland Tribune; SFE* for *San Francisco Examiner; BB* for *Berkeley Barb;* and *DJ* for *Daily Journal.*

2. The following segment of this chapter draws heavily on Collier and Horowitz (1981).

3. Mainly newspaper articles, a long magazine article by Collier and Horowitz (1981), and many discussions with Joan Morris.

4. Also see Williamson [*SFC*], 1979, for a similar statement.

5. None of the numerous commentators on the Stender attack have even hinted that her gender might be relevant, although one *San Francisco Chronicle* reporter—Nicholas Von Hoffman—has suggested that her Jewishness may have been.

References

Collier, Peter and David Horowitz. 1981. "Requiem for a Radical." *New West* (March): 64–71, 133–47.

Congbalay, Dean, and L. A. Chung. 1989. "Top Security for Suspect in Huey Newton Slaying." *San Francisco Chronicle*, 30 August.

Daily Journal. 1987. "Two Folsom Convicts Guilty in Stabbing of Third." 8 September.

Isabel, Lonnie. 1983. "Convict Says He, Not Brooks, Shot Stender." *Oakland Tribune*, 23 June.

Jackson, George. 1970. *Soledad Brother: The Prison Letters of George Jackson.* New York: Coward-McCann.

Reiterman, Tim and Don Martinez. 1979. "Prisonwork Link in Stender Shooting." *San Francisco Examiner*, 30 May.

Scott, Austin. 1979. "Did Prison-reform Pullout Nearly Cost an Activist's Life?" *Los Angeles Times*, 5 June.

San Francisco Chronicle. 1979. "Charles Garry Says He's on a 'Hit List.' " 23 June.

_____. 1984. "Fay Stender's Assailant Slain." 28 March.

Von Hoffman, Nicholas. n.d. "When Good Friends Fall Out." *San Francisco Chronicle*.

Wallace, Bill. 1979. "After the Stender Shooting: "I'm No Hero!" *Berkeley Barb*, 19 July–1 August.

Williamson, George. 1979. "Courtroom Brawl in Stender Case." *San Francisco Chronicle*, 19 June.

_____. 1980. "Drama in Court—Stender Testifies." *San Francisco Chronicle*, 1 January.

Part 6

❖ ❖ ❖

WOMEN FIGHTING BACK
AGAINST FEMICIDE

Take Back the Night march, San Francisco, 1990. The names and pictures of several victims of the 1989 Montreal mass femicide are shown, backed by a banner proclaiming that erotomisogyny, or pornography, incites femicide. Photo Jane Philomen Cleland.

Introduction

In devoting the concluding section of this anthology to the efforts of women fighting back against femicide, we have attempted to close on a note that emphasizes women's strength and powers of resistance. Resistance to femicide is, in fact, a theme that runs through the book. The very act of speaking out against femicide is itself an act of resistance, and in this sense every contribution to the book belongs in this last section. The selections that follow illustrate some of the many ways that women have organized to challenge femicide.

This section opens with an activist statement, a press release from angry women protesting the Yorkshire Ripper killings in England. The next selection, "Fighting for Justice," articulates the activities of a group dedicated to the memory of Gurdip Kaur, who was beaten to death by her brother-in-law. The Gurdip Kaur Campaign describes how its participants drew on a range of activist strategies in an explicitly antiracist struggle aimed at bringing Gurdip Kaur's husband to justice for his part in her death. As well as describing the pain occasioned by the murder of Gurdip Kaur, the failure of the police to act against her husband, and their efforts to thwart the campaign, this reading speaks of the campaign's determination "not to mourn her death in silence."

The Southall Black Sisters outline several campaigns waged over the femicide of Asian women in London. In "Two Struggles: Challenging Male Violence and the Police," the Southall Black Sisters document their anger and sorrow at the deaths of Kirshna Sharma and Balwant Kaur, both of which could have been prevented by effective police intervention. The piece points to the particular problems experienced by Asian women in the United Kingdom following incidents of violence. It emphasizes that the struggle against male violence and femicide is inseparable from the struggle against racism, particularly police racism, in Britain.

Direct action against femicide by individual women and women's groups in the United States is discussed in the balance of the readings in part 6, beginning with Suzanne Lacy's "In Mourning and in Rage," which explores the use of performance art in protests against femicide. Lacy describes a specific action taken to commemorate the victims of the Hillside Strangler, demands effective police action against male violence, and protests the voyeuristic and woman-blaming coverage in the press.

Next is a group of readings collected under the heading "Nikki Craft: Inspiring Protest." Diana Russell introduces these writings, which analyze and describe protests against pornographic portrayals of sexual violence. Nikki Craft, a committed feminist activist, directed, inspired, or in some way influenced these imaginative, extralegal protests.

Finally, in "What Can We Do about Femicide?" the author, Anonywomen, returns to the theme "We will not mourn her death in silence" by proposing a commemorative day of mourning and anger against femicide. The proposal outlines ways of raising consciousness and expressing anger about femicide. Although the actions suggested include book burning, a particularly controversial act in Europe because of its association with fascism, the idea of an international annual day of protest against femicide is valuable.

The means of protest described in the following pages are neither exhaustive nor appropriate to all situations. Our purpose in including them is to acknowledge some of the protests already taking place and to encourage more such acts of resistance.

Take Back the Night march, San Francisco, 1990. Photo Jane Philomen Cleland.

Women, Angry at Male Violence, Say: "Resist the Curfew!"

DUSTY RHODES AND SANDRA McNEILL

Hundreds of angry women staged a militant protest in Leeds last Saturday [28 November 1980]. Angry at advice to stay indoors since the last "Ripper" killing, five hundred women marched with torches through town, stormed into the Odeon Cinema (which was showing the film *Dressed to Kill*), and challenged men in the street, asking them where they were at the time the "Ripper" killed Jacqueline Hill. The march was organised by Women Against Violence Against Women. We reprint their statement in full below:

> We mourn Jacqueline Hill, and all the other women who have died at the hands of the "Yorkshire Ripper." And we are angry.
>
> We are angry at being told to stay at home after dark. Why must we women restrict our lives when it's men who are to blame? Many women work at night: they can't stay at home. Anyway, home may not be safe for many of us. A quarter of all the crimes of violence reported is wife battering. And we're expected to take this without defending ourselves.
>
> On Monday this week, Charlene and Annette Maw were sentenced to 3 years for killing their drunken violent father in self-defence. We demand their immediate release, and the right of every woman to defend herself against male violence.
>
> We totally reject the way the press label women "respectable" or not. We will not be judged and divided into the "pure" and the "fallen."
>
> We know that when this "Ripper" is caught, women will not be safe. Everywhere women are murdered, raped and battered by men daily. We will carry on fighting until every woman can live without fear of being attacked by men. We demand:
>
> > Police—release your information on the "Ripper!"
> > Every woman's right to self-defence!
> > Curfew on men, not women!

Reprinted from *Women against Violence against Women,* ed. Dusty Rhodes and Sandra McNeill (London: Onlywoman, 1985).

Fighting for Justice

THE GURDIP KAUR CAMPAIGN

On 11 May 1986, Gurdip Kaur Sandhu was brutally beaten by her brother-in-law, Harbax Singh, in the presence of her husband, Gurbax Singh. At the inquest on 28 August of that year, her death in hospital was ascribed by a Home Office pathologist to "heart and lung failure from a fractured larynx," injuries consistent with her having suffered continuous blows to the throat.

Gurdip Kaur was born in Africa in 1952, and came to Britain from India when she was a teenager. At sixteen she married Gurbax Singh Sandhu and moved to Reading. From then on she was subjected to persistent physical violence and mental cruelty from her husband, and had to suffer frequent beatings and humiliation in front of her children and family. In 1984 Gurbax Singh was given a three-year prison sentence for a drugs offence. He was released in December 1985, having served half that time. Four months later, Gurdip Kaur managed to obtain an emergency court injunction which gave the police power of arrest against her husband, and they separated. For the next few weeks she tried to live an independent life with her children, free from violence, despite the lack of support from the Asian community, with their constant reminders of *izzat* (her "family honour"). Her separation and planned divorce was said to bring disgrace on her husband and their joint families, and there were many pressures to return to him and attempt a reconciliation.

On 11 May 1986, Gurdip Kaur agreed to allow her husband to come to the house to pick up some clothing. He arrived about 8 P.M., closely followed by his brother, Harbax Singh Sandhu. Both men had been drinking. Gurdip Kaur was alone in the house, apart from the youngest of her three sons, twelve-year-old Ravinder. After a few minutes she went into the kitchen to put her tea cup in the sink. Harbax Singh, her brother-in-law, followed her in, grabbed hold of her,

---

Reprinted from *The Boys in Blue*, ed. Christina Dunhill (London: Virago, 1989).

bashed her head against the kitchen unit and punched her repeatedly in the throat. When Ravinder saw what was happening he rushed in and tried to drag his uncle away, but found himself collared in a half-nelson by his father, Gurbax Singh, who thrust him out of the room. Ravinder picked himself up and ran to call the police, but finding the front door locked, came back through the house. He saw his mother lying on the floor, looking "as if she were asleep," and his uncle pushing a glass to her mouth. After hearing the kitchen drawer open, he saw his father, clutching a large knife, blade downwards, like a dagger in his fist. Gurbax Singh aimed the knife at Gurdip Kaur, saying he was going to kill her, but was stopped by his brother. Gurdip Kaur was then bundled into a borrowed van and driven away by Harbax Singh to the house of a friend of his. After he'd left, the friend called the police. Harbax Singh then dumped Gurdip Kaur in the hospital casualty department and went back to his friend's house, where he was arrested. Gurdip Kaur was put on a life-support machine. Five days later, it was switched off and she died.

The information above was heard in Winchester Crown Court in January 1987, when Harbax Singh Sandhu was tried for the murder of Gurdip Kaur. The medical evidence showed that Gurdip Kaur had died as a result of a fractured larynx; the prosecution alleged that this had been caused by Harbax Singh when he punched her in the throat, and that therefore he had murdered her. The prosecution's case was largely based on the testimony of Gurdip Kaur's youngest son Ravinder, who presented a clear and unshakeable account of the events of the night of 11 May. The defence contested that a punch could not have caused the fatal fracture, but that the damage had been inflicted by Gurdip Kaur's husband, Gurbax Singh, who had stamped on his wife's throat while she was on the ground. In his summing up, the judge told the jury that if they were not satisfied that the punches from Harbax Singh had caused the fracture then the verdict should be "not guilty." However, if the punches had caused the fracture then he was responsible for her death. If this was the case and he had intended to kill her, or to do her really serious bodily harm, then he would be guilty of murder, but if that had not been his intention then he should be found guilty of manslaughter.

The jury was out for nearly four hours at the end of the three-day trial, coming back twice for clarification of the law. They returned with a verdict of "not guilty of murder, but guilty of manslaughter." The court then heard that Harbax Singh had already served time in prison. In 1981 he had received a three-year prison sentence (of which he served two years) for twice attempting to employ men to kill his own wife. This news appeared to shock and distress the jury.

Harbax Singh Sandhu had not only tried to have his own wife murdered, he had also subjected her to a level of violence that sent her to hospital twice. After his term in prison, he had abducted their son, and escaped to India. His wife had finally managed to win back the child through the Indian courts, but she and her son were then hounded by Harbax Singh and forced into hiding.

The British laws of evidence made it impossible to present this information in court during the trial. Legally, it would be said to have no bearing on the case in hand which involved his brother's wife's death. However, Harbax Singh had also persistently threatened the lives of Gurdip Kaur and her family. Over the telephone he had frequently told Gurdip Kaur that she was going to die. The police were well aware of this fact; on several occasions they had listened to these calls, but nothing about the threats was mentioned in court, not even as a prosecution question to the defendant.

The prosecution has complete discretion as to what information it wishes to present in court. Had the jury known of these phone calls, even as hearsay evidence, perhaps the verdict would have been different. Harbax Singh was not the only man threatening Gurdip Kaur and her family. After her death, when Harbax Singh was in custody, the phone calls continued. The family were blamed for the charges against Harbax Singh, blamed for the existence of the Gurdip Kaur Campaign, and told that they would die. On the last day of the Crown Court trial, Ravinder was told over the phone that he would not live another day. Some of these threats are known to have come from his father's family. Gurbax Singh had stopped his son from trying to save his mother; he had brandished a knife on the night she died; he had played no part in getting his fatally injured wife to hospital; he had not even rung for an ambulance. The defence counsel alleged that he had killed Gurdip Kaur. But Gurbax Singh Sandhu made no appearance at the trial of his twin brother, not even as a witness to the events of the night of 11 May.

Gurbax Singh was arrested after the attack on his wife. But he has never been called upon publicly to account for his actions at the time of the assault—all charges against him were dropped on the advice of the Chief Prosecuting Solicitor for the Thames Valley Police, and the reasons for this are not known to us.

When a number of local women became aware of these facts, they came together to start the Gurdip Kaur Campaign, a group mainly comprising Black women, most of whom were Asian. The campaign demanded justice for Gurdip Kaur: that Gurbax Singh be tried for his involvement, and that the public be made aware of this horrific example of male violence against women. It was felt that if the state would not bring Gurbax Singh to justice then the campaign would, even if this meant instigating a private prosecution. Information about the case was circulated through leaflets, mailings and articles in the women's media. The campaign soon received the support of individuals and organizations from all over the country. There were many letters and donations, and hundreds of women signed the petition demanding justice for Gurdip Kaur. Women also joined pickets outside the magistrates' court in Reading where Harbax Singh had his remand hearings. There was a demonstration at Winchester, where Harbax Singh had been tried for murder.

The campaign also attracted the interest of the police, who soon started to investigate the group. The organization which acted as the contact address for the campaign, and members of the local alternative newspaper that had carried information about the case of Gurdip Kaur, were visited by police officers from outside the Reading area. They said that they were following up a complaint received by the Director of Public Prosecutions from the family of Gurbax and Harbax Singh, and that they wanted the names and addresses of the members of the campaign so that they could talk to them about any planned demonstrations during the trial. It was suggested they write to the campaign to arrange a meeting, but no correspondence was forthcoming. The police officers also wanted to know where the campaign's leaflets had been printed, what machine had been used and how the campaign was being funded. They advised that they would continue their investigations should the campaign continue its demonstrations.

The family of Gurdip Kaur were also visited and questioned about the campaign by these police officers. During the committal hearing at Reading Magistrates' Court reference was made to the campaign as a factor in deciding where the Crown Court trial should take place, with an assurance made that the police were aware of the involvement of several local activists. The trial therefore took place nearly fifty miles away from Reading in Winchester, "due to the strength of local feeling"—presumably an attempt to shake off the "local" demonstrators. At Winchester, the judge warned the court that demonstrators could be imprisoned for carrying placards. The protesting women outside the court were moved, but continued the action with an impromptu march around the town.

The campaign has always been very cautious about promoting itself. The whereabouts of meetings and the names of members were kept very quiet. This was originally due to wariness of Gurbax Singh and his family, who were still threatening Gurdip Kaur's relatives. However, caution then became a habit due to harassment from the police. The campaign could understand a fear that its activities might prejudice the trial (and it was careful not to do so), but the police could have written to the group had that been the problem. We would have thought that in some ways we were on the same side, wanting to see a criminal brought to justice, and those under threat safeguarded. How ironic therefore that a perfectly legal campaign organization should be pushed into hiding by the police themselves.

Gurdip Kaur and her family might certainly have expected a more sympathetic reaction from the police, who had been aware for some time of the violence suffered by them, having had to remove Gurbax Singh for the night on more than one occasion. However, when asked for help, they could only suggest that Gurdip Kaur move house. They offered her no assistance with getting an injunction. This she finally obtained with the help of Social Services. The police had listened to telephone death threats from Harbax Singh and his brother, but when asked for protection could only suggest a change of telephone number. They said they could not do anything until something definite happened and that such a situation was only to be expected within the Asian community.

After the death of Gurdip Kaur the family were treated very insensitively. Ravinder, who was only twelve, underwent intensive questioning for several hours at a time, and other members of the family were heavily interrogated about their activities in attempting to bring Gurbax and Harbax Singh to justice. After Gurbax was released the police warned the family that if they threatened him in any way, they would be the ones in trouble.

At the time of writing the campaign still exists. Harbax Singh is in prison, Gurbax Singh is free and Gurdip Kaur is dead. There was some media interest after the trial, but many of the national papers, television and radio did not consider the case significant, or sufficiently newsworthy, despite the highlighting of the issue of domestic violence at the time. A private prosecution now seems impossible for many reasons. Apart from the expense, and other inherent difficulties, such as the need to collect statements and persuade witnesses to give evidence, the court case of his brother makes it appear that Gurbax Singh has committed no crime. Although a court has heard evidence that he was involved in the events for which his brother has been imprisoned, that he tried to stop his son from protecting her, that he made no attempt to call the police or an ambulance, that he played no part in getting his wife to hospital, there is no such charge as "accomplice to manslaughter." A jury has decided that the death of Gurdip Kaur was an accident.

The campaign appears to have no option but to keep pressurizing the Department of Public Prosecutions to reopen the case, although the letters of many women and men, including sympathetic MPs, have so far resulted only in rare and disappointing replies, which generally say that there is not enough evidence for a conviction.

The police failed Gurdip Kaur for seventeen years. She had visibly suffered violence at the hands of her brutal husband, had often been seen with cuts and bruises, or had been publicly degraded by him. She and her family had made the police aware of this, and of the threats to her life, and yet the police failed to take action to protect her, or even to take this information seriously. This once again demonstrates the lack of interest shown by police everywhere in crimes that can be termed "domestic," their inability to recognize the danger confronting so many women, and their reluctance to face the issues involved. The police still seem to have the attitude that violence in families is not their concern; in such a case they seem even more inclined to regard male violence as an inherent part of family life, to be dealt with by the community to which the woman appears to belong.

The judicial system failed Gurdip Kaur by denying her the means to protect herself. Later, it did not effectively punish those responsible for her death. The court failed to present to the public all the available information about her case, or to give anyone the opportunity to speak for a woman no longer able to speak for herself. The court also encouraged racist assumptions, such as the argument that Sikh men will be more affected by alcohol—a statement which no doubt added to the "mitigating circumstances" in the minds of the jury, and which once again allowed alcohol to become an excuse for men killing women.

The Asian community failed Gurdip Kaur—failed to allow her to live her life without violence. An Asian woman in Britain is prevented from challenging her husband, brother or father, not only by the state's external controls on her, but by the community's internal controls. For her to leave a violent situation is to leave the family completely, away from the disapproving Asian community in a society which is both racist and sexist. Those women who take such action are often accused of staining the family honour or *izzat* of their husbands and relations. For members of the Asian community to have allowed Gurdip Kaur to live free of violence would have meant recognizing the existence of such violence within the home and within the community. They would have had to challenge it as oppressive, rather than accepting it, as many do, as a vehicle by which men exert their authority and power over women.

These basic facts of male violence are, however, universal in all societies and cultures. Women all over the world are subjected to male violence in all spheres of life—a violence which induces fear, and as a result, subjugation. Everywhere we see the covert sanctioning of this oppression, and thus the implicit condoning of male violence against women. The police, the courts, our communities and society as a whole allow women such as Gurdip Kaur to suffer violence and die, through the unthinking and unspoken belief that domestic violence is a natural part of family life, indeed expected as an instrument of the patriarchy that upholds the status quo.

The Gurdip Kaur Campaign brought together Black women and white women from all over the country to demand justice for Gurdip Kaur and for the thousands of women who every day suffer violence at the hands of men. All of us who have grieved for Gurdip Kaur must ensure that she is not forgotten, using her memory to strengthen our struggles for change.

We will not mourn her death in silence.

Two Struggles: Challenging Male Violence and the Police

SOUTHALL BLACK SISTERS

In June 1987, the Metropolitan Police issued a "Force Order" relating to domestic violence to all police stations in the London area, which directed officers' attention to new provisions in the Police and Criminal Evidence Act 1984. It also recommended close liaison between the police and groups in order to deal with domestic violence jointly.

Southall Black Sisters do not believe that the Order's emphasis on prosecution and its recommendations for liaison with local groups are serious attempts to address the problem of how the police should respond to domestic violence. Women have always criticized the police for not acting on powers that they already have and for not providing an effective emergency response to violence in the home, regardless of whether prosecution takes place in the final instance or not. Without such an emergency response women remain at risk from violence and in danger of their lives. The Force Order guidelines do not address this issue. Instead, they emphasize the need for the police to "liaise" closely with local groups. This is known in police language as the "Multi-Agency Approach" and was one of the key recommendations of the Metropolitan Police Internal Working Party Report on domestic violence. Exactly what the Multi-Agency Approach is, what it means and why it should be adopted at this particular moment are all questions central to any discussion of current policing, including police response to domestic violence.

For black people, the police in this country have always represented the most overtly repressive face of a racist state. The uprisings in London's Southall and in virtually all other inner cities in the last twenty years have been urgent and spontaneous expressions of the despair, anger and frustration of many blacks in the face of growing homelessness, unemployment, immigration

---

Reprinted from *The Boys in Blue*, ed. Christina Dunhill (London: Virago, 1989).

controls and racial attacks on the streets. The state's response to the uprisings and growing unrest has been to strengthen the police force by giving it new powers through legislation and increased resources as a way of diffusing protest and resistance.

In recent years, the state and the police have redefined their priorities and objectives, so that the very attempts of black people to organize themselves have become criminal offences (for example, with the prosecution of the Newham Seven and the Newham Eight—youths who sought to defend themselves against racist gangs). Nor is this onslaught restricted to the black community. Increasingly, sections of the white community have come under attack. The Thatcher government's campaigns in respect of the inner cities do not stem from a concern for urban decay, poverty and deprivation but from a need to control the unrest that arises from these conditions. They ignore the real issues at stake: unemployment, homelessness, health and education. The police, for their part, have ensured that their policies and objectives are in line with the government's aims. They are intensifying a process begun in the late seventies which sees targeting, surveillance and control in the inner cities as the main policing priority.

Ironically, for black women, in the face of harassment, intimidation and violence from our communities, the police have continued to be the only agency to whom we are forced to turn for immediate help. The majority of women have no faith or confidence in the police, but because of a lack of any alternative, women have had no choice but to make demands for protection and safety from them. For black women, challenging an issue like domestic violence within our own communities and challenging the racism of the police at the same time is often fraught with contradictions. On the one hand, we are involved in campaigns against police brutality, deaths in police custody and immigration fishing raids. On the other, we are faced with daily beatings, rape and sexual harassment. We are forced to make demands of the police to protect our lives from the very same men along whose side we fight in anti-racist struggles. The struggle against racism cannot be waged at the expense of the struggles within a male-dominated and patriarchal community whose traditions and customs confine the woman to the home and deny her the right to determine who she wants to live with and how. Many of us feel that to make this struggle secondary to the struggle against racism means at best to ignore women's experiences and at worst to passively collude with those patriarchal practices. Instead, our view is that somehow both struggles have to be waged simultaneously without losing sight of the consequences each can have on the other. Our demands must take both struggles into account.

Asian women have challenged the idea that the "honour" of their families rests on their behaviour and their silence. Women like Krishna Sharma and Balwant Kaur dared to "break the silence" by asserting their right to live independently, free from violence. Both women were killed by their husbands, precisely because they posed a threat to their husband's authority, and by implication to the male-dominated community. The deaths of both Krishna Sharma and Balwant Kaur were preventable, if only the police had bothered to act on their pleas for help hours before they were murdered.

Kirshna Sharma died in Southall in May 1984, after suffering violence from her husband for years. Finally, unable to bear it any longer, she called the police for help. The officer who turned up at her door said he could find no evidence that Krishna Sharma's husband hit her, although he had admitted to slapping her sometimes. He advised her that she would have to bring a private prosecution against her husband. Within a matter of hours Krishna Sharma was found hanged, with her clothes torn and with several bruises on her body. Yet later an inquest into her death returned a verdict of suicide.

Balwant Kaur, a young Asian woman and mother of three, was murdered in Brent Asian Women's Refuge on 22 October 1985. Having already lived through eight years of abuse and violence at the hands of her husband, she had finally managed to escape to the refuge in July 1985. Previously, whilst at her marital home, the police had been called but had failed to provide protection. Balwant Kaur's husband, Bhagwant Singh Panesar, unable to bear the fact that he was no longer able to "possess" her, tracked her down to the refuge. On the night of 18 October he came to the refuge with two hired accomplices. He had told the two men that he intended to burgle the refuge, but when they learned of his real intention to kill his wife, they abandoned him. Those same two accomplices returned to the refuge the following day and warned Balwant about her husband's intentions to kill her. The refuge immediately informed the local police and asked for protection in the form of a twenty-four-hour patrol. The police sent an officer who spoke to the residents of the refuge and then went away. No further action was taken. Several days later, Balwant was stabbed to death by her husband in the presence of her three young daughters. Not only had the police failed to respond to the threats made on Balwant's life, but soon after the murder they divulged the whereabouts of the refuge to the media, who broadcast the address all over London and thus endangered the lives of all the other women in the refuge. The total disregard for the safety of women and children and of the refuge shown by the police meant that the refuge had to be evacuated within twenty-four hours of the murder.

The deaths of both Krishna Sharma and Balwant Kaur show with frightening clarity that the police choose to direct their resources at priorities other than violence against women, and that as a result the lives of many women are at risk. We believe that the problem here is one of the ethos of "success" in police operations. The police measure their success in terms of rates of prosecution and conviction, and not in terms of the safety and protection they can provide. The problem is also one of police priorities. Whilst police officers are readily deployed to control protests against loss of civil liberties, poverty and deprivation, countless women who live in fear for their lives at home are ignored.

More than a year after the issuing of the Force Order, it seems to us that the police have failed to implement their own guidelines. In our experience, it has been left to individual officers to interpret the Order in the way they choose to do so. Moreover, the majority of officers seem not to know of the Order's existence and still refuse to acknowledge that domestic violence is a serious crime.

However, what we have found, certainly in Ealing, is that the local police force as a whole is following the Order's recommendation of a "Multi-Agency Approach" to domestic violence. This approach is presented in terms of close co-operation between the police and local statutory and voluntary agencies, but in reality, it has less to do with providing an immediate emergency response to domestic violence than to building up a profile of each community. The terms of reference for such "co-operation" are set by the police. In the process of "working together," agencies such as social services, schools and the DHSS move away from the original ethic of social welfare, and are transformed into a role where they are there to aid the police. The consequences for black people as for all other disadvantaged sections of the community are all too clear.

In Southall we have experienced directly how the Multi-Agency Approach to domestic violence is taking shape. In February and March 1987, we attended meetings called by the Southall police in order to discuss their response to domestic violence. During the course of these two meetings the police were very clear and frank. Their proposal was to set up a "domestic violence panel," composed of social workers, probation services, psychiatric nurses, volunteers from the local victim support schemes, and of course the local women's groups. This panel would meet regularly in order to hold case conferences. The terms of reference for the panel were set by the police. All the different agencies were asked to provide information on "problem families" and as part of this, we were to pass on our domestic violence cases to the police. The police gave no indication of what they intended to do with the information.

Needless to say we decided to play no part in this scheme. Its terms of reference clearly reflected the police attitude and policies on domestic violence. Domestic violence was redefined as characteristic behaviour of "problem families," who would then become the subject of police attention. These families might be stigmatized solely on the basis of the whims, prejudices and assumptions of individual officers. We were at pains to point out that domestic violence can occur in any family, regardless of race, religion and class, at any time. It is not confined to "problem families" however that expression may be defined. The role of the police is not to take away women's initiative in this respect. It is rather to respond swiftly and effectively when women call, whatever their family circumstances.

Throughout our meetings the police maintained that domestic violence was a "family" problem and so argued that it was not possible to intervene to enforce the law. They were worried about the negative image that men might have of the police force if they did act! In an area like Southall, with its predominantly Asian population, this reluctance was also backed by racist assumptions. Factors such as arranged marriages and a different culture were cited as reasons for lack of intervention on the part of the police. They also argued that older Asian women are supposed to have a higher tolerance level and therefore be less in need of immediate help. One wonders whether such assumptions were responsible for their inaction when confronted with cries of help from Krishna Sharma and Balwant Kaur.

The approach to domestic violence adopted by the police in Southall, as elsewhere, ties in neatly with police rhetoric of community policing and consultative meetings. Working panels on problem areas such as racial harassment and domestic violence create the illusion of police concern and a readiness to "involve the community," and at the same time allow the police to shift the focus away from their own responsibilities. Ultimately, the police's approach is a distraction which shifts the emphasis away from demands for police accountability in dealing with these issues.

In the light of the experience of black people in such areas as Southall, Brixton, Notting Hill, Handsworth, Toxteth, St. Paul's and Tottenham, black people cannot place any trust in such schemes as the Multi-Agency Approach. These and other schemes only confirm to us that the police will use increasingly sophisticated tactics to control black people.

Experience has shown that the police are not on the side of women and blacks. It is therefore no accident that the police have chosen to prioritize domestic violence by targeting "problem families." The Multi-Agency Approach remains a propaganda exercise aimed at a section of the community, that is women, who for years have suffered violence and even death as a result of police inaction. At the same time the Multi-Agency Approach serves to extend the net of corporate policing.

The deaths of Krishna Sharma and Balwant Kaur have raised important questions for those of us who know that we have to continue making demands of the police in the absence of any alternative. However, we must recognize that the police force itself is becoming increasingly sophisticated in its operations and in setting its own priorities. It has taken upon itself the task of social control, and it has been campaigning vigorously for the powers and resources to carry out that task. It is our responsibility in the light of our own experiences to fight for the powers and resources of the police force to be redirected to meet our needs.

In Mourning and in Rage
(with Analysis Aforethought)

SUZANNE LACY

*Activist political art is not a simple product of inspiration or a well-meaning
and fortunate arrangement of images. It is composed, as well, of social analysis
and a strategy for audience involvement. In this article I would like to offer
some brief observations toward an analysis of news reporting on rape murders,
using the example of the Hillside Strangler Case to describe how the reporting
of sex crimes serves to intimidate women and perpetuate mythologies about
violence against them. This analysis, developed by Leslie Labowitz and myself,
with the inspiration of Women Against Violence Against Women (WAVAW)
activists, is the core of the art performance "In Mourning and in Rage . . ." we
created for Los Angeles media on December 13, 1977.*

1. FACT AND FANTASY

In early November 1977, the second of what was to become a string of sex murders broke into the Los Angeles media. Two weeks earlier the discovery of the
nude and strangled body of Yolanda Washington passed essentially unnoticed
by the press; violence was commonplace in the lives of prostitutes. But when
Judith Miller, a fifteen year old who frequented Hollywood Boulevard, was
found strangled the day after Halloween, newspeople began to question the
relationship between the incidents. As one after another lifeless body was
uncovered during that month (a total of ten by December 1), the "Hillside Strangler Case" was born. No one knew who invented the phrase, police or press, but
its graphic description of the crime scenes made it a crucial element in the
media coverage.

Reprinted from *Ikon*, second series no. 1 (Fall/Winter 1985): 60–67.

During the winter months in Los Angeles, the Hillside Strangler Case was created as a literal entity in the minds of mass audiences through the exchange between police and reporters and the communication of that interaction to the public. The murders, of course, *did* actually occur, as tangible as the abandoned bodies of women found scattered around the city, as real as the grief expressed by their loved ones; and they were linked to the same killer or killers through painstakingly gathered evidence. But the public's *awareness* of the Hillside Strangler Case was the province of the local news industry, and as soon as rudiments of a story were in, reporters set out on the trail of what would eventually become the biggest story to hit the city in years. "I was living this television fantasy," admitted one columnist. "I'd known guys to get calls from criminals who were afraid of the police and wanted to turn themselves in to a reporter. . . . I got to admit, I got so caught up in my own fantasies that I even left numbers where I could be reached 24 hours a day. . . ."[1] The fantasy involvement of reporters, mostly male, in the drama of the Hillside Strangler murders was transmitted to their audience. Throughout the city, men's jokes, innuendos, and veiled threats (I might be the Strangler, you know) revealed an identification that was at the very least fueled by reporters' enthusiasm, if not generated by it.

In one incident after another, reporters' zeal, public pressure on the police, and the antagonisms between police and newspeople accounted for an elaborate series of reporting inaccuracies. One reporter formulated a theory of bizarre ritual torture based on the placement of the victim's bodies; he withheld the details of this theory at police request, although the police knew all along that the body position was a reflection only of how it had been carried. "We tried to help the press as little as possible," said a sheriff's department investigator; ". . . an erroneous conclusion on a reporter's part was encouraged . . . (for) if the real killer ever confessed, he or she would mention details that had not been read,"[2] thus verifying the authenticity of the confession. At least twice confessions known to both police and reporters to be false were released or allowed to remain uncorrected in the media to heighten suspense.

Within this complicated panorama of fact, fictionalization, and deliberate falsehood, one has to ask, what is the purpose of reporting such crimes? How do they serve their chroniclers and affect their audiences? Reporters maintained that each detail gave women more information to protect themselves. The effect, however, of explicit descriptions of locations where bodies were discovered, veiled hints of ritualistic sexual murder, and similar elaborations fed women's hysteria. Their responses, spurred by fear, were then duly reported. Women carried kitchen knives and police whistles, bought out lock supplies in hardware stores, and began to severely curtail their movement throughout the city.

If the end result of such "media events" is the intimidation and terrorizing of a mass of women, then news reporting might profitably be subjected to a feminist analysis along the lines of that applied to entertainment and pornographic media. This analysis is complicated by a rationale used by entertainment barons but perhaps more applicable here: the public has a right to know what is happening in their environment, and it is the role of media to (objectively) represent that information. Of course, the lie here is that real objectivity is, or can be, maintained in symbolic representations. But, believing that it can, viewers often confuse the account of an incident with the incident itself.

To state the obvious, news reporting in a large urban environment is actually the interface between the real event and the public's perception of it. What is not so obvious is *how* so called "facts" are selected and construed to reinforce or shape audience belief systems. Hand in hand with police working on a case, the media creates a crime-series from isolated incidents, fabricating a construct the public will recognize over and over. That construct, in the case of violent sex crimes, is often as close to a murder mystery fiction as any T.V. detective program or film could ever hope to get. Facts, framed according to the myths about rape and sexual violence that are preserved in much of our fiction, create a reality contextualized not by the social forces and conditions that are causal to such violence, but, curiously, by the entertainment industry. Hence, in unraveling just how news reporting might serve the hidden social purpose of intimidating and containing women (in the manner of pornography, for example), we must look at the forms and themes it chooses for its information.

2. CONSTRUCTING A NEWS STORY

What are the makings of a good story, a thriller that will keep newspaper readers buying papers, television audiences coming back for news updates? Reporters, competing with Hollywood for viewers, and influenced as members of audiences themselves, arrange their stories to reflect the elements of drama: a recognizable theme, coherent plot, antagonists you can hate and protagonists with whom you can identify. Throughout fiction certain themes recur, their appeal rising and falling with variables in the social climate. Consider this scenario: a maniacal killer stalks young, beautiful and helpless women. He is caught in the end, but not before a good deal of graphic violence has been accomplished for the satisfaction of the audience. Given the current appeal of such themes in popular entertainment, it should not surprise us to see the Hillside Strangler news coverage following this paradigm.

The first necessary ingredient to selling a newstory over a period of time is to reinforce a familiar theme with a recognizable image. The coining of the phrase "Hillside Strangler" fixed the series of crimes in the public imagination. It had all the makings of a good title. It was evocative of sexual violence and it dramatized one of the peculiarities of the case that seemed most horrible in the absence of other specifics: the encountering of nude corpses on populated hillsides by local residents. Discretion on the part of major newspapers and T.V. channels prohibited actual portrayal of these bodies in the fields where they were found (although other sources, not so delicate, revealed obscenely objective photographs of the dead women in situ); but photographs of officers bending over a concealed body served the same purpose, as viewers completed the picture in their own minds with images borrowed from entertainment and art. Variations on a constantly repeated verbal description, "the nude, spread-eagled body of a woman was found strangled today on the side of a hill" became the icon, the major image, around which the drama progressed.

The plotline, which revealed itself sporadically in police news releases, false confessions, and continuing murders, could not advance toward a conclusion faster than actual events would allow. So to expand the narrative, reporters constructed a past tense by investigating the lives of each victim. Visuals established who the victim's family and friends were, what their homes looked like, where their bodies were discovered, and, of course, the appearances of the victims themselves.

Overlooking the obvious connection—each victim was a female in a sex-violent culture—reporters ransacked the pasts of the dead women, searching with the police for clues as to why *these* particular women had been singled out. Mistaking causation for the similarities in each killing, reporters inadvertently upheld the common myth that victims of sex violence are somehow culpable, if only in their choices of action. If they could just uncover some commonly held fatal mistakes, readers would be able to protect themselves! Thus, when it was discovered that the first two women were frequenters of Hollywood Boulevard, reporters fell eagerly on the information. Here was a possible cause: the women were either prostitutes or had been mistaken for prostitutes by the killer. This clue neatly satisfied the notion that assault victims are promiscuous (until recently a victim's sexual history could be used against her in California courts) and coincided with speculations that the killer was motivated by rage against a seductive mother. No one seemed inclined to make an alternative hypothesis: the availability of prostitutes makes them vulnerable to sex-criminals who are just beginning to learn the ropes. Though the prostitution theory was soon proven unfounded the taint of it remained. Undaunted, reporters continued to create, soap opera fashion, such stories as "She Looked For Love, Found Strangler."[3]

The fear-motivated actions of women through the city (all of them potential victims!) heightened the suspense and embellished the basic storyline. Self-defense was put forward in several feature articles, although the visual message frequently demonstrated the most ineffectual, rather than powerful, moments—a woman crying from the mace sprayed in her face by an instructor, another revealing a small paring knife hidden in her purse as she stood in front of a Safeway market. In one television special for women, the lead segment featured a woman's feet walking alone at night with anonymous male feet stalking her. Following the sensationalist style of crime fiction, many images reinforced the idea of women's helplessness.

In the absence of real information, the killers possible motivations were largely culled from popular mythology. Psychologists in the media speculated that his mother was dominating, perhaps erratically cruel and seductive; that she may have been a woman of easy virtue (especially popular during the time of the prostitution theory); and that his father was absent. A sex killer is assumed to be driven by rage toward women, but his hatred is explained by hateful women. After the confessed killer was caught, one author again adhered to this version of reality, describing Kenneth Bianchi's vascillating and neurotically aggressive mother, his dead father, and his deceitful first wife. (Interestingly, while the author notes Bianchi's intense interest in pornography from the early teens onward, he makes no attempt to ascribe this particular detail to a motivational construct.)[4]

While the similarities in the history of some sex killers, where these are in fact found, may be part of a picture of personal distress, they do not explain *why* this distress is enacted in sexual violence, or how such incidents are upheld by our entire social fabric. Unfortunately, the analysis and contextualization needed to understand how sex-violent crimes occur and what we can do about them is rarely part of hard news coverage. The Hillside Strangler Case, as detective story par excellance, galvanized an entire city, gluing its citizens each night to television sets. It sold newspapers, locks, guns, and dogs; became the subject matter of jokes and nightmares; was responsible for destroying marriages and careers. But in the telling of this story the news media perpetuated the same images and attitudes, ironically appealed to the same prurient interests, that created the social climate for the crime itself.

3. WHAT WAS TO BE DONE?

Early one morning in December, Leslie Labowitz and I sat over coffee and the morning newspaper, sickened by the headlines. The Strangler had killed another woman, his tenth, and the body had just been discovered. In sharing our own pain and feelings of powerlessness, we decided to throw our energy into a performance, a personal expression but one which would also fulfill, as well, two important goals: to create a public ritual for women in Los Angeles to express their grief, their rage, and their demands for concrete action, and to present, within the media, a feminist perspective of the case. We would use the media's own language of high drama and intriguing visuals to create a newsworthy event of our performance. We would design it to fit the form of a news broadcast. For the next thirteen days we worked with Bia Lowe and other members of the Woman's Building to produce "In Mourning and in Rage . . ."

On December 13, 1977, seventy women dressed in black gathered at the Woman's Building in Los Angeles. The women received instructions for the event which began when ten actresses dressed in mourning emerged from the Building and entered a hearse. The hearse and two motorcycle escorts departed from the Building, followed by twenty-two cars filled with women. Each car had its lights on and displayed two stickers: "Funeral" and "Stop Violence Against Women." The motorcade circled City Hall twice and stopped in front of the assembled members of the news media.

One at a time, nine seven-foot-tall veiled women mourners emerged from the hearse and stood in a line on the sidewalk. The final figure emerged, a woman clothed in scarlet. The ten women faced the street as the hearse departed while women from the motorcade procession drove slowly past in silent homage to the mourners. Forming a procession three abreast, the mourners walked toward the steps in front of City Hall.

Women from the motorcade positioned themselves on either side of the steps forming a chorus from a modern tragedy. They unfurled a banner which read "In Memory of Our Sisters, Women Fight Back."

As soon as the media had positioned itself to record this second part of the event, the first mourner walked toward the microphone and in a loud, clear voice said, "I am here for the ten women who have been raped and strangled between October 18 and November 29!" The chorus echoed her with "In memory of our sisters, we fight back!" as she was wrapped with a brilliant red scarf by the woman clothed in red. She took her place on the steps, as the second mourner walked to the microphone. The strategy of this performance was to study media reporting conventions and systematically subvert them. If the media focused on ten victims' individual histories, we would use the representation of ten performers to describe a continuum of violence. When the second woman spoke, she decried the four-hundred or so women raped in Los Angeles

From a performance by Suzanne Lacy and Leslie Labowitz. "In Mourning and in Rage." Los Angeles 1977. Photo Susan Mogul.

during the same six-week time period. Another represented those women battered in their homes, still another the one out of four victims of incest.

Each of the nine women made her statement which connected this seemingly random incident of violence in Los Angeles with the greater picture of nationwide violence toward women; each received her red cloak; and each was greeted by the chorus, "We fight back." Finally the woman in red approached the microphone. Unveiled, speaking directly and powerfully, she declared, "I am here for the *rage* of all women. I am here for women fighting back!"

All visual and temporal elements of the artwork were carefully designed to fit into the news format, including the size and shape of the banner and the shouting chorus, presenting notions of aggressive defense, a response counter to the expected convention of mourning. The ten women on the steps, the chorus and their banner, served as a background against which the remainder of the piece unfolded. A short statement, known today as a soundbite, was directed at the press, explaining the artists' rationale for the piece. A member of the Los Angeles Commission on Assaults Against Women read a prepared list of three demands for women's self-defense. These were presented to members of the mayor's office and City Council. The final image consisted of a song, "Fight Back," written especially for the event by Holly Near. The audience joined in this and a spontaneous circle dance as the artists and political organizers met with and answered questions from the press.

Political art can have many functions, many of them overlapping. The artist can use her understanding of the power of images primarily to communicate information, emotion, and/or ideology. She may, additionally, provide us with a critique of popular culture and its images or of current or past social situations. Sometimes her work can inspire her audience toward action in the service of a cause. Or the artworks might function best as a model for other artists or activists. These varied possibilities lend themselves to several ways to assess a political artwork's success.

4. DIRECT RESULTS AND CONCLUSION

As to direct results of "In Mourning and in Rage," how it affected immediate action, those we know of can be listed simply. Following the event, one reporter confronted a telephone company representative in his office. Although they had been stalling on the emergency listing of hotline numbers, promoted by feminist activists for over a year, he assured the reporter that favorable action was pending. Shortly after, the phone company did indeed list rape hotlines in the front of the phone book, although they were removed the subsequent year.

The $100,000 reward money that had been offered by the county for the arrest of the Strangler was converted into funding for free self defense workshops throughout the city, an action that was started prior to our event by the County Commission on the Status of Women, but one which received a favorable boost as a result of our publicity. In addition, two self-defense workshops for city employees, offered by Councilwoman Picus, and a Saturday session sponsored at our instigation by the rape hotlines, were put into motion that day.

In terms of audience attitude changes, a much more difficult area to assess, we can only report that the media coverage of the performance was, for the most part, consistent with our design and strategy. The performance was featured that evening on most major television newscasts in the area and received some national airplay. Leslie supervised a PBS follow-up program—students at the Woman's Building discussing sensationalist news coverage—and appeared on talk shows and at meetings with reporters to discuss issues raised by the performance. Within the general television audience we had very little feedback as to the effectiveness of the newsclip in changing anyone's perspective about the Strangler case or its coverage, but we received a lot of warm response from the Los Angeles feminist community at large (in sharp contrast to the suspicion and disinterest with which artists were previously greeted). It's fair to suggest that this performance, its coverage, and the word of mouth report of it considerably enhanced future interaction between artists and feminist activists in the city.

Although the empowerment we felt by successfully realizing our intentions is not to be underrated, it is important not to count heavily on a single three to four minute interruption to change a steady flow of counter information. The victory may ultimately be most important in demonstrating one strategy for people to air oppositional attitudes—one way artists can contribute valuable skills to social change. And perhaps the latter is most important of all: for the past three decades the path of visual art in this country has diverged from that of social reform and political protest. A generation of feminists and leftists have grown up distrusting the elitism of visual art. Although throughout these years a few committed leftist artists in this country continued with political critique in their art, the rise of feminism during the seventies gave a significant boost to the visibility and potential in activist political art. As we enter the eighties and increasing repression demonstrates the necessity of coalition building, it is imperative that activists embrace the models developed by artists over the past ten years, exploring as they do so how artists can play an active role in the politics of social change.

Notes

1. Ted Schwartz, *The Hillside Strangler* (Doubleday, 1981), p. 83.
2. Ibid., 61.
3. *Los Angeles Times,* Sunday, December 18, 1977, p. 30, pt. 1.
4. Schwartz, *The Hillside Strangler,* ptl. 147.

Nikki Craft: Inspiring Protest

INTRODUCTION

Diana E. H. Russell

If I were to be on the selection committee for a Nobel Prize for feminist activism, I would have no hesitation in nominating Nikki Craft.

For almost 20 years I have followed her efforts to stop violence against women, and I have been in awe of her brilliance. Her extraordinary abilities emerge as she uses her art in pursuit of her political goals: her sharp wit, her inventive sense of humor, her instinct for good strategy, her understanding of what will interest the media, to say nothing of her courage, her ability to inspire and mobilize others, and her willingness to act alone and to swim against the tide if necessary. Craft uses all her talents and intelligence in the service of her profound determination to make the United States a less violent country for women to live in.

Craft has attacked many different forms of woman hating in our contemporary U.S. culture, including rape, pornography, sexist ads, products that promote bulemia and anorexia, beauty pageants, and anything that requires women to mutilate their bodies to meet prescriptive standards of female attractiveness. In addition, Craft has been one of the few feminists to consistently demonstrate against femicide (although she only recently started using this particular word). However, these protests do not stand out from her actions on other issues, partly, I believe, for lack of an accepted word—until now—to describe the misogynist killing of women.

Note: Those interested in having Craft present her inspiring slide show about her political work should write to her c/o Clearinghouse on Femicide, P.O. Box 12342, Berkeley, Calif. 94701-3342. Donations to help Craft keep a roof over her head and food in her stomach while she keeps on trying to make the world a safer place for all women can be sent to the same address.

The following five readings provide typically daring examples of anti-femicide protests by Craft and her sister activists. In "The Incredible Case of the Stack o' Wheat Prints," Craft describes how, in 1980, she destroyed a collection of 10 prints housed in the Special Collections Library at the Santa Cruz campus of the University of California. These photographs eroticize the murder of women by glamorizing representations of their corpses. Craft was nearly expelled from the university for this action.

I remember Craft asking me to write to the chancellor of the university in support of her action—an easy task for me. In the end, not only was she not expelled, but she was nominated for a chancellor's ethics award by 400 students, her arresting officer, the provost of her college, and the socialist feminist mayor of Santa Cruz.

Next, D. A. Clarke analyzes Craft's one-woman Stack o' Wheat action, arguing that defense of the prints on the grounds that they constitute art "is specious at best." She points out that the established definition of what constitutes art is discriminatory, and she analyzes how male art is frequently used to silence women.

The following two selections describe the destruction of *Hustler* magazines by the Preying Mantis Women's Brigade, a fly-by-night underground feminist group in Santa Cruz, where Craft lived for many years. This group engaged in many illegal actions designed to attract media attention in order to confront issues of violence against women. These acts of rage were dedicated to one of the victims of murderer Kenneth Bianchi, the so-called Hillside Strangler of Los Angeles, who was sentenced to life imprisonment together with his accomplice, Angelo Buono, for the torture and murder of 10 women. The victim was 20-year-old Cindy Lee Hudspeth. Craft selected her from the others because a "joke" was published in *Hustler* referring to her murder as Bianchi's "latest accomplishment."

One of the many lessons that Craft's life can teach us is how powerful and effective one dedicated, courageous woman can be. I have often thought that if there were many more Nikki Crafts in our movement, women in the United States would be much closer to achieving basic feminist goals. Those who have worked closely with Craft, such as Ann Simonton and Melissa Farley, two other remarkably brave and committed feminist activists, exemplify Craft's ability to inspire.

I regret that I have never lived in the same community as Craft because I fancy that I might have become—like Simonton and Farley—less willing to allow my fear of arrest and imprisonment to stop me from doing what needs to be done. I believe I would be less intimidated by the police and courts and would get more enjoyment from my activist work. The injection of humor into demonstrations is not only effective, but fun. Anyone who hears Craft talk or attends her rousing and informative slide presentations about her work will learn that she doesn't merely rage and scream. She also laughs a lot.

In the final reading of this group, Melissa Farley describes what she and Craft called a "rampage" against the femicidal images published in a particular issue of *Penthouse*. Their many acts of civil disobedience during this 18-month rampage in 1985–86 resulted in 95 arrests of many different individuals. Craft was arrested 17 times and Farley 13 times, in different states.

THE INCREDIBLE CASE OF THE STACK O' WHEAT PRINTS

Nikki Craft

The print shown in the breakfast setting was reproduced from a collection of 10 photographs in the University of California Santa Cruz Special Collections Library called *The Incredible Case of the Stack o' Wheat Murders*. In each print, a woman appears to have been murdered. She is attractive, nude—and in the words of the accompanying informational pamphlet, "the postures are far less telling of struggle than of surrender, provocativeness, and sensuality."

Streaming from her body and swirling onto the floor are enormous quantities of what seems to be blood. The reviewer comments, "Of course the epitome of the series' humor resides in all the Hershey's chocolate used." Beside the victim in each photograph is a stack of pancakes. Purchasers of these 14" by 17" prints (at a cost of $450) also receive 8 ozs. of Hershey's Chocolate syrup and "enough pancake mix to make one complete Stack o' Wheats."

Presumably, the prints have been kept in Special Collections for their redeeming artistic/intellectual qualities. But the choice of the model, her poses, and the use of coke bottles, half-eaten bananas, etc., as props, make it difficult to view them as anything more than violent pornography. No matter what the artist's intent, the erotic language used to market them destroys any justification for them to remain in the sanctuary of the UCSC Library. For example, the reviewer observes that "There is a chance that discrete pleasure will be received from the portrayed transgression of another body—a profound ecstasy. . . ." He also notes that the "blood" "did little to hide the body's harmonious lines, but rather gave it new beauty." He refers to "utterly exquisite corpses." The inclusion of the pancake mix is the final insult to all womankind, the implication being that the purchaser can construct his own scene—create his own victim.

Violent pornography is an expression of something profoundly real in male psychology. Violent pornography is the theory; rape is the practice. To expect women to tolerate the protection of this sadistic chic in their school library is

---

Nikki Craft's Stack o' Wheat prints press release (31 March 1980) and speech "In Defense of Disobedience" (written Spring 1980) have been merged and edited for this volume by Diana E. H. Russell, with Craft's permission.

Nikki Craft destroying photographs that eroticize the murder of women. Photos Bill Reynolds, 1980.

unreasonable. Blacks would not tolerate the "humorous" prints of Klan lynchings. Jews would not tolerate the satirical depiction of Jews in baking ovens. To ask women to be good civil libertarians at a time when we are being mutilated, raped, and murdered in massive numbers is to ask us to passively accept our own victimization.

The day after I viewed these prints, I read on the front page of the *San Francisco Chronicle* of the murder of Barbara Schwartz, who was stabbed to death while jogging on Mount Tamalpais. She was described as "curled in the fetal position, the front of her blouse drenched in blood as she lay in the shadows under the redwoods—her dog's nose pressed against her lifeless arm."

I was reminded of another *Chronicle* story about another San Francisco area jogger, Mary Bennet, 23 years old, who died after a violent struggle defending herself against a "frenzied killer" rapist. She was stabbed 25 times, with multiple stab wounds on her face, neck, and chest. Golfers stated that they heard her "long, agonized screams," but did not investigate because they saw a police car in the area. Her body was discovered "much later by a party of hikers when they followed a trail of blood and saw one of the woman's feet protruding from a shallow grave of leaves."

As I continued reading the grisly account of Barbara Schwartz's death, I remembered the satirical pamphlet I had seen in the University library the day before—how "the epitome of the series' humor" resides in all the chocolate syrup used as blood.

In the same *Chronicle* article the chairman of the San Francisco Council on Physical Fitness warned all women of the "extreme danger of jogging in any city during the day . . . " and advised all women to jog in groups, preferably on specified jogging tracks.

When I went jogging that day, I wondered what beach I should go to—which one was safe. As I jogged I was wrenched by the image of Barbara Schwartz curled in a fetal position. I felt Mary Bennet's long, agonized screams that went unanswered to be the screams of all women everywhere.

It was then that I decided to destroy the Stack o' Wheat prints in the McHenry library. The Stack o' Wheat prints were destroyed as they were born: with chocolate syrup poured on torn pieces. Les Krims has taken the torn pieces of all womankind, poured chocolate syrup on them, and served them on a platter to reinforce the preconceptions of a violent, woman-hating society. I have taken torn pieces of Les Krims' work, poured chocolate syrup over them, and served them to make an artistic statement, to bring some very vital issues into focus, and to try to change the circumstances of women's and men's lives.

I destroyed these woman-hating prints in the name of all women who must live moment by moment with awareness of possibly becoming the next statistic on some police file; for all women who must live as if in a war zone, constantly on guard. I did this with the understanding that destroying violent pornography will not solve the problem of how men think and feel about us, but that assertive, direct actions such as this will affect the way we think and feel ourselves; and with the understanding that our very lives rest on our commitment to refuse to collaborate in our own destruction.

What I have done has been referred to as "censorship." But there is a distinction between official censorship and a moral decision by one individual to destroy a publicity packet that violates all of humanity. And my insistence that such illustrations of the mutilation of a woman's body and spirit are not art does not mean that I feel it should be subject to government censorship.

Official censorship is dangerous—it can be used against all of us. And my own action, without the educational process that accompanied it, would have been inexcusable. I am not opposed to the use of these prints for educational purposes: they were shown at the Forum at my insistence, and I have displayed them at tables I have set up on campus. In fact, I have requested their public display in the lobby of the library. But as they were in Special Collections, they were without a context other than the accompanying promotional pamphlet. In this light, their presence is inappropriate and offensive, itself an instance of violence against women.

Although I continue to object to official censorship, I support illegal actions such as this one, undertaken by individual women and groups of women and men who commit themselves to these acts—not taking them lightly, but evaluating creatively their responsibility to other women and men, to their communities, to the world, and to themselves. Those who choose these kinds of actions must consider every possible consequence they may incur, personally and politically, long-term and immediate. It is of utmost importance that we be willing to take moral responsibility for our actions, whether publicly as I have done, or privately, as some will choose to do.

I support the actions of Red Zora in West Germany, who stole $50,000 worth of merchandise from sex shops, leaving a leaflet signed, "avenger of the oppressed"; I support the Bluebird Five who spray-painted and pasted leaflets on a local porn shop—as I support all women who realize the urgency of our circumstances and take responsibility for dealing with the sexual violence that is pervading our lives. These efforts, our energy, our time, our money, and our lives, we give to change the course of history. We do this so that our children and their children will not be forced to live with the same fear that women of past generations have grown to accept.

If I have learned anything in my years of volunteer social service work in this area, it is that stopping the rape, mutilation, and murder of women rests in our hands. Even after reading the grisly headlines, society in general, and, perhaps, men in particular, may have uttered a dutiful "how terrible"; but little active interest has been shown in the battle against this violence and its climate of fear. And until stopping this violence becomes a societal priority, we are left with the enormous task of finding a solution. Our desperate attempts may be controversial and at times illegal. However, no matter how we choose to deal with this monstrous burden, until drastic changes occur in attitudes and the way we are forced to live our lives each day, we have little to lose.

I refuse to align myself with any individual or group whose goal is sexual repression. I will work to defend freedom of access to any information or expression of any ideas concerning honest sexuality or erotica of any kind. Explicit sexual material has its place in literature, art, science, and education, and most of all in the public domain. What I do think is that we need a new definition of obscenity that focuses on violence, not sex—on the intent to degrade and dehumanize the female body for sexual stimulation. What I am unalterably opposed to is the female body being stripped, bound, raped, tortured, mutilated, and murdered in the name of entertainment and free speech.

As long as we read of women murdered by misogynist men—women like Karen Mondic, Diane Wilder, Laura Collins, Yolanda Washington, Judith Ann Miller, Lisa Theresa Kastin, Kitty Genovese, Jill Barcomb, Kathleen Robinson, Kristina Weckler, Mary Vincent, Sonja Johnson, Dolores Cepeda, Mary Bennet, Jane Evelyn King, Laura Rae Wagner, Kimberly Diane Martin, Cindy Lee Hudspeth, Edda Kane, Barbara Schwartz, Andrea Joy Hall, Jackie Doris Gilliam, Jacqueline Leah Lamp, Lucinda Schaefer, Shirley Linett Ledford, Mary Ann Pesce, Anita Luchessa, Aiko Koo, Cynthia Schall, Rosalind Thorpe, Alice Liu, Clarnell Strandberg, Sara Hallett, and Diane Steffy—we must examine the portrayal, by all forms of media, of women as unwilling victims.

It is not just a matter of our personal distaste for this material. It is a matter of our very lives resting on the false conceptions about women that Les Krims has perpetuated in his series. Even though there is a debate as to whether there is in fact a direct correlation between violent acts and pornography—and I happen to believe there is—women cannot afford to wait until definitive results come in. No matter how pornography affects men, in order to maintain our self-respect, we must refuse to allow *anyone* to portray us as victims in the manner Les Krims did. And we must attack all others who financially profit at our expense from this type of degradation.

I agree that censorship is a deadly menace. It silences us and destroys our spirit. When it is enforced, people live in fear of expression themselves. But violence against women is the ultimate silencer—it destroys women's lives. It makes us afraid, not only of expressing ourselves, but of being ourselves. And when night closes in, it comes like a prison.

THE EVIDENCE OF PAIN

D. A. Clarke

On March 31, 1980, long-time feminist activist and ceramicist Nikki Craft walked into the Special Collections room of the University of California library at Santa Cruz and tore up a set of photographic reproductions; she then poured

Reprinted from *City on a Hill,* 3 April 1980, with permission from City on a Hill Press, University of California, Santa Cruz.

Hershey's syrup over the shreds. She claimed, in a public statement, that the prints' unquestioned presence in the protected collection was an insult and a threat to all women.

Craft was arrested, as was professional photographer Bill Reynolds, who documented the event. They were both charged with felony conspiracy, questioned, and released. Later, the arresting officer was to add his signature to many others recommending Craft for a Chancellor's Award for "significant contribution to campus understanding of ethical principles."

Controversy raged on the small campus, some individuals going so far as to call Craft a "censor" and a "fascist." Heated correspondence was printed in the student newspaper; many members of the Aesthetic Studies department were outraged at the destruction of "art" and demanded punitive action against Craft.

> It saddens me deeply that this campus has been in more turmoil over the symbolic destruction of a $3 set of prints than over the murder of Diane Steffy last November. Diane Steffy was a student at our university and she was silenced forever.
>
> I agree that censorship is a deadly menace to the human spirit—it silences—it destroys our spirit. When it is enforced, people live in fear of expressing themselves. But violence against women is the ultimate silencer—it destroys women's lives. It makes us afraid, not only of expressing ourselves, but of being ourselves. And when night closes in, it comes like a prison.
>
> —Nikki Craft

The photographs were part of a boxed packet by New York photographer Les Krims, *The Incredible Case of the Stack o' Wheat Murders* (published in 1972). Each sepiatone print shows a woman, stripped either from the waist down or completely, lying in what appear to be pools of her own blood. Apparently dead, she is usually gagged and bound, sometimes her entire head is wrapped in a bag or cloth; in several prints she bears realistic knife wounds. She is always in a mundane, familiar setting, and near her in every picture is a stack of whole wheat pancakes.

Curator Robert Sobieszek, whose critique accompanies the prints, finds the series a "humorous" treatment of what are often called *signature murders:* murders in which the victims are subjected to a characteristic mutilation, or in which some idiosyncratic object, symbol, or message is left at the scene. Sobieszek writes, "Of course, the epitome of the series' humor resides in all the chocolate syrup used as blood."

In every picture, the woman's partial or complete nudity, as well as the photographer's penchant for posing her with spread legs, strongly intimate that she has been raped either prior to or after her death. In the kitchen scene, there is an upright Coke bottle left standing between her thighs, a clear allusion to the horribly common device of rape with an object (Coke bottles, as well as guns, are particularly favored by real-life rapists.)

Police and concerned citizens are aware that the incidence of rape in the United States is approximately one "successful" rape every four and a half minutes. The molestation of girl-children occurs about once every ten minutes; both types of assault are accompanied by varying degrees of additional brutality, up to and including mutilation and murder. Sobieszek, however, did not find Krims' imagery evocative of the terror and torment inflicted hourly upon the women and children of America by American men.

> No police file contains . . . such an array of utterly exquisite corpses. . . . By meticulous design the streams of blood . . . did little to hide the body's harmonious lines but rather gave it a new beauty . . . despite the somewhat romantic exaggeration.
> —Robert Sobieszek

Sobieszek managed to find the image of a raped and butchered woman "exquisite," "harmonious," even "romantic"; indeed, possessed of "a new beauty" in disfigurement and death. Granted, he knew that the blood was really chocolate; he knew the model, said to be Krims' wife, was the same in all the prints. But surely he also knew, as anyone must who reads the paper, that there was no exaggeration, that these scenes, and worse, are enacted daily—not in "artistic" sepiatone, it is true, but often photographed by their perpetrators.

There is no exaggeration. What there is is an insidious and perilously selective understatement, a glossy dishonesty. The Stack o' Wheats, in essence, is a lie about women and about violence.

As Sobieszek notes, "the postures are far less telling of struggle than of surrender, provocativeness, and sensuality." Let us leave aside, for the moment, the familiar and vile conception that women somehow provoke the violence men commit upon them, and also the weighty question of whose sensuality is gratified by the mutilation and degradation of the female body and soul. The simplest lie is the first one: *there is no struggle.*

There are no bruises on the model's exquisite shaven skin—presumably they were not sensual enough for the artist's purpose. There is no sign that she fought, as women have and do and will, for her dignity and her life. She is shown as the docile victim of every femicidal fantasy, who gracefully accepts her place as object and target and sacrifice to male hatred, who obediently abnegates her own humanity and goes smiling to the slaughter. She has never existed, except in the misogynist imagination.

We are not meant to identify with the victim; the prints are designed to prevent us from doing so. Her face is obscured by a gag or entirely hidden; she is only a female body. We cannot see her eyes—through which she might look back at her rapist, her murderer, or the omnipotent photographer. We cannot see her mouth—through which she might communicate her agony and anger, requiring our response. Like shaven-headed and uniformed concentration-camp victims, she is reduced forcibly to anonymity, deprived of individual personality.

Furthermore we see her from above, looking down, from the vantage of the murderer as he looks back on his work. This technique of viewpoint has become more and more prevalent in films about anti-woman violence of late, decoying the viewer into an identification with the invisible male protagonist as he rapes and kills.

On the other hand, though Krims' work stands out by its inhumanity and offensiveness, his basic aesthetic is simply an exaggeration of that prevalent throughout traditional, male-dominated art. It is essentially a political aesthetic, its prime premise being the humanity of men and the non-humanity of women—a male supremacist aesthetic. In photographic shops one still comes upon those "how to" books for the amateur: *Photographing Flowers, Landscape Photography, . . .* and of course, *Photographing Women.*

The imposition of a male-invented standard of beauty for women, which traditionally requires the imitation of the child in manner and appearance, doubly diminishes the individuality of the anonymous female model. When all women photographed by an artist are selected according to the same narrow criteria, they become more and more standardized, aesthetic *things* to be placed in attractive settings—still lifes.

The beauty standard, moreover, since it requires that women look other than they are, necessitates the alteration of the female form, its variations over time only changing the manner and degree of alteration and not the fact. Woman-as-world becomes not merely part of the landscape to be stared at, but raw material to be *made into art.* The practices of "beautification" imposed by the arbitrary standard range from time-consuming inconveniences (painting, plucking, shaving) to minor health hazards (corseting, high heels) to agonizing mutilation (clitoridectomy, binding)—but these practices all have two things in common.

One is that all are employed to convert the "raw material" of the natural female body into an aesthetic object for the pleasure and approval (and occasional purchase) of a male or males. There is very little pretense that women would endure these painful rituals for themselves or each other—judgment comes from the male "artist." The second common point is that all, in their particular time, have gone from being optional adornment to being cosmetic and necessary. In the end, all have been seen as required repairs to the flawed or unartistic female person; and the normal adult female body and personality, unmutilated, have been perceived by men as ugly.

> *Il faut souffrir pour etre belle.*
> —Old French saying

We note that the person referred to in the saying is always female; she is made *belle* not *beau,* by her suffering. The premise is intrinsic to a culture where female beauty is perceived only as the imposition of artifice, in short as Art. In fact, where all the details of female appearance which are perceived as beautiful are the evidence of inconvenience and pain, it is but one short step to the premise that *the evidence of pain is what is beautiful in women.*

This in fact appears to be Sobieszek's interpretation of the Stack o' Wheats—that blood, simulated knife-wounds, torn clothing, all the evidence of pain and defeat, are what make Krims' model so very "exquisite." Perhaps the most important aspect of the Krims/Sobieszek work is that it is the logical extension of an aesthetic which eulogizes and perpetuates male supremacy. It is central to the hostility with which the female artist is often received by critics and so-called (male) colleagues; it is central to the atrocities daily perpetrated upon women, and to the lies told about those atrocities.

> Les Krims has taken the torn pieces of all womankind, poured chocolate syrup on them, and served them on a platter to reinforce the preconceptions of a violent, woman-hating society. I have taken torn pieces of Les Krims' work, poured chocolate syrup on them, and served them to make an artistic statement, to bring some very vital issues into focus, and to change the circumstances of women's and men's lives.
>
> —Nikki Craft

Les Krims offered, to anyone who bought the full size (14" x 17") Stack o' Wheat print set, one can of Hershey's syrup and enough pancake mix to make one stack of wheats. Sobieszek found this another facet of the work's "humor." Perhaps it was the do-it-yourself offer which spurred Craft to drastic, if symbolic, action (symbolic, because at her own expense she provided the library with a replacement set of prints).

All the visual arts communicate. Les Krims' art communicates, in this case, an adherence to the use of woman as aesthetic object, and a profound callousness and disregard concerning the fear and pain of real women; it further communicates a constant identification with the rapist/murderer, adopting his violent hatred as the *artistic viewpoint.*

Nikki Craft's art communicates, in this case, an urgent rage and grief—grief, for thousands of raped and butchered women who will never again live unafraid *or who will never again live;* rage, that anyone can carefully produce and market lies about those women and their pain, that anyone can deliberately mythologize and identify with their murderers and rapists, and call the killer's handwork aesthetic. Craft's art attempts to educate, to educate men to the depths of female desperation and thirst for freedom, to educate women to our own power as artists, as shapers of the world.

Les Krims' art tells the viewer that women are helpless, unresisting victims who look and act like the pornographic fantasies of male invention; that we die faceless and mute; that our murderers can pause to consider our "harmonious" corpses, leave ludicrous clues, and get away with it—to kill and kill again. Nikki Craft's art tells the audience/reader/viewer that women are not helpless, that we can defend ourselves and the truth, that we can indeed take apart the products of a male supremacist art, and with its pieces build an essay in anger and courage. Her message is one of faith: that we can confront and defeat the violence which threatens any moment to overwhelm us.

It is this grief and rage and confirmation which form the basis for a feminist aesthetic, a women's art which does not merely imitate more and more skillfully the male supremacist style. It is the aesthetic of struggle, shaped in part by the hostility of a surrounding culture.

A feminist art recognizes and cherishes the individuality of all women—with both gravity and satire, it describes the reality of female experience and its diversity. A feminist art draws upon a deep and constant anger, and a deep and constant love, for the courage to assert the truth about women's lives.

STRIKING FLYNT

Irene Moosen

The 38th floor of a 45-story office building on Century Park East in Los Angeles belongs to Larry Flynt Publications, home of *Hustler* magazine. The morning sun glints blindingly from the side of this awesome structure as the lunch hour traffic picks up its pace.

If Larry Flynt, *Hustler's* editor, had been in his office last Monday, he could have looked out of his window and seen the Preying Mantis Women's Brigade stage a protest and leaflet passersby below his office. If he had come down one of the six elevators which open onto his entryway, tipped his hat to the three guards who maintain a constant vigil over his business chambers, he would have received a poster with his own face shining up at him. He would have seen himself under the WANTED sign with the charge below his picture—"for inciting the violent rape and murder of women and children."

The Santa Cruz-based group traveled south on this first business day after International Women's Day to confront *Hustler's* publication of violent pornography and to discuss the First Amendment. The dozen women and two-man auxiliary who comprised the group held picket signs and talked with the press which gathered for the noontime demonstration.

The "Porn Machine" stood on the sidewalk, a conceptual monument to the powerful millions that *Hustler* represents: 1.5 million in circulation and millions in revenue. The machine is a black box with pictures from the magazine of naked women being sexually brutalized, and cartoons mocking such things as the Hillside Strangler and domestic violence. This black box is the foundation for a large gold phallus with an American flag, which waves back and forth atop the machine.

At 12:00 the street theatre began with three women lying beneath the Porn Machine, while others read scripted dialogue to the crowd.

The demonstrators discussed censorship and whether violent pornography breeds the acts that it depicts, as the group believes. The skit ended with several

Reprinted from *City on a Hill*, 12 March 1981, with permission from City on a Hill Press, University of California, Santa Cruz.

women tearing up copies of *Hustler,* breaking eggs over them and dousing them with chocolate syrup. The group called upon people to destroy *Hustler* at the newsstands and to pressure vendors enough to discontinue selling the magazines. Nikki Craft, one of the organizers of the protest, stated: "*Hustler* has been tearing up women for long enough, now it's time for women to tear up *Hustler.*"

The demonstration brought reluctant response from Flynt Publications. A press release was brought to reporters on the street acknowledging Preying Mantis' First Amendment rights and calling for the group to respect *Hustler's* First Amendment rights in turn.

The most vivid and perhaps most candid response was offered by Althea Leasure, Larry Flynt's young wife, throwing a copy of the latest *Hustler* at Ann Simonton, a participant in the demonstration, and remarking, "Read this. Maybe you'll learn something."

Jess Grant, one of the men supporting Preying Mantis, explained, "We're not calling for censorship. If we wanted a law, we would be in Sacramento. We want private individuals to see it and then communicate their anger and disgust any way they can."

"We're calling for corporate responsibility," said Nikki Craft. "Drug and automobile companies must prove their products are safe for the market before they are released; we ask Larry Flynt to prove that what he prints does not lead to acts of violence."

ACTIONS AGAINST *HUSTLER*

Preying Mantis Women's Brigade

At this time the Preying Mantis Women's Brigade and its active supporters take responsibility for the destruction of over 550 *Hustler* magazines on newsstands in the Santa Cruz area. Men and women have worked individually and in groups, as drivers, diverters and destroyers. Various techniques used were squirt bottles filled with black India ink, Verathane, motor oil and toothpaste; many copies had the first pages torn down the center. There were many "accidental" spills of coffee and Coca Cola over the publication. Red paint is also aesthetically appropriate.

These magazines were destroyed in memory of Cindy Lee Hudspeth, age 20—a victim of the Hillside Strangler, Kenneth Bianchi. They were destroyed in retaliation against *Hustler's* "joke" which aggrandized Bianchi. *Hustler* refers to her murder as "his latest accomplishment." Then goes on to state, "You gotta treat 'em rough. After knocking off a couple of bimbos the Hillside Strangler likes to kick back and relax with Dewar's Lite Label."

Leaflet distributed in Spring 1980. With permission from Nikki Craft.

Hustler, Bianchi, and other mass murderers of women work in direct collusion with each other. The media's ability to mold mass consciousness and affect behavior makes the connection between violent pornography and sexual crimes against women undeniable. News accounts document the political atrocities being committed against women daily. Women must gauge their lives by the setting sun and in our community we are warned not to walk in public parks in daylight hours.

Now let us discuss freedom and 1st Amendment Rights. Larry Flynt maintains his rights to abuse and degrade women. He strips, binds and mutilates women to humor and entertain his male audience. He reinforces social hatred and malice against women. As he profits, women pay—with their dignity and their lives.

We support the 1st Amendment. We do not want official censorship. We demand corporate responsibility. Flynt's product incites the rape and murder of women and children. Any publication that panders to the idea that women are merely objects for sadistic mutilation cannot expect to be immune to the outraged response of women and men who know better.

We know that men and women across the country will join with us in the systematic destruction of *Hustler* through individual and group acts of civil disobedience. Store owners and distributors take no financial loss. All unsold magazines are returned to Flynt Publications with the message that we are fed up with his violence.

Flynt's call to violence has been directed against human beings; our call to destruction is aimed against property and objects that seek to destroy our bodies and our lives. As soon as Larry Flynt expresses concern for our safety as human beings, we will concern ourselves with the safety of his publication.

We recognize the importance of education and encourage people to write or call stores that carry *Hustler,* respectfully requesting the removal of this publication from their stands. We are currently compiling for publication a list of establishments that stock *Hustler.* Future boycotts of those stores are also planned. We appreciate notification of any store in your area that carries this magazine, as well as documentation of any additional actions against it.

Postscript by Nikki Craft: As a result of these actions, and at the time of this writing [1981], only one out of 18 stores raided has reported the incident to the Santa Cruz police. Six merchants have ceased to sell the magazine in their stores, four more are considering doing so. The Preying Mantis Women's Brigade plans to organize boycotts against any store that tries to press charges against our guerilla actions. Women in the brigade have managed to photograph some of the actions by pretending to be photography students. They are calling for systematic national destruction of *Hustler* on the newsstands in the hope that if enough community dissent is expressed over violent pornography, news dealers will be pressured to take the magazine off their racks.

THE RAMPAGE AGAINST *PENTHOUSE*

Melissa Farley

The December 1984 issue of *Penthouse,* continuing a history of publishing images that teach men to eroticize dead and battered women, did one other thing: it sparked my collaboration with Nikki Craft on what evolved into a two-year series of political and economic actions against pornography, femicide, and *Penthouse* in particular.

Nikki Craft, a radical feminist activist for ten years when I met her, had recently presented her antipornography slide show in several areas of the Midwest. Her slides were a combination of pornography and her own powerfully creative responses to violence against women.

In 1984 I worked at a feminist psychotherapy collective, Hera, in Iowa City. At that time I'd worked for a number of years with survivors of incest and sexual assault. I regularly heard women's accounts of the role pornography played in their sexual assaults. Psychotherapy addresses solutions on an individual level—I found that women really can and do heal from these experiences, especially when they participate in groups with other survivors. As a therapist, however, I had reached a point where I needed to take some action, outside of my office, that would strike at some of the root causes of these violent acts against women. Nikki Craft's carefully articulated feminist activism appealed to me.

The December 1984 *Penthouse* contained nine images of Asian women tied up with heavy rope, bound tightly with ropes cutting into their ankles, wrists, labias, and buttocks. Two of the images show women bound and hanging from trees, heads lolling forward, apparently dead. Another woman is masked, trussed up, and lying on a floor, appearing dead. In another image from this issue, an adolescent girl is proffered by an older female to the camera/pornographer/consumer/misogynist. The younger girl is bound harshly with heavy ropes around her neck, around her torso, which cut painfully into her labia. She has no pubic hair, so she looks quite young. The lack of pubic hair also permits the viewer to see precisely how the rope cuts tightly into her genitals. Her hands appear to be tied behind her back. The older woman, collaborator with the camera, herself has only a sheet draped around her, but with her hands on the young woman's shoulders, she seems to be pushing the resisting younger woman toward the viewer. Both women have their eyes closed, with their heads bowed slightly, in deference/sacrifice. Two of the images are of women who have been tied up and dumped onto rocky cliffs, looking limp and dead. The pornographer shoots these dead women lying on their stomachs, with their genitals viewed by the camera in a position a rapist might tie an unconscious or resisting woman in order to rape her. In only one picture do we see a woman looking into the camera, looking at her own death, standing on a cliff with her face painted white, a rope around her neck and chest. Throughout these murderous images are sprinkled "artsy" haiku quotes that exude dominance and subordination.

Our response to this issue of *Penthouse* marked the beginning of what we came to call the National Rampage against *Penthouse*. We used civil disobedience as our primary strategy, then later expanded the Rampage to include guerrilla theater, consumer boycotts, and corporate confrontation. Our goal throughout all these actions was to educate the public about the pervasiveness of pornography, the way in which pornography promotes the epidemic of violence against women and children, and the urgent need for individual and collective responses to these issues.

In two years, Nikki was arrested 17 times and I was arrested 13 times in 9 different states. We traveled to many communities, and in each we invited feminists to join us in civil disobedience. When we counted all the others who were arrested with us on these different occasions, there were more than 100 individual arrests during the years of the Rampage against *Penthouse*.

I want to tell you some of the details of our modus operandi. For two years, this was essentially a two-woman organization, although we could not have carried out the Rampage without the intense commitment of feminist activists from communities throughout the United States. They helped organize the actions and helped us with media contacts and sign painting, and they were arrested and went to jail with us. We had support and creative ideas from close friends, but we worked with only a shoestring budget. My income dropped by a third for the two years because I was spending so much time on the Rampage, and I spent my own money on transportation, photocopying, and mailing costs. Nikki spent even more, often going into debt as a result of Rampage expenses. We received a few financial contributions, but basically the two years of activism were fueled only by our fury at violence against women.

After contacting local feminist groups about participating in our action, Nikki's antipornography slide show was the organizing vehicle that inspired women and men to join us the next day. For example, in December 1984 five of us burned an effigy of Bob Guccione (owner and editor of *Penthouse*) in front of a bookstore in Madison, Wisconsin, that sold the magazine. We did a brief press interview, then entered the store; each of us picked up a copy of *Penthouse* (without paying for it, of course!) and ripped it into shreds in symbolic retaliation for the distribution of images that eroticize the murders of women. We always notified the police and the press in advance, and on this occasion we were arrested twice in one day for these acts. In most other locations we were detained in jail before being released on our own recognizance, so we couldn't get to our next action until the next day. We posted bail to get out only once in two years.

We performed our acts of civil disobedience almost ceremonially. Often, those of us who are rape and incest survivors spoke publicly of our experiences as we ripped up pornography. Soon after we began the Rampage, a North Carolina man was charged with the kidnap, rape, and murder of an eight-year-old girl, Jean Kar-Har Fewel. In February 1985, two months after the December 1984 *Penthouse* images of hanged Asian women were published in *Penthouse*, this orphaned Chinese child, in the process of being adopted, was found raped and killed, with ropes around her neck, attached to a tree. We mourned her tragic death and dedicated several of our actions to her memory.

Usually, each woman destroyed only one copy of *Penthouse* per demonstration, in keeping with our philosophy that the goal of these actions was not censorship but education. Following each action, there would be a flurry of news coverage during which reporters grappled with the issues we held up for public debate (with widely varying success). We handed out a flier that outlined our views on sexuality and censorship as well as pornography.

Our goal was first to promote public thinking about the harm done to women by pornography. Our second aim was to confront the pornography industry, which netted about $8 billion annually by 1985, and to pressure it to take some responsibility for the harm it was doing to women. We described our approach as educative, extralegal, and civilly disobedient. Although civil disobedience has been widely used in the black civil rights movement and in the antiwar movement, amazingly enough feminist civil disobedience had not been used much in the United States since women gained voting rights. (One of the suffragists' major strategies was to illegally enter voting booths.)

Some argued against our "destruction of property" (that is, the single copy of *Penthouse* each of us ripped up in each one of our actions). We responded that since we viewed pornography as a "clear and present danger" to women's lives, we felt justified in taking some extreme actions to publicize that danger. We further noted that pornography itself has more legal protection as "speech" than do the *real women* who appear in pornography and whose injuries are trivialized. We wanted people to see how pornography threatened women's very survival.

There was one exception to our practice of destroying only a single copy of *Penthouse* in our actions. At one bookstore in Waterloo, Iowa, an employee called the owner and informed him of our destruction of a single copy of *Penthouse*. He told the employee to let us do whatever we wanted to because we were "nice girls who meant well." On that occasion, we proceeded, with the owner's blessing, to rip up copies of *Penthouse* and *Hustler* until we were literally knee-deep in pornography.

We also emphasized that we were pro-sex, pro-nudity, and pro-sensuality. At the height of the Rampage against *Penthouse,* Citizens for Decency through Law, a right-wing Christian based group, began a series of its own actions against pornography, objecting to "explicit sexual material," extramarital sex, homosexuality, sex education, and abortion. Nikki named our new organization Citizens for Media Responsibility without Law, a takeoff on the right-wing Citizens for Decency through Law. Both groups, on one bitterly subzero day in January 1985, picketed 7-11 stores in Cedar Rapids, Iowa. We carried signs expressing our opposition to *both* sexual repression in peoples' lives *and* violent pornography. We handed out a list of all the sexual acts we could think of—and said we approved of them.

Years later, liberal pro-pornography organizations and much of the media still simplistically assign us to the same camp as the right-wing antipornography fundamentalists. Women have told me that they fear ostracism from liberal feminists as prudish and "antisex" if they oppose pornography. The antipornography movement among feminists encompasses a variety of points of view, including legal approaches such as the legislation proposed by Andrea Dworkin and Catharine MacKinnon, as well as civil disobedience and economic sanctions. Feminists who are incest survivors have begun to look at how their abuse is repeated in sadomasochistic sex. These women are not "antisex." They are "anti" abusive, injurious sex. I was thrilled to hear one woman describe herself recently as "in recovery from sadomasochism."

We found that in many communities—Lincoln, Nebraska; Iowa City, Iowa; Santa Cruz, California; Minneapolis, Minnesota; Madison, Wisconsin—women and men were ready to participate in civil disobedience against femicide. We wanted to include many more people in the actions against *Penthouse's* femicide-promoting images and to demand corporate responsibility from Guccione's *Penthouse* empire. The Rampage expanded to include economic boycott as well as civil disobedience. We reviewed back issues of *Penthouse* to ascertain who advertised in it—that is, which corporations provided the financial backing for dissemination of femicidal images. We could have selected many, but we chose

Feminist protesters tear up pornography, emphasizing that they are not opposed to nudity and sexuality. Photograph by Jeff Myers published in *Press Citizen,* Iowa City, Indiana, 21 December 1984.

to target for boycott five corporations that had a relatively benign public image and that we thought would not appreciate our public joining of their names with the *Penthouse* images: Panasonic, Canon, Casio, Sanyo, and Magnavox. We also appealed to several of these corporations on the grounds that they were Asian corporations sponsoring images promoting the bondage and enslavement of Asian women. We had previously targeted local distributors of pornography, but now we also focused on a bookstore chain, B. Dalton's, which sold *Penthouse*, as well as Meredith Corporation, the printer of *Penthouse*, located in Des Moines, Iowa. Soon, National Organization of Women state chapters in Wisconsin, Texas, and North Carolina endorsed our boycott. In August 1985 we received word that Magnavox had decided to stop advertising in *Penthouse*. We considered that a major victory for the Rampage. In late 1985 *Advertising Age* noted a 25 percent decrease from the previous year's level in corporate advertisers in *Penthouse*—as compared with ad pages in 1984. We were exultant about this loss of advertising income to *Penthouse*, although aware that some of the decrease may also have been due to pressure from right-wing groups.

Throughout the time of our Rampage, women came forward with their personal accounts of the killings of women for men's sexual entertainment. On International Women's Day, March 1985, Margaret Zack of Santa Cruz, California, participated in the Rampage by destroying a copy of *Penthouse*. Before her arrest she spoke to feminists and reporters about her decision to devote her life to ending violence against women. Margaret Zack's 18-year-old daughter Tania had been found raped and bludgeoned to death after having been abducted from her car.

Another phase of the Rampage was the formation of Minors against Violent Pornography. This group of six 10- to 13-year olds from Iowa City, Iowa (including my daughter, Darca Morgan) organized its own boycott of local stores that sold *Penthouse*. They also engaged in at least one civil disobedience action with no adults present. The children made a number of public statements about sex education and discussed their own reactions of fear and disgust about violent pornography. One child spoke of her fear when she saw a friend's father reading pornography. Another spoke with concern regarding a sexually abused friend of his. A 13-year-old boy said: "We think *Penthouse* is the wrong textbook to teach anybody about sex."

Guccione continued, in 1985, to pump out images promoting the murder of women, images linking men's sexuality with violent assault on women. One piece of fiction in a January 1985 *Penthouse* included the following passage: "Hold a woman at the end of a gun and you can't tell how she'll react. Sometimes they cry. Sometimes it's quite the opposite. They want to make love to you." In May 1985 *Penthouse* printed a centerfold of a woman on her knees looking invitingly at the camera/consumer/murderer while she reads a newspaper with the headline: "Woman Found Strangled." We know that as men masturbate to these images, their sexuality is trained to violence, even to murder, of women. In March 1985 *Penthouse* published an article about the torture of

Latin-American women. While smugly spouting liberal anti-contra rhetoric, the article in fact was a home torturer's how-to manual.

At about this time we came up with a sticker that we started selling to feminist organizations. It read "Rape Manual." Once the backing was peeled off, it bonded firmly with paper. We were pleased to learn that these stickers had been used to glue shut *Penthouses*, and the covers had to then be ripped in order to see what was inside.

In late fall 1985 we decided to focus our efforts on the printer of *Penthouse*, Meredith Corporation, which proudly listed in its annual report all the publications it printed *except Penthouse*—for example, *Better Homes and Gardens*, *Metropolitan Home*, *Sail*, *Seventeen*, and *Successful Farming*. In response to our demand that Meredith stop printing *Penthouse*, thereby demonstrating a degree of corporate social responsibility and accountability, one of its public relations men wrote: "No corporation should appoint itself as a conscience for society." He then proceeded to sanctimoniously defend the First Amendment. Nikki designed a glossy brochure about the Meredith/*Penthouse* connection, with captions under the *Penthouse* images such as "People might think the printers of *Penthouse* would be outcasts . . . but we're successful white businessmen, and people, too." We handed out thousands of these brochures to the people of Des Moines, Iowa. Several women purchased one share of stock each to ensure that we'd be able to enter Meredith's annual stockholders' meeting, where we planned to confront stockholders about the sources of their profits.

We formed an organization called Meredith Stockholders against *Penthouse*, which urged Meredith to divest itself of the *Penthouse* printing contract. Meredith did not permit us to hand out literature or speak, but at their annual meeting we removed our coats, revealing the *Penthouse* images of bound and dead Asian women that we had ironed onto our shirts.

Throughout the Rampage, Nikki and I wrote articles, spoke with the press, raised money, lectured, and gave legal testimony on the violent effects of pornography on men's attitudes and behavior, and consequently, the danger to women and children. The time I spent in jail and in dealing with the court system was not particularly pleasant—at one point I developed an anxiety response whenever a police car came near. By far the most stressful aspect of the Rampage, however, was the constant reading and viewing of pornography. I began to wonder what the women in the pictures had felt and what had happened to them. The pornography had a depressing, demoralizing, sexually stifling effect on me at times. I felt caged in by it. On the other hand, looking at pornography just prior to an act of civil disobedience was a spur to our rage, to action. It became—and still is—impossible for me to not see, even for a moment, the constant threat of violence that pornography poses to women in this culture.

The conviction in January 1990 of Dwaine Tinsley, creator of "Chester the Molester" cartoons, on five counts of child molestation, validated the relationship we saw between pornography and sexual assault. As Tinsley told his coworkers, "You can't write this stuff all the time if you don't experience it."

Penthouse has expanded its misogynist repertoire to articles that deal with incest (December 1989). Under the guise of concern about "shattered innocents," the *Penthouse* article graphically describes sexual assaults on children in a manner that no doubt appeals to pedophiles. The article eroticizes sexual violence against children and reads like the pornography it is: "What terror Adam must have felt . . . mixed as he grew older with the excitement of sexual arousal—long before nature intended it—an excitement that must have added to his guilt from knowing that what his grandfather was doing had been forbidden since time immemorial." I see the *Penthouse* incest article as a carefully planned propaganda piece aimed at mystifying the real causes of sexual assaults on women and children. The incest is considered by *Penthouse* to be the result of *individuals* who are "selfish, warped, emotionally disturbed, or lecherous." Socially sanctioned violence, objectification, sexism, and misogyny are, of course, not mentioned as causal factors. *Penthouse* carefully suggests to the reader that it is far more important to address *child* sexual assault than the assault, exploitation, or murder of "grown women." This is, again, cleverly divisive propaganda.

There is a lot of work left to do. I've rested now for a few years since the Rampage. Is anyone out there ready for some action?

What Can We Do about Femicide?: A Proposal

ANONYWOMEN

Canadian women have declared 6 December a Day of Mourning for Women. I propose that, following their lead, we in the United States stage 6 December memorial demonstrations to publicize our grief *and* our rage over victims of femicide. I propose that our demonstrations include graphic photographic documentation of the horrors suffered by victims of femicide and that such illustrative documents be taken directly from the commercial and sexualized gore we find in magazines, record albums, movies, videotapes, computer games, and posters. At every demonstration, let us testify to the outrages endured by each woman who was slaughtered that year by misogynist hate.

FEUX DE JOIE

After testifying, anyone who wishes to may burn the hate literature she has brought, as an expression of our hope that hate crimes against us will vanish from the earth. Imagine lighting a fire, one that *we* control! In honor of our Canadian sisters, let's name these memorial demonstrations *Feux de Joie,* or Fires of Glee.

These annual demonstrations will forcefully advance women's interests by focusing public attention on femicide, by raising the consciousness of people who have been desensitized to the murder of women and mass media presentations of femicide, by embarrassing and exposing the producers of this type of "entertainment," and by giving isolated women the kind of support they need to take a stand against viewing femicidal images and other misogynist propaganda. For those of us who participate, 6 December will be a day on which to reaffirm our commitment to women's dignity and sisterhood.

Candida Ellis's editing of this proposal is greatly appreciated.

Every year on 6 December, let women everywhere stand on stages and in public parks, on the steps of capital buildings and courthouses, speaking out with their friends, in their communities and in their churches. Let us tell our stories of how femicide has snuffed out the lives of our sisters, to television cameras and radio microphones. Or, perhaps for the first time, some of us can simply sit with a group of our friends and recount what happened to us (femicide attempts) and to those we know—those awful stories we have kept to ourselves for too long. When we have finished talking, we can display femicidal photography from *Hustler* magazine or a videotape like "Drive-in Massacre" (by Magnum Entertainment, Inc.) to remind ourselves of the profits being made off women's agony. We will publicly mourn the brutal femicides of Kitty Genovese, Christina Ricketts, Andrea Faye, Rebecca Wight, the 48 victims of the Greenriver Killer, Renu Puri and Marie and Ruth Richards and Zeinab, and Malatina, and the Montreal engineering students, and the millions of other women we will *not* forget. In their memory, and in the knowledge that we are threatened with the same deaths they suffered, we will continue to expose the misogyny. We will demonstrate how misogyny leads to femicide. And we will commit ourselves to stopping femicide.

SUMMARY AND CONCLUSION

Where Do We Go from Here?

JILL RADFORD

One purpose of this anthology has been to name femicide and to identify it as an urgent issue for feminists and others concerned with violence against women. Diana Russell and I have defined femicide in the context of sexual politics to call attention to and challenge the violence that underlies patriarchal oppression. We see the anthology as a beginning in the work needed to create a political climate in which the death of any woman as a result of femicide cannot go unnoticed but is recognized as an event worthy of comment, anger, and protest. It is, then, a part of the feminist enterprise of creating a world in which the violent subordination of women to men is no longer a fact of life. Imagining a world that is safe for women, safe from male violence, free of sexism, racism, classism, and heterosexism, may in the 1990s seem a Utopian dream. But feminism should not lose sight of its dreams, hopes, and ideals. Without these our politics lose purpose and meaning. Given that this volume is one of the first to deal specifically with femicide, it is perhaps premature to attempt definitive conclusions. Instead, I would like to draw together some of its central themes and to locate these within a feminist analysis.

In gathering writings on femicide from three continents and across a wide historical range, we have illustrated that femicide, far from comprising only random or isolated incidents of sexual terrorism, is extensive. Femicide has cost the lives of thousands of women. If as many deaths had been caused by a disease, there would be a massive outcry—unless, of course, the disease was one like AIDS, which initially afflicted those living on the margins of white heterosexist society. Femicide is a phenomenon that patriarchal interests have taken pains to deny. Rather than allow the extent of femicide to be acknowledged and addressed as a matter of social and political concern, the powerful institutions of patriarchal society, namely, the law, the judiciary, the police, and the media, have largely denied the existence of femicide.

Central among the strategies developed to obscure the issue of femicide is that of individualization. Instances of femicide are constructed as unusual and isolated incidents, or if patterns are noticed and connections made between a series of killings, then these are held to be the results of the actions of isolated and crazed psychopaths rather than a recurring expression of male sexual violence. Jane Caputi makes a similar point: "We are now expected to understand the contemporary terrorization of women, not in political terms, but as the aberrant behavior of mysterious sexual maniacs, preternatural monsters, or in the most acceptable jargon, *psychopaths and sociopaths*" (1987, 109 [Caputi's emphasis]).

Perhaps the most common strategy used to deflect blame from the killer is to blame the victim or some other woman in the killer's life, often his mother, for the killer's psychopathology. Her failure to meet some alleged need in the killer's past is then claimed to have precipitated his act of femicide.

Woman-blaming explanations are used so routinely that they have become a credible part of mainstream discourse, even encoded in law. In English law, for example, *provocation* ("she made me do it") is an accepted defense to murder. The law, in its failure to treat all forms of femicide as violent crime, provides little check on men's behavior and sometimes, as with the defense of provocation, effectively excuses it by refusing to see it through eyes other than those of the "reasonable man" so favored in English jurisprudence.

When it is the victim who is blamed, the dead woman's life-style, behavior, and personality are subject to public scrutiny in the courtroom and in the media. Often it is the killer's reconstruction of the woman's life that is put on trial. Thus the woman has taken from her not only her life but her identity. The ensuing pain to her family and friends is documented throughout this volume. At an ideological level, the image of women as deserving of death is constructed. Through the interactive processes of individualization and woman blaming, the existence of femicide is masked, and men and masculinity are protected as responsibility is shifted onto women, who are then defined variously as inadequate or provocative.

Another theme of the anthology is the failure of the state through its law enforcement and judicial system to offer women protection from femicide. The way the law reaches for defenses to diminish men's responsibility simultaneously denies the dignity of the dead woman and puts other women at greater risk. This failing reflects the general absence of legal protection for women in situations of domestic violence, especially in England. It was only in February 1990 that the British government agreed to reconsider outlawing marital rape, which led to a change in law in 1991.

The failure of the police to act in ways that might protect women from male violence has been well documented by feminists. In relation to femicide, many of the contributions to this volume detail failures in the law enforcement process that have resulted in the deaths of women. The complaints take different forms: failure to recognize deaths by femicide as resulting from the actions of serial killers; failure to give priority to investigations of women's deaths; and failure to respond to calls from women asking for assistance in relation to domestic violence. Underlying this neglect is a failure to value women's lives and to recognize the threat sexual violence poses to women. Parallel to this disregard for women is the problem of police racism. Racism and misogyny often interact to deny black and ethnic minority women the police protection they need. The complaint of police neglect is cross-cultural and long-lived. It cannot be dismissed as the result of the odd mistake in police practice or aberrant actions on the part of individual officers. On the contrary, a structural basis to the problem must be located and repaired.

The failings of the media to represent femicide as a serious crime have also been documented in this anthology. Feminists have long been critical of the media's voyeuristic approach to violence against women and its reproduction of woman-blaming ideology. The treatment of femicide is no exception. The killing of a woman by a stranger in a public place may get front-page coverage, exploited for its ability to sell newspapers. Instances of domestic violence, however, unless somehow spectacular, are subsumed under the category of "family tragedy" and given less attention. The portrayal of femicide in TV dramas and the celebration of famous murderers such as Jack the Ripper also attest to the media's failure to take femicide seriously. The exploitation of femicide as sexual fantasy in pornography is deeply troubling. As Diana Russell argues, although the actual annihilation of women has not been institutionalized, women's annihilation in media representations has.

Radical feminist analysis locates male sexual violence as the form of violence securing the gendered power relations of patriarchy. Liz Kelly and I have argued that "the presence of sexual violence is . . . one of the defining features of a patriarchal society. It is used by men, and often condoned by the state, for a number of specific purposes: to punish women who are seen to be resisting male control; to police women, make them behave or not behave in particular ways; to claim rights of sexual, emotional and domestic servicing; and through all these maintain the relations of patriarchy, male dominance and female subordination" (Kelly and Radford 1987, 238-39). Within this analysis, femicide represents an extreme form of sexual violence. As Diana Russell points out, it is not necessary to argue that the preservation of male supremacy is an actual goal of the men committing femicide to see that it is at the very least one of the consequences of these crimes. What difference does it make for the victims of femicide if their killers are considered mentally ill? Being mentally ill does not free men from their misogyny or racism, so their "illness" is irrelevant to the contention that their femicidal attacks are misogynous acts that serve to perpetuate misogyny. Given that sexual violence and femicide are central to the power relations of patriarchy, challenges to this violence constitute a profound challenge to patriarchy itself. In this way working against femicide is fundamentally political work.

In light of recent developments in work on sexual violence in the United Kingdom, I want to argue that it is vital not to lose sight of the essentially political nature of resistance to it. The United Kingdom is witnessing a trend on the part of the police, social workers, lawyers, professional counselors, and therapists to engage in and build careers on work dealing with sexual violence. Long criticized for their failure to respond to the problem of sexual violence, these professionals have now begun to move in. Their response to male violence is at the level of service provision, but it often takes place within a political framework that defines women and children as helpless victims who are responsible for the violence they experience by virtue of their assumed inadequacies. Consequently, they are seen as being in need of professional help to relocate them within their role as defined by patriarchy. This trend is illustrated by the establishment of nonfeminist refuges for women who have experienced domestic violence in which therapy is a condition of entry; victim support programs in which men are encouraged to support women who have experienced rape to try to ensure that these women will not reject men and to facilitate their rapid readjustment to active heterosexuality; the provision of family therapy for survivors of child sexual abuse that locates responsibility for the abuse within the entire family and defines mothers and survivors as collusive in that abuse.

While some feminists have demanded state recognition of and action against male sexual violence, the ensuing response often severely compromises feminist values. The danger lies in the tendency of those who accept patriarchal values to force a separation of feminist support services from their political roots. This separation has allowed the mental health community to appropriate service provision, with perhaps some lip service to feminist work. But the political base is transformed into one that can be comfortably accommodated within an antifeminist professional practice. In this process feminist politics are negated and replaced by an antifeminism rooted in an ideology that essentially blames the victim. The divisiveness of this response is posing difficulties for feminist activists working in the area, particularly because the state, having developed alternative professional services, is withdrawing funding from feminist services, such as rape crisis centers and women's refuges.

Because of the nature of femicide, in which there is no victim to be offered support, the attending issues are somewhat different. But the potential for a similar divisiveness exists here, too. It is important to demand that the problem of femicide be recognized; yet it is also important that professionals in mental health, law enforcement, and the judicial system be prevented from appropriating the problem of femicide and relocating it in their own agendas, agendas that may be informed by antifeminism, racism, and heterosexism. This is why it is necessary to recognize the political nature of the struggle against femicide.

The radical feminism outlined here, however, is different from that of the early 1970s. It is a feminism that perceives male sexual violence as the basis for securing the gendered power relations of patriarchy. But it is also a feminism that recognizes the differences among women in terms of their relationship to the other power structures present in patriarchal societies, differences that structure both femicide itself and the state's response to it.

In Western industrialized societies women are divided by the class relations of late capitalism; the racism of postcolonialism; sexuality (where heterosexuality, and with it male control of women at the most personal of levels, is deemed compulsory); and ageism. In theoretical terms, contemporary radical feminism recognizes the complexity of these interactive structures and their different impacts on women. In activist terms, many radical feminists have recognized both the power and the limitations that attend such politics. While identification with one's own group can be an important source of strength and confirmation, it also has the potential for creating divisiveness and reproducing the oppressions of the larger society, namely, classism, racism, heterosexism, and ageism. In response, many activists are beginning to explore the possibilities of creating alliances against sexual violence and femicide that cross over these boundaries.

The readings in part 6 of this book, "Women Fighting Back against Femicide," explore the challenges facing coalitions and alliances made up of women from different backgrounds and with different political priorities. While this kind of work will take time—to build trust, to work out nonexclusive ways of working, to plan, even to make mistakes—it does seem to have a greater potential for mounting a stronger challenge to the threat of femicide than does a partial-politics approach that can be easily appropriated by defenders of patriarchy into agendas of their own.

Traditionally, state reforms are limited; they address problems that prior political campaigns have forced onto the agenda. A typical response is for the state to recognize a problem in order to contain the protest, doing so in a way that poses no real threat to established interests or values. This suggests that if and when the state is forced to recognize femicide as a problem, it will seek to redefine it in a way that minimizes its threat to the patriarchal status quo. This will require a reformulation of the problem that inevitably excludes feminist analysis. It is possible to imagine, for example, an authoritarian government interpreting a feminist concern about femicide as support for law-and-order politics.

Even if some acknowledgment of the gendered nature of femicide is accommodated, it would of necessity be partial. Likewise any remedy would be partial. Existing protections against male violence—the laws around rape, for example—protect only those women defined as "deserving" according to patriarchal standards, that is, women privileged by class, race, and relationship to heterosexuality. If antiracism, antiheterosexism, and anticlass privilege are foregrounded in our politics, perhaps this bias can be resisted.

A lot can be learned from the formation of alliances among women with different positions in relation to patriarchy. From reading black women's accounts and by networking, I have come to understand why the issues of race and racism are inseparable from any struggle they enter. The selections by and about black women in this anthology demonstrate that a struggle against femicide must be a struggle against racism as well, whether it is the racism of femicidal killers, the police, the legal system, pornographers, or the racism of white feminists participating in the struggle. It is uncomfortable for white feminists to be confronted with their own racism. As white women, we are accorded a certain privilege so routinely that it is hard for us to see it. Identifying the ways in which this racism can disable us in our work with black and minority women is difficult, as is acknowledging how much we need to learn and unlearn. But the alternative, in my experience, is resentment, confused silences, political inaction, and failure of feminism.

Similarly, recognizing heterosexuality as a major force in society is essential to understanding the impact of femicide on lesbian communities. Without such an understanding, any analysis of femicide will be partial, distorted, and inadequate. Heterosexism, as is documented in the anthology, can motivate and legitimize femicidal attacks on lesbians. It can result in the femicide of known or suspected lesbians not being taken seriously by the police and in the acceptance of antilesbianism as mitigation in the courts. From the United Kingdom there is evidence that lesbians who report violence are harassed and arrested by the police and that the police use murder investigations as "trawling exercise" to obtain and record information about the lesbian community that is spurious to the investigation at hand but useful to police data banks.[1]

Another way in which femicide affects the lesbian community is that it can lead to the denial of lesbian relationships. History is full of examples of how lesbian partnerships are denied, how the most significant relationships of lesbians sufficiently well known to have biographies published about them are excluded from those biographies. The denial of a woman's lesbian identity represents a posthumous insult and a gross lack of respect for that woman's life. It also hurts some of the individuals who were close to the dead woman. Bereaved lesbians may find their relationships are not recognized in grieving rituals, for example, making the nightmare even harder to bear. The development of support services for the bereaved is one way the gay community has had to respond to the AIDS crisis. Similar support work is necessary in the short term to deal with instances of antilesbian femicide. In her poem "Womanslaughter," Pat Parker writes,

> I will not pick the right flowers
> I will not celebrate her death
> and it will matter not
> if she's black or white—
> if she loves women or men.

This is the spirit we must embrace if we are to combat femicide successfully .

There are presumably as many ways to fight femicide as there are women willing to engage in the struggle. Our campaigns may be waged in our communities, our places of work, around centers of government, in the courtroom, or in the media. Letters can be written to parliamentarians or legislators and to the press; informed comment can be made in poems, novels, plays, performance art, the visual arts, music, and dance; protest can be joined through participation in marches, vigils, or abseilings.[2] The history of women's struggles is testimony to our powers of imagination once an issue is named.

There is also a need for more research on femicide. Feminist concepts of research are broad. They include academic work, as illustrated in some of the selections here, but also networking in the community, reading local newspapers and magazines, and listening to other women's stories. One huge gap we discovered in putting together this book was our limited knowledge of the impact of and resistance to femicide in cultures other than our own, particularly in the Third World. Eastern Europe is another area about which Western knowledge is limited. It may not be our place as First World women to tell these women's stories in their stead, but we can make ourselves accessible to them and offer support in terms of access to our resources. Global resistance to femicide requires an international network that includes those women most often excluded.

Another important area is support work with women who have lost friends, family, or lovers as a result of femicide. Having been there, I know there is a need. This means finding ways of reaching women, knowing when to offer support and when this might be an intrusion, learning how to support one another through grief and anger, learning how to hear the pain without having it undermine one's own strength, learning the skills of survival. As firm as we are in our resistance to femicide, we must be equally firm in our support for one another. Work on femicide is one of the most grueling feminist enterprises. It can, unless we are careful with one another, burn us out quickly. To avoid burnout, I would also argue that it is essential to hold onto our ideals and dreams of a world free from sexism, racism, heterosexism, and other oppressions that divide us from one another. It is in these cracks and divisions that woman hatred, the ideology of femicide, is nurtured.

Notes

1. Lesbian and Policing Project, *Annual Report* (London: LESPOP, 1988).

2. "Abseiling" is a reference to a celebrated action in which several lesbians in 1988 abseiled, or descended, from the public gallery to the debating floor of the House of Lords to protest Parliament's attempt to legalize discrimination against lesbians and gay men in the provision of local authority-funded services such as education, library services, social services, and arts programs.

References

Caputi, Jane. 1987. *The Age of Sex Crime.* Bowling Green, Ohio: Bowling Green State University Popular Press; London: Women's Press.

Kelly, Liz, and Jill Radford. 1987. "The Problem of Men." In *Law, Order, and the Authoritarian State,* ed. Phil Scraton. Milton Keynes, England: Open University Press.

is not so gd to be born a girl (I)

NTOZAKE SHANGE

Is not so gd to be born a girl/ some times. that's why societies usedta throw us
away/ or sell us/ or play with our vaginas/ cuz that's all girls were gd for/ at least
women cd carry things & cook/ but to be born a girl is not good sometimes/
some places/ such abominable things cd happen to us. i wish it waz gd to be
born a girl everywhere/ then i wd know for sure that no one wd be infibulated/
that's a word no one wants us to know/ "infibulation" is sewing our vaginas up
with cat gut or weeds or nylon thread to insure our virginity/ virginity insurance
= infibulation/ that can also make it impossible for us to live thru labor/ make it
impossible for the baby to live thru labor/ infibulation lets us get infections that
we cant mention cuz disease in the ovaries is a sign that we're dirty anyway/ so
wash yrself cuz once infibulated we have to be cut open to have you know what/
the joy of the phallus/ that we may know nothing abt/ ever/ especially if
something else not good that happens to little girls happens/ if we've been
excised/ had our labia removed with glass or scissors/ if we've lost our clitoris
because our pleasure is profane & the presence of our naturally evolved clitoris
wd disrupt the very unnatural dynamic of polygamy/ so with no clitoris, no
labia, & infibulation/ we're sewn-up, cut-up, pared down & sore if not dead/ &
oozing puss, if not terrified that so much of our body waz wrong & did not
belong on earth/ such thoughts lead to a silence/ that hangs behind veils &
straight jackets/ it really is not so good to be born a girl when we have to be
infibulated, excised, clitorectomized & still be afraid to walk the streets or stay
home at night.

i'm so saddened that being born a girl makes it dangerous to attend midnight
mass unescorted. some places if we're born girls & some one else who's very
sick & weak & cruel/ attacks us & breaks our hymen/ we have to be killed/ sent
away from our families/ forbidden to touch our children. These strange people

Reprinted from *Black Scholar*, May–June 1979, 28–29.

who wound little girls are known as attackers, molesters, & rapists. they are known all over the world & are proliferating at a rapid rate. to be born a girl who will always have to worry not only abt the molesters, the attackers & the rapists/ but also abt their peculiarities/ does he stab too/ or shoot/ does he carry an ax/ does he spit on you/ does he know if he doesn't drop sperm we cant prove we've been violated/ those subtlties make being a girl too complex/ for some of us & we go crazy/ or never go anyplace.

some of us have never had an open window or a walk alone/ but sometimes our homes are not safe for us either/ rapists & attackers & molesters are not strangers to everyone/ they are related to somebody/ & some of them like raping & molesting their family members better than a girl-child they don't know yet/ this is called incest & girl children are discouraged from revealing attacks from uncle or daddy/ cuz what wd mommy do/ after all daddy may have seen to it that abortions were outlawed in his state/ so that mommy might have too many children/ to care abt some "fun" daddy might have been having with the 2 year old/ she's a girl after all/ we have to get used to it/ but infibulation, excision, clitorectomies, rape, & incest/ are irrevocable life-deniers/ life-stranglers & disrespectful of natural elements/ i wish these things wdnt happen anywhere anymore/ then i cd say it waz gd to be born a girl everywhere/ even though gender is not destiny/ right now being born a girl is to be born threatened/ i dont respond well to threats/ i want being born a girl to be a cause for celebration/ cause for protection & nourishment of our birthright/ to live freely with passion, knowing no fear/ that our species waz somehow incorrect.

& we are now plagued with rapists & clitorectomies. we pay for being born girls/ but we owe no one anything/ not our labia, not our clitoris, not our lives. we are born girls & live to be women who live our own lives/ to live our lives/
    to have/
    our lives/
    to live.

Sources

SELECTED BIBLIOGRAPHY
Compiled by Diana E. H. Russell

Books

Abrahamsen, David. 1985. *Confessions of Son of Sam*. New York: Columbian University Press.

Banks, Harold K. 1967. *The Strangler: The Story of Terror in Boston*. New York: Avon Books.

Barnard, Alan, ed. 1953. *The Harlot Killer: Jack the Ripper*. New York: Dodd, Mead & Co.

Bean, Constance. Forthcoming. *Women Murdered by Men They Love*. New York: Haworth Press.

Beattie, John. 1981. *The Yorkshire Ripper Story*. London: Quartet Books.

Biondi, Ray, and Walt Hecox. 1988. *All His Father's Sons: Inside the Gerald Gallego Sex-slave Murders*. Rocklin, Calif.: Prima Publishing.

Blashfield, Jean F. 1990. *Why They Killed*. New York: Warner Books.

Cameron, Deborah, and Elizabeth Frazer. 1987. *The Lust to Kill: A Feminist Investigation of Sexual Murder*. New York: New York University Press.

Caputi, Jane. 1987. *The Age of Sex Crime*. Bowling Green, Ohio: Bowling Green State University Popular Press.

Cheney, Margaret. 1976. *The Coed Killer*. New York: Walker & Co.

Chimbos, Peter D. 1978. *Marital Violence: A Study of Interspousal Homicide*. San Francisco: R & E Research Associates.

Crimes and Punishments: A Pictorial Encyclopedia of Aberrant Behavior. 1973. England: Phoebus Publishing.

I am grateful to Laura X, Jane Caputi, Roberta Harmes, Jill Radford, and, most particularly, Chris Domingo for their assistance in compiling this bibliography.

Cullen, Tom A. 1965. *When London Walked in Terror*. Boston: Houghton Mifflin Co.

Daly, Martin, and Margot Wilson. 1988. *Homicide*. Hawthorne, N.Y.: Aldine de Gruyter.

Daly, Mary. 1978. *Gyn/Ecology: The Metaethics of Radical Feminism*. Boston: Beacon Press.

Dillman, John. 1986. *Unholy Matrimony: A True Story of Murder and Obsession*. New York: Macmillan.

Dworkin, Andrea. 1974. *Woman Hating*. New York: Dutton.

Ehrenrich, Barbara, and Deirdre English. 1976. *Witches, Midwives, and Nurses*. London: Writers and Readers.

Ewing, Charles Patrick. 1990. *When Children Kill: The Dynamics of Juvenile Homicide*. Lexington, Mass.: Lexington Books.

Farsen, Daniel. 1972. *Jack the Ripper*. London: Michael Joseph.

Frank, Gerold. 1966. *The Boston Strangler*. New York: New American Library.

Frondorf, Shirley. 1988. *Death of a "Jewish American Princess": The Story of a Victim on Trial*. New York: Villard Books.

Gaylin, Willard. 1982. *The Killing of Bonnie Garland*. New York: Simon & Schuster.

Gordon, Paul, and Phil Scraton, eds. 1984. *Causes for Concern*. London: Penguin.

Gore, Tipper (Mary Elizabeth). 1987. *Raising PG Kids in an X-rated Society*. Nashville: Abingdon Press.

Hanmer, Jalna, and Sheila Saunders. 1984. *Well-founded Fear: A Community Study of Violence against Women*. London: Hutchinson.

_____, and Mary Maynard, eds. 1987. *Women, Violence, and Social Control*. London: Macmillan.

_____, Jill Radford, and Elizabeth A. Stanko. 1989. *Women, Policing, and Male Violence*. London: Routledge.

Hawkins, Darnell F., ed. 1986. *Homicide among Black Americans*. New York: University Press of America.

Hester, Marianne. 1992. *Lewd Women and Wicked Witches: The Dynamics of Male Domination*. London: Routledge.

Holliday, Laurel. 1978. *The Violent Sex: Male Psychobiology and the Evolution of Consciousness*. Guerneville, Calif.: Bluestocking Books.

Holmes, Ronald M. 1989. *Profiling Violent Crimes: An Investigative Tool*. Newbury Park, Calif.: Sage Publications.

_____. 1991. *Sex Crimes*. Newbury Park, Calif.: Sage Publications.

_____, and James De Burger. 1988. *Serial Murder*. Newbury Park, Calif.: Sage Publications.

Kelly, Liz. 1988. *Surviving Sexual Violence*. Cambridge, England: Polity Press.

Kendall, Elizabeth. 1981. *The Phantom Prince: My Life with Ted Bundy*. Seattle: Madrona Press.

Klausner, Lawrence D. 1981. *Son of Sam*. New York: McGraw-Hill.

Krafft-Ebing, Richard von. 1965. *Psychopathia Sexualis*. New York: Stein & Day.

Larsen, Richard W. 1908. *Bundy: The Deliberate Stranger*. Englewood Cliffs, N.J.: Prentice-Hall.

Levin, Jack, and James A. Fox. 1985. *Mass Murder: America's Growing Menace*. New York: Plenum.

Leyton, Elliott. 1986. *Hunting Humans: Inside the Minds of Mass Murderers*. New York: Pocket Books.

Lindecker, Clifford L. 1990. *To Love, Honor, and Kill*. New York: Knightsbridge Publishing.

Lunde, Donald T. 1976. *Murder and Madness*. New York: W. W. Norton.

McGinniss, Joe. 1983. *Fatal Vision*. New York: New American Library.

Malette, Louise, and Marie Chalou. 1991. *The Montreal Massacre*. Trans. Marlene Wildman. Prince Edward Island: Gynergy Books.

Masters, R. E. L., and Eduard Lea. 1963. *Sex Crimes in History*. New York: Julian Press.

Meyer, Peter. 1982. *The Yale Murder*. New York: Empire Books.

Michaud, Stephen C., and Hugh Aynesworth. 1983. *The Only Living Witness*. New York: Linden Press.

_____. *Wanted for Murder*. 1990. New York: Penguin Books.

Morneau, Robert H., and Robert R. Rockwell. 1980. *Sex, Motivation, and the Criminal Offender*. Springfield, Ill.: Charles Thomas.

Mowat, Ronald R. 1966. *Morbid Jealousy and Murder: A Psychiatric Study of Morbidly Jealous Murderers at Broadmoor*. London: Tavistock.

Norris, Joel. 1988. *Serial Killers: The Growing Menace*. New York: Dolphin/Doubleday.

O'Brien, Darcy. 1985. *Two of a Kind: The Hillside Stranglers*. New York: New American Library.

Pagelow, Mildred Daley. 1984. *Family Violence*. New York: Praeger Publishers.

Ressler, Robert K., Ann W. Burgess, and John E. Douglas. 1988. *Sexual Homicide: Patterns and Motives*. Lexington, Mass.: Lexington Books.

Rhodes, Dusty, and Sandra McNeill, eds. 1985. *Women against Violence against Women*. London: Onlywomen Press.

Rule, Ann. 1980. *The Stranger Beside Me*. New York: New American Library.

Rumbelow, Donald. 1975. *The Complete Jack the Ripper*. Boston: New York Graphic Society.

Saldana, Theresa. 1987. *Beyond Survival*. New York: Bantam.

Schechter, Harold. 1989. *Deviant: The Horrifying True Story of Ed Gein—The Original Psycho*. New York: Pocket Books.

Schwartz, Ted. 1981. *The Hillside Strangler: A Murder's Mind*. Garden City, N.Y. Doubleday.

Secrest, William B. 1967. *Juanita: The Only Woman Lynched in the Gold Rush Days*. Fresno, Calif.: Saga-West Publishing.

Wilson, Colin. 1969. *A Casebook of Murder*. London: Leslie Frewin.

_____, and Robin Odell. 1987. *Jack the Ripper: Summing Up and Verdict*. New York: Bantam.

Winn, Steven, and David Merrill. 1979. *Ted Bundy: The Killer Next Door*. New York: Bantam.

Articles, Pamphlets, and Parts of Books

Anony Ms. 1984. "Mr. Normal Meets the Beast, or How 'The Yorkshire Ripper' Became Peter Sutcliffe." *Women Studies International Forum* 7, no. 1.

Baig, Tara Ali. 1988. "Sati, Women's Status and Religious Fundamentalism." *Social Action* 38, no. 1.

Bal, Vidya. 1990. "Fighting Wife Abuse in India." *Off Our Backs*, March.

Barnard, George W., Hernan Vera, Maria I. Vera, and Gustave Newman. 1982. "Till Death Do Us Part: A Study of Spouse Murder." *Bulletin of the American Academy of Psychiatry and Law* 10.

Black Coalition Fighting Back Serial Murders. 1991. "Counting Women's Lives: Organizing for Police Accountability in Black Communities." Sample organizing packet.

Blue, Woody. 1991. "Billboard Action Delivers." *Off Our Backs,* February.

Bordewick, Fergus. 1986. "Dowry Murders." *Atlantic Monthly,* July.

Brownmiller, Susan. 1975. "Rape-murder." In *Against Our Will,* ed. Susan Brownmiller. New York: Simon & Schuster.

Burgess, Ann W., Carol R. Hartman, Robert K. Ressler, John E. Douglas, and Arlene McCormack. 1986. "Sexual Homicide: A Motivational Model." *Journal of Interpersonal Violence* 1, no. 3.

Campbell, Jacquelyn. 1980. "Misogyny and Homicide of Women." *Advances in Nursing Science* 3, no. 2.

Caputi, Jane. 1989. "The Sexual Politics of Murder." *Gender and Society* 3, no. 4.

_____. 1990. "The New Founding Fathers: The Lore and Lure of the Serial Killer in Contemporary Culture." *Journal of American Culture,* Fall.

_____. 1992. "To Acknowledge and to Heal: Twenty Years of Feminist Thought and Activism on Sexual Violence." In *The Knowledge Explosion,* ed. Dale Spender and Cherris Craneberry. New York: Teachers College Press.

Carpenter, Teresa. 1980. "Death of a Playmate." *Village Voice,* 5-11 November.

Clarke, D. A. 1981. "The Incredible Case of 'The Stack o' Prints Mutilations.'" *Quest: A Feminist Quarterly* 5, no. 3.

Clover, Carol J. 1987. "Her Body, Himself: Gender in the Slasher Film." *Representations* 20 (Fall).

Combahee River Collective. 1981. "Twelve Black Women: Why Did They Die?" In *Fight Back,* ed. Frédérique Delacoste and Felice Newman. Minneapolis: Cleis Press.

Cowles, Kathleen V. 1988. "Personal World Expansion for Survivors of Murder Victims." *Western Journal of Nursing Research* 10, no. 6.

Craft, Nikki. 1992. *Nemesis.* Rancho Cordova, Calif.: A.C.L.U. Nemesis Publishing Concern.

Crompton, Louis. 1980-81. "The Myth of Lesbian Impunity: Capital Laws from 1270 to 1791." *Journal of Homosexuality* 6, nos. 1-2.

Daly, Martin, and Margot Wilson. 1988. "Evolutionary Social Psychology and Family Homicide. *Science* 242.

_____. 1990. "Killing the Competition." *Human Nature* 1.

Davids, Diana. 1992. "Inside Story: The Serial Murderer as Superstar." *McCall's,* February.

Davis, Lisa. 1991. "I Remember: Daddy Did It." *This World, San Francisco Chronicle,* 29 September.

Dietz, Park E. 1985. "Hypothetical Criteria for the Prediction of Individual Criminality." In *Dangerousness: Probability and Prediction, Psychiatry and Public Policy,* ed. Christopher Webster, Mark Ben-Aron, and Stephen Hucker. New York: Cambridge University Press.

_____. 1986. "Detective Magazines: Pornography for the Sexual Sadist?" *Journal of Forensic Sciences* 31, no. 1.

_____. 1986. "Mass, Serial, and Sensational Homicides." *Bulletin of the New York Academy of Medicine* 62, no. 5.

_____. 1987. "Patterns in Human Violence." In *American Psychiatric Association Annual Review* 6. Washington, D.C.: American Psychiatric Press.

Dobson, James. 1989. "Interview with Serial Sex Killer Theodore Bundy." Pamphlet distributed by CDL, copyright by Focus on the Family, March.

Domingo, Chris. 1990. "We Are More Than Fourteen." *Off Our Backs,* February.

Doudna, Christine. 1990. "Ending the Rape of Our Liberty." *McCall's,* May.

Dreschler, Debbie. 1979. "Silkwood Family Sues Nuclear Plant." *New Women's Times*, 16 February.

Dufresne, Martin. 1990. "Focus on Gynocide in Montreal." *Between the Lines*, 18-31 January.

Dworkin, Andrea. 1981. "The Marquis de Sade (1740–1814)." In Andrea Dworkin, *Pornography: Men Possessing Women*. New York: E. P. Dutton.

Edwards, Susan. 1986. " 'Provoking Her Own Demise': From Common Assault to Homicide." In *Women, Violence, and Social Control*, ed. Jalna Hanmer and Mary Maynard. London: Macmillan.

Egger, Steven A. 1984. "A Working Definition of Serial Murder and the Reduction of Linkage Blindness." *Journal of Police Science and Administration* 12, no. 3.

Ehrenreich, Barbara, and Deirdre English. 1976. "Burn Witch, Burn." *Women: A Journal of Liberation* 3, no. 2.

Ericksson, Brigette. 1981. "A Lesbian Execution in Germany, 1721: The Trial Records." *Journal of Homosexuality* 6, nos. 1-2.

Firstman, Richard C. 1990. "The Last Year of April LaSalata." *Newsday Magazine*, 28 January.

Frenkel, F. E. 1964. "Sex-crime and Its Sociohistorical Background." *Journal of the History of Ideas* 25.

Friedman, Deb, and Lois Yankowski. 1976. "Snuffing Sexual Violence." *Quest* 3, no. 2.

Frye, Ellen. 1978. "Abused Women: Two Freed, Three Murdered, Wife-killer Walked." *Off Our Backs* 8, no. 2.

Goodman, Melissa. 1988. "Who's on Trial Here? Four Other Victims Who Were Blamed." *Redbook*, June.

Graysmith, Robert. 1986. *Zodiac*. New York: St. Martins.

Hazlewood, Robert R., and John E. Douglas. 1980. "The Lust Murderer." *FBI Law Enforcement Bulletin* 49, no. 4.

Heise, Lori. 1989. "Crimes of Gender." *World Watch*, March-April.

_____. 1989. "The Global War against Women." *Utne Reader*, November-December.

Holmes, Helen B., and Betty B. Hoskins. 1985. "Prenatal and Preconception Sex Choice Technologies: A Path to Femicide?" In *Man-made Women*, ed. Gena Corea et al. London: Hutchinson.

Humphrey, John A., R. Page Hudson, and Steven Cosgrove. 1981–82. "Women Who Are Murdered: An Analysis of 912 Consecutive Victims." *OMEGA* 12, no. 3.

Jarvis, Michaela. 1989. "The Meaning of Fear." *Express*, 8 December.

Jordan, Nick. 1985. "Till Murder Do Us Part." *Psychology Today*, July.

Kannabiran, Vasantha. 1986. "Report from SSS, a Women's Group in Hyderabad, Andhra Pradesh, India." *Feminist Studies* 12, no. 3.

Karkaria, Bachi J. 1972. "Raped Women of Bangladesh." *Illustrated Weekly of India*, 18 June.

LaFuente, Chris. 1991. "Stopping the War against Women on the Homefront." *Off Our Backs*, April.

Lastreto, Nikki, with William Winans. 1989. "The High Price of Marriage in India: Burning Brides." *This World, San Francisco Chronicle*, 2 July.

Laurino, Maria. 1987. "Prosecuting Jennifer Levin's Killer: A Sensational Homicide Presents a New Challenge for Assistant D.A. Linda Fairstein." *Ms.*, September.

Leidholdt, Dorchen. 1983. "Coalition Stops 'Snuff.' " *Newsreport (Women against Pornography)* 5, no. 2.

Levy, Jerrold E., Stephen J. Kunitz, and Michael Everett. 1969. "Navajo Criminal Homicide." *Southwestern Journal of Anthropology* 25, no. 2.

Lindsey, Robert. 1984. "Officials Cite Rise in Killers Who Roam U.S. for Victims." *New York Times*, 21 January.

The Link—The McGill Daily; Joint Special Issue [on the Montreal Massacre]. 1989. Montreal: McGill and Concordia Universities.

Magnuson, Ed. 1976. "Death by Gun: America's Toll in One Typical Week." *Time*, 17 July.

Mahoney, Martha R. 1991. "Legal Images of Battered Women: Redefining the Issue of Separation." *Michigan Law Review* 90, no. 1.

Mani, Lata. 1990. "Contentious Traditions: The Debate on Sati in Colonial India." In *Recasting Women*, ed. Kumkum Sangari and Sudesh Vaid. New Brunswick, N.J.: Rutgers University Press.

Matalene, Carolyn. 1978. "Women as Witches." *International Journal of Women's Studies* 1, no. 6.

Mercy, James A. Forthcoming. "Men, Women, and Murder: Gender-Specific Differences in Rates of Fatal Violence and Victimization." *Journal of Trauma*.

_____, and Linda E. Saltzman. "Fatal Violence among Spouses in the United States." *American Journal of Public Health* 79, no. 5.

Patel, Vibhuti. 1989. "Sex Discrimination and Sex Preselection Tests in India: Recent Techniques in Femicide." *Reproductive and Genetic Engineering* 2, no. 2.

Pharr, Suzanne. 1990. "Hate Violence against Women." *Transformation* 5, no. 1.

Piers, Maria W. 1978. "About Wet Nurses." In *Infanticide Past and Present*, ed. Maria W. Piers. New York: W. W. Norton.

Pogrebin, Letty C. 1989. "Boys Will Be Boys?" *Ms.*, September.

Ressler, Robert K., Ann W. Burgess, Carol R. Hartman, John E. Douglas, and Arlene McCormack. 1986. "Murderers Who Rape and Mutilate." *Journal of Interpersonal Violence* 1, no. 3.

_____, Ann W. Burgess, John E. Douglas, Carol R. Hartman, and Ralph B. D'Agostino. 1986. "Sexual Killers and Their Victims: Identifying Patterns through Crime Scene Analysis." *Journal of Interpersonal Violence* 1, no. 3.

Revitch, Eugene. 1990. "Gynocide and Unprovoked Attacks on Women." *Journal of Corrective Social Psychiatry* 26, no. 2.

Rimmel, Lesley. 1983. "Seeing Snuff." *Newsreport (Women against Pornography)* 5, no. 2.

Roggencamp, Viola. 1984. "Abortion of a Special Kind: Male Sex Selection in India." In *Test-Tube Women: What Future for Motherhood?* ed. Rita Arditti, Renate Klein, and Shelley Minden. London: Pandora Press.

Ruether, Rosemary. 1974. "The Persecution of Witches: A Case of Sexism and Ageism?" *Christianity and Crisis* 34, no. 22.

Russell, Diana E. H. 1982. "Femicide: The Murder of Wives." In *Rape in Marriage*, ed. Diana E. H. Russell. New York: Macmillan.

_____. 1989. "Sexism, Violence, and the Nuclear Mentality." In *Exposing Nuclear Phallacies*, ed. Diana E. H. Russell. New York: Pergamon Press.

Schwartz, Ted, and Kelli Boyd. 1981. "Kenneth Bianchi: Inside the Mind of the 'Hillside Strangler.'" *Hustler*, August.

Sedgwick, John. "A Case of Wife Murder." *Esquire*, June.

Sen, Amartya. 1990. "More Than 100 Million Women Are Missing." *New York Review of Books*, 20 December.

"7 Deadly Days." 1989. *Time,* 17 July.

Showalter, C. Robert, Richard J. Bonnie, and Virginia Roddy. 1980. "The Spouse Homicide Syndrome." *Bulletin of the American Academy of Psychiatry and Law* 8.

Smith, Joan. 1982. "Getting Away with Murder." *New Socialist,* May-June.

Smith, Pamela. 1989. "Perfect Murderers." *New Statesman and Society,* 7 July.

Soman, Alfred. 1986. "Witch Lynching at Juniville." *Natural History* 95, October.

Sonnenschein, Allan, and Hugh Aynesworth. 1985. "Serial Killers: Henry Lee Lucas, 'Killing Every Way Know to Man.' " *Penthouse,* February.

Stanko, Elizabeth. 1985. "The Rhetoric of Protection." In *Intimate Intrusions: Women's Experience of Male Violence,* ed. Elizabeth Stanko. Boston: Routledge.

Stanley, Liz. 1985. "Accounting for the Fall of Peter Sutcliffe, and the Rise of the So-called Yorkshire Ripper." *Manchester University Occasional Papers* 15.

Starr, Mark. 1984. "The Random Killers." *Newsweek,* 26 November.

Stuart, Ellen P., and Jacquelyn C. Campbell. 1989. "Assessment of Patterns of Dangerousness with Battered Women." *Issues in Mental Health Nursing* 10.

Summers, Anne. 1989. "The Hedda Conundrum." *Ms.,* April.

Swigert, Victoria L., Ronald A. Farrell, and William C. Yoels. 1976. "Sexual Homicide: Social, Psychological, and Legal Aspects." *Archives of Sexual Behavior* 5, no. 5.

"Symposium on Feminists Targeted for Murder: Montreal 1989." 1991. *Feminist Issues* 11, no. 2.

Walker, Lenore E. 1989. "Facing My Own Terror." In *Terrifying Love: Why Women Kill and How Society Responds,* ed. Lenore Walker. New York: Harper & Row.

Walkowitz, Judith. 1982. "Jack the Ripper and the Myth of Male Violence." *Feminist Studies* 8.

Weaver, Carolyn. 1984. "The Killing of Laura." *Mother Jones.* February-March.

West, Rachel. 1987. "U.S. PROStitutes Collective." In *Sex Work: Writings by Women in the Sex Industry,* ed. Frédérique Delacoste and Priscilla Alexander. Pittsburgh: Cleis Press.

Wilbanks, William. 1982. "Murdered Women and Women Who Murder: A Critique of the Literature." In *Judge, Lawyer, Victim, and Thief,* ed. Nicole Rafter and Elizabeth Stanko. Boston: Northeastern University Press.

Wolfgang, Marvin. 1956. "Husband-wife Homicides." *Journal of Social Therapy* 2.

Women We Honour Action Committee and Rosemary Gartner. 1990. *Annotated Bibliography of Works Reviewed for Project on Intimate Femicide.*

Women We Honour Action Committee and Rosemary Gartner. 1990. *Final Report to the Ontario Women's Directorate: Research Project on Homicides Related to Domestic Violence against Women.*

Wood, Chriss, Deborah Shug, Doug Smith, and Tom Regan. 1988. "Killers at Large." *Maclean's,* 18 July.

Wowk, Maria. 1984. "Blame Allocation, Sex, and Gender in a Murder Interrogation." *Women's Studies International Forum* 7, no. 1.

ORGANIZATIONS

Compiled by Chris Domingo and Diana E. H. Russell

Black Coalition Fighting Back Serial Murders, P.O. Box 86681, Los Angeles, CA 90086-0681. Founded in January 1986 out of concern for the many unsolved serial femicides of mainly black women occurring in south central Los Angeles.

Body Counts, published monthly by the Lesbian Community Project's "Urban Amazons," P.O. Box 5931, Portland, OR 97228. First published in 1991 to provide a comprehensive chronological listing of and commentary on acts of violence against women, including femicide, in the metropolitan Portland area.

Campus Violence Prevention, Administration Building, Room 108, Towson State University, Towson, MD 21204. Conducts nationwide surveys on campus violence. Research specialist available for consultation.

Clearinghouse on Femicide, P.O. Box 12342, Berkeley, CA 94701-3342. Founded in 1989 as a loose collective of women engaged in research, education, and protest action. Publishes a quarterly newsletter, *Memory and Rage,* and makes research materials available through an extensive computer bank and archive. Also coordinates a support network for women who have lost a family member or friend through femicide.

Clothesline Project, P.O. Box 822, Brewster, MA 02631. Founded in 1990 and run by a coalition of women who invite others to make shirts for clotheslines in more than a dozen states in memory of women who have been victimized by violence, including, but not confined to, femicide. The shirts are color coded according to type of violence; shirts in memory of femicide victims are white. For information on where to send shirts, write to Rachel Carey-Harper at the above address.

Coalition to Stop the Green River Murders, 2536 Alki Ave. SW, Box 129, Seattle, WA 98116. Formed in Seattle in 1983 as an educational and political action group to try to stop the Green River serial killer. The coalition conducts archival research and indexes information about national and international cases of serial murder.

Donna Fitzgerald Daigneau Fund, First National Bank, 324 State St., Portsmouth, NH 03801. Established in memory of Donna and three of her friends, all killed by Donna's husband. Raises money for women's shelters in New Hampshire and Kentucky.

Family Violence Network, P.O. Box 854, Lake Elmo, MN 55042. The Minnesota Coalition for Battered Women monitors information about femicides throughout Minnesota and reports them in the Family Violence Network newsletter, *Networker.*

I.L.K.A. (Information, Love, Knowledge, Action), P.O. Box 357, Arnold, MD 21012. Gisela Dibble founded I.L.K.A. after her daughter, Ilka, was murdered, then raped, by a boyfriend. Dibble is waging a battle in Maryland to establish sexual assault on a dead woman as a crime so that such offenders can be charged with first-degree murder.

Justice for All, 11 Park Place, New York, NY 10007. Founded in 1989 by Ellen Levin and Dennis Holland to advance victims' rights through legislation. Levin's daughter, Jennifer, was raped and murdered by Robert Chambers in Central Park; Holland's sister, Kathleen, was murdered by her boyfriend. Both attorneys for the murderers used the "rough sex" defense.

Security on Campus, Suite 105, 618 Shoemaker Rd., Gulph Mills, PA 19406. Founded by Connie and Howard Clery, whose daughter, Jeannie, was raped, tortured, and murdered on a university campus by a fellow student in 1986. Provides the information needed to pursue legal cases against colleges and universities on behalf of the victims and survivors of campus violence. Has lobbied successfully for state laws requiring colleges to disclose crime statistics on their campuses.

Vigil Project, P.O. Box 21105, Santa Barbara, CA 03121. Assists women in developing creative forms of protest. Organized a 24-hour vigil, "Facing Our Worst Fears," for example, in memory of the 53 women and girls who were victims of femicide in Santa Barbara County between 1980 and 1990.

Women's Monument Project, Comptroller, Capilano College, 2055 Purcell Way, North Vancouver, British Columbia V7J 3HF. Established to raise money for a monument to the women who died in the mass femicide in Montreal, 6 December 1989.

Women's Project, 2224 Main St., Little Rock, AR 72206. Documents hate crimes, including femicide, in Arkansas, and publishes the information in the annual *Transformations*. Also engages in annual protest actions (for example, arranging a public tombstone display for murdered women). Major goal is to include violence against women in hate crime legislation.

Women We Honour Action Committee, 22 Parfield Drive, Toronto, Ontario M2J 1B9. Conducted first of its kind study of intimate femicide in Canada. Compiled data in Ontario for the period 1974-90 from the files of the Office of the Chief Coroner and from unofficial sources, such as newspapers, shelters, women's advocates, and victims' families and friends. The three primary goals of the study are to document the incidence of intimate femicide, to describe the characteristics and circumstances of the people involved, and to present the stories of a small number of women killed in this way. Inquiries should be directed to Women We Honour Action Committee, c/o The Denise House, P.O. Box 146, Oshawa, Ontario L1H 7L1.

FILMS ON THE MASS FEMICIDE IN MONTREAL

Compiled by Chris Domingo and Diana E. H. Russell

After the Massacre. Directed by Gerri Rogers. Studio D, P43, National Film Board, Box 6100 Station A, Montreal, Quebec H3C3H5. This documentary connects the massacre with male violence against women. It contains commentary from feminist authors, students, reporters, a sociologist, and a woman who recovered after being shot in the Montreal mass femicide.

Beyond the Sixth of December. Directed by Catherine Fol. Studio D, P43, National Film Board, Box 6100 Station A, Montreal, Quebec H3C3H5. A controversial film focusing on the experience of Nathalie Provost, an engineering student wounded in the massacre. The film shows her to be an assertive woman who refuses to consider herself a victim of systematic male violence.

Emergency. Directed by Adele Brown. 7 Barbara Lane, Binghamton, NY 12903-2755. This film addresses issues of gendered violence, with emphasis on the Montreal massacre. It is accompanied by a study guide and is intended for classroom viewing and discussion.

Riposté. Directed by Suzanne Vertue. In French. Reseau Vidi-Elle, 4013 des Erables, Montreal, Quebec H2K 3V7. Suzanne Vertue calls the Montreal massacre a "crime politique contre les femmes et les lesbiennes"—a political crime against women and lesbians—who died for the sole reason that they were women. In keeping with this viewpoint, the film contains only female voices.

Index

The Editors

Jill Radford is a feminist activist, researcher, teacher, and support worker. She currently works for Rights of Women, a feminist legal project in London, and tutors women's studies and criminology for the Open University in London, Central London Polytechnic, and Roehampton Institute for Higher Education. She has published articles about male sexual violence and the judicial system with both feminist and academic presses, and is coeditor of *Women, Policing, and Male Violence* with Jalna Hanmer and Elizabeth A. Stanko. Ms. Radford is active in the campaign to establish a defense for women and children charged with the murder of a man who has a history of violence or abuse. She is working toward the freeing of Kiranjit Ahluwalia, Sara Thornton, and other women serving life sentences in such cases.

Diana E. H. Russell is a Professor Emeritus of Sociology at Mills College in Oakland, California, where she has taught for 22 years. She holds a postgraduate diploma from the London School of Economics and a Ph.D. from Harvard University. Dr. Russell is the author or editor of nine books, including *The Politics of Rape; Crimes against Women: The Proceedings of the International Tribunal*, with Nicole van de Ven; *Rape in Marriage; Sexual Exploitation: Rape, Child Sexual Abuse, and Workplace Harassment; The Secret Trauma: Incest in the Lives of Girls and Women*, for which she received the 1986 C. Wright Mills Award for outstanding social research; and *Lives of Courage: Women for a New South Africa*. She is working on a book on pornography, *Making Violence Sexy*.